The Autobiography of
William Allen White

William Allen White in the first Emporia *Gazette* office in 1896. Courtesy White family collection, William Allen White Memorial Library, Emporia State University.

The
Autobiography
of
William
Allen White

Second Edition,
Revised and Abridged

Edited by
Sally Foreman Griffith

 University Press of Kansas

Publication was made possible in part by a grant from the William Allen White Foundation. Founded in 1945, the Foundation seeks to perpetuate William Allen White's ideals, and it supports the School of Journalism that is his namesake at the University of Kansas.

Published by the University Press of Kansas (Lawrence, Kansas 66045), which was organized by the Kansas Board of Regents and is operated and funded by Emporia State University, Fort Hays State University, Kansas State University, Pittsburg State University, the University of Kansas, and Wichita State University

Library of Congress Cataloging-in-Publication Data

White, William Allen, 1868–1944.
    The autobiography of William Allen White.—2nd ed., rev. and abridged / edited by Sally Foreman Griffith.
        p.   cm.
    Includes bibliographical references.
    ISBN 0-7006-0470-7 — ISBN 0-7006-0471-5 (pbk.)
    1. White, William Allen, 1868–1944.   2. Journalists—United States—20th century—Biography.   I. Griffith, Sally Foreman.
II. Title.
PN4874.W52A3   1990
818'.5209—dc20
[B]   89-49050
                                                                        CIP

British Library Cataloguing in Publication is available.

Printed in the United States of America
10 9 8 7 6 5 4 3 2 1

The paper used in this publication meets the minimum requirements of the American National Standard for Permanence of Paper for Printed Library Materials Z39.48-1984.

Contents

Editor's Acknowledgments *vii*

Editor's Introduction *ix*

1   "As It Was in the Beginning!" *1*

2   The Story of Will (Sometimes Billie) *17*

3   I Choose a Foster Father *34*

4   Destiny Rolls My Dice—"Come Seven" *47*

5   A Reporter in College *63*

6   I Become a Blind Leader of the Blind *81*

7   A Gilded Metropolis *95*

8   I Cross the Rubicon *109*

9   The New Editor and His Town *130*

10   I Awaken to Fame *148*

11   At the Century's Turn *159*

12   I Discover Reform *174*

13   Happy Days *188*

14   I Join a Rebellion *203*

15   The Europe Which Has Vanished *209*

16   The Battlelines Form *215*

17   Armageddon *234*

18   The Birth of a Party *248*

19   Decline and Fall *262*

20   A World Aflame *275*

21   The Peace That Passeth Understanding *282*

22   Through the Valley of the Shadow *297*

23   Mostly Personal *305*

24   The Downhill Pull *313*

Biographical Notes *333*

Editorial Notes *345*

Selected Bibliography *355*

Index *357*

Editor's
Acknowledgments

This new edition would not have been possible without the active support of William Allen White's family. Mr. and Mrs. Paul David Walker have been most helpful and understanding of our hopes for the project. The late Katherine K. White, in particular, first gave me the idea of doing an abridged edition when she commented that she had always thought that her father-in-law's famous autobiography "could have stood some editing." Throughout the lengthy process of preparation, the staff of the University Press of Kansas has been understanding, supportive, and infectiously enthusiastic. I am grateful also for the assistance of the staffs at the Kenneth Spencer Research Library at the University of Kansas, the William Allen White Collection at Emporia State University, and the Manuscript Division of the Library of Congress. I was aided at a particularly opportune moment by a grant from the H. V. Kaltenborn Foundation. The long process of entering the text into a word processor, aided by a grant from Villanova University, was made easier by the enthusiastic assistance of Maurita Scola.

Editor's Introduction

When William Allen White died in January 1944, a few days short of his seventy-sixth birthday, he was eulogized as "one of the truly great Americans" of his age.[1] He was certainly one of the best known, and probably one of the most beloved, Americans of his day. White had in his half-century in public life become an influential figure in state and national Republican politics. He was a respected journalist and author of biographies, novels, and short stories, and his shrewd, kindly commentaries on contemporary events were widely circulated by the national media. He had helped to found the Progressive party in 1912 and continued throughout his life as an advocate of social reform and individual rights. During and after World War I he had become a world traveler, and he consistently argued thereafter that the United States must assume a responsible leadership role in international affairs. He had watched with alarm in the 1930s as aggressive fascist governments seized control in Germany, Italy, and Japan; as a second world war loomed in 1939, he helped found the Committee to Defend America by Aiding the Allies, popularly known as the White Committee. His leadership of this cause helped weaken the political power of isolationism, enabling the U.S. government to send military aid to Great Britain in its moment of greatest need.

Such national reputation and influence seem particularly remarkable for a small-town newspaperman. But what may have endeared White most to his contemporaries was that he accomplished all these things while remaining in his home town of Emporia, Kansas, as publisher and editor of the *Gazette*. Although millions of twentieth-century Americans pursued economic prosperity by moving to large cities, many continued to believe that the nation's principal strength and virtue resided in its farms and small towns. To them White represented the best qualities of the traditional American character. As *Life* proclaimed in celebrating White's seventieth birthday in 1938: "He is the small-town boy who made good at home. To the small-town man who envies the glamour of the city, he is living assurance that small-town life may be preferable. To the city man who looks back with nostalgia on a small-town youth, he is a living symbol of small-town simplicity and kindliness and common sense."[2]

White's *Autobiography*, published posthumously in 1946, had been long awaited by his contemporaries.[3] For them it provided a fascinating account of the career of a beloved national figure and an insider's view of the many political events in which he had participated. A bestselling Book-of-the-Month Club selection, it was awarded the coveted Pulitzer Prize for biography. For later generations of Americans, to whom White may be less familiar, it offers more as well: It presents in a particularly vivid and engaging way a wide stretch of American history, the half-century spanning the American Civil War and the First World War. As American history students know from their textbooks, these are the years when the United States industrialized, changing from a mainly rural and agrarian society to a nation of cities and factories. The *Autobiography* breathes life into such abstractions as "industrialization" by telling the story through that most accessible of lenses, individual human experience. In these pages we have a picture of frontier life as seen through the eyes of a child; of the booming, reckless Gilded Age through those of heedless youth; of the era of progressive reform through those of an active young adult; and of the First World War and postwar reaction through the rueful eyes of mature middle age. We consequently learn the concrete human effects of large-scale social changes. For a small boy the coming of the railroad translated into the fact "that homemade sleds and little homemade wagons would pass; that the bows and arrows which boys made by seasoning hickory behind the stove and scraping and polishing them with glass would as an art disappear forever" (13). Through White's stories of his initiation into and early exploits in politics we learn volumes about the attractions of that most popular of all participatory sports in the nineteenth century. In his accounts of his hero-worshiping friendship with Theodore Roosevelt and his growing dissatisfaction with the political and economic status quo we see the mixture of hope, fear, enthusiasm, and adulation that propelled many middle-class Americans to become reformers in the two decades before World War I.

From the age of seventeen until his death, White made his living as a journalist, and his *Autobiography* consequently describes vividly the transformation of journalism that accompanied and contributed to the industrialization of American life. White's accounts of his journalistic experiences convey the feeling of the newspaper business in those years in which it changed more rapidly than ever before, in which the technology, the economics, and the very philosophy of journalism were transformed. In his years as apprentice printer and reporter, White learned not only the mechanical steps by which a small-town newspaper was produced but its wider social underpinnings as the handmaiden of party politics. Far different from the mass-circulation commercial metropolitan papers, the typical small-town newspaper—which was what most Americans read in the nineteenth century—depended for its very financial survival upon such outside support as the patronage that White's father provided for the little Butler

County *Democrat*. Such newspapers knew nothing of today's journalistic norms of "objectivity"—their job was to get their candidates elected and, they hoped, to secure the high-paying job of postmaster for the editor himself.

But even as William Allen White first set out on his own in 1895 as publisher of the *Gazette*, journalism was beginning to change. The rise of national name-brand advertising and modern merchandising methods brought substantial new revenues to even small-town papers, and their daily circulations were swelled by the institution of Rural Free Delivery, which enabled outlying farmers to subscribe to daily newspapers. These new sources of income brought journalists greater independence from their political patrons, and many like White exerted this independence in defying their former bosses and participating in reform movements. At the same time, however, to attract new advertising dollars, a newspaper was compelled to continually increase its circulation. This required investing considerable money in improved machinery and, above all, appealing to as wide a range of readers as possible. As this process continued into the twentieth century, journalism, in White's words, ceased to be "a profession" and became "a business and an industry" (329).[4]

WHITE HAD been thinking about writing his autobiography for a long time. He had, in fact, written a draft as early as 1927, when he was fifty-nine. He shelved that first effort, though he would incorporate passages from it into the final version.[5] A decade later he signed a contract with the Macmillan Company, his long-standing publisher, for an autobiography to be entitled *Recollections of a Country Editor*. He made a second attempt in the late 1930s but was no more satisfied with it.[6]

What may have finally spurred White to begin writing in earnest was that many others were responding to public interest in him by writing biographies. Although they were all basically laudatory, they inevitably presented a picture of his life that differed from White's own perceptions of himself. The first full-length biography, which appeared in mid-1941, was by Everett Rich, a professor of English at a local college. Charles Vernon, a newspaperman who had started his career as a *Gazette* reporter around 1900, when White was still a conservative Republican, read Rich's biography and complained to White: "He describes a noisy, conceited and ignorant jay while the Mr. White I fell for seemed even then a considerable of a man."[7] White replied that Rich "did not know the young man that you knew and loved. He only saw the exterior. He did not know that when I was being that smart-alecky jay on the paper, my emotional nature was gradually growing and that through my sympathies my understanding was broadening."[8] White was the only one who could tell that story from the interior.

Far more troubling was the discovery in January 1941 that Hollywood producers were working on a movie of his life. White appealed to his Republican colleague Will Hays, chairman of the Motion Picture Producers and Distributors organization, to help him put a stop to it. "I just don't want it," he fumed. "A man in his lifetime just can't stand by and see a full-length picture of himself on the film. It would be too much." Hays sympathized and saw to it that the project did not materialize.[9]

After he resigned from the White Committee in January 1941, White set about in earnest to write his life. To refresh his memory of his early days he re-read old letters and pored through the large collection of boyhood memorabilia that his doting mother had accumulated. He appealed to old friends for help in recalling half-remembered events or anecdotes. He even asked a former playmate to help him piece together a picture of the young Will White. "I wish you would sit down and write something about the boy you knew then," he wrote. "I mean how he looked, was he thin or fat, was he smart-alecky or shy, was he a bit of a snob or something of a democrat or neither or both."[10]

Many of his friends and reform colleagues were also writing their memoirs at this time, and White was able to compare memories and to muse about the larger meaning of their collective experience. After reading the recently published autobiography of fellow progressive Ray Stannard Baker he wrote to praise the book and comment, "The thing that got me was the parallel of our lives. I, too, played in the woods which the Indians had just left but a few years before. . . . I, also, grew up in a pioneer environment." He continued,

> It has been a great life and we have seen great changes in the world. I have an idea that when this era from 1900 to 1936 is seen in the perspective of history, it will be called the Day of the Dinosaur, when we erected great organizations of men in corporations and in governments somewhat in the democratic form, with huge bodies of great power and no brains, and they shall have to pass. In some ways they are amiable creatures. In others they are bloodthirsty, ruthless and terrible. But we have lived in the epoch that made them. We have tried futilely to shoot them with our own pellets of copy paper. Their hides were too thick. But they were dumb.[11]

By the summer of 1941 he had begun to write, dictating for an hour or two each morning to his stenographer, Minnie Yearout. Though hampered by ill health and repeatedly drawn from his work by the demands of public affairs, he continued to work on his autobiography until he learned in October 1943 that he had inoperable cancer. His great work remained unfinished at his death. His son, William L. White, and his widow, Sallie Lindsay White, prepared the manuscript for publication after his death.

White was undoubtedly distracted by his many public commitments, but it also seems that he found the task somewhat daunting. After all, writing an autobiography is more than simply recalling all the events in one's life. White realized this, for he announced at the outset of the book that "this Autobiography, in spite of all the pains I have taken and the research I have put into it, is necessarily fiction." Telling one's life story is a creative process that requires the author to select from the millions of possible events in his or her life and to shape them into a coherent narrative. The kind of story chosen depends upon how one sees the overall meaning of one's life.

What might have made the task particularly difficult for White was that he had changed very much over his long and productive life. When he became a progressive between 1900 and 1905, much of his thinking changed accordingly. Similarly his progressive hopes for social regeneration had been dashed by war and subsequent disillusionment, to be revived only in part in the far different conditions of the Depression. Above all, he wrote his autobiography during the darkest days of yet another world war, when the conflagration seemed to mock his fondest beliefs in human progress. Which "White" was he to portray? Which understanding of world history should shape his interpretation of his life?

He attempted to resolve the problem by acknowledging that his lifetime had encompassed many different identities. The draft that he left at his death contained an introductory statement: "I knew all seven! Being the autobiography of six other fellows whom I knew and was. By a sedentary old gentleman named William Allen White."[12] He planned to divide the work into a series of books, each with the name by which he was best known in each incarnation: "Willie" during his infancy and early childhood; "Will" or sometimes "Billie" during boyhood and youth; "Will A. White" during his early days in journalism; "W. A. White" during his emergence as a progressive; "Bill White" during his middle age; and, presumably, "William Allen White" during his later years. He was not, unfortunately, able to fill out the scheme, reaching only early 1923 before he became incapacitated by his final illness. It was, in any event, an awkward scheme to work out, for during his adult years White fulfilled several different identities simultaneously. He perhaps best captured a sense of his multiple identities in a letter he wrote in 1910, responding to a friend's request for a photograph. He sent two pictures, explaining:

I don't seem to be able to get all my various split-up characters under one canvas. Of the two pictures that I am sending you one is Bill White of the Emporia *Gazette* who is rather handy in the fourth ward and sometimes does business on the county central committee, a good advertising solicitor and sometimes takes a hand at reporting and is not highly regarded in our best circles. The other picture is the statesman who has terminal facilities at Topeka and traffic agreements in New York.

Now about the author; I have never been able to get him before a camera. He is no friend of mine and I have never seen him. . . . His work, when it is good, surprises me as much as anybody. I should like to have his photograph as well as you, but I have never got it.[13]

There was no easy way to separate the stories of these different personalities. The version published in 1946 omitted the introduction about these six "other fellows" and contained only the first four of the projected six or seven books. The last book, of "W. A. White," encompassed more than half the entire work.

In selecting and organizing his life story, White had many models to choose from, for the autobiography has assumed many different forms as it has developed over the centuries. The first great autobiography and the model for many that followed was the *Confessions of St. Augustine*, wherein the fourth-century bishop recounted the sinfulness of his pagan life before and the blessedness of his life after his conversion to Christianity. As with the many spiritual accounts that followed over the centuries, the moment of conversion forms the climax and the focus of Augustine's autobiography, for it is God alone who gives meaning to his life. Although fictional, the widely read religious allegory *Pilgrim's Progress*, by John Bunyan, also provided a powerful model for early autobiographies. First published in 1678 and reprinted countless times in the following three centuries, it told the tale of Pilgrim and his lifelong journey in search of the Celestial Kingdom.

Another autobiographical type is the exemplary tale, or "success story," a sort of secularized version of the religious confessional that explains how the author made his or her career. The model and most famous example of this form is Benjamin Franklin's eighteenth-century *Autobiography*, which he claimed was intended solely for the education of his descendants: "Having emerg'd from the Poverty & Obscurity in which I was born & bred, to a State of Affluence & some Degree of Reputation in the World, and having gone so far thro' Life with a considerable Share of Felicity, the conducing Means I made use of, which, with the Blessing of God, so well succeeded, my Posterity may like to know, as they may find some of them suitable to their own Situations, & therefore fit to be imitated."[14] It was published after his death and widely read in the nineteenth and twentieth centuries as a "how-to" guide to worldly success. The form has been emulated by self-made men and women ever since, from P. T. Barnum in the mid-nineteenth century to Lee Iacocca in the twentieth.

Until the middle of the nineteenth century, autobiographers in general tended to focus upon their adult years, when they had assumed active participation in the world; but in the late nineteenth century, many began to dwell most lovingly upon their childhoods, when life was carefree and irresponsible. The "childhood," as one critic has termed such autobiographies, attempted to recapture a way of existence very different from the world of adults, to re-create "an autonomous, now-vanished self which formerly existed in an alternative dimension."[15] Finally, the simplest and least introspective of all autobiographical forms is the political memoir, the political leader's retelling of the inside story of the events in which he or she participated. Such memoirs tell only of the public person, leaving aside the inner feelings or the personal background that shaped the author.

In keeping with the multiplicity of roles that he played and with the transitional character of the period in which he lived, White's autobiography contains elements of all these different forms, giving the work a rich but often contradictory quality. At times, particularly when he recounts the founding of the Progressive party in 1912 and its collapse in 1916, it is a political memoir, in which he gives his version of the important events in which he had participated. At other times, the autobiography is a success story reminiscent of Franklin's classic account. This is particularly true of his lively account of his arrival in Emporia as the *Gazette*'s new proprietor, so evocative of Franklin's famous tale of his arrival in early eighteenth-century Philadelphia with only a Dutch dollar in his pocket. White's version of the founding moment of his career might well have been based upon his memory of Franklin's, which was the most widely read autobiography in the nineteenth-century United States. As he became increasingly well known, White delighted in retelling, and his readers seemingly in rehearing, how he had come to Emporia. As *Life* put it in 1938: "Every small-town boy who ever dreamed of becoming a newspaperman knows the story of how William Allen White, with 27 years behind him and $1.25 in his pocket, rode the Santa Fe into Emporia, Kans., one day in 1895, borrowed $3,000 and bought the Emporia *Gazette*, and next year wrote an editorial called 'What's the Matter with Kansas?' which made him nationally famous overnight." Like Franklin's, too, White's autobiography is peppered with wise, Poor Richard–type sayings about the sources of his success. Describing the moral of his initiation into the printer's world, he noted, "We are ashamed for the things that men know, not for the things we do" (51). And he concluded that his college career gave him "the habit of trained attention to the printed page" without which "the going in the modern world is tough" (66).

Yet in telling the story of his early life as "Willie" and "Will (sometimes Billie)," White adopts the tone of the "childhood" form and dwells lovingly upon the unfettered, often magical world of his own childhood and youth, when he roamed the woods and prairies that surrounded his home, playing with his fellows games that no adult understood. In fact, White had much earlier in his career taken advantage of the public delight in such idyllic Huck Finn– and Tom Sawyer–type portraits of boyhood. *The Real Issue*, his first volume of short stories, published in 1896, contained a story entitled "In the Court of Boyville," about the exploits of one "Piggy" Pennington and his friends. S. S. McClure, publisher of the popular *McClure's Magazine*, republished the story and commissioned White to write others to accompany it. The resulting "boy stories," as White called them, appeared in book form in 1899. White's nonfictional account of his own childhood, written over four decades later, reveals that many of those stories were autobiographical. Nonetheless, although White painted the story of his childhood and boyhood in the sunniest of hues, the *Autobiography* does not suggest that these were the best years of his life or that his experience was downhill from that point. Instead he emphasizes that his life was a gradual unfolding of personal identity from one age to the next.[16]

White's interpretation of his early years and of most of his life was shaped by ideas about evolution that had influenced so many Americans in the late nineteenth and early twentieth centuries. Charles Darwin's theory of evolution— that all species, including humans, evolved gradually through the process of natural selection—prompted many educated Americans to reassess their conceptions of human nature and of social progress. Many were particularly impressed by philosopher Herbert Spencer's application of Darwin's ideas to human society. Society, Spencer asserted, followed the same laws of development as other organisms—progress occurred automatically through the unplanned competitive behavior of individuals who made up the social organism. During the Gilded Age, conservative Americans asserted that the emergence of great fortunes and giant corporations like John D. Rockefeller's Standard Oil Company merely reflected Spencer's principle of "the survival of the fittest." By the beginning of the twentieth century, however, reform-minded men and women, including White, rejected Spencer's argument that government must not attempt to interfere with the natural evolutionary process; they insisted instead that through government, humanity could give evolution a helping hand. Nonetheless, they did accept the Social Darwinian notion that through evolution, society was continually progressing.

White also adopted the common evolutionary belief that "ontogeny recapitulates phylogeny," that the individual's development follows in miniature the same pattern that the human race had traced in its evolution from savagery to modern civilization. Consequently he documented his childish customs as though they were those of a vanished prehistoric tribe, noting for example that he had done household chores cheerfully "in the primitive, savage simplicity of childhood" (6), or referring to the "gang instinct of boyhood" (27). For White his childhood had indeed been a Golden Age, but its passing was inevitable and necessary for his development.

For some Americans Darwin's theories challenged their faith in God, but many like White were able to reconcile evolution with religious belief. His chance conversation with a philosophically inclined stranger while a seventeen-year-old student at the College of Emporia laid the foundation for his faith: "He held Jesus up to me as the greatest hero in history and asked me to read the story of the two thousand years that had followed his death and to watch how slowly and yet how inexorably the world had changed, veering to human happiness as it accepted little by little, phrase by phrase, the philosophy he preached and made it a part, even a small part, of human institutions" (45). White described this meeting as the beginning of "the road to Damascus" (46), but it was clear that his "conversion" to progressivism was an evolutionary process rather than the work of a single moment.

Although on its surface, White's *Autobiography* is far less religious than St. Augustine's *Confessions*, much of its language and its underlying structure derive from White's own religious understanding of the world, with its fusion of Christianity and evolutionary progress. As a boy he had attended Sunday School regularly, he claimed, mainly to be with the other children, but the education he gained gave him a deep knowledge of the Bible. Biblical phrases and metaphors abound in his autobiography, as in all his writings. The central theme of his novel *A Certain Rich Man* was drawn from the New Testament parable of the prodigal son, the restless younger son who leaves his father's house and dissipates his inheritance in wild living, but who eventually returns to his father empty-handed and repentant. White admitted that the story "was the story of my own inner life" (195). For him the moment of return to his "father's house" was his own "evolutionary" conversion from conservative Republican to progressive reformer. As he explained to his former reporter Charles Vernon, it involved a gradual broadening of his understanding based upon the natural growth of his "sympathies": "And so I burst out of the biological chains that held me, a mean conservative, and became what I hope was a fairly consistent liberal."[17]

The years around 1904 that saw this breakthrough and up to the beginning of world war in 1914 are clearly the high point of White's *Autobiography*. He felt at his full powers and engaged in strenuous endeavors that seemed to be at the center of world history. On the other hand, he entitled his discussion of postwar politics "The Downhill Pull" and seemed genuinely to feel that turning fifty in 1918 was the end of the most exciting era of his life. White had begun to write about the postwar years by late spring of 1943 but made little progress in the months that followed. Undoubtedly his health was waning, but one is tempted to think that at some level he lacked the will to finish the account of his last twenty years. Despite his many genuine accomplishments in the 1920s and 1930s, much of White seems to have gone to the grave with Theodore Roosevelt in 1919 and his beloved daughter, Mary, in 1921.

Nonetheless the perspective of the *Autobiography* is not that of William Allen White in 1912 singing "Onward, Christian Soldiers" with his comrades in the new Progressive party; it is the gentler, more tolerant perspective of one who has lived to see many of his enthusiasms wane and his dreams disappointed. Throughout the work the "William Allen White" of his last years comments bemusedly upon the foibles of his younger incarnations. A recurring theme is human blindness—our inability to truly understand the meaning of our experiences at the moment in which we live them. Only in hindsight can we begin to see the truth, he seems to argue, but even this understanding is imperfect and uncertain, for it will be modified by yet later developments.

White, looking back upon his life from the perspective of a world again at war, perceived many of his life's efforts as but "bubbles on the stream." Many of his contemporaries saw the wars in which twentieth-century humanity seemed to be repeatedly embroiled as proof that faith in progress was an illusion and that human beings were essentially irrational and brutal. But to the last White refused to give in to this hopeless view of life. Our vision is simply too limited, our lives too short, he concluded, to enable us to see the full truth. Yet looking back over his own relatively few years on earth, he felt that he had begun to catch an inkling of that truth. In March 1942, as Japanese forces continued their relentless conquest of the South Pacific, White wrote his friend Paul Hutchinson, a lay columnist for *Christian Century*, who had written him in despair.

I am pretty well satisfied that this whole show, from Sarajevo to Pearl Harbor, is some kind of a deep struggle in man's heart with his destiny, man seems to be trying to pass from a civilization which for four thousand years man has been erecting on the basis of family, town and national self-sufficiency, to the vast interdependence made necessary by the coming of a machine age, where not only raw materials must move freely but the finished products thereof must not be bound or hampered. In that evolutionary struggle has risen a deep fear of the man of one talent that he will not survive. So he has turned for fifty years, in the politics of the world, slowly to collectivism, and at the same time, the world tendency was too largely, too narrowly nationalistic, and the clash has just blown the whole world clear, plumb to hell and gone, speaking not profanely but with all the piety of my ardent nature.

So, my dear Paul, don't feel uneasy if you don't know where the world is going. Nobody does. God knows—He who planted deeply in the heart of man the pattern of his ultimate destiny which has been unfolding since man's first conscious hour when he knew good from evil—I repeat, God knows![18]

These words could well have been used to conclude William Allen White's great, unfinished autobiography.

ABOUT THIS EDITION

William Allen White composed his autobiography in the last years of his life, typically by dictating to his stenographer; he planned to edit the typed transcripts later. He did make preliminary changes in wording on early chapters, but he was not able to complete his work before he died. The evening before undergoing the exploratory surgery that discovered his incurable cancer, he asked his son, William Lindsay White, to edit the work and see it through the press. White noted that "it needed cutting, particularly for repetition."[19]

Consequently many decisions that went into the edition of White's *Autobiography* published by the Macmillan Company in 1946 were made by someone other than the author. We can, of course, never know exactly what changes he himself would have made. Examination of several drafts of the manuscript available at the Kenneth Spencer Research Library at the University of Kansas and the William Allen White Memorial Library at Emporia State University showed that changes both in wording and in content were made throughout the publication process by his son, by his wife, Sallie (who had been his lifelong editor), and by editors at Macmillan. In many cases these changes corrected factual errors. A few cuts were made, but these were not extensive, and more drastic cuts suggested by Francis Brown of the New York *Times*, probably at the request of Macmillan editors, were largely rejected by the Whites.

The purpose of this new edition is to make the *Autobiography* available to new generations of readers: first, by bringing it back into print after many years; and second, by making it shorter and eliminating digressions. Because the first published edition is widely available in libraries, I did not think it was necessary to provide an identical edition, nor did it seem desirable to seek to recapture some ideal "original" version, because the author had not been able to fulfill his own intentions for his work. Accordingly I have made extensive cuts and have sometimes rearranged passages in order to provide greater coherence and continuity. Nonetheless I have sought to maintain a readily identifiable relation to the 1946 version by marking all cuts with ellipses (. . .). An Editorial Notes section at the back of the book describes where cuts and rearrangements have been made in the 1946 edition. These notes will enable readers who are curious about the altered passages to refer to that work.

In many cases I have made cuts to eliminate repetition. Where further cuts were necessary to reduce the length of the book, I gave priority to the following areas: (1) political and social movements with which White had direct experience; (2) magazine and newspaper publishing; and (3) the culture of the small-town Midwest during White's lifetime. Also in the interests of brevity and coherence, I decided to omit the final chapter of the 1946 edition in which William Lindsay White described the last two decades of his father's life, quoting extensively from his letters and editorials. For one thing, more detailed information on these years is now widely available in other biographies, which also quote heavily from William Allen White's writing.[20] Further, as his son acknowledged, it was impossible to duplicate the tone and perspective of the preceding chapters by quoting from contemporary letters and editorials, "for in his account of the previous five decades he tempers what he then wrote and thought with that mellowness which only comes with the years."[21]

Punctuation has been altered throughout to conform with more modern usage. Although words and passages have been cut and some passages rearranged, I decided to make no changes within the sentences themselves beyond those made by previous editors. I compared the manuscript that was sent to the publishers with the edition as finally published in 1946. In some instances where the sense was clearly improved by the Macmillan editor, I adopted these changes; but in others where changes seemed to alter the historical value of the passage I retained the wording of the manuscript. On occasions where it was necessary to insert a word or phrase to maintain continuity, I placed brackets around the inserted words. I have commented in footnotes upon factual inaccuracies in White's statements but have made no effort to deal with how his interpretations might differ from mine or those currently held by other historians. Finally, in keeping with the goal of making this work accessible to a wide range of readers, I have inserted short notes to explain many of White's allusions. The more prominent people whom White mentions in the text are identified in Biographical Notes at the back of the book.

NOTES

1. Oklahoma City *Times*, quoted in Walter Johnson, *William Allen White's America* (New York: Henry Holt and Company, 1947), p. 4.

2. "William Allen White of Emporia: An American Institution Is 70," *Life*, February 28, 1938, pp. 9–13. Edward Gale Agran describes White's appeal to a newly urbanized middle class in " 'Too Good a Town': William Allen White and the Emerging Rhetoric of Middle America" (Ph.D. dissertation, University of Wisconsin–Madison, 1986).

3. White, *The Autobiography of William Allen White* (New York: Macmillan Company, 1946).

4. For further details about these changes, see Sally Foreman Griffith, *Home Town News: William Allen White and the Emporia* Gazette (New York: Oxford University Press, 1989).

5. The manuscript of this early draft is in the William Allen White Collection, William Allen White Memorial Library, Emporia State University.

6. White to George P. Brett, Jr., June 22, 1943, William Allen White Papers, Manuscript Division, Library of Congress (hereafter cited as LC).

7. Charles M. Vernon to White, September 15, 1941, LC. Appearing almost simultaneously were Rich's *William Allen White: The Man from Emporia* (New York: Farrar and Rinehart, 1941), and Frank C. Clough, *William Allen White of Emporia* (New York: McGraw-Hill Book Company, 1941). Clough was city editor of the *Gazette*.

8. White to Vernon, September 30, 1941, LC.

9. White to Will Hays, January 8, 1941, LC.

10. White to Charles W. Harvey, September 13, 1941, LC; see also White to Harvey, June 20, 1941, LC.

11. White to Ray Stannard Baker, October 20, 1941, LC.

12. This statement was included in the preliminary material of the manuscript as it was sent to Macmillan, now in the William Allen White Papers, Kansas Collection, Kenneth Spencer Research Library, University of Kansas, Lawrence.

13. White to Jay E. House, August 6, 1910, LB17, LC.

14. Benjamin Franklin, *The Autobiography and Other Writings*, ed. Kenneth Silverman (New York: Penguin Books, 1986), p. 3.

15. Richard N. Coe, *When the Grass Was Taller: Autobiography and the Experience of Childhood* (New Haven, Conn.: Yale University Press, 1984), p. 293; see also Patricia Meyer Spacks, "Stages of Self: Notes on Autobiography and the Life Cycle," in *The American Autobiography: A Collection of Critical Essays*, ed. Albert E. Stone (Englewood Cliffs, N.J.: Prentice-Hall, 1981), pp. 44–60.

16. *The Real Issue* (Chicago: Way and Williams, 1896); *The Court of Boyville* (New York: Doubleday and McClure, 1899).

17. White to Vernon, September 30, 1941, LC.

18. White to Paul Hutchinson, March 5, 1942, LC.

19. W. L. White, "Life with William Allen White Was Lively," Kansas City *Star*, September 22, 1968, p. 9F.

20. These include Johnson, *William Allen White's America*; Rich, *William Allen White: The Man from Emporia*; Clough, *William Allen White of Emporia*; David Hinshaw, *A Man from Kansas: The Story of William Allen White* (New York: G. P. Putnam's Sons, 1945); John DeWitt McKee, *William Allen White: Maverick on Main Street* (Westport, Conn.: Greenwood Press, 1975); and E. Jay Jernigan, *William Allen White* (New York: Twayne Publishers, 1983).

21. W. L. White, "The Last Two Decades," in White, *Autobiography*, p. 629.

THIS AUTOBIOGRAPHY, in spite of all the pains I have taken and the research I have put into it, is necessarily fiction. The fact that names, dates, and places seem to correspond with such things that may have occurred in real life does not guarantee the truth of these stories. So, in all candor, I wish to warn the reader not to confuse this story with reality. For God only knows the truth. I am hereby trying in my finite way to set down some facts which seem real and true to me. At best this is only a tale that is told!

—*William Allen White*

1

"As It Was in the Beginning!"

I was born February 10, 1868, between nine and ten o'clock of a Thursday morning at Emporia, Kansas. I was born "Willie," though named William Allen, a name which did not occur to me nor any of my friends for long years, even decades afterwards. A few days after my birth, this item appeared in the Emporia *News*, which referred to my father, Dr. Allen White: "There is another man in town they call Pap. He wears a stove pipe hat and carries a cane, and weighs (since the event) eight hundred pounds. He talks of sending the 'young man' down on 'Warnut' to take charge of the branch store."

I, Willie, was that young man, a baby of whom I know nothing except what has been told: that is that I was husky, always fat, with lusty bawling lungs, and that I was a nursing baby. . . . Soon after I was born my father began looking for a new location. Emporia was getting too thick. A town of five hundred was more civilized and sophisticated than he could bear. So he went sixty miles southwest to what then was known as "the Walnut"! The town was El Dorado. Probably less than a hundred people lived in El Dorado when he opened his store, in a rambling one-story frame building with a black sheet-iron stovepipe sticking out of the roof over each of the six rooms, and naturally it was known in the countryside as "the foundry." The long procession of settlers moving out of the eastern Mississippi Valley into the western watershed of the Mississippi passed our house every day. We could hear the rumbling wheels far into the night. The dust settled over everything and my mother [Mary Hatten White], who was a ferret for dust, worked day and night to keep things clean. . . .

I have often wondered how it happened that my father took charge of that town. Everyone agrees that he was its moving spirit. He was a Democrat in a land where the returning soldiers of the Civil War made an overwhelming flood of Republicans, yet he took leadership. A county-seat fight arose with the adjoining town, Augusta. The El Doradoites built a courthouse with their own

1

funds and turned it over to the county. He headed the subscription list. They hired a man at the county-seat election to commit a palpable election fraud, voting names from the city directory of Buffalo, New York, wrong end to: "Jones, William; Smith, John; Robinson, Harry," and so on down the line. And when the artist who committed the crime was convicted, they paid his family a good round monthly sum while he served his term in the penitentiary, until they could wangle him out. . . . We were so near the frontier that law and order and the decent amenities of civilization often were but scantily observed.

One night in the midst of this county-seat war, El Dorado had word from its spies that a cavalcade was coming from Augusta, armed to the teeth, to take away the county records. Within an hour a hundred young men with their old army rifles, blue-coated soldiers of the Civil War, were in the courthouse and on the roof and in the windows thereof. The cornice of the roof bristled with gun barrels like quills upon the fretful porcupine as Augusta's procession, headed by an ox team and a great dray to carry the records, rolled into town in serried ranks—a little army of invasion. It was a pitch-dark summer night. My father was in command of the defenders. But as he went out of our house, where he had dropped in on some errand, my mother begged him to take off his white clothes, for he was a shining target in that Panama helmet, his pleated shirt, his light suspenders, and his nankeen trousers. But he waved her aside and remarked gaily: "Well, Ma, when they are aiming at me they won't be shooting at the courthouse!" And he walked out gaily with his cane over his arm and my little dog following him, a funny, fussy, pudgy little fat man, five feet four, playing grotesquely at Richard of the Lion Heart. I have a notion that maybe he cut such a festal figure, more or less ridiculous, that Augusta could not bear to get a bead on him. For he mingled in the crowd, joking with the invaders—whom he knew, of course, behind their masks. When, finally, fearing to rush the armored courthouse, the grim columns from Augusta turned tail and marched home in the gray dawn, the mob had an indignation meeting where Augusta had gathered to welcome the conquering heroes. They hanged a little fat figure made by stuffing flour sacks with straw and vented their anger by shooting it to pieces. And that was the end of the county-seat war in Butler County.

My father's next job was to organize the Democratic party in Butler County. I can remember, as a little boy, going with him in the buggy for days and days as he rode from one neighbor to another, exhorting the Democrats in the various townships in this county, larger than the state of Rhode Island, to come to a county convention. When they came they put out a full ticket and went home with instructions to trade every candidate on it for votes for Vincent Brown for county clerk. To the amazement of the Republicans, he won and the party had a toehold in the courthouse and so was duly founded. . . .

The first emotional disturbance in my life came when I was about two years old, probably a little older. A baby brother was born. I cannot now remember why I hated him. Of course it was jealousy; but I hated him with a bitter, terrible hate. And this I am sure I can remember: I sneaked around the corner of the house to the east porch where his crib was, of a summer afternoon, and began pounding him with my little fists. They caught me when his screams called them. I had no remorse that I remember. I cannot bring back any pictures of his early death and recall nothing of his funeral.

I was three years old then and had a sense of my environment. For me it remained a strange and lovely world. Two elderly, devoted, and adoring persons, whom I called "Pa" and "Ma," guided me and bowed down before me and I knew it and ruled them ruthlessly. I was spoiled, as what child born of parents in their late thirties and forties would not be? I could draw a picture today of my home, the old foundry, with its long kitchen where the dining table stood, its attached woodshed with the trapdoor into the cellar. And between the woodshed and the kitchen, in a covered corridor, they hung my little swing where I would swing for hours, singing a little bee song—a kind of long ah-h-h-h of sheer delight. I was a happy child and found a thousand things to please me. The world was made to bring me delight.

There was a living room, ruled in fall and winter by a big, round, sheet-iron stove. On our walnut table the tall lamp sat, and here always newspapers were piled and books strewn. A spare bed filled a far corner. Our very best room, the parlor, I rarely entered, for it was dark there by day and I was afraid of it. My own little bedroom and my parents' larger bedroom adjoined the living room and the parlor. Of course, I went in and crawled in between them in the morning and seemed to give them much delight. . . . In that Elysian childhood where I first opened my conscious eyes to the world about me, I was shielded from pain and sorrow and lived, if ever a human being did live, in a golden age. . . .

I seemed to turn everything into song. The little bee song of my babyhood became a long cantata which I made up, perhaps—words and tune and all—as I sat, a solitary only child, in the shade of the morning-glories or, best of all, in the barn at the end of our town lot. That barn was my first enchanted palace. Modern childhood has no equivalent to my barn. I don't know how young I was when I invented the story that it was haunted, and scared the daylights out of other children as I pointed to the barn's high rafters, pretending to see faces and fairies which they also pretended to see; and we scared ourselves and wrestled on the hay loft and smelled the nice smell of the horses and the cow. Sometimes we sat in the corn crib and watched the pigs beneath, and the chickens. It was all strange and adventurous. The old pig that woofed at us and that we were sure would eat us if she caught us, made us feel that we were in the presence of a dragon as authentic as that which St. George went forth to slay.

Of Sunday afternoons, Pa and Ma walked with me to the timber between our creek and its junction with the Walnut River. Pa made me hickory whistles and taught me how to tell different trees by their leaves and bark. It was before they had cut out the buckbrush, the wild raspberries, the blackberries, elderberries, and pokeberries. Above this wood's brush were the one-story trees—the papaws, haws, buckeyes, and the redbuds that I loved. Far above these rose the sycamore, the hickory, the elm, the oak, the walnut, the ash, the coffee-bean tree or locust, and the cottonwoods. Walking with Pa and Ma of a Sunday afternoon, I saw squirrels, rabbits, and, once in a while, Pa would show me a coon at the river's brim, or a helldiver. Pa had been born in the Ohio woods and loved timber, and he taught me from earliest childhood to know and love the woods.

But the thing which gave the woods their glamour for me was that only a few years before the Indians had moved out of this timber, onto the prairie lands far to the west and the south. I used to play little games by myself in the woods with mythical little Indian boys. And in some way—I never exactly knew how—I imagined or fancied or dreamed it, and I believed that I turned into a little Indian boy and indeed was one. So I believed, or most seriously fancied, that some day soon the Indians would come back and take me with them. I was scared and happy at the fantasy, which hung about me a long time—maybe a week, a month or half a year.

Indian scares were common in those days. As a baby, my mother took me into a log house across the street from our home where all the women and children of the town, fearing an Indian raid, were gathered while the men did sentry duty. . . . Stories of Indian uprisings, of murders and kidnappings, of brushes, skirmishes, and battles with soldiers not so far away, from a hundred to five hundred miles, were often told in the town. Naturally, El Dorado boys knew these stories by heart as they played in the woods.

Once when I was a little fellow, probably eight or nine years old, half a dozen of us were playing in the underbrush of the timber half a mile from town. . . . Suddenly, looking into the road, we boys saw a great company of Indians on horseback, halted in the road where it forked a few rods from us. We did not run into the timber because they were obviously friendly Indians and we were familiar with them. We walked over shyly to look at the red cavalcade in blankets, one or two of them in feathers, men, women and children. Why they addressed me, I don't know. . . . But they asked how far to town, and I told them. And then one of them, a squaw and a leader, said in perfectly good English, "Boy, will you ride with me and show me?"—and I climbed up and the other boys stood envious. We rode into town, I straddling the horn of her saddle, a little fellow whose bare toes toyed with the mane of the Indian's horse. And as we crossed the bridge to ride up Central Avenue and the town turned from its affairs to watch the Indian procession, they saw me. I knew that I was a person of consequence and I swelled up. Many is the time I moved in pride in later years, but never in such vainglory as when I rode up Central Avenue and the squaw dropped me gently at the town pump and said, "Good boy!" Often bands of Indians like this passed through town, little more than gypsies. These were Sioux going from their Dakota home to visit their comrades, the Comanches, in the Indian Territory.[1]

Then, of course, I had the prairies, the wide illimitable stretches of green in their spring and summer verdure, stretching westward from my front door, with not a dozen rivers or important streams, to the Rocky Mountains six hundred miles away. As a child, I did not know how far they went. To me, they were merely illimitable beyond the horizon and nothing could happen to me except the bite of a rattlesnake, and I never heard of a boy being bitten by a rattlesnake in my childhood. . . . Prairie fires raged up to the outskirts of El Dorado, and I have no lovelier memory in my heart than the night picture of a prairie fire on the high hill horizon east of town, a great raging fire. We would see in silhouette the little figures of men fighting the fire with wet gunny sacks.

I remember the delight of the prairies in the spring and summer when the grass was green and the wild flowers grew everywhere. I used to bring them in little sweaty handfuls to my mother with much delight—foolish little bouquets that I thought were lovely. Two or three hundred yards from our house where I used to play on these prairies as a child, was a little rock-bottomed creek. In later years they dammed it. But before the dam filled up its channel I was allowed, when I could not have been more than four or five years old, to go down to its banks to play. In the riffle we had a little water wheel which gave me great delight. Here and there, as this brook wormed its way across the prairies, were little pools into which the water ran over the sparkling brown and golden pebbles, and in them silversides, sunfish, and minnows played and could be had with a string and a pinhook. But I caught few. I loved better to watch them, for long minutes, swerving about in tiny schools with tadpoles and sometimes a little turtle, which I brought home and kept in a can or the rain barrel until it got away.

I wonder now—I have often wondered—about those little brooks and the courses that they cut in the prairies. For sixty years streets and houses have wiped out those kindly rivulets and springs. In all the prairies across these latitudes, the plow has come and filled the brooks. Even the verdure of the prairies and the pastures is different. The brooks are dry. The land has changed. The white man has come with his presence. The primeval fairyland has gone—fled before the grim reality of man's harrow and his plow, his highway and his house,

---

[1]Popular term for the area between Kansas and Texas set aside for the Indians removed from the southeastern United States between 1820 and 1845. In 1907 this land was united with Oklahoma Territory to the west and admitted to the Union as the state of Oklahoma.

his horse and his cattle, and all the ugly realities of man's fight to live by the sweat of his brow. The red man, who did not sweat much nor stop to drive away the fairies, knew in some ways how to live more easily in this land than his proud white brother.

As a little child, before they caught and bound me to a school desk, I remember spring, summer, and golden autumn as though I had lived always out of doors. In winter I ranged around the rooms of the foundry. My mother had pasted copies of the old Emporia *News* on the kitchen walls to make it warmer there. And while she worked I used to stand and pick out my letters from the advertisements and spell little words and play with my blocks and toys around the big sheet-iron heating stove. The chunks it ate were too big for me to carry, but I cannot remember when I did not have to fill up the woodbox back of the kitchen stove. And there were chips to rake up around the woodpile and bring in for kindling, and cobs to gather. I cannot remember when these duties began, so it must have been early. We called them chores. I am ashamed to admit that the machinations of grown-ups at first concealed from me the fact that they were evil and onerous. I did chores cheerfully in the primitive, savage simplicity of childhood. . . .

My father was then keeping a drugstore and practicing medicine a little. . . . He loved medicine but never could make it pay because he did not keep his collections up. So every few years, being a Yankee and a natural trader, he would retire from practice and make some money, pay his debts, get a little ahead, and then go at medicine again. [His drugstore] had great bottles of colored water in the window, five- or ten-gallon bottles, shining red or blue or green. On the left hand as one went in was a soda fountain with half a dozen flavors—lemon, strawberry, banana, raspberry, and "don't care," which was a mixture of the odds and ends of all of them. In the top of the screen that shielded the prescription case was a huge mortar and pestle. Bottles, gold-labeled with names of drugs, stood on one side of the store, and an amazing array of patent medicines adorned shelves on the other side. A short counter of stationery and a case of cigars was opposite the soda fountain. . . . The store was so profitable that within a few years my father was able to trade it for a good farm and have enough capital to run this at a loss for a year or two. . . .

Until we moved there, "the farm" had been a halcyon place where I had my own little brook, my own little bull calf, my own pigs, and a colt that was growing up to be my pony. A farmer and his wife lived in its little clapboard house, but it never occurred to me that we proud folks, who kept a store and lived in the great rambling foundry, could go to the farm actually to live. But there we went—my mother protesting at the top of her good Irish lungs, but nevertheless going.

For my father had built on the farm a large log cabin with a huge fireplace. At first there was no floor, but at this my mother raged and then, lo and behold, there was a floor. My father's idea was to duplicate exactly the cabin in back-woods Ohio where he was born and grew up. He thought he could go back to the golden days of his youth. . . . So there was a loft in our log cabin where the hired men slept. And hanging over the rafters, the first autumn, were strips of dried pumpkin, bunches of onions, tufts of sage, and Heaven knows what other nonsense groceries. I remember my father standing at a table, in a lean-to which we had built on the narrow end of the log cabin, cutting up beef to corn and to dry and putting away pork to pickle. We had a smokehouse where we cured hams and bacon, and of course a pit where we buried cabbage, turnips, pota-toes, carrots, beets, and apples. To carry out his romantic dream of another day, my father had the carpenter build a little trundle bed that rolled under the big bed by day and was pulled out for me to sleep in by night. But clearest of all my recollections is the vast, continuous indignation of my mother at the sentimen-tal tomfoolery of this whole business. . . . The farm was no place for a woman who was five feet four and weighed even then less than a hundred pounds. Hired girls would not go to the farm even seventy years ago, and my father, be-ing in his fifties, had to hire all his share of the farm work done. . . .

I had as much delight on the farm as my father. I fed my own pig; I tried to break my own steer calf for an ox; I romped with my pony and I played long hours by the little brook that trickled through the gravel in the pasture. Some-times I took a little pinhook and brought home a silverside or a sunfish, or took a can and brought home a tadpole, a little turtle, but Ma would yank them out of the rain barrel as fast as I would sneak them there. Pa did not care. He would always say: "Why, Ma, let the boy have his fun.". . .

I don't know how long we stayed on the farm. I can remember spring there and summer and late autumn. I know it was a year of drouth. For the prairie chickens and the quail came to the yard to eat with the hens. And once an ante-lope leaped the stake and rider fence which my father, in his reminiscent folly, had built for the cattle corral, and ate hungrily with the bony cattle in the cor-ral. Way down on the branch, nearly a mile from home, the neighborhood boneyard grew, and I remember in the spring the coyotes had gnawed the bones white, and it was a place of fear and desolation and great offense. Then, like a quick flash in a motion picture, we were back in town.

My father had traded his drugstore for the farm. So, when we came back to town, I could no longer go into the store and get a glass of soda water free from his fountain. I had to ask politely for the empty cigar boxes under the counter. I was no longer permitted to take a handful of almanacs and distribute them among my friends. It seemed strange, and the strange seeming still lingers in my memory, that I could not go into that store and make free of it. So came the sense of property to my childhood.

In the meantime, I was sent to school. What a day! Ma started to take me but Pa objected. He always objected when she coddled me. Of course, I liked to be coddled and I sided with her, but he had his way. The compromise was that he said, "I'll take him!" And so we started out. She was in the doorway and I left her with her eyes full of tears, for she knew, having taught school, that I would never come back her baby! She knew that I was gone out of her life as a child and would return that noon a middle-aged young person, out in the world for good and all. Pa took me two blocks on my way to the schoolhouse, still three blocks away, and when he was out of sight of Ma and the doorway he prodded me with his cane in pride and affection and said:

"Now, Willie, you are a man. Go to school!" and turned and left me. He could not bear the shame of bringing me into the schoolroom, shame for him and shame for me, and we both knew it. And I trudged on and was glad. And then, for the first time, I remember Albert Ewing coming along the same way, and he and I walked into the schoolhouse together—my first boy friend. After that day we were inseparable for ten years.

The influx into the western Mississippi Valley in the seventies was unbelievable. Every day a score of young soldiers and their wives drove into town, either to settle in the village or to locate land in the Walnut Valley. In the school, new children were entering every day. Albert and I and Leila Heaton and the Betts boys were old settlers there—a haughty aristocracy who lorded it over the newcomers for a few days until they also became scornful of the newcomers, and so it went.

The public schools in El Dorado, and all over the West in those days, were the best that money could buy. We had the largest building in town, a two-story stone one with four rooms which soon afterwards became six—the largest edifice in Butler County. The rooms were well equipped, with good seats and desks and blackboards. We had no pioneer hardships in our Kansas schools. All over the Missouri Valley, the settlers first built a sizable schoolhouse and then built their towns around it. But our school, graded from the primary to the high school even in the seventies, was ahead of the civilization about it.

We sang gospel hymns every morning and the teacher read a chapter in the Bible and there was no nonsense about that. For we were all little Protestants, and no one thought of objecting to Teacher reading the Bible. She made us say the Lord's Prayer after the Bible reading, and then we were started off right for the day. At noon we sang another gospel hymn and loved it. The words did not mean much, but it was fine exercise for our lungs. And, a few grades higher than the primary, we were taught to read music and were given secular songs to sing.

As for playgrounds, we had everything west of the schoolhouse to Denver. The prairies came to within a hundred yards of the building. And sometimes, when prairie fires rose, we boys—little and big—took our coats off, soaked them in tubs of water from the school well and flopped out the fire, standing with the men of the town. Once the flames almost reached the woodpile that fed the big, potbellied iron stove in every room. Each room had its own water bucket and its own tin cup. And you were supposed to quench your thirst at recess and not bother Teacher between times. At recesses and at noon, we played ball, sometimes one-old-cat, or two-old-cat, town ball and baseball, marbles in season, pullaway, stink base, and hide-and-seek. Any new boy had to fight his way into the lodge of boyhood with Byron Snow, Dow Blair, or Ed Dupee, who were ordained to pick a fight for that purpose by the school masonry. . . .

It was about that time, possibly a year or so later, that politics first entered my young life. Before that, almost as far back as I can remember, I knew I was for Horace Greeley, though I hadn't the faintest idea who Horace Greeley was, nor what "bein' for him" implied. But when Hayes and Tilden ran for president, because my father was a Democrat I had to suffer the flings and arrows of outrageous Republicans[2]—sons of the young soldiers; even Albert Ewing turned against me. Only Leila Heaton remained faithful.

She saved my life. I came to school in October, when the campaign was at its height, wearing a little scarf on which were woven "Tilden" and "Hendricks." Naturally the Republicans, the big boys and the little ones, got me down, tied the Tilden and Hendricks scarf around my neck and began pulling it and dancing about with great glee. The world went black. Only Leila Heaton, running screaming to the teacher and tattling on the boys, saved me from garroting, for I was unconscious when the teacher came, loosed the noose, and threw a bucket of water on me. I was a sight to see. No valiant defender of Democracy lay there on the brown prairie grass, but a little pop-eyed, redheaded, freckled-faced, gasping, ashy-blue Democrat, with two teachers and Leila Heaton hovering over him! I opened my eyes and saw Albert Ewing—a renegade to his party, "whence all but he had fled!"[3] But I slowly came to and grinned. I know I grinned, for they told me so. I know I tried to look brave. Leila Heaton and my adored teacher bent over me and I was a happy little polygamist, proud of their solicitude.

Sometime between the days when I fished with a pinhook for minnows under the bridge and the time when I suffered valiantly for Tilden and Hendricks, the river east of town was dammed and the water backed up under the bridge, and there was no riffle for a mile upstream. . . . [We swam] in the millpond and [fished] off the dam, and the riffles were only below the dam. It was all a wonder,

[2]This is White's version of Hamlet's "slings and arrows of outrageous fortune" (*Hamlet*, Act III, scene i).

[3]From Felicia Hemans's famous poem "Casabianca," which begins "The boy stood on the burning deck / Whence all but he had fled."

full of joy and beauty. The grove around the mill was the town park. And a new bridge spanned the stream.

And El Dorado was a big town, maybe six hundred people. We had three saloons, and little boys could pick up corks for fishing bobbers back of the saloons, and sometimes find salable bottles, mostly flasks. Most gay and gorgeous of all, sometimes back of the saloons we could find a drunk sleeping it off and take dares for going closest to him and throwing weeds and other debris upon him. So life was full of dangers. We had two new livery stables in town, and one of them kept a stallion until our mothers complained, thinking we did not know! So then the stallion was moved out of town. And one summer day we discovered a camping place deep in the woods above the town where there was often a covered wagon and some strange girls. We used to peek through the brush at what was going on there until Merz Young, who was the protector of the innocent, came and chased us off with yells and curses, throwing rocks. And the knowledge of good and evil came to us, even as to the Pair in the Garden. . . .

I was eight years old when I stepped out into society. A note in beautiful Spencerian handwriting,[4] on pink paper with gilt edges—I have it yet—came to me, declaring: "Master Willie White is invited to be present at the birthday party of Miss Alice Murdock at their home on Star Street, March 23, 1876." And so I was dressed to kill in a little blue suit, bound in black braid with shiny little golden buttons, white stockings, and black shoes. My hair was wet and pasted down, and my neck washed even behind the ears. It was an afternoon party, bright and gay, and little Alice, with her spinal curvature, was the sunshine of it all. . . . We played games (kissing games I think—post office, clap-in-clap-out, and forfeits) and then went on the lawn, shot arrows at a target, and rather wickedly played hide-and-seek in the barn and had ice cream and cake and lemonade, sitting around like little angels eating their ambrosia. It was all very exciting.

In the meantime, at home things were changing. My father, who had been elected to the city council once or twice, and twice was elected city treasurer, had bought a large square of land—a city block—four or five blocks westward from the creek, and we were planting it to trees. He and I used to water them. We planned to build a house there. My mother was happy, for she did not like to live on the street where the old foundry stood on the highway, less than half a block from Main Street. The other women of the town lived on the hill, and my mother felt that some sort of disgrace came from living downtown. . . . Only poor folks lived down there in little homes scattered back of the Main Street.

---

[4]A popular slanting style of handwriting created by nineteenth-century American calligrapher Platt Rogers Spencer.

Then I think that subconsciously she felt that if we lived on the hill, five blocks from Main Street, the Doctor would not always be inviting people in for dinner. Our house was less than two hundred feet from the stage hotel. It was her complaint that she fed more people from the stage than did the hotel. This meant hard work, for she never would keep a girl. She always said she would rather do the work than bother with one. So when anyone whom my father knew came through on the stage from Emporia, Cottonwood Falls, Council Grove, Leavenworth, or Lawrence—and he knew nearly everyone—we fed them, with Pa, sitting at the head of the table, prouder than punch of his wife's cooking. He had a baronial air and knew his greatest joy as a host. It was the source of a good deal of bone-picking between my parents after our company was gone. He was always crestfallen when he realized the amount of work he had caused. For my father was a kindly man and had been the head of a home too many years not to realize, when he thought of it, how many extra steps it makes when company comes. But he could not resist "company."

But he always helped her. He always wiped the dishes, made the fire in the cookstove in the morning, and filled the woodbox, with my help even when I was little more than a toddler. I have seen him sweep, fetch, and carry, trying to make up to her for the trouble he had caused. He was an addict to hospitality. He could not take it or let it alone.

Then one day the storm broke. He wanted to sell the lot on the hill, and he wanted to build the big house there where the foundry was, tearing that one down. . . . She raged and wept and would not sign the deed for days and days. Times were tough in those days for a little boy of nine or ten, and it sometimes took two or three minutes of play with the gang in the barn, or on the vacant lot, or down along the river, to wipe away the clouds of sadness that hovered over his heart at home. But, finally, the deed was signed, and then we moved across the street while the foundry was being torn down and the new house was built.

It was a grand house. Probably my father tried to make up for its location by making it much the biggest house in town. It had eleven rooms and a cellar under all, and one hundred forty-four linear feet of porches, which he enjoyed and elaborately bragged about when he showed it to visitors. The porches made it possible to get a breeze from every angle—north, east, south, west. We also bought a houseful of new furniture from Leavenworth. . . . Then we had a big party and housewarming. Whether my father and mother gave the party or whether the town just moved in, I do not remember, but it seems to me it was probably the latter; maybe at a wink and nod from my father, who loved company, reveled in it and was really a glowing host. . . .

I am afraid I shared my father's sinful pride in the house—in its grained dining-room wainscoting, in the painted yellow and black squares on the dining-room floor, and in the big kitchen and in the parlor with body Brussels carpet and a gaudy parlor suite, most expensive, in the comfortable living room, crawling with half a dozen rocking chairs, large and small. The house was heated downstairs with three hard-coal base-burners, each glittering with nickel-plated fenders and fancy doodads—glowing household idols!

And the house had such a woodshed as a boy prince could dream of in his palace! There was room even for a trapeze. The worm in the bud was that I could split wood there even when it rained, a drawback but not a major flaw. For on rainy days boys gathered there, and, being host, I acquired some prestige, if not quite leadership. In the woodshed I tied my pet coon and kept my trapped mockingbird, also my little lonely bluebird and my voiceless drooping redbird, until my father persuaded me to let them all go, though I could have traded them for a king's ransom.

In the woodshed I assembled from the house and from the barn the various tools of my trade, being a boy, what might be called the hereditary appurtenances[5] of Will White: a thick piece of glass that was used for scraping and polishing cowhorns; a drawknife; skates with runners, rubbed with bacon rind to keep away rust; bits of iron that had no use but were potentially of extreme value for only boys know what reason; a rawhide quirt—an eight-strand, square-braided whip of my own construction, a priceless treasure; rows and ranks of cigar boxes filled with nails, screws, tops, marbles, and Heaven only knows what of the wampum of boyhood. So the place, indeed the entire woodshed, glowed with the warm and comfortable feeling of great riches in my boy's heart. I was an acquisitive kid, with methodical ways, and stored my treasure there in the woodshed with something like a capitalist's delight in great treasure, good investments.

I was ten years old when we tore down the foundry. El Dorado was only a year older, but it had grown by that time to be a town of nearly a thousand people. It was a self-sufficient community. We had shoemakers who made my father's shoes, although my mother's came from St. Louis where he traded in his merchant days. The town tailor made Pa's Sunday clothes; my mother made his everyday clothes. She, or other women whom she hired, knitted our socks. The food of the town was mostly raised on the townsite or near it on the farm. A small packing house put up hams and bacon and cured beef. A wagon shop back of our lot made carriages, and one of the town's most distinguished artists was a wagon painter who striped buggy wheels and painted the elaborate designs—cornucopian or the seal of Kansas—on the sides of wagons. The town had two or three blacksmith shops, which were busy all day. Ringing anvils

---

[5]White is playing upon traditional legal terms: "appurtenances" referred to things belonging to another thing; and "hereditament," to kinds of property that can be inherited.

woke me in the morning and tolled like bells when I went into the house at dusk. Busy places were those blacksmith shops, which mended and made a score of gadgets for house and farm. We had three harness shops, where I loved to play and listen to the stories of the soldiers who sometimes gathered there, for one harness maker was a noted soldier. A little tannery was established, and a small furniture factory made the chairs, tables, and beds of the pioneers. Native lumber—walnut and oak—stood behind these factories curing, and we boys used to play on the lumber piles and hide between them in our games.

Then the railroad came and everything was changed. I did not know that the smell of coal smoke, which first greeted my nostrils with the railroad engine, was to be the sign and signal of the decay of a town and indeed of pioneer times, when men made things where they used them—all the things necessary to a rather competent civilization.

In the boy's world, it meant that homemade sleds and little homemade wagons would pass; that the bows and arrows which boys made by seasoning hickory behind the stove and scraping and polishing them with glass, would as an art disappear forever out of the life of American boys. The railroad meant that the woodpile would slowly disappear, and that on the far horizon great engines were gathering to wreck the barns, and that the town herd, which I drove for a time, would vanish before the onslaughts of the milk bottles in another fifty years. What a revolution for boys came chugging into the world with that iron horse!

We boys in El Dorado saw colored people for the first time—railroad laborers sweating at their work and singing. We caught their songs and echoed them in our play, building little railroads with whittled ties, imitation rails, grades, and ballast. Our hands were so deft, our imaginations so quick, that we imitated the very things that would rob boys of their skill and their homely work.

Let us look for a fleeting moment at this little fellow just edging eagerly out of childhood. He has been two or three years in school. He is in the second reader,[6] but has read all the readers through to the fourth. He knows the multiplication tables because he was nagged all over the house to learn them—pounced upon at odd times by fierce, merciless parents with: "What's nine times three?" or "Eight times twelve?" or "Seven times six?" And he has drawn fuzzy little mountains on his maps of the United States, of North America or Europe, and colored them after the fashion of schools with red, yellow, blue and green chalk. . . .

His mother is reading to him every night while his father protests that she is spoiling him; reading the Dickens stories which he understands and the Cooper

---

[6]McGuffey's Readers, a series of six textbooks, were used by generations of nineteenth-century American schoolchildren.

Indian stories which he loves, and *The Mill on the Floss* by George Eliot, which bothers him a little, and a story by George Sand about a dark pool,[7] which scares him. He knows his Mother Goose by heart. His gospel hymns are engraved on his memory for life. He is going to four Sunday Schools for purely social reasons—because the boys are there and he is a gregarious kid. And, because his memory is a malleable tablet, he has learned hundreds of verses and, being a bit of a smarty, likes to show off. . . . In summers at Sunday School he wears a little nankeen suit made of the same material as his father's, of which he is quite proud. And the boys, who nickname everybody, have begun to call him "Doc"—and "Doc White" he is to remain, through more than sixty years to a score of oldsters. He is Willie only at home and to his teacher and to Leila Heaton. . . .

As far as I can learn from honest boys who knew me, and from old people who saw me, this Willie had no exceptional qualities, nothing outstanding in his heart. He knew he was a coward so he did brave things sometimes to prove that he was not, but did them in fear and trembling and always showing off. At an early age, the hired man had taken him along when he took the horses to swim. First off, the hired man waded with the little scared kid to where the current was swift and, holding the little fellow high in his arms, threw him as far as he could and cried: "Swim, damn you, swim!" So he had to swim. And the hired man laughed when he came up—spouting, paddling, and yelling. But he learned to swim.

One thing he could do so well that all the boys in El Dorado remember even today: He could dive clear across the creek, and sometimes he would dive so far upstream beyond the swimming hole and hide under a stump where there were supposed to be snakes—but weren't—that the whole parcel of young savages at the swimming hole would be scared white, fearing he was drowned. No bathing trunks were ever heard of in that young savage band. They loved to smear themselves with mud and make indecent patterns with sticks upon their bodies and stand near the railroad bridge, yelling when Number Four passed, waving and making obscene gestures at the passengers. For they were dirty little devils, as most kids are when they are leaving the portals of babyhood and becoming boys. He knew ribald rhymes and Rabelaisian[8] catches and catcalls. He and his fellows released their vague, unformed romantic impulses in the venery of the barn and haystack and swimming hole.

Probably four major influences made this child: the home, where there was reading and considerable intelligent guidance which only later did he perceive,

---

[7]White is probably referring to Sand's popular story *The Devil's Pool* (*La Mare au Diable*, 1846) which is set in an idyllic pre-industrial French countryside.

[8]Refers to François Rabelais (1494?–1553), whose satirical novel *Gargantua and Pantagruel* was noted for its broad, even crude humor.

as he recalled certain attitudes of his parents; then came the barn, with its ancient lores and skills, its trapeze swinging from the rafter, its haymows full of somersaults, forward and backward, where gangs of boys tried to reproduce circus gyrations; after the barn, the river—swimming, fishing, rowing in summer, and skating in winter; and the roaming through the timber, trapping quail and redbirds and mockingbirds and rabbits and cutting stick horses in spring. Probably the stick horse has passed out of childhood. But this Willie, who developed his acquisitive faculty early, kept a stick-horse livery stable and was a stick-horse trader before he was seven. The woods also yielded walnuts for all the boys who would go after them, and a few hard hickory nuts and papaws after frost in autumn, and coffee beans and buckeyes, which had a certain commercial value in the primitive swapping commerce of childhood. The woods was a storehouse of all boys' treasures. . . .

Probably marbles and fighting were extracurricular activities attached to and surrounding the school—also footracing and ball. Willie was a fairly good shot at marbles. His mother lived in the pink cloud of innocence that Willie did not play for keeps. Pa knew better and never betrayed him. But here is a curious thing. The little devil had an acquisitive faculty and he found, watching the wiles of the older boys, that by setting up a fancy marble for boys to shoot at from a hazardous distance and charging two or three commies or a white alley a shot, then giving the prized marble to the man who hit it, he could accumulate marbles faster by running this thing he called a bank than he could by playing for keeps, although he was fairly deft at that. So he set up a bank. But, alas, one day his father discovered that his child had a whole cigar box full of glassies, potteries, and agates which he had accumulated running his bank. That was the end of the bank. Said Pa: "Now, Willie, whatever you get playing keeps is yours. It's a fair game. But these are dirty marbles. You didn't win them and you didn't earn them. Your bank was a swindle." And so, the bank was closed and the career of a future capitalist was nipped in the bud.

The home, the barn, the river, and the school made this Willie White. The school only taught him superficial things—to read, write, and figure and to take care of himself on the playground. But those other ancient institutions of learning taught him wisdom, the rules of life, and the skills which had survival value in the world of boyhood. . . .

It was in those days when I was nine years old, or thereabouts, that Leila Heaton, who had left El Dorado for the little town of Chanute, died of scarlet fever. Albert Ewing told me. I carried a heavy heart for days and days, and was probably mean and hard to get along with. I remember this picture of Willie and his grief. It may have been the Saturday after I had the news, which would have been the first holiday when I could go to the woods of a morning. It was a sunny spring day. I was alone, down where the ravine empties into the creek. The berry blossoms, the raspberries and blackberries were out and, even now, when I smell them their perfume brings back a poignant pungency. I sat for a long time, as it seemed, but maybe for only a few minutes, in the berry brambles, silent and dumb. Then I went down under a hard mud bank to a tree where a pool was backed up into the ravine from the millpond. I sat there, playing with some old pignuts dropped from a hickory tree the autumn before, and found under my hand some coffee beans from a locust tree. I was only thinking, just stringing wandering fancies through my brain about life, and death, and Leila Heaton—a dirty little boy with a bruised scab on his cheek from a fight with John Knowles, not too clean a nose, and very filthy hands. I whispered her name many times and then, looking cautiously about, I said it aloud, and began to make up a little song—with Heaven knows what words. Of course they were silly, but they seemed beautiful. They are gone now. Heaven also may know the tune I used; probably the mélange of all the tunes I knew was my song of sorrow, little above a bee's hum—repeating over and over weird meaningless phrases, lifting my voice sometimes and suddenly muffling it in shame. I can still see the gaudy woodpecker on the dead beech tree across the pool and hear him drum. Some hogs came down to drink and wallow near me in the mud. Above the fence that hemmed the pond in from the creek, a log had lodged at flood time. Under the bright spring sun came a turtle and I clodded it back into the water and so broke the spell of song. In my pocket, among treasures of string and marbles, was a jew's-harp with a bent tongue. I straightened it out, sitting there on my haunches in the spring's sunlight, thrummed the jew's-harp to some sad old tune, and so looked out of my childhood far forward into my teens, and thus through sorrow, at the mystery of life. I felt there in the sunshine of the hog lot something strange approaching, something bright and sad and wonderful. It was youth. And that day and time Willie began to pale and pine away and pass. A boy appeared.

2

The Story of Will
(Sometimes Billie)

I was Will White, not Willie, when I came to my tenth birthday. The town of El Dorado had lost its tough pioneer character. Brick buildings were appearing on Central Avenue and Main Street. Substantial residences, with east and south porches, were rising up on the hill beyond the town. The big stone schoolhouse acquired an addition. It was a six-room grade school with a high school, for which I was headed intrepidly. . . .

Two events make me remember my tenth birthday—a sheet and pillowcase party, at which all the children who went to Alice Murdock's party, that is to say the nobility and gentry, were assembled; and the glorious fact that on my tenth birthday my parents gave me a Mason & Hamlin cabinet organ, most ornate, most gorgeous, with a chromo of an autumn field on the centerpiece at the top. . . . It came from Chicago and was the town pride. That it was the most splendid organ in town, where not more than three or four pianos rivaled it, of course did not make me humble. . . .

Music, since I can remember, has always been one of my chief delights. I can recall now, after seventy years, hearing the El Dorado silver cornet band playing down in Burdette's grove by the mill. The strains wafted across our creek to our place. I remember even that I was sitting under the grapevines preparing my little stomach for a gorgeous bellyache, eating the half-green grapes and listening to what I felt was heavenly music. It was the first band I had ever heard. . . .

Of course I "took lessons" in music, first from a Mrs. Charley Hobson and then from a most accomplished musician—a Mrs. Fannie DeGrasso Black. In vain she tried to keep me to my exercises; but I could learn by ear almost as well, and certainly more rapidly, than I learned by note. Time and again she would catch me using my ear, and time and again she would try to bring me back to my "one and two and three and four and. . . ." So, finally, she yielded and gave me pieces. I never had to be lashed like a galley slave to my practice at home. I was up and at it as soon as I had visited my traps in the morning down in the timber, and probably before I had got my woodbox filled for the day. . . . Always I had my lesson, for I loved to play the pieces I heard on the street or at school or at the minstrel show or at a circus. The atmosphere of my life seemed to be charged with song and dance. . . .

My father saw it a year or so after the organ came. One day he pointed out an old whiskey-soaked failure, whom the town jeered at, a man who gave fiddling lessons and played for dances, drank like a fish as everybody knew, and never paid his debts. Even I knew at eleven or so that he ran after women and had every other fault that beset a man with emotional unbalance. And one day, as he passed, my father called me to his chair on the front porch, where I stood between his legs, and he put his arm about me and said:

"Willie, see old Professor Mechem! Pretty poor pickin's of a man, isn't he?"

I agreed.

"Just about frazzled out and gone to hell."

Again I agreed.

"Do you know what's the matter with him?"

I certainly knew. At least when my father went on I was not surprised:

"Music! Just too damned much music. He wa'n't such a bad feller when he was young. I knew him back in Leavenworth. Kinda dressed to kill and very sporty. But he just let himself go on music. And he's a dead beat and a whiskey sot and everything else that's mean, and it's music. And now, Willie, what do you say that we stop music lessons? I don't want you to grow up like that."

So we stopped. And again my mother sighed herself into a good cry, for she was tremendously proud of my music. . . . She would sit by the hour when she ought to have been at work, drinking in the crude music that I made by ear and note so slovenly and so carelessly in my ignorant pride. My father was not unappreciative. He heard me play a tune and he whistled it—and he was a great whistler—with an exact ear, but he would have died before he would praise me openly as my mother did. . . .

Only when my mother got down a book and offered to read to me could I be lured from the organ. She read widely. I would give a great deal to know what became of the two-volume edition of poems by the Tennyson Brothers which she owned, and from which she sometimes read to me what seemed like heavenly music. But for poetry, mostly I had Felicia Hemans and verses from selections of poetry that the book agents sold her—good old standard pieces of the early nineteenth century, or maybe the late eighteenth, full of jig and jingle and jump of the sort that I had read over and over in the school readers. . . . She fed me liberal doses of Anthony Trollope, Wilkie Collins, Charles Reade, after Dickens had played out.

She had been one of the founders of the El Dorado City Library which still functions in the town after more than sixty years. And, of course, I had my own books from that wellspring. It was there that I ran across *Tom Sawyer*, and *The Jumping Frog of Calaveras County*, and *Innocents Abroad*, and loved them. I went stark mad over Mark Twain at a dozen years. My mother was shocked, for Mark Twain was accounted an atheist. But my father did not care. . . . While he set great store by the Bible as literature and as a code of morals, [he] had very little use for its theological implications. I gathered from their arguments that my mother was still afraid of hellfire and still hoped for wings. . . .

I look back upon my boyhood there in the big house, when I was going to school in the grammar department, with a sense of well-being. My father was somebody. Occasionally he took me to Topeka, when there was a Democratic state convention; or when he was delegated from the town to represent it at some statewide meeting or enterprise, where his leadership rose above his party. And I remember once playing around the naked foundation of the west wing of the Kansas statehouse while my father, inside at the Democratic convention, was running for state treasurer. It was then, when we were passing along the streets, that we ran into some sort of a city election or informal primary. We saw a long queue of Negroes, holding their ballots high so that the checker could read them and pay them when they came out of the voting booth. And my father said angrily to me, "Willie, look at that! In this state the year before you were born they voted a constitutional amendment which gave those men the right to vote and denied it to women like your mother. I voted for woman suffrage, but against this damn shame!"

He wanted me to know it. I have always remembered it. And it is a tradition of family pride that we entertained Susan B. Anthony in the sixties when she was campaigning in Kansas for woman suffrage. And Elizabeth Cady Stanton was my mother's friend. My father also was a prohibitionist back in the seventies when the issue was pending in Kansas. Democrat though he was, we entertained at our house John P. St. John, the Kansas Republican hero of prohibition. Senator Plumb, whom my father knew in Emporia and who had gone to Washington and was a power there, a black Republican, enjoyed our hospitality—as did Senator Ingalls, an erudite Massachusetts man who honored Kansas as a senator. These house guests gave me a sense of belonging to the ruling class, and maybe I was a little snob, though I hope not. But it could have been, easily. . . .

If I was a snob, Agnes Riley took it out of me. She was a farmer's daughter. In those days, when boyhood was young, my world revolved around her, and there was no snobbish nonsense about Agnes. She walked a mile and a half to school. On cold days she wore a scarlet shawl that I could see from the second-story window of the schoolhouse more than a mile away. And I watched it come across the prairies with delight and mounting joy. A tall, thin, black-eyed girl, with high coloring, was Agnes Riley. It seemed to me her black eyes glowed with a fire I had never known before. I certainly "thrilled with delight when she gave me her smile" though I do not remember that I trembled with fear at her frown.[1] For she never frowned. But after my birthday party, where I looked for her among the sheeted and pillowcased ghosts and finally found her, she was the center of my cosmos. . . . It was boy and girl—newborn adolescence moving youth for the first time. It is an exquisite sensation, feeling the blood coursing through strange channels, taking new delightful ways, or running from the heart through life's spring erosions to the brain, reporting there great news of ineffable happiness. We were boy and girl going furtively, almost stealthily perhaps, but eagerly into the new wide land of youth, the promised land of the wicked Canaanites, those grown-ups where all the milk and honey of new untasted joy lay vague before youth to lure it on; boy and girl and youth!

If Agnes Riley, in those first days of my young boyhood, was the center of my cosmos, and if I spent more time than I should, of early morning, plucking my mother's roses and tying them on a wire cross which my own hands made, and if I gathered wild flowers for her and not my mother, and if I watched eagerly in the morning after I had slipped the rose wreath in our desk for the red shawl coming over the horizon, I did not moon about it. . . . Always I had an eye on the main chance. For I was born with an acquisitive sense. My little bank on the clock shelf at home was always well filled. I was always looking for a chance to run errands for someone with a dime. I remember vividly my father coming up behind me one summer day on Main Street and whacking me with his cane across my upturned bottom, to the astonishment of a stranger before whom I was kneeling, shining his shoes: "Get up from there, Willie—not that, by God! You go home!" And I grabbed my kit, for which I had traded a heavy outlay of marbles that I had won in my marble bank, and scurried home. How he ever explained it to the stranger, I do not know. But when he came home he called me to his chair and said, very gently: "Now Willie, . . . there are some things you just can't do unless you have to, and you don't have to shine any man's shoes." He explained it all in language which I have forgotten. It was the only time in all his life that I can remember when he implanted a sense of caste in my heart. . . .

I had come into the zone where a boy runs in wild gangs. I was a born gangster. The town was not large enough for more than one or two gangs. Ours dug a cave by the river bank. We stole chickens from a nearby farm, and roasting ears and watermelons and tomatoes in summer. And in fall, each of us had an apple stealer, a horseshoe nail driven through a cork, with feathers at one end, tied to the end of a string to keep it upright. We would throw it into an apple peddler's wagon on the street, or into a bushel basket of apples before a grocer's

---

[1]White is paraphrasing a popular song, "Ben Bolt," from a poem by Thomas Dunn English about Sweet Alice, "who wept with delight when you gave her a smile, / and trembled with fear at your frown!" The song appeared in George Du Maurier's popular 1894 novel *Trilby*.

door, spear an apple, yank it, get it into our pockets in the wink of an eye. Then, bulging with apples, we would hie us to our cave and eat in gloating, guiltless glee, proud of our prowess. Old man Young, the city marshal, once took after us with our pockets bulging. Albert Ewing, Bill Betts, Charley Harvey and I started together down an alley, and with a natural criminal instinct, broke—running four ways; and while the old man hesitated for a moment before deciding which to follow, we were gone. We made the wide circuit of the town, like hunted criminals, before we rounded up, with panting and beating hearts, to the cave. Old man Howe, whose chickens we stole, reported to my father. He paid for the day's chicken and told me at dinner that night the difference between having fun and being a thief, and said that any time we wanted a chicken he would give me money for it. Even my mother joined him in reprobation, though she did think old man Howe might be in better business than tattling about boyish pranks. . . .

The town changed swiftly. It, too, was going from its childhood into youth. The railroad seemed to shrivel and wither its little industries, though I did not realize it until many years afterward. The tin shop slowed down. The harness shop was not what it had been; harness came ready-made from Kansas City and St. Louis. The tannery disappeared and only the tanbark marked where it stood. Even the slaughterhouse was not the busy place it had been when I was a child and gloated and gagged at its stinks and ghastly sounds. The shoe shop seemed to be making no more shoes, only mending them. The plaster of Paris hat molds that I had first known around Leila Heaton's mother's millinery, we no longer found around El Dorado's new millinery shop. Hats came in from afar, ready molded.

The self-sufficient village was becoming a country town in my early boyhood days. Its population had grown to more than a thousand. It was a bustling place. New houses were going up all over the hill where my father sold his lot. Two-story houses were now becoming common. No one had quite so many feet of porch as we, but wide porches were common, and yards began to be fenced in paling where the cattle had grazed in my childhood. Streets were lined out and bluegrass lawns appeared. Elm trees, moved in from the creeks, lined the streets, and evergreens dotted the lawns. A few women now had time for flower gardens. The wide place in the dusty road where the movers' wagons rumbled, where the movers themselves trudged along, and where the little boys followed herding their cows—all this was going or was gone.

By 1880 Kansas was fairly well settled and the era had begun—a time when machinery was beginning to dominate the farm, and the mortgage to buy farm machinery was being plastered over the new state. For there was no economic surplus, no savings to draw on. Credit was easy. Labor-saving machinery piled up in front and behind all the hardware stores. Business was good. . . .

It was about this time that my father, who had been enjoying our grand new house with its twelve rooms, its "hundred forty-four running feet of porches," its gorgeous gingerbread ornamentations crawling all over the pillars of those porches and under and around the twenty-two windows and half a dozen doors, decided that he owed it as a public duty to the town to open this house as a hotel. And maybe that did not start a volcano, an earthquake, and a family cataclysm! I remember the disturbance, but the only sentence of it that hangs in my memory is this: "Well, Doctor, we might as well have a hotel; they might as well pay something as long as you keep bringing them in!" . . . So my mother yielded. The hotel opened.

I, a little boy of ten or a dozen years, had charge of the cigar stand. I bought and sold my cigars, paid the bills, and kept the profit, under the stern accounting eye of my father. . . . I stuffed the little bank with the profits. My father turned the pennies, dimes, and quarters into five-dollar gold pieces, and I always had a little money to spend for the fundamental necessities of boyhood, though he made me pay for my first suit of store clothes out of that bank. But I was proud enough not to begrudge the price. He was teaching me thrift, economy, and the rules of business, though I did not know it. Neither did my mother appreciate it. But she was too busy in the kitchen to know, or probably care much, what happened. For while my father preened around the place in his white clothes and Panama hat, on his majestic stretch of porches, greeting his guests, entertaining them, and going to market with his basket like a maharajah to a durbar, she did a husky woman's work—this woman with pink and white complexion and bronze hair which she curled so carefully until we opened the hotel. She wrestled, wrangled, and roughed it, trying to get along with two or three girls in the dining room and kitchen who soldiered on her, knowing that she would rather do it herself than quarrel with them about how to do it. In the midst of it, she was attacked with inflammatory rheumatism. She lost all of her teeth, and they cut off her hair. . . . Before she was up and at work again, we closed the hotel. It was a sad farce, that hotel venture.

My father seemed to have some hidden pride in not making money out of the hotel, though he was a shrewd trader in real estate. Probably he hesitated at capitalizing his hospitality, for he was vastly proud of his table. We used only the breasts of the quail and prairie chickens, generally broiled on hickory coals, and, in season, we had them once or twice a week. He bought only the best cuts of beef. I remember as a little boy going with him many times to market to bring home the market basket, and he taught me where to find the tenderloin, the sirloin, the T-bone, and the rib roast in a beef carcass. He always saved the bones for soup! Not, I suppose, because he liked to save so much as because he liked to serve good soup. We bought mackerel in the kit, and salt codfish by the case. In rush times I waited on table. I had to learn the bill of fare and sing it off for each of the guests. I also learned how to set the table expertly, and niftily pyramid knives and forks and spoons with a napkin on top. . . .

It was during or just before our hotel experience that I began my newspaper experience in a curtain raiser, a quick seriocomedy piece that was to forecast my career. When I was eleven years old, or such a matter,[2] my father thought I should work. He was forever singing that ancient father song that came, probably, from Father Adam, telling the boys of the marvelous industry of his childhood. If fathers, when they were boys, really had done all the things they brag about, the world would have been strutted into its millennium ten thousand years ago. So my father is not to be blamed if . . . he felt that I should be chained and shackled to the machine of life. . . .

Mothers are different; my mother was. She had had a little brother, as most mothers had, and she knew how naturally reckless and unchainable a little boy is. So she did not want me to go to work. But the Puritan blood in my father, and a vast phantasm of his own industry and exemplary childhood, backed him up when he would harness me to the harsh, hard work of the world. We did not need the money. . . . But, alas for me, he was a Democratic politician and naturally had money invested in the poor little starved-to-death Democratic weekly published in a tiny, unpainted, cigar-box-shaped pine building with a false front, straggling on the outskirts of the mean little business street of the county-seat village that hoped some day to be a city. In order to secure me employment he had only to take me by the hand the day after school closed in the spring, lead me up the street, and present me to the Editor. We shall meet this Editor later.

In the printing office were three racks of type and a small-job printing press—a Gordon I believe—on which were printed noteheads, letterheads, and small handbills. Near that was an old Washington hand press of an ancient and honorable lineage. It was secondhand—secondhand so many times that no one knew when it came from the foundry. It had crossed the Mississippi before the Civil War, that was all one knew definitely. Its Kansas lineage could be traced from Leavenworth to Lawrence, to Topeka, to Ottawa, and so, following the stream of immigration, to El Dorado for a few years, after which it was to march westward into the wheat country and thence into the great desert of the Southwest. A composing stone stood in the midst of the room, on which were the forms of type for the two pages which the paper set up and printed. Its outer pages came from Kansas City, ready printed. The walls of the room were unplastered, as well as unsealed. It being summer, the stove sat—cold and rusty—by the press, with paper sticking out of its mouth and a pot of ancient printer's tableting glue on its top, cold and petrified in disuse. A dejected attempt to cover the

[2]White was at least thirteen, for the Butler County *Democrat* was not founded until March 24, 1881.

rough, splintery board walls and joists of the room with handbills and so beau-
tify it, disclosed the portraits of a number of stallions and jacks, a Fourth of July
bill or two in red, white, and blue, some theatrical handbills revealing the fact
that "Pygmalion and Galatea" and "Sparticus, the Gladiator" and "The Hidden
Hand" and "Uncle Tom's Cabin" had been played by strolling players—Lillie
Lord and her company, the Goldens and Spooners, in the courtroom across the
street. . . .

Here in this sanctum, . . . barefoot, with a clean Monday-morning shirt on,
and with pants rolled decently to my knees, I was left by my father. The Editor,
the foreman, and the printer formed the dramatis personae of the establishment. I was to be the devil.[3] I have a scant memory of my work in the printing
office at that period. I remember picking up type from the floor in the evening
and sweeping out the room. I remember carrying water from a well down the
street and across an alley to the printing office. I remember standing on a box
and rolling an ink roller across the type on the bed of the Washington hand
press—hard, sweaty work from which, probably because I did it badly rather
than because he pitied me, the foreman took me after what seemed a long time,
possibly half an hour. I remember folding papers for subscribers which the Editor addressed in lead pencil. And I remember carrying the papers to the post office in a great wash bucket, going several times.

Finally, Saturday night came. I sat around, saw the Editor come over to the
printer and make some financial arrangement with him and saw him slip some
paper—possibly a check, possibly an order for groceries, Heaven knows what,
but not coin of the realm—to the foreman. Nothing came to me. I was to have
had a dollar and a half a week. I was not a brash child, except on the playground. I said nothing. The Editor walked grandly out. The printer winked at
me with some cryptic meaning being behind his wink, which disconcerted me
deeply, for I went home that night full of wrongs, wrongs which my mother
abetted. When I went to bed I overheard her upbraiding my father. It seems he
had forgotten to leave the money for my wages with the Editor, as per previous
agreement.

The discovery of this fact, that I was being paid by my own father, was dis-
concerting. My mother told me the next day that when I had worked a whole
week I should have my wages. So I went back—a galley slave scourged to the
dungeon—and worked Monday, Tuesday, and Wednesday. Wednesday night I
waited—no wages came. I came home surging with unjustice and wept, being inside the threshold where tears did not disgrace a boy. Again my mother assured
me that I should have my money the next morning; my father had forgotten, or
maybe the Editor had forgotten. Someone had blundered.

---

[3]The apprentice in a print shop was commonly known as the "printer's devil."

I went back Thursday morning. The Editor came breezing in, cheerful, happy, and apparently innocent of the great wrong he was committing. It was a hot summer day in June. The printer and the foreman drank much water. The water in the bucket was two-thirds gone and was stale. The order came to get another bucket of water; this was just before noon. The air was wavy with heat outside. Grasshoppers and locusts were rasping their clatter in the trees and high weeds through which I went for the water. At the well, throwing rocks at the hornets working in the mud around the curb by way of diversion, were my fellow citizens and peers in the free Kingdom of Boyville. I set down the bucket and took a mild detached interest in the hornets. My peers knew that I was no longer of their rank. I had become a bondman not of their caste. And, being boys, they taunted me: "We're goin' swimmin'." "Wouldn't you like to go swimmin'?" "New boy down there says he can take a big rock to weight him down and walk across the creek under water. Betcha he can't." "How many buckets of water do you have to carry?" "Is it hot in that buildin'?" "Who's your boss?" "Does he jaw you?" "Whatja do?" So they twisted the spears of captivity in my entrails. They started up and casually went away, throwing clods at me by way of contempt and derision, and I fired back rocks, looking wistfully at the straggling procession roaming down the path between the high weeds, through the ravine that led to the creek.

All that morning I had furtively watched that Editor for some sign of his intention to establish justice in that shop, as between him and me. I had had no sign; not a flicker of an eyelash. The last tagging toddler of the gang disappeared into the weeds.

And I, lifting my face to high heaven to witness the justice of my cause, kicked the bucket into the mud, swarming with hornets, and went running down the path toward the swimming hole. So fell the curtain on the prologue of my career.

As I look back across the years, my father seems to have been hurrying my education with some kind of premonition that his time was short. He was taking me to places where I should see interesting things—to Kansas City to see steam power engines and the great trotting horses, Maud S. or Rarus (I forget which), to the State Fair to see the first electric light when it crossed the Mississippi River. It was on a high pole, a sputtering lavender star which was supposed to light a whole neighborhood. On the same trip, probably at the fair, I saw James G. Blaine. It was in the early eighties. His beard was lighter than an iron gray. His skin was fair. His smile was electric, even a little boy knew that. His voice was gentle and persuasive. My father explained to me who Blaine was, in language that a boy in his early teens could understand. He gave me a low opinion of Blaine. Indeed, my father's heroes were few. Even Tilden, whom he thought a martyr, he accepted only at a liberal commercial discount. He came greatly to admire Abraham Lincoln. Andrew Jackson was his ideal. From both my parents, I had but scorn for the Republican leaders of Reconstruction days and the things they were doing to the South. In Kansas, in the seventies and eighties, the Democratic party was in a hopeless minority. The soldiers of the Civil War, whom I saw in my childhood coming into Kansas and appearing on high days and holidays in their army blue with their visored caps, dominated the state.

Here may be a place where I can set down the photograph upon my child's mind of the first memorial parade I ever saw. It was headed by the El Dorado silver cornet band in splendid regalia—splendid to my child's eye at least. Following that was the volunteer fire department pulling the old pumping engine that took its water from the great cistern at the corner of Central and Main Streets. Then in the town's one open carriage sat Peter Telyea, a veteran of the War of 1812—a man well into his nineties who owned the town carriage works and who toiled amid his lathes and shavings every day until he died. Behind him, on horseback, were the veterans of the Mexican War. Colonel Gibson, our town banker, rode at the head of that small squadron of fifty men or so, all bearded. Then, in order of rank, were the veterans of the Civil War. General Ellet, the hero of Island Number Ten in Grant's campaign on the Mississippi, led the long line. After the general came the half-dozen colonels we had, and captains, all sashed and horsed and panoplied in military pomp; and following them walked the blue-clad soldiers of the lower ranks. Behind them marched citizens on foot and women's organizations.

It was a long parade—a picture I shall never forget. And my father, who had no part in the military glory, held my hand as we stood on the sidewalk. He explained to me the meaning of it all and left to me no great sense of the pomp and circumstance of glorious war.[4] My Uncle Frank Hatten, my mother's brother, captain of the First Michigan Cavalry, who enlisted and re-enlisted three times and after the war went West to fight the Indians, rode in the parade. My father clapped for him, and so did I. But he dismissed certain sections of the parade with the phrase: "A lot of damn bounty jumpers!" and carefully explained to me that a "bounty jumper" was a man who was paid to substitute for a drafted man and who then deserted from the army with his bounty in his pocket, turned up in another part of the country, got another bounty, and enlisted again. It was a fairly profitable career in a country which had a wide, unsettled frontier to which the bounty jumper could go, and from which he could return to ply his trade in a new and strange community. . . .

I cannot remember, and I have often tried, just when it was that our gang of cave dwellers who played "Injun" with our bows and arrows . . . came indoors

---

[4]Shakespeare's Othello, a powerful military leader, recalls the "pride, pomp, and circumstance [pageantry] of glorious war" (*Othello*, Act III, scene iii).

and began to be "housebroke." Somehow I believe the girls got us in. We began to attend parties—somewhere between eleven and fourteen. There also we ganged up, but with the female of the species, and I remember early in our middle teens we who cast ourselves as Indians and desperadoes, bandits and horse thieves, suddenly found ourselves playing post office, dancing the Virginia reel, taking our apples to girls instead of to the teacher, and sending valentines. We called our gang—male and female—the "Spring Chicken Club," and Mr. Murdock in his newspaper in El Dorado named us "Trundle Bed Trash." And we liked the name.

Our social diversions, even when we had a party in the town restaurant, could not have cost us more than a quarter, for in those days one could get a fiddler, a pianist, and a cornetist, or any combination of three dance-music makers, for five dollars. But the apex of social distinction was to hire "the Italians," who came from Wichita or possibly Kansas City, and made the rounds of the country towns. They played on the streets for dimes and nickels and were hired by the young blades of the town, men in their late teens and early and middle twenties, and we Trundle Bed Trash trekked along for a price, and the music—a violin or two, a flute, or a harp—seemed to me exquisite.

Hearing "the Italians" was a step up in my musical education. I followed them about the streets. I passed the hat for them among the traveling men at our hotel so that they would play on the porch a long time. I had never before heard such music and my ears drank it in greedily. When they were gone, I went to my cabinet organ, tried to play by ear the tunes I heard and made some kind of a fist of it—probably a pretty poor fist. But it pleased me immensely.

It was curious to note, and I suppose I see it more clearly in the perspective of nearly sixty years, how the gang instinct of boyhood changed so swiftly and so surely from the wild life of the male to the mixed society which formed the Spring Chicken Club. Certainly it thought itself the elite, but the same kind of ganging that the boys knew, where there was no line of marked wealth or parental distinction back of the crystallization, governed the unconscious organization of the Spring Chickens. It was not the rich little boys and the rich little girls in a community where we had few riches who set the social pattern. Some boys and some girls who were Spring Chickens were dirt poor. But not all the dirt-poor boys and girls got in, which also was true of our horse-thief gang in the caves. Childhood and youth, left free as we were in a new place and a verdant time, were drawn together in their organized social cliques and clans, somewhat by their natural qualities—their capacity for crystallization. Whatever it may be, I know now and I knew then, that we—the elite, the Spring Chickens—were envied. I realized that we were a lot of little snobs and were proud of it. . . .

Let us take a look at this Will White, the schoolboy. He is of medium height for a boy, with the one pancake freckle of childhood breaking into crumbs of freckles at his neck under his ears. Here comes his chiefest sorrow—pimples all over his jaw and chin and cheek, miserable disfiguring pimples that he could not help squeezing, pinching, scratching, black-headed pimples that broke his pride. Other boys teased him and shamed him about them. For there was a boy scandal about pimples which had no reference to a boy's diet. . . . He was still a good footracer and proud of his straight, hard legs.

Clothes interested him. He began to learn to tie a four-in-hand and knew that a made-up tie was not quite the thing. And he tried to learn to waltz. Square dances, of course, were simple enough. A boy hobbled along and kept some sense of the rhythm of the music in his feet, but waltzes were different. I can see myself now, a chunky, nimble youth carrying in his arms a big, brown rocking chair with a cane seat, whistling a waltz. . . . On summer afternoons he used to lie in the hammock on the east porch of the big house reading, with maybe another boy or two about, whose nose also was in a book. . . . By way of being human, the other boys played baseball and went out to wallop or be walloped by the Augusta High School team, or the Douglass team, or Towanda, or Benton, or Eureka, or Rosalia. The El Dorado ball players were the Red Socks. I kept score and looked after the bats and catcher's masks, and so learned to be methodical and punctual and precise about material things, while the other boys learned highly laudable skill.

As for the girls, even the worst of us—the more venereal-minded—set them upon a pedestal. They were apart, though often in school one of us would sit with a girl to sing in the music hour. All of us beaued the girls to the little dances and to the kissing parties, which still lingered along in the middle teens half surreptitiously in our social life. But on the neighborhood vacant lots girls played with us. Sometimes, if they were tomboys and not afraid of showing their legs, they joined in footraces; and I can remember that Dora Rector, who because she was husky, commanded our respect, could without scandal do turns on the bar and was not ashamed if her skirt flopped over her head and showed her chaste and ruffled drawers while she hung by her legs and dropped from a knee hold to a toe hold on the swinging broom handle that was our trapeze. Other girls envied her, tried to imitate her, but certainly did not talk about her. . . . I recall today with boyish glee the pride that I had in Dora Rector when she gathered her little skirts and petticoats up to the bulge in her panties, with her eyes set, her jaw fixed, her chin forward and her head down, the best runner in the east part of town. And I backed her with all the pins, marbles, tops, pennies, and other wampum of boyhood that I could scrape together.

This recollection deserves space here because it marks the passing of a pioneer sport, the footracer who went from town to town, generally staging crooked races with local runners. He must have been known since the very beginning of man's earthly pilgrimage. In El Dorado he passed on westward with the sun and we boys and girls merely imitated him—the ancient sportsman who lived on the prowess of his legs. He could not thrive in coal smoke or around the hum of machines. But he was a real figure in my boyhood.

It was in those days in my very early teens that I tried to write what I thought was poetry. Agnes Riley had written a poem, "To a Sand Bur," and published it in the El Dorado paper. She had an aunt, May Riley Smith, who published a book of poems and whose name we saw in *Harper's Bazaar* and other publications designed for women. My first poetical effort was deeply philosophical. I remember writing the title first, "Whatever Is, Is Right." And I have a notebook now, which my mother preserved, in which I set down a list of words which rhymed with "right": "fight" and "blight," "kite" and "tight." How I must have patted myself on the head in pride when I plunged into the depths of my vocabulary and turned up the word "wight"! A quatrain or two stand there in my little notebook, threescore years, to remind me how well *Lalla Rookh*[5] and Byron and "Lucile"[6] and Whittier and "Hiawatha"[7] and Will Carlton's poems bore their fruit. I had not yet come to James Whitcomb Riley, so I spelled my words correctly. . . .

The summer of 1882, I crossed the final branch of the Rubicon Valley[8] and came out of childhood ultimately and finally into boyhood. I was fourteen years old. The carpet slippers which I wore on Main Street in my latter barefoot days were discarded and they put shoes on me. Two women practically tied me to get them on—my mother and Agnes Riley. Their disapproval of my bare feet lured me into captivity. Maybe as a consolation, I bought, traded for, or received as a reward for soliciting subscribers for the *Youth's Companion*, an accordion and mourned through it the passing of the golden days. I wonder what boys and girls today do without the premium list of the *Youth's Companion*. That little book opened the door to so many desirable things: a scroll saw, which Albert Ewing got; Barney and Berry skates, which later I acquired; musical instruments, balls and baseball bats and masks, books of games and magic, dumbells, boxing gloves—all to be had for new subscribers to the *Youth's Companion*. My father caught me crooking it a little by persuading a boy whose subscription was expiring to renew in the name of another family. Pa stopped that swindle. But I worked hard on the *Youth's Companion* job in those days and captured much loot.

[5]*Lalla Rookh* (1817), by Irish poet Thomas Moore, was a romantic narrative poem with an Oriental setting.

[6]*Lucile* (1860) was a popular romantic novel in verse by "Owen Meredith," the pseudonym of English diplomat Edward Robert Bulwer-Lytton.

[7]Henry Wadsworth Longfellow's poem *The Song of Hiawatha* was published in 1855.

[8]The Rubicon was a small river separating ancient Italy from Gaul, the province governed under an agreement with the Roman senate by Julius Caesar. Fearing his growing power, the senate ordered him to return to Rome without his army. When in 49 B.C. Caesar crossed the Rubicon in defiance of this order, he precipitated a civil war. Hence "to cross the Rubicon" is to take an irrevocable step.

My father seems to have been with me a good deal that summer. I remembered afterwards, and I remember now, that he sat on the front porch in his white summer regalia, trying to coax me away from the natural diversions of the hour to tell me about his boyhood in Ohio: something of his father and mother who died when he was about my age; and how he and his elder brothers cleared the timber from the farm on which he grew up; and of the friendly Indians that were around Norwalk, Ohio, in the twenties and thirties. He was pointing morals, which at the time bored me, for a fourteen-year-old boy is essentially amoral. I was probably a little to the left of amorality by nature and disposition. Life had to beat honesty into me by the club of experience. My father's wise saws and modern instances may have sunk deeply into my consciousness and they may have bobbed up later—I don't know. But I do believe that Solomon's emphasis on the word "old" has not been sufficiently understood when he said: "Train up a child in the way he should go: and when he is old, he will not depart from it."[9]

One certainly departs from that way in youth, also in early manhood. But whatever one has planted inside him in youth, in the way of spiritual and environmental inheritance, comes bursting into his life around forty and thereafter. Probably I did not really appreciate my father nor mourn his loss with real filial piety until I was old in the biblical sense of the word. . . .

One day that summer Pa and I were alone together. I remember I was lying on my belly, idly thumping my toes on the floor, with my nose in a big leather-bound copy of Plutarch's *Lives*,[10] which Pa had in the bookcase. . . . He had been silent for a long while, drumming with his fingernails on his chair the rhythmic skeleton of some old tune singing in his heart. The bee song that he often hummed was silent. I looked up, and his eyes were glistening as he caught my attention. An open letter was on the table beside him. . . . He saw that I noticed his moistened eyes. He smiled and said: "Willie, this letter tells me about the death of a girl I knew when she was not much older than you. She was an awfully nice girl and she thought I was nice too. And she was about your age. She was my girl and I was her beau and that was a long, long time ago. And now she is dead! Her sister wrote me here, and sent me a lock of her hair. She said she wanted me to have it. And it's gray! Goddlemitey, Willie, it's gray! It's gray!" He paused a moment, began drumming again and then: "Well, I suppose it ought to be really. But it's gray!"

He repeated that phrase like a gentle protest to Providence. Pretty soon he got up, took his cane, and toddled off the porch down the sidewalk to the thick of the town. And Plutarch interested me no more that morning. I looked at my father going down

[9]Proverbs 22: 6.

[10]Plutarch's *Parallel Lives* was composed of paired biographies of Greek and Roman statesmen and generals, who served as models of character and bravery for centuries of readers.

the street and suddenly realized that once he had been a boy and had had a girl like Agnes Riley—maybe! After that it was as though we were brothers-in-law in the great family of romantic intrigue. So, initiated into that brotherhood, I never told my mother—not to her dying day. But I did tell Albert Ewing, who had Lizzie Ruddick on the string, and Agnes, and we marveled much at the ways of men.

That summer my father took me with him on various trips to Topeka, to Kansas City, and to Wichita. And I remember that he talked to me a lot, but what he said is gone from my consciousness. He talked politics with me, that I remember. And, being a rock-ribbed Democrat, he was greatly interested in a young New Yorker who had been a reform mayor of Buffalo and who was reigning as governor of New York. His name was Grover Cleveland. He was my father's kind of a Democrat in those days, and my father so deeply impressed the name of Grover Cleveland on me that later, when school opened and the high school teacher, seeking to interest us in politics, asked everyone to name his guess for the next president of the United States, I rose and said bravely, "Grover Cleveland!" The schoolroom laughed. They had never heard of him. I suppose that tradition lived in the El Dorado High School for a dozen years. The teacher, who afterwards became a lawyer, never let me forget it. He did not know that I was not abnormally prophetic but merely was echoing the wishful prophecy of an old-fashioned Jacksonian Democratic father.

My father, like most Kansans of substance and some little consequence there in those days, was an ardent believer in prohibition. . . . [He] frowned upon the movement in his party to make the resubmission of the prohibition amendment its cause in Kansas at the election that year. He headed the Butler County delegation to the state convention at Emporia that year. There the Democrats nominated a good old Tennessee silk-stocking Democrat, . . . [named] John Martin. But in the platform upon which John Martin was to run was a plank denouncing prohibition, promising to annul the amendment by disuse or something of the kind. John Martin took the platform and declined to run with that plank in. Whereupon the convention nominated George W. Glick—a man whom my father called a "whiskey Democrat from Atchison."

He came home heartbroken. He did not whistle. He would lose his cane. All I can remember is that I heard him tell my mother: "Ma, I lived through the hell of one time when the Democrats stood for nullification,[11] and I just can't stand it again!" His politics meant that much to him! He finally took to his bed. I did not know it then, nor for many years afterwards, but he was suffering from diabetes or shock, and the worry killed him. He died on October 4, 1882.

---

[11]Nullification was the principle, first stated by Thomas Jefferson, that each state had the right to reject, or "nullify," federal laws it found contrary to the Constitution. It was frequently raised in pre–Civil War debates over slavery. It refers here to Kansas Democrats' opposition to enforcement of the 1880 amendment to the state constitution that banned alcohol.

His death came to me suddenly. I was not allowed to go to school the morning that he died. I had no idea he was so near death, but I sensed something dreadful in my mother's manner and in the fact that two doctors had come. They went away, and I followed them down the walk. I cannot remember what they said, but I know they shook their heads, and then I was frightened. In the mid-morning, my mother called me to the bedside where she and a neighbor woman were working—rubbing my father's hands and feet and applying hot cloths to his legs and arms. He could not speak. He seemed in a coma. I thought it was sleep, though his eyes were slitted, and I too began rubbing his feet and crying and calling "Pa," and looking at his slitted eyes to see if I could get one glimmer of recognition. I was a frightened little boy. Suddenly and desperately I tried to call my father back. He passed away about noon, and the world grew black for me, though I did not cry much. That I remember. Indeed, I tried to comfort my mother, who mourned with racking sobs and unchecked tears, as we stood alone there by the bedside when we knew he was gone. Then my memory rings down the curtain.

I only remember that in the evening I tiptoed along into the room where my father lay upon his bier, covered with a sheet, lifted it up, and saw that his face was bloated and colored with the poison that killed him. I let out one moan of terror and fled, and never looked upon him again. I could not bear, even when they told me that the undertaker had cleared away his blotches, to see him again. I would not go to his coffin when it was opened. But I remember that my mother consulted with me about the hymns they would sing at his funeral. I remember that she said he liked the tune "Rock of Ages" and she also picked a gospel hymn called "When the Mists Have Cleared Away"—the burden of which was: "In the dawning of the morning we shall know each other better when the mists have cleared away." I knew even then that she was expressing the anguish in her own heart that she had not understood "the Doctor," that she had not realized her dream of love and romance with him.

We had a really notable funeral for the town. He had been elected mayor the spring before, and El Dorado turned out, filled our yard, and stood far down in the streets beyond. I was not without my pride, looking back as we rode along, and made the turn half a mile from home, and headed for the East Cemetery, to see the long line of carriages and wagons and carts still moving into the procession on Main Street. My pride probably conquered my sorrow for a little while, which is a natural conquest in a boy's heart.

I should have been heartbroken at the loss of my father. I was not. After the first few hours or days of acute grief, I went about my business and resented the tender solicitude of those who supposed I would be mourning deeply. Yet I know now, and probably knew then, that he was a good father to me and a good man in all of his relations. . . . I am sure that, spiritually, he made me—not by blood inheritance so much as by the unconscious guidance he gave me, the example he set, which I know now I tried to follow, and by the practical ideals he established. He was tolerant but never uncertain of his convictions, which he held courageously but never cantankerously. He hated argument and wrangling. Above everything, he was humorously self-deprecating, perhaps even consciously clowning a bit—an attitude a short man sometimes takes to compensate for the fact that he is a runt. . . .

He was a man of books and reading, as those things go among pioneers. . . . Among his books, which included a book on horticulture, another on agriculture, was Plutarch's *Parallel Lives*, a large volume which he tried to make me read, but for years it was too heavy for me in avoirdupois and in intellectual weight. But I remember that he read it often. . . . All of his books, which I imagine he brought over from his life before my mother came into it, I read. When I begin to look back at them and to see my father in perspective, I realize that he was in some ways an exceptional man who sought real leadership and tried to keep it anonymous; who loved power but always pretended he had none; who made money easily and spent it wisely and never had a miserly desire to be rich. I know that one of his hidden vanities was to be the first man on the subscription paper with the largest donation. He was a great hand to pass the paper himself to help various causes. He helped to build every church in El Dorado. . . . I know he helped to pay the El Dorado preacher in at least three churches and never went inside a church himself, though he was familiar with the Bible and its phrases were forever creeping into his speeches, especially in his merrier moments. . . .

I am setting down these things here at my father's death. But, alas, I understood their meaning only when I saw him in the retrospect of my own manhood and middle age. A boy of fourteen could not comprehend such a man as he was. But when my memory put him together again, I could mourn him deeply. I have never ceased to sorrow that he did not stay with me for another twenty years, to help me and to guide me from the follies which he may have seen ahead of me. I know now what I did not know then—that I was the apple of his eye. He loved me and hoped for me and maybe, to whatever gods he knew, he prayed for me. And when I was old I did not depart from the way! . . .

3

I Choose a Foster Father

My father had been ill in bed two weeks the October that he died. The crops on the farm near town, for which he had traded the farm on the West Branch, were ready for harvest—a little wheat, some oats, corn and millet. It was my job to get [my mother's] share from the tenant. I remember riding on the farmer's wagon to mill when the wheat was threshed, taking the millet to the feed store and the corn to our crib in town by the barn. I got my check from the miller for the wheat and I took it to the bank, but I did not know how to deposit it. The bank clerk showed me carefully how to make out a deposit slip and told me to go and get my father's bank book. I deposited the money in his name, then later changed the account to my mother's name. I collected the rent on the two or three little one-story frame buildings with false fronts that he owned, occupied by real estate men, lawyers, and such like, on the fringe of Main Street, and on one rather nice residence in the best part of town. I put that money in the bank and my mother and I kept the household account together. But, at fourteen, I was the man of the house. For I took to responsibility as a duck takes to water.

After a few months—maybe by the first of the year 1883—my mother realized that our income would not keep us. . . . So she opened the house to roomers, had two or three families, and charged well for her rooms. And sometime in the spring she began to take her roomers as boarders. Her cooking was famous over the town, and before spring she had the dining room filled with boarders, and at a good price. She was a close buyer and a good marketer. Moreover, she could send me to market, for my father had trained me, and so we did well. . . .

It was in those boarding-house days that T. B. Murdock came into my life—a man who greatly influenced me, an exceptional man whom my father deeply respected and, I think, held in affection. He ran the Walnut Valley *Times* and I can remember him in my childhood as a straight natty figure of a man who sometimes, for full dress, wore his army uniform of blue with brass buttons and his visored cap. He had a short goatee and a moustache which, also for full dress, he waxed at the ends. He was a light-footed, fully faced man, later in life inclined to paunch a little. He had a soft, self-deprecating voice—a bit ingratiating, not exactly a cooing pigeon's; but a voice that pleased women. He and my father had swapped books and read much for busy men in a frontier town. He had no formal education except that which he acquired in his trade as a printer. The thing that gave him distinction in my life was that he could write. . . .

He was a survival, a holdover, from post-bellum America. He had zeal without moral restraint for holy causes. His amiable casuistry justified doing evil for good. He was a warm-hearted man with a child's love of giving joy, a child's vanity in dressing up, and a wanton's way with him which made his friends trust him further than he would trust himself. For he was never a sanctified winner. He knew too well his grievous weaknesses. . . .

In the seventies Bent Murdock brought his first wife to the wilderness of Kansas from a sheltered little town in Ohio—from a white house with green blinds under spreading elms inside a white paling fence, to a man's world, a tough-shooting, wide-open frontier town, where half a dozen horse thieves were hanged one night in a village nearby, where her neighbors might be strumpets or gamblers, and where Mr. Murdock was, with my father, leading a dirty county-seat fight, always verging on felony and often toying with manslaughter. She was a pale, frail, shy, sensitive thing, and one day she looked out of the window of her two-room home on the main street of El Dorado. She saw a group of rowdies carrying a rope and roaring in their liquor that they were "looking for old Bent Murdock"—old at thirty-three! She went stark mad, cut her throat and her son's throat and, still flourishing the bloody razor, fell fainting from loss of blood on her front porch as she was chasing her little crippled daughter Alice, . . . who ran screaming to the neighbors. They brought the dead boy and the dying mother to our house, and there held both funerals. . . . Then, after only a decent period of mourning, Mr. Murdock married Marie Antoinette O'Daniel—a schoolteaching widow who had come out of the Eastern Shore of Maryland to our wilderness to escape only Heaven knows what little hot hell that was sizzling for her at home.

My father, though he was a Democrat, supported Mr. Murdock, a Republican, in 1876, when he was elected to the state senate. He was a notable figure in the state. When he was defeated for reelection to the state senate by the people of Butler County in 1880, he sold his newspaper, left the town in disgust, and took a job writing editorials for the Topeka *Commonwealth*. Then, after my father's death, he came back, started a new paper—the El Dorado *Republican*—and lived for a year or so at our house with his family. . . .

Marie Antoinette Murdock—later "Aunt Net"—was one of the women who made a deep impression on my life. I first saw her teaching elocution. She was reciting "The Raven"[1] and scared the wits out of me. And her next selection at the evening's entertainment was a poem with the refrain: "I am not mad, I am not mad"—a long dramatic pause, then in a voice of horror, "But soon shall be!" Woops! but that scared a little tad of six! But she was a lovely thing, that Marie Antoinette—a hothouse flower. . . . For she never touched reality. To her, reality was loathsome. She played her life away. I don't think she ever touched dishwater. I never saw her, when she lived in our house, in the backyard on any pretense—any whatever! I lived with her or near her for a long generation and never saw her slouchily dressed, never saw her when she wasn't sitting for her portrait, dressed for a grand ball.

She read wisely and well. From her . . . I had many modern books and magazines. She wrote well and sometimes reviewed books for her husband's newspaper. I remember her review of Ed Howe's *The Story of a Country Town*,[2] and her review of the first edition of *The Rhymes of Ironquill*.[3] A decade before those books were acclaimed across the land, she assessed them for their real value. . . .

Sometimes of winter evenings when the others—my mother and the Murdocks—were out . . . I used to go to their room and sit with her beside the glow of the glittering base-burner while she read to me, beautifully, elocuting elaborately some tale or poem or magazine article. . . . I sat there in the firelight's ruddy glow, fancying that I was Pip to her Miss Havisham![4] Probably we needed each other: I was the audience she always craved; she was the dramatic actress that I yearned to know. I still can hear her proud voice crying: "The tintinnabulation of the Bells—the Bells, the Bells!"[5] Even now I do not know what the poem meant; but it certainly did something to me that I needed in my business as a teenage boy who desired to be a sophisticated young gentleman. . . .

A few years later when the Murdocks bought a home on the hill above town, they bought one with a circular stairway leading to a wide hallway. It gave her the chance she needed in her life. She never came down those stairs that she did not look like Maria Theresa coming to meet her conquerors. . . . And certainly the Murdocks were a handsome pair—Aunt Net and Uncle Bent—in their thirties, a distinguished and more than commonly cultured couple. They served the best table in town. They danced well when they led the Grand March at the

[1]"The Raven" (1845) by Edgar Allan Poe had the well-known refrain, "Quoth the Raven, Nevermore."

[2]Howe published this pioneering realistic novel in 1883.

[3]Kansan Eugene F. Ware's *Rhymes of Ironquill* (1885) were widely read in his day.

[4]Characters in Charles Dickens's novel *Great Expectations* (1861). Pip is strongly influenced as a young boy by the rich, eccentric recluse Miss Havisham.

[5]Poe's poem "The Bells" (1849) evokes the sound of bells through the rhythm and timber of his words.

Firemen's Ball. They read the new books and magazines. They dressed in the latest style. Mr. Murdock bought his clothes even then from Brooks Brothers. . . .

I knew even then that Mr. Murdock ran Butler County politically. I knew casually that he was a director of the Florence, El Dorado and Walnut Valley Railroad, a Santa Fe Branch, and often a private car came and picked him up and took him on journeys. I knew that he associated in Topeka with the rich and the great and with the ruling class of our state. I was proud of it. And I . . . was to all intents and purposes a member of their family. He was my foster father. Because my father held him as his little brother Benjamin,[6] he took me on as his spiritual child. I was proud of him, grafted him into the wound that death had left when my father went, and gave him a son's affection and respect which I never withheld.

The winter after my father's death, my voice was changing and, curiously enough, I realize now why I began to be interested in singing. It was the pinfeather rooster starting to crow, though I did not know that my urge to sing, and that of other boys in school, had its biological root. I thought it just happened. Anyway, the next winter a half a dozen of us organized what we called a male quartet, though it sometimes ranged from a quartet to an octet, and we did our harmonizing by ear. They learned the tunes; I played them on the organ. Lew Schmucker's brother had a banjo. I could use the accordion. Ed Harvey had a guitar. . . .

So we young roosters used to roam about the town at night serenading—chiefly our various "girls," though sometimes singing under windows of prominent citizens for the very joy of it. We called ourselves "the Screech Owls." We sang sentimental ballads of that day, the leftovers from the Civil War, Stephen Foster's folk songs, dolorous ballads like "Marguerite," and waltz songs. . . . And, of course, we used the real spirituals like "Go Down, Moses," "Swing Low Sweet Chariot," "Nobody Knows the Trouble I See," and "The Old Ark's A-Moverin'." It was a wide repertoire and anything we heard in a show or on the street we picked up.

It was in those years after my father's death that I began to earn my first real money, in terms of dollars, playing for dances with a blind fiddler named Dol Cowley, who was good as fiddlers go, and with a cornetist named George Yonkman. We played at dances in the country, where they took down the beds, moved all the furniture outside except the cookstove, and danced in three rooms—leaving only the cabinet organ which I played to clutter up the floor. We played and they danced, chiefly square dances, some polkas, a few schottisches, but rarely a waltz. . . . Because the fiddler was blind and the cornetist otherwise busy, it was my job to call off the square dances. My changing voice I trained to

[6]In the Old Testament, Benjamin was Joseph's beloved younger brother (Genesis 45).

some powerful register so that I could unlimber it and throw it, on a clear moon-light night, all over the township as I bellowed the promptings of the dizzy maze. That voice afterwards stood me in good stead in open-air meetings. In those days I got three dollars a night for it, a dollar more than the other two musicians because I called off. So I had money to burn and Agnes Riley got more buggy rides than I could have given her earning an honest dollar.

But after all, probably in those days I was more interested in school than in any other one thing. School, to me, satisfied the gang instinct. There . . . I was someone. I liked to boss and always at school a lot of boys not only needed boss-ing, but liked it. . . . Two boys at the El Dorado High School period colored my life, Albert Ewing and Lew Schmucker. Both were good at their studies in school. . . . But Lew Schmucker's reading range was wider than Albert's or mine. And because Lew was a year or so older than I, he led me far afield in books. We both patronized the city library, reading almost exclusively fiction and poetry, as befitted boys in their middle teen age. We rollicked through Mark Twain. We roared at Bill Nye. Lew could read *Don Quixote*[7] with appreciation, but it stalled me. We bought the current humorous papers—the *Texas Siftings*, the *Detroit Free Press*, the *Arkansas Traveler*—and read with howling glee the first newspaper syndicated humorist that I remember, who wrote the "Spoopendyke Papers"—pieces which raised their laughs by making grotesque metaphors. . . . Other boys were reading dime novels, stories that filled the place that movie "Westerns" hold today. . . . But Lew and Albert and I . . . looked down with vast scorn on more vulgar dime novels. Probably it was a bit snobbish. But John B. Alden, the mail-order book dealer who sold cheap pirated editions of British authors, got most of our spare change. We bought his "Red Line Poets," bound in gaudy colors and printed on gilt-edge pages. We could have had the same books from the city library, but it was our delight to collect books just as other boys collected bugs and stamps.

Looking back and remembering, I have often wondered if when I called on Agnes Riley, hugging under my arm *A Tale of Two Cities*[8] or *Les Misérables*,[9] I really seemed the little pimple-faced, mild-eyed, redheaded prig that I was. . . . The poor girl must have paid heavily for the few buggy rides, the occasional or-gies in the ice cream saloon, and the one or two, or perhaps half a dozen, rides she took to parties on rainy nights in the town's only musty hack. But she was a gentle soul, patient and long-suffering, with most luminous, lovely eyes. So when, in its mid-teens, the Trundle Bed Trash felt that they were a bit too old for kissing games at parties, those eyes tormented me without recompense or ade-

[7]Don Quixote (1605) by Miguel de Cervantes Saavedra is generally considered the first modern novel.

[8]A novel about the French Revolution by Charles Dickens published in 1859.

[9]A ten-volume novel by Victor Hugo published in 1862.

quate reward. But some way, to meet them at school over the top of a geometry for a fleeting second, or over the railing in the hall, or going in the door when the bell rang, paid well for the torture. I was happy. I even made fun of Albert Ewing, who was running the same gauntlet of unrequited affection past Lizzie Ruddick. We talked about the girls a good deal and Lew Schmucker hooted and jibed us. For he had been to boarding school and he knew a lot of things about girls that we were not supposed to know—the dirty little devil.

I was sixteen years old when I finished the El Dorado High School. . . . After we marched out of high school the last afternoon, before the graduating exercises, Albert Ewing and I hung around the building until all the other children were gone and went up, hand in hand, to stand and look over the little puddle of empty desks, and had a real sentimental souse. . . .

The night of our graduation is burned in my memory, for there, before a whole skating rink packed with people, I had my first public failure—the greatest disgrace that ever came into my life. I had helped the others with their essays. Because I could write fluently and well, I had dashed off my own offering on "the jury system." It was a palpable plagiarism from Mark Twain. When I got going I could not stop in my writing. It was in my own handwriting, which was never good, and because I had felicity in writing, Professor Olin, the high school principal, read it swiftly, not realizing its length. So when I rose and began to read, I stumbled with my own handwriting and read on, and on, and on. Someone held a lamp over my shoulder that I might see better. The lamp made me sweat. But I stumbled and mumbled on and on. I could sense that the crowd was restless but I did not have the gumption to skip and stop. Pretty soon there was a whistle from the rear gallery. . . . I felt that pretty soon real trouble would begin. Other whistles came. Then someone began to clap his hands. And finally, when only Heaven knows how long I had been on my feet reading that interminable essay, which I once had thought was funny, uproar stopped me and, with my face redder than my pimples, I backed off, sat down, and the crowd laughed and laughed. The day when I am hanged by the Nazis will not bring me such shame as I saw and felt sitting there waiting for Professor Olin to announce the last song on the program:

> Oh, if for me the cup be filled,
> Oh, fill it from the gushing rill!

I do not know what exactly that night's experience taught me—if anything. But I do know that it gave me stage fright and kept me off the public platform for well-nigh a dozen years. Probably that also was good, a gift of the gods. For I might have been a spouter who thought he was an orator.

In summer, after my graduation, I was an idler, a wastrel, for the first time in my life and, sadly enough, for the last time. I flitted like a young butterfly in and out of the county teacher's institute, giving man's natural polygamist instinct full range with the little country girls of my age who had come to town to prepare for the teacher's examination. Lots of girls in those days in Kansas were teaching who were fifteen or sixteen years old, just out of the eighth grade in the country schools. Thirty dollars for an eight months' school meant a lot to a girl whose family was struggling under a farm mortgage. They studied hard and the county teacher's institute was a place of some distinction then. . . . Albert Ewing and I and the other boys of the Screech Owls trod the primrose path with the little school teachers and took them downtown and filled them with ice cream, lemonade, and walked home shyly trying to hold their hands— sometimes getting our ears boxed for our trouble, but always in good humor. By day, after the institute was closed, I sat on the porch and read John B. Alden's treasures or, feeling that I was a little too old for the swimming hole and the little tads, sneaked to the creek with my classmates at odd times when we thought the place would be abandoned. . . .

Another thing that I remember: Whenever I went into the barn, especially into the hayloft where my highest, happiest boyhood moments passed, it all seemed strange. I seemed to be looking back into a world that had been. I had passed on and was a disembodied spirit visiting its earthly habitat. Yet only a year or two had gone since that barn was my earthly home. I have had several retrospective glimpses like that as life has moved on and I have come back from the dead into other scenes and times, from another life I have lived in these earthly habiliments. It was Henley who wrote:

> So many are the deaths we die
> Before we can be dead indeed. . . .[10]

Late that summer my mother and I began to consider college. It must have been in August that a tall, pale, attenuated man, perhaps in his fifties, with an ascetic face, gashed and furrowed with the claws of suppressed desires, showed up at the boarding house one day. He was the president of the College of Emporia, campaigning for students. Because the college was near at hand, and I was timid, and my mother lonesome, we chose it without knowing anything about it. Before I knew it, I was bound for college.

The College of Emporia, in the autumn of 1884, was without a building. It was located on the third floor of a brick structure at the corner of Sixth and Commercial in the throbbing heart of Emporia, which then held six or seven thousand people. There the College opened in half a dozen rooms. Seventy-five boys and girls were herded by six or eight teachers. . . .

[10]The lines are from Henley's poem "Rhymes and Rhythms."

I got very little out of that college. I had a year of third-year Latin and my first year of Greek, which I presumed that naturally all college students had to have. There was no nonsense in the curriculum of the College of Emporia to disabuse me. I tried a term of French. I had been through Hill's *Rhetoric*[11] twice in high school—once to learn it and the second time to enjoy it, and probably to show off my knowledge of it. So I took it again in college, and had advanced algebra and a little primitive physics. There was no chemistry laboratory and they did not teach chemistry. And, of course, I had English literature, an advanced course over the high-school course, which I enjoyed.

I lived with a widow, a preacher's widow, Mrs. Jones, who had a boy my age. I brought from El Dorado to college a small box of books: my Red Line poets; a pirated edition of Longfellow's early poems; *The Wandering Jew*, by Eugene Sue; the Deerslayer[12] stories; and a one-volume condensed copy of the *Works of Thomas De Quincey*. The last contained "The Confessions of an English Opium Eater," which that year was my favorite literary diversion. And, however poor the college was as an intellectual stimulus, Bob Jones . . . was a joy and stimulation to me. He read my books and I read his, for a preacher's son generally has books. And we roamed the woods together Saturdays with our lunch—gay sixteen-year-olders. We carried a sack for walnuts and a club with which to knock them down; also always a book or two. So we rowed on the Cottonwood and stripped betimes and jumped in and stretched out on our bellies, kicking our toes in the mold in the woods, reading Tennyson and Byron, talking bashful big talk that little boys in their teens enjoy. . . .

But the lifelong blessing which the College of Emporia gave me was a boy— Vernon Kellogg. The thing that brought us together was that he also was buying books from John B. Alden. And so far as I know, he was the only boy in the College of Emporia who had much bookish interest. . . . We both came from the ruling class. His father [had been] the president of the State Normal School, . . . had studied law, had been probate judge of the county, was elected state senator the year I came to college; and his stepmother also was a lawyer, her husband's partner. And their house, when I entered it to visit Vernon, was the first house full of books that I had ever seen—bookcases around the walls, books on the table.

That year the big thing that Vernon Kellogg did for me was to take me across the street from the college into the second floor of the bank building where the city library was housed. The gray-haired librarian, Mrs. Carpenter, who was a glamorous figure for me because her husband had been killed in the Quantrill

[11]This was either *The Science of Rhetoric* by David J. Hill (1877) or *The Principles of Rhetoric and Their Application* by Adams Sherman Hill (1878).

[12]Popular adventure tales by James Fenimore Cooper that featured the noble frontiersman Natty Bumppo, also known as Leatherstocking.

Raid,[13] let me loaf there and brought me books. . . . The Emporia City Library was a vastly different place from the El Dorado Library; more books, better books, and a fulltime librarian were in Emporia, and all of the magazines that one could want, even from England, and illustrated papers—*Harper's*, *Leslie's*, the *London Illustrated News*, *Puck*, *Judge*. To add warmth to the glamor, often across the table sat Vernon Kellogg and we whispered and giggled; and when he found a sentence in a bird book, or bug book, or zoology book that pleased him, he shoved it across the table. And I did the same when a poem or essay pleased me. . . . It made little difference to me whether the college across the street kept or not. I was not bold enough to skip classes, but I doubt if I learned much from them. So I walked in the new heaven and the new earth. And I became in the College of Emporia the willing slave of Vernon, a few months my senior. . . .

But that winter the college students, because there were a hundred of them, could do what the Spring Chickens in El Dorado could not do. Often a sled—a great hayrack on runners—was hired and we all sat in the bottom, boys and girls, and tangled our legs together and felt very warm and wicked as we slyly held hands, slipped arms about each other, and were quite sinful in our own Presbyterian eyes. I had qualms about Agnes Riley, but I went every time I was asked. . . .

During vacations, of course, I went home; indeed I went home between vacations, sometimes over weekends, and always brought back literally trunks full of food. My mother did not realize how Bob Jones' mother was stuffing me—how good a cook she was. So to keep my soul and body together, my mother baked cakes and pies and roasted a chicken, and tucked in doughnuts and glasses of jelly. Craftily I widened the circumference of my college influence by inviting boys to my room, where we devoured the feasts that I brought from El Dorado. So I had some distinction in the college which had nothing to do with my scholarship, and other boys deferred to me. . . . Without these things, which are granted to boys from the ruling class, I would probably have been just a little bashful, measly-looking boy, afraid to say his soul was his own and craven at heart. Instead of which, I read Emerson's "Self Reliance" and had my first rebirth on earth.

In El Dorado I had been thrilled by Emerson's line in the essay . . . : "Trust thyself: every heart vibrates to that iron string." And I asked Mrs. Carpenter for the essay. I can remember that it was on a snowy February day when I had just turned seventeen, and as I read that essay my spirit expanded as though I had heard the trumpet call of life. I was thrilled and stirred and literally overturned. I

[13]In 1863, during the Civil War, a Confederate guerrilla band led by William Clarke Quantrill destroyed much of Lawrence, Kansas, an abolitionist stronghold, and killed about one hundred and fifty residents.

doubt if I have ever been moved so deeply by anything else that I have read. So I read all the essays and other Emersonian books and was glad to live and proud to feel that I was beginning to understand something of the puzzle of life.

For Emerson seemed to correlate all the world for me, the spiritual world. Deep within me a philosophy was forming. Probably I was just imposing Emersonian transcendentalism upon the theology of the Sunday School of my childhood. . . . Nor did Emerson, who probably justified my rambunctiousness by preaching self-reliance, make me less of a conceited ass.

But he did give me courage, always backed up by Vernon Kellogg, to survive a Moody revival which shook the school. Vernon and I were scared stiff that it would get us and pledged ourselves to stand against it. . . . It took the town as well as the school, and I can remember Moody yet—a soft-voiced man with a high and lovely tenor singsong to his incantations, a bearded man, paunchy, with fat jowls and wonderful eyes, and with all that a really spiritual face. . . . I had two roommates who knelt and prayed every night by the bedside and, like a soldier upheld by Emerson, I ducked into bed and turned my face to the wall and said my little "Now I lay me's" in secret, scorning what seemed to me the profanation of their public promiscuity with God.

But after the revival I noticed the college gradually slumped back to its normal life. I can remember still the curious spiritual squint-eyed, wordless questioning I put to Rankin Hendy, the president's son, who being a preacher's son, the devil's dear and mischievous child, proposed to illustrate some precept in our psychology class, wherein we were studying "surprise." He picked up a three-legged chair in the back of the room, a discarded recitation chair, and when I asked him what he was going to do, he went to the open window there on the third floor above the busy street, and said: "Let me show you some surprise and see how it reacts."

He balanced the chair a minute on the window sill and I stood beside him, wondering what was in his mind. We both looked out and down into the street. It was almost deserted. Fifty feet to the westward of us, going east, was old man Cross, a pompous banker with side whiskers, who wore a high, sawed-off, stiff felt hat and swung a cane which he flicked at dogs and boys who got in his way. And as he approached, Hendy said to me: "Now look!" And he dropped the chair three stories down on the sidewalk, not a dozen feet in front of old man Cross, who literally jumped into the air, threw his cane in the gutter and, hearing the thing crash and seeing it splinter, ran for his life. It was a noble sight, and I can laugh at it yet after nearly sixty years. And I know now how surprise works as a biological process. But a second after we had ducked back from the window I thought: "Hendy's a hell of a Christian. ". . .

In 1884 I got a lesson that lasted me all my life by scaring the daylights out of me. James G. Blaine was running against Grover Cleveland. I was supposed to be a Democrat. . . . And I was hoping heartily for Cleveland's election. . . . But the day after the election, Blaine seemed to have won. A great crowd surged on Commercial Street and Sixth Avenue as the news came seeping in, and the Democrats, for all the Republican clamor of delight, were still cocky and they were still betting on Cleveland. That morning I had received from my mother the twenty dollars to last me through the month of November. It was in four five-dollar bills. Treacherously but greedily, thinking to make money out of the foolish Democrats, I bet five dollars on Blaine and lost. Five dollars out of a twenty-dollar allowance was a burden too grievous to be borne. I have never made an election bet of over fifty cents since. Experience is a dear school and fools learn in no other; and I have always had to get my experience in the foolish way. I was ashamed to tell my mother that I had bet on her candidate. I just sweated it out!

When I came home for Thanksgiving, I learned a story that shamed me more. When Cleveland's election was finally beyond a doubt the week following, the Democrats in El Dorado put on a great torchlight parade and hired the band, indeed a couple of bands from neighboring towns, and literally tore the roof off of El Dorado. It was their first victory since Buchanan in '56. While I was betting on Blaine my mother had been rejoicing in every way a woman can. But the night of the big Cleveland torchlight procession and jubilee, she was heartbroken. She believed that the rebels were coming up out of the South to run the country. But she knew how my father would feel. So that festive night she put a lighted candle in every one of the forty windows in our house except the kitchen. There she pulled down the curtains, blew out the light, and sat and rocked in sorrow, yet I suppose in a certain proud glamor of loyalty that his house, his big house with a hundred and forty-four feet of porch, where the band stopped three times and serenaded that night, his house was with him—all lighted up in jubilation at the victory.

The spring semester found me grinding away with the college freshman classical course. I cared little for any of it except the English literature, the English composition, and Vergil's *Aeneid*.[14] But I was tremendously interested in books and magazines. . . . In Emporia the *Atlantic Monthly* was placed in my hands by the librarian. And there I had my first taste of William Dean Howells. . . . I read Howells's *A Modern Instance* and realized that I was opening a new door. Here was a novel different from the Dickens I adored. . . . I read it and reread it, and some way felt that I had made a great discovery. Mr. Howells was not anywhere near the zenith of his fame in the spring of 1885. I was always proud that I spot-

[14]Vergil's epic Latin poem the *Aeneid* tells the story of Rome's legendary founder. It was often used as a textbook because of its perfection in structure, diction, and meter.

ted him early. When he came to Emporia I asked him to write in my book, and when I told him how I had found him and taken him to my heart, he wrote in my book: "W. D. Howells—Mr. White's discovery!"

I was a seventeen-year-old boy and was passing out of gangdom and becoming an individual. Looking back now, I know why I made long and lonesome walks into the country. . . . One Sunday night in the early spring I was walking alone, because I felt it was too hot to go to church. I plodded up Commercial Street with my hands behind me, as is my wont today when I am mildly curious and interested about the universe and the immediate environment thereof. Along came a man whom I had never seen before and have never seen since, but I have remembered him for a lifetime—a slim, good-looking, well-dressed, ready-speaking man. I thought he was a traveling man—probably a salesman. He boarded me with some light remark, slowing down his pace and catching step with me, and we began to talk about Heaven knows what. But before we had gone much more than a block we began to talk religion. And because he was a stranger, I unbuttoned my heart to him and he sensed that I was in some sort of a conflict. I myself do not remember what it was. For an hour we walked and he talked and set me right with the world.

Whatever religious faith I have is based upon his wise words. And the wise thing he said was that it made little difference how the Bible was put together but a great deal of difference that it had held up through the centuries and for many thousands of years, because its wisdom some way matched and covered human experience. I remember also that he said not to fret too much about the miracles and the story of the virgin birth, that the same stories would be found in many religions. He talked about the tragedy of the life and death of Jesus, pictured him as a young man who found his country and his people in bondage and sought to free them by pointing their way to a philosophy of peace through humility, through tolerance, through charity, rather than by appeal to arms. He held Jesus up to me as the greatest hero in history and asked me to read the story of the two thousand years that had followed his death and to watch how slowly and yet how inexorably the world had changed, veering to human happiness as it accepted little by little, phrase by phrase, the philosophy he preached and made it a part, even a small part, of human institutions. Then my companion turned our talk to a discussion of the futility of force and the ultimate triumph of reason in human affairs. He explained his theory that Jesus died to save the world by demonstrating, through his crucifixion and the symbol of his resurrection, the indestructibility of truth.

My ears had been opened by Emerson. That unknown man turned over the sod of my spirit and uncovered an understanding heart. That, to my youth, was the night of the Great Light. Yet it was only the seed and not the harvest of the truth that came to me as the unknown sower walked with me on that evening's pilgrimage along Commercial Street toward "the way, the truth and the light!"[15] He may have been a preacher and not a traveling salesman at all. Or, more likely, he was some young divinity student in his early twenties. And I have often wondered whence he came and where he went. But because I was seventeen, because youth opens its heart in those days to the great mysteries, the faith this stranger preached has been with me through all the years.

So at last I was on the road to Damascus![16]

[15]John 14:6.

[16]St. Paul was converted from a persecutor of early Christians to a tireless apostle of the new religion while he was traveling to Damascus (Acts 9:1–8).

4

Destiny Rolls
My Dice—
"Come Seven"

In early May of that year 1885 I came to the conclusion that it was rather mean and miserable for a big, healthy, strapping seventeen-year-old boy to let his mother keep boarders to send him to college. Both of my roommates were working their way through school. One was a janitor in a bank; the other was a printer at the case. So I sat down . . . and wrote three letters to El Dorado: one to our only Jewish merchant at the time, Cass Frieburg, who kept a dry-goods store, one to George Tolle, who ran a grocery, and one to T. P. Fulton, who ran the Butler County *Democrat*. I asked all three for a job in exactly the same language and told them why I wanted to earn some money and, more than that, to learn something about a business where I could earn money and go to school. The dry-goods merchant and the grocer replied courteously that they had no job. But the editor offered me a job which he said, with more truth than he realized, would not bring me much money but would give me a chance to learn a trade that was profitable and that I could use when I went back to school.

As I took that letter out of Box 10 at the Emporia post office, I did not realize that I had received my life's calling; that I had channeled my entire life without deviation or break from the letter that I held in my hand. Yet there stood destiny pointing over my shoulder to a road that I should never leave. . . .

I had a job. It was in early June 1885 that I walked into the office of the [Butler County] *Democrat* one fine Monday morning. And as I came in, the editor, with a broad and affectionate smile, rose to shake hands with me. I was from college then, mind you, and could be respected as a gentleman. And as he stood with hand outstretched, he said: "Well, Willie, you better bring back that bucket from the well before you go to work again." So rose my curtain of destiny. . . .

Now it is my pleasure and honor to introduce Thomas Parker Fulton, "Tee

47

Pee," my first and dearest boss. . . . He is of southern Ohio extraction and possibly has some of the fiery blood that before the Civil War percolated across the Ohio River from Kentucky and the Virginias. He has a loud but caressing voice. He wears good clothes and always a flower in his buttonhole; a black cutaway, or Prince Albert, generally is his coat, and with it gray trousers and shiny shoes. No slouchy sloven is he, but a scholar and gentleman, and also at proper times a judge of good whiskey.

Tee Pee could sling a pen. His was known as a vitriolic pen. And he was always ready to back it up with his trusty gun. It mattered little that he was the world's worst shot. . . . He wrote rapidly and well. His copy was as meticulous as his clothes and manners. He leaned to editorial rather than news. Our paper still had only four pages; and still the two outside pages, printed in Kansas City, contained news of the world on the first page, a love story and miscellaneous items on the fourth. So the editorials and the local items, on the paper's inside pages, were all that Tee Pee contributed to the news end of the paper. He solicited advertising and, after the manner of editors of his day, as a solicitor he was half blackmailer and half mendicant—from Democrat merchants he begged, from Republicans he mildly insinuated threats! Also he solicited subscribers and job work. He intrigued diabolically for the county and city printing and was in politics heels over head.

He was the typical country editor of sixty years ago. His little office would not have invoiced more than fifteen hundred dollars; yet with that weapon he wielded much influence in his town and county and state. He was an artist who owned the tools of his trade. "Owned" may be too strong a word, but the men who had bought it and given it to him to run a Democratic paper, and went through the grotesque formality of taking a mortgage for it, had long since lost any flickering hope of interest upon the note or even title to the mortgage. So the weapon rested in his hand, a flaming sword for what he regarded as justice. . . .

When the fitful fever of the Kansas boom broke in the late eighties, he was one of its casualties and went outward with the tide—a gay, noble, but futile figure, affectionate to the point of passion, generous to the point of larceny, irresponsible to the point of heroism, the product of an older, more primitive, and courageous civilization. He was too young to fight in the great Civil War, but his youth had been shattered by war's warped ideals. After the mad, glad boom of the eighties, sad unromantic paydays came to America. Men simmered slowly down to humdrum living on a cash basis, or thirty days and a 5 percent discount. Tee Pee, to whom money meant little and credit meant much less, looked about with dazed, hurt eyes at a sordid, grasping world wherein he could not function after the manner of the days of his youth and early manhood.

In the office of the [Butler County] *Democrat* in the summer of 1885, we were still without a newspaper press. We had two job presses—an old Gordon and a Colt's Universal. They were foot-power presses. On these little presses we printed our job work. To print our paper we went to the office of our less loathed and more highly esteemed contemporary,[1] the El Dorado *Republican*, and used its cylinder press—a mechanical marvel of that day. In the *Democrat* office we had four racks of type and upon each rack was a case of body type in which we set the paper. . . .

It was my job to open the office in the morning at six-thirty, sweep it out and start the day. Theoretically, the printers came down at seven o'clock. Tee Pee generally sailed in between eight and nine, with an expansive greeting for everyone. [Then] industry began to hum in the office. The foreman, the printers, and the apprentice, who had idled during the early hours—chatting, standing around looking out of the windows, piddling with the types, possibly throwing them in and filling up their cases—set busily to work. Tee Pee began stuffing the copy hook. At ten o'clock the click of the types in the sticks began to indicate that the long day was well begun. After I had swept out the office I was supposed to kick the pedals of the job presses, if they were to be used, or to assort the rules and reglet from the forms upon the composing stones, or to run errands for Tee Pee; or, wanting anything else to do, I was put to setting type. . . .

As a little boy in the office five years before, to my shame, I had during my short apprenticeship been sent around by the printers to borrow a square auger, to get a left-handed shooting stick, to get the italic chases, and upon certain indecent errands which were covered from my innocence. But now, as a young gentleman out of high school with a year of college behind me, I was too wise to be fooled by the old tricks of the trade. Still I had to be taken down, to be put in my place as the office devil.

Of course I was proud of my job, and the printers knew it. I dramatized myself as a heroic young gentleman of the ruling classes, manfully learning a trade years after other young gentlemen had begun their professional apprenticeship. In the evening when work was done, I put on my round-cornered starched cuffs and white collar and sailed out in what was termed in the vernacular of those times "high sassiety." . . . But the journeymen printers, who worked for a living and chewed plug tobacco, had a rather low opinion of their devil. So they laid for me.

Here is the way they brought me low. General Grant died in the summer of 1885. Prohibition was four years old in Kansas then and at times unsteady on its feet. One could order liquor from outside the state then and have it shipped in by the bottle or case or carload without let or hindrance. So, by way of drown-

---

[1]Nineteenth-century journalists often jestingly referred to their local competitor as "our loathed but highly esteemed contemporary."

ing their sorrow at the death of the General, the printers of the town combined and ordered two or three cases or kegs of beer; they took them to an adjacent grove near town where on the Saturday night of Grant's funeral they proceeded to saturate the beer with a waste basket full of buns, cheese and ham sandwiches. They made the night hideous with their caterwauls.

Naturally I went along. Naturally also, being an exemplary young person, after paying my share of the expenses I participated in the orgies rather vicariously. I did not drink, not a drop, which also greatly amused the printers. Then at midnight's stilly hour, we collected all our bottles, sent for all three of the town's hacks, loaded the entire printing fraternity of the three El Dorado printing offices into them, and went out baying at the moon, serenading, kicking and rattling the bottles between anthems. Thus we attracted the attention of the sedentary old gentleman with the heavy cane, whom the Grand Army of the Republic had political pull enough to keep in the marshal's office. He piously shooed us off Main Street. Then the war council of the printers' party decided to go out to the leading Presbyterian elder's home and commit some deep outrage on him and his. So we deposited our empty bottles by stealth upon the front veranda of his palatial residence, a long, shiny, gorgeous row which greeted the morning sun. The elder, being a late Sunday-morning sleeper, did not know of the shiny jewels glistening on his outer portals. The town next morning filed by, hooting with delight. Now I participated eagerly in all these orgies and, being sober, possibly added certain grotesque details which the befuddled mind might have overlooked. . . . So I hied me, giggling, to the *Democrat* office Monday morning with my little tin halo of virtue carefully and firmly set above my shining brow. When the first printer came in, he nodded at me cordially and said: "Have you paid your fine?" And, to my inquiry, he casually said that the marshal was arresting the participants in General Grant's obsequies and that they were pleading guilty and paying a ten-dollar fine, with seven dollars' costs, for being drunk and disorderly! The second printer and the foreman came in with the same information and indicated that if I did not go down and pay my fine, the marshal would be up soon to drag me off to durance vile. I protested that I did not take a drink. They protested ignorance and astonishment at my disclaimer. The office was in an uproar of denial and recrimination. The men said they had seen me drink, had even seen me reeling drunk, and were sorry that they could not testify as to my sobriety.

I made an errand to the other office. There I was greeted with the same hailing sign of distress. There also, popular opinion acclaimed me a hypocrite and a liar. I sneaked through the alleys to avoid the good old marshal. With a fear-stricken face, I went about my morning's work, listening for every noise on the stairs as the doomed man listens for the hangman's footsteps.

I could not plead guilty for I was not guilty. Anyway, I had decided rather denitely to be president of the United States, and I could not see that record on the police court blotter rising up against me in future years to bar my way to the White House. . . . I slipped home through the alleys, ate my noon meal in silence, for the cloud of turpitude was on me. I was learning a great lesson—that it is far more shameful to be caught than to be guilty.

That afternoon came the *thump, thump, thump* up the stairs of the marshal's feet, syncopated with the rattle of his cane. He came in solemnly, walked over to me, put his hand on my shoulder, said that he knew and respected my father and would make it as easy for me as possible, and if I would hand him seventeen dollars and fifty cents he would go down and make the record. I had no seventeen dollars and fifty cents. I knew no one who would lend me that vast sum. To get it of my mother would be to confess. I tried to borrow it in the office. I might as well have tried to get the printer to underwrite the national debt. I begged for time and that night after work I looked up a young lawyer and laid my woes before him. He also told me there was nothing to do but to pay my fine, let the record stand, and turn in the future to a holy life—perhaps take monastic vows instead of going to the White House, which I regarded as a sad compromise. All night I tossed upon a sleepless bed and came to the office the next morning, irritable and forlorn.

The marshal came up again. Again I begged for time. There I was, caught in the great iron-toothed trap of fate, ruined for life at the threshold of a brilliant career. Another day passed, another conference with the young attorney, and another sleepless night. I grew haggard and contemplated suicide or flight. And then in the evening again I heard the *thump, thump, thump* of the marshal's step upon the stairs.

We were standing around the wash pan, the common office wash pan, and the common, old stinking office towel, when the marshal entered with his gyves and shackles. It was an awful hour. The other printers hooted at me. Then when I had writhed in my torture enough to satisfy their esthete, degenerate, and sadist hearts, with an awful guffaw in which the marshal joined, clanking his spectacles on his belly watch chain, they told me that the whole thing was a practical joke and indicated in a general way that it would cost me a case of beer for that particular offense, which they would pay for and take from my wages from time to time as I could spare it. I jumped out of the accusation of guilt and rushed into the arms of crime with free and eager feet. I bought that illegal beer, again clinching the great lesson that unjust public accusation brings more shame than undetected obliquity. We are ashamed for the things that men know, not for the things we do. And so, learning this lesson of life, I was put in my proper place as a printer's devil. It was a good lesson anyway.

As the summer wore on, I learned more and more about the printing office. My high school education and my year at college doubtless quickened my wits.

Music had nimbled my fingers. I learned to set type quickly and fairly accurately. I could make up a job for the job press and run it off, adjust the impression, distribute the ink, and my legs travelled thousands of unmeasured miles, kicking the old Gordon and the man-killing Colt's Universal job presses. Occasionally when Tee Pee, a man given to large leisures, left town or felt lazy—being full of politics and a letch for fishing—I wrote local items and cut out reprint to keep the copy hook filled. Joe, the foreman, had no taste for these tasks, which were his by all right. And because I had some white-collar talent, he drafted me and smoked a peaceful pipe while I worked. . . .

Then came a fine, fair autumn day when Tee Pee, in a new and gorgeous suit with rather more scarlet in his geranium boutonniere than usual, sailed down to the office before the morning Santa Fe train went north and told us in his fine, clear, dramatic voice that he was going to Washington to get the post office. He sat down, quickly filled the hook with copy, said he would be back in two or three weeks, waved his hand like a prince's wand at the office, and said: "Well, you boys get out the paper anyway, and when I come back I will fix it up with you."

It was the post office that made us stay. Without that lure, Joe and the printer would have gone. For Tee Pee had queer ways about money; not that he was dishonest, not that he was careless of our rights. But in those days Saturday night was a hollow, empty form in the office of the [Butler County] *Democrat.* Tee Pee generally put on a Saturday ritual, something like this: He would bustle in briskly Saturday morning while we were all throwing in type at our cases and when there was little need for much copy on the hook, greet each of us cordially, almost affectionately, stand in the midst of his realm, and say, "Well, well, boys, Saturday, isn't it? Saturday!"

Joe Cox, the head printer, being a malignant and courageous spirit, would probably answer back with the voice of the devil's hellions filing a saw, "You're right, it is!"

And Tee Pee would blink at him with a hurt and injured look, then turn to his desk and busy himself getting up copy. In the course of an hour or such a matter, after a subscriber had come in, or a statesman, to discuss the local situation, shortly before noon Tee Pee would rise again and begin the ritual: "Well, boys, I must go out and see the sheriff. He owes me something for some sheriff sales. And I think I will get a little money from George Tolle, or maybe from Ed Denny, on account. You boys be in this afternoon and I may be able to make you all happy."

Then Joe Cox, out of the deep malignity of his heart, would cry: "All right, Tee Pee! We'll be here waitin' for you."

And Tee Pee would walk out briskly, with a businesslike air, go clattering down the steps as one who was hurrying to a fire, and the place that knew him that day would know him no more. Late in the afternoon, Joe, the foreman, being a family man, would sneak out on the pretense of ordering some groceries, and we knew he was going to waylay Tee Pee somewhere on the streets and get either money or an order for groceries, or coal, or clothing, or whatever his needs might require. Sometimes Joe Cox, the printer, would sally forth. But as the evening shadows lengthened in the office we would sit in droning and drowsy talk around the cold office stove, smoking and spitting and hoping against hope for the foot upon the stairs that never came. At odd times, Tee Pee would pass me a dollar, or two dollars, or a five-dollar bill. I kept no account. At first I did not know that he kept no account.

But when he went to Washington . . . we four, representing the working class, made a solemn pact that we would take in all moneys and other collateral evidences of wealth that came to the office, keep them, distribute them in proportion to our wages, and make no accounting of it to the boss. We collected what we could and found that he had no books and that he was none the wiser for our wholesale hypothecation of his funds. We caught up with ourselves a little and, while he was gone, we four thieves enjoyed a degree of prosperity that we had not known before. . . .

Joe, the foreman, put me in charge of writing the local items and getting up the reprint copy for the editorial page. I was proud of my job as printer-reporter. It gave me no more status in the office than I had had, but it gave me outlet to the street where I gathered items. The girl clerks in the dry-goods stores greeted me on familiar terms. I was a "person" on the street. And coming back to the office I set my items in type. Naturally I pressed the extraneous matter from my items so that I might hurry back to the street and be a reporter again.

There was a flavor in those days about the printing office. Printers were supposed to graduate into editors, editors into statesmen, statesmen into leading citizens, and so rise to empyrean heights in the state and nation. This was the natural road to the White House. No printer ever had gone to the White House, but in general all young printers expected to go there.

Of a Sunday the printers would gather in the office and read the exchanges, comparing the typographical excellences of other papers and their own and discussing matters of the craft: the secret of glue making, how to mold rollers, how to cast slugs, and how to stop the encroachment of women compositors into the back rooms of the printing offices. Women in that day had acquired no rights in the printing offices. They came in under protest, remained in scandal, and sometimes left either to marry the foreman or to satisfy the jealous rage of his wife. Every printer in an office which employed women was looking—indeed, was hopefully, passionately expecting—to trap the foreman in some intrigue with the office printer girl. Of a Sunday, in our office which was free of the female taint, we gossiped bitterly and salaciously about the foreman and the printer girls of the other shop. Perhaps all this was the intuitive fear of a tide of feminism. In our heart's heart we heard its rising murmur. . . .

One day that summer a young god appeared in the shop. He was a journeyman printer wandering over the state and was hired in some rush of work, possibly caused by the annual appearance of the tax-sale notices in our paper. His name was Ewing Herbert. He stood six feet, with an olive skin, black eyes that twinkled, and a mop of stiff, raven-black hair that brushed his broad, low, handsome brow. He had an organlike bass voice. He was young and full of gay and malignant adventure. He had been out and around in the great world. He was a swift compositor and an intelligent one. He too had one eye on the White House. Ambition had her prod forever at his back. I became deeply fond of this young knight errant, two years my senior. I followed him about, was his willing slave, accepted his opinion, served him, and probably bored him to a crisp. It was I who, from my meager peculations, bought the watermelon which we ate in the office at the noon hour or after work hours, throwing the rind through the window at leading citizens who passed along the street, and ducking out of sight after letting drive. . . .

Ewing Herbert and I spent some time of evenings loafing around a big camp meeting that was held a few miles below El Dorado. Revivals, protracted meetings, and, in summer, camp meetings were not new things to me. . . . But here was a camp meeting larger than any I had ever seen. Ewing and I used to lie on the grass on the bank that rose above the wooded dell, gossiping and philosophizing. . . . And through the years I can bring back what we talked about one night. That camp meeting, with its rich and shimmering golden heaven and its glowing, frightful hell, was patronized only by the poor. No El Dorado merchants were there, nor lawyers, doctors, or teachers. Occasionally a clerk came. But here were the workers, the failing farmers, and their fading wives. Ewing, who had been reading the meditations of a German philosopher called Jean Paul Richter, the "only one" to match my Emerson, said:

"Will, look at that crowd. Too poor to skin. They've just got to have heaven to square it up with themselves for falling down, and they've just got to have hell for people like us who are having such a good time. They can't figure out a just God without a heaven and a hell."

And it has stuck with me all these years. But our philosophizing did not lessen the joy we had joining in the camp-meeting hymns, considering the camp-meeting emotional upset, the hallelujahs and the imprecations to the Lord for forgiveness—all the outbursts of overwrought minds and burning hearts that made the spectacle so weird, so terrible, so fascinating. . . . After camp meeting, we two would trudge back to town indulging in tall talk about the vast mysteries of life, chiefly love and religion, women and God, after the manner of boys who are in the presence of strange forces that they cannot comprehend. We did not realize that our questioning, our bewilderment, our yearning to know the truth of the mystery was as old as the race. . . .

It was I who bought the *Century Magazine* and sat in the office of a Sunday and heard, with Heaven only knows what delight, Ewing read *Huck Finn*, all about the king and the duke and the raft on the Mississippi—a glorious odyssey which fired both our souls. . . . When in the fall Ewing went away to the College of Emporia, where I had gone, my heart followed him. But I stuck to my job. I was not swift enough as a compositor to earn a living. . . .

Tee Pee did not receive the post office as a victor's laurel wreath when he went to Washington. He stayed week after week, yet he came back without it—but hopeful! Also, he came back to trouble. No reformer was Tee Pee. It was not the day for reformers. However, his young reporter in a mad moment essayed to run a four-line item about the town poker game, intimating rather broadly that the "officials should do something." Why I did it, I do not know, looking back over the years. That town poker game was an ancient institution. Possibly it was protected by the officials, possibly they participated in its profits. Possibly the ancient and honorable poker game was like the liquor joint in the livery stable on South Main Street where, in a rank-smelling empty box stall in a tub with ice, covered by a gunny sack, one could go on a hot day and get a bottle of beer, or fish a black bottle of red liquor out of the hay in the manger and leave the price in the feedbox. Possibly the town poker game was like the sordid palace of gilded joy down across the railroad track which ran with little molestation as a necessary evil in that gorgeous established order. I do not know. But when Tee Pee came home he found that four-line item staring him in the face, threatening libel, riot, manslaughter, and sudden death. So I went back to my printer's case, and Main Street and Central Avenue knew me no more. My career as a reporter was ended. . . .

So came Christmas and New Year's. Then, being able to set a galley and a half of type a day and throw in my case to boot, and two galleys if the copy was flat, I hied me away to college to join Ewing Herbert and the high gods of the academic Parnassus.[2]

I had, on the whole, a low opinion of those high academic gods. Vernon Kellogg was writing to me from Lawrence about the glories of Kansas University, urging me to go there. I was torn, perhaps not so much between the grandeur of the university and the shabby ways of the college as I was between Ewing Herbert and Vernon Kellogg. Ewing won. We roomed together; we worked together on the *College Life*, which he had founded. In spare time he earned money as a reporter for the Emporia *News*, and I went to work as a printer on the third

---

[2]A mountain in Phocis, Greece, whose two summits were consecrated to Apollo, the Muses, and Dionysus; consequently it was regarded as the seat of poetry and music.

floor of the *News* office. The College of Emporia had that year left the tall building on Sixth Avenue. It operated in two adjacent frame store buildings on North
Commercial Street. It was a measly affair. I had no happy memories of that
spring semester at the college. . . .

The composing room of the *News* was on the third floor of a ramshackle old
firetrap. It had a few slim south windows, never washed, and a large stove in the
middle of the room. . . . Half a dozen printers, pale and generally emaciated
men hurrying toward tuberculosis from bending ten hours a day over dusty
cases of type, stood in their alleys, and two or three inky cubs in various stages
of apprenticeship roamed about, dodging the foreman's eye in an industrious
endeavor to loaf. A grimy, foul-smelling, filthy place it was. Yet to me, out of the
little country printing office where I was a personage, it seemed to epitomize the
great city. For Emporia was two or three times as large as El Dorado.

I entered the portals of the *News* office with fear and trembling. I did not
dream that I was a discontented proletarian when I grumbled in my heart that
twenty-five cents a thousand ems[3] for setting type was measly pay for a high
school graduate and a collegian. I was just a poor devil applying for work and it
was anything to beat the boss. So I told the foreman that I was a journeyman
printer, which was not true. The lie was a part of the class struggle, but I did not
know it. All I knew was that I could stick type with the best of them. Whereupon my lie stuck and the foreman gave me what was known in that day as a
sub-case. That is to say, I substituted in the afternoon when a printer wished to
lay off, or when there was a rush of work. I went to my case. Probably as I pulled
my printer's rule from my pocket and picked up my stick, I showed the old
printer standing by his case beside me that I was young and green and nervous.

"You don't know what to do, boy, do you?"

I shook my head.

"Go over to the copy hook on the foreman's desk and bring back a piece of
copy and I will tell you."

The piece of copy I chose was telegraph flimsy, which was without *and*'s, *the*'s,
any's, *or*'s, and lacked many an obvious verb in the simple indicative mood. It
might as well have been written in Greek. Moreover, it was a part of the market
report. The old man smiled. The market reports were fat takes, for experienced
printers would pick them up already set in type from the day before and correct
them for that day. I could not have done this without elaborate instructions. He
took my "take," gave me a piece of reprint which he had, easy copy, showed me
how to dump my stick and where and how to identify my take with my own
slug, and guided me all through the day. One of the few passionate impulses

---

[3]An em is a unit of measurement in printing, equal to the width of a capital M.

which have kept me in the narrow path through all these years is a desire to go to heaven and offer old Slug Nine, who stood beside me that day, the choice of my harp and crown and robe if he needs them.

Work was plentiful that winter in the *News* office. The industrial revolution was going well, though I did not dream what it was. When Saturday night came, Ewing Herbert and I went to a gaudy restaurant in the town, ordered a thick, rare beefsteak with canned mushrooms, dined like gormandizing young princes, and saw the future shimmering before us—an iridescent dream. Of course the gulf that lay between Ewing and me was unbridged. For he was earning his way through college as a reporter on the *News*, while I was a mere printer. Moreover, he had won an oratorical prize in the college in a day before football, when intercollegiate oratory made him as important as a football star would have been fifty years later in the college world. Night after night, when he came home from a social gathering in the town, from which most collegians were barred, he pulled the clothing off me to keep me from going to sleep in the cold room, and recited his prize oration to me—gestures, modulations, and all—while I, shivering like a wet dog, coached him. I could say that oration today.

In the spring when the state intercollegiate oratorical contest was held in Topeka, the College of Emporia—with Ewing Herbert as its hero—chartered a special car and went cheering and ballyhooing across the state to support him. I came down from the composing room to the editorial rooms to hold Herbert's place for a few days as a local reporter. . . . I pounded the streets in the afternoons for items, went to the railroad station, rode the fire wagon, chased the runaway horses of the grocer delivery wagon, and made myself generally useful in the literature of the time and the place—prouder than Pontius Pilate of my reporting job in the big town newspaper office.

At Topeka, the great night came. Herbert, representing the College of Emporia, walked magnificently out on the stage in a borrowed dress suit, a regal figure. . . . He opened up, spoke the first sentence with his melodramatic manner, paused as was his wont to let it sink in, then moistened his lips, opened his mouth and uttered—not a word. He stood there a few seconds, and the seconds piled into a minute! Then three grew into four awful minutes of stage-struck silence. Finally, with the dignity that befits a thwarted god, he bowed, turned, and walked off the stage. Shame kept him from coming back to Emporia. He could not face the town or the school, and no one today who does not know how the white light of fame glittered upon a college orator should blame him. His college was disgraced; his town eclipsed. He threw up his job, and I never went up to the third floor of the composing room again. I was a reporter for life.

The next summer I went back to El Dorado and found a job as reporter and city circulator for Mr. Murdock's paper, the *Daily Republican*. He gave me eight dollars a week, a princely salary. It was my duty to hire the carriers, to collect the monthly subscription from the town subscribers, to solicit new subscribers and also, which pleased me most, to write local items betimes. . . .

That summer working on the El Dorado *Republican* was probably the proudest summer in my life. I was eighteen and full of sap. The familiar world of my childhood and boyhood I saw through the eyes of youth. I felt consciously that I was a young man, even a young man rejoicing! I was associating on something like equal terms with grown men and women. I realized that as a reporter I had rather ill-concealed powers of life and death over my contemporaries. I could wave my wand and bathe them in valuable publicity; or I could withhold the baton and keep them in outer darkness. I was bright enough to realize that my power would vanish if I used it too brashly. . . .

We had few sacred cows in the *Republican* office in those days. Mr. Murdock was an easy boss. He liked to hear the paper talked about. He liked to have a stir and rumpus going on. So he never pulled the rein on me as I roamed about the town seeking whom I might bedevil, providing he was not a good advertiser, a political ally, or someone connected with the county printing. The county printing was our reason for being. For that, we would sacrifice anything! For that, we wrangled and rowed with the other editors of the town and the county. . . . In every western country newspaper in that golden day, the county printing, which amounted to five or six thousand dollars a year, was chiefly profit and it was, as a matter of fact, almost our only profit. For that we lived, moved, and had our being. So the county commissioners who dispensed the county printing were sacred cows. At the weddings of their daughters, we printed the full list of gifts. At the funerals of their families, we turned black rules of sorrow. If they dallied with the public funds, we defended them against the onslaughts of the less-favored newspapers in the county.

The politics of the day was full of intrigue and the intrigue was greased more or less with corruption. Railroads were being built across the Missouri Valley; legislators were being elected and governors chosen who would carry water for the iron horse. The spirit of the times, which we called the spirit of progress, was a greedy endeavor to coax more people into the West, to bring more money into the West. It was shot through with an unrighteous design for spoils, a great, ugly, riproaring civilization spun out of the glittering fabric of credit. Everyone who owned a white shirt was getting his share of some new, shiny, tainted money in those days of the mid-eighties in our boundless booming West. We sought to establish industries and spent much of the investor's money in salaries of promoters. We laid out town additions for colleges and sold town lots to establish these starved little institutions on the prairie half a mile from our towns in sun-baked, rococo stone buildings without endowment and without reason for being—colleges which struggled along for a generation and then sometimes gave up the ghost became city high schools or crumbled into disuse.

We voted bonds for anything—schools, courthouses, city buildings, railways, factories without economic reason, streetcars, waterworks, electric lights— anything. Wherever we could borrow capital with bonds we got it, spent it riotously, with never a thought of payday. So later, when the crash came, the delinquent taxes piled up, and newspapers waxed fat in advertising those delinquent-tax sales, and the county commissioners, who awarded tax-delinquent printing contracts, remained as they were in my halcyon days with Mr. Murdock, little tin gods in our newspaper cosmos!

It was in that gaudy civilization—stalking trivial personal items about the nobility and gentry of the times, riding on the rear step of the bedizened new red fire wagon, chasing runaway horses up and down Main Street, running panting to trains that unloaded their daily spawn of suckers, who in turn became a part of the vast swindle that was the Middle West of the eighties—that I, a strawhaired reporter in my teens, began to learn the newspaper business in the fool's hard school of experience. But that summer of '86 was all grand to me. I had no perspective. I was as mad as the craziest and no better than the worst, when it came to the vast conspiracy of the times.

I had the special privilege of my craft. I rode free to the railroad stations and to public ceremonies in the new varnished hacks that rattled about the streets. I had passes on the railroads. At the eating houses I was a favored guest. All reporters had these special privileges. The opera house opened its door for me when I flashed my old printer's rule. I consorted with the judiciary in return for advertising the dignity and wisdom of the court. When junketing excursions of councilmen started on big drunks, to view municipal improvements in other towns on the taxpayers' money, reporters were taken along and treated as young princes—maharajas of the first class. I had two summers of this in El Dorado. . . .

I was learning to write. I was learning that the way a thing was said, even a three-line item, was quite as important as the item itself. Probably I had some facility of expression. Even if the Emerson microbe in my mind was for the time dormant, my reading of Mark Twain and Bill Nye and the newspaper humorists of that day had given me some knack of putting words together grotesquely. And I tried to make all of my items snappy. The printers—this I know, for they told me so—frankly thought I was a smart-aleck, an opinion they may have drawn from the town at large. Then one day I learned that language used recklessly was dynamite. It happened this way:

A woman came to town selling corsets. Cass Frieburg, the dry-goods merchant, and one or two others . . . nagged me into assailing all itinerant merchants and making my assault generally, but rather particularly and pointedly, directed at this corset saleswoman. And when I came downtown the next morning, as I started upstairs to the editorial room of the *Republican*, the devil from the printing office told me that the woman was waiting up there for me with a rather ill-concealed rawhide that she had bought down at Jimmie Dodwell's harness shop. So I did not go up to the office but began collecting my news. The first batch I took up the back stairs and gave to the foreman and learned that the angry woman was looking for me on the street. Whereupon I haunted the alleys that day, going into back doors of the stores and collecting my news, sometimes standing not more than fifteen or twenty feet from the lady who was laying for me with that "patient watch and vigil long,"[4] which controls the conduct of a "woman scorned."[5] For two days and a half this contest lasted, and finally the woman left town. That was my first lesson in the perils and penalties of indiscretion. . . .

I reported my first murder case that summer. It was a mystery. I helped to solve it, for I had become correspondent for El Dorado of the Associated Press, the St. Louis *Globe-Democrat* and the Kansas City *Star*. Here is what happened: Ten miles from El Dorado a summer flood uncovered the body of a man which had been buried hastily in a ravine. Only one clue was left to guide us to the murderer: a broken spade handle nearby, on which were carved the letters "O. L.". . . . I wrote the story for the El Dorado *Republican* and wired it abroad. Several weeks afterwards, a sheriff came from North Dakota with a theory about a man named Orin Larriway, who owned that shovel. He was a hired man on a farm. He and the farmer had left their North Dakota home, bound for Texas to buy a farm. A few weeks after their departure the farmer's wife and child disappeared also. The sheriff's theory was sustained by neighborhood gossip that Larriway had murdered his boss, sent for the boss's wife and child, and that they had gone Heaven knows where.

That hypothesis was verified. Larriway was picked up, brought to El Dorado for trial, and I reported the murder case. He was convicted and sent to the penitentiary. Probably I was mean to him, for in jail he grumbled that I had caused his conviction by printing and coloring the evidence. The Lord knows, I cannot say that he was not right. For I had no sense of justice then and had great pride in my power. My reporting gave me a little local fame. I sent a day-by-day story to out-of-town papers and was paid for it decently. I was somebody, or thought I was; probably strutted my pride. . . .

That same summer another significant and memorable episode in my newspaper career occurred. George Gardner, a noted criminal lawyer in our town, helped the new county attorney, Charley Lobdell, try his first case. . . . Gardner made an eloquent plea and I wrote down a column of it. . . . At noon the next

[4]From Byron's poem "Mazeppa": "There never yet was human power / Which could evade, if unforgiven, / The patient search and vigil long / Of him who treasures up a wrong."

[5]English dramatist William Congreve wrote in *The Mourning Bride* (1697), "Heav'n has no rage, like love to hatred turn'd, / Nor Hell a fury, like a woman scorn'd.

day Gardner met me in the most conspicuous place in El Dorado—at the corner of Central and Main Streets, on the lid of the Fire Department cistern—and grasped my hand and slipped a five-dollar bill into it and said, "Will, this is for you!" and hurried away. I went to the office feeling that I had been bribed and corrupted. I went straight to Mr. Murdock with the bill still in my hand, told him the story, and said, "What shall I do?"

The old man looked at me quizzically and broke out: "Tried to bribe my reporters, eh! The damned scoundrel! Hasn't he got any moral sense left?" He saw the bill still in my hand and said, "Willie, give me that bill. By Godfrey's diamonds, ploughing with my heifer, eh? I'll show him he can't buy my reporters!" And, slipping the bill in his pocket, he gave me the funniest, quizzicalest, and chucklingest smiles and added, "Now go to work!" He kept the bill! . . .

Sometime in that summer of 1886 Vernon Kellogg persuaded me to go to the state university . . . [and] my mother decided to rent our house and establish a home for me in Lawrence. One Sunday in late August, I went to the livery stable and got my favorite team, Tom and Jerry, early in the morning and set out for Agnes Riley's home, and we two went on an all-day picnic excursion, headed eastward into the Flint Hills—I had never seen them. I had no idea of their loveliness. As we passed Rosalia, on the high tableland that soon breaks into the great ravines and canyons that are gouged beneath this upland to make the rolling hills, we were both astonished and delighted with the beauty that unfolded before us. We were eighteen. I, at least, had never had a consciousness of beauty in landscapes. . . . The hills were clad in summer green and in those days the deep ravines were wooded and the road, a dirt road, a farmer's road, ungraded, wound around the contour of the hills, crossing the ravines on wooden bridges which rumbled under the horses' feet and the buggy wheels as we passed.

We knew that when I went to the university and Agnes went to the State Agricultural College at Manhattan, our ways were parting. I do not think we ever talked of marriage. . . . At eighteen, a boy with two years before him in college and a deep-seated desire to be somebody, sometime, perhaps a self-centered little intellectual snob, could feel the conflict of emotions, the dread of a parting, which would make him sad in silence, and also an alternating curve of joy and delight at the new world dawning before him. What Agnes felt, I do not know. But I do know that we were happy and took a deep joy in the vast monotony of curve and lines. The colors in different shades of green, all innocent of the plow, brought us a delight that only youth can have in those first experiences which bring new stimulation to the senses. To see a new world in youth is to approach the ineffable.

So, at noon, we found in a deep ravine a quiet grove and ate our lunch there

by a spring. It "were happiness enow!"[6] We rode home through the long afternoon and the late twilight and saw the hills in the new light when the horizon-
tal light lines from the west made strange shadows. The pleasure that had run
through the day was turned, at night, into exquisite silence. Thus we rode back
across the upland under the stars. And when I had helped her out of the buggy
at her father's door I wound the reins around the whip socket on the dashboard,
curled up in my seat, and let Tom and Jerry go clattering along their well-known
beat. I was awakened only when I heard the roar we made crossing the bridge
near town. I sailed into the livery barn, yelled at the stable boy, and went home,
tired, exalted, happy—with that happiness which is screened through sadness
and purified. . . .

[6]White is probably referring to the famous passage from *The Rubaiyat of Omar Khayyam*: "A
Book of Verses underneath the Bough, / A Jug of Wine, a Loaf of Bread—and Thou / Beside me
singing in the Wilderness— / Oh, Wilderness were Paradise enow!"

5

A Reporter
in College

Here is the way Vernon Kellogg said I looked when I struck Lawrence. He wrote it, in a reminiscent mood, thirty years after: "He was a little taller than a middle-sized boy, with a long neck and what would be called a chunky body. It was clothed in a good, hand-me-down brown suit with braid around the coat edge, and a made-up necktie, hand-painted. In the necktie was a golden bull's head with chipped diamond eyes. Over it all, skimmed-milk-colored eyes, a blond splotched skin, a broad wide forehead, reddish hair topped and crowned with a rather wide white hat with a narrow black band—the type of headgear worn by western cowmen and gamblers. He was not a prepossessing figure."

Yet that was what Vernon had on his hands as fraternity material. For he was bound that I should belong to his fraternity, Phi Delta Theta, and Vernon then and always was a resourceful man, canny, not above intrigue, quietly determined. . . . That young man . . . had considerable self-assurance for his age. . . . He had been accepted as a man among men in a printing office and as a reporter on the streets of El Dorado. . . . Later I heard it said in the university by fraternity scouts who looked me over that I was fresh. "Too damned fresh" was the criticism which the Betas passed upon me. . . . I made a bee line for the college newspaper called the *Courier*, and with Vernon's fine Italian hand was installed as one of the local editors and choked the editor, Cyrus Crane, our local college orator, with copy—all sorts of copy. I wrote personal news items, smart-aleck cracks at the various foibles of the university, and dug up some news which other, less-skilled reporters had overlooked. That did not reduce my hat band either.

Moreover I wrote articles in the El Dorado *Republican* about the university—bumptious articles, critical articles—with an impudence uncalled for. I signed these articles in brash conscious audacity with the name of a then nationally famous anarchist, Herr Johann Most. The El Dorado *Daily Republican* in the university library was widely read. One of my "Herr Most" screeds was copied in the local paper. The finger of, if not exactly scorn, at least unpleasant disapproval pointed my way, which pleased me greatly—appealing to my naturally exhibitionistic nature. . . . I was pleased to be a "figure" on the Hill. I herded around in the college for the first few months, finding my place in half a dozen classrooms, letting the faces of my fellow freshmen photograph on my memory. I was soon calling them by their names, without either Mister or Miss to the jug handle of their surname. Indeed I was calling most of the girls by their first names and I am quite sure I was busy polishing apples for all of my teachers.

On the other hand, I was most sensitive, deeply sensitive to the beauty I saw as I stood many a quarter of an hour on the porch of the university on Mount Oread looking over the Kaw Valley for miles and miles. On a clear day, with proper light, one could see the smoke in Kansas City. I had never been so high above the environing plane in my life before, and I had never before seen so much land. It was a lovely prospect and moved me deeply. So I wrote some verses about it. . . .

I had been in the town but a few days when I went to the office of the Lawrence *Journal* and tried to make a connection there to report university news. I got an assignment on space, fifty cents a column—not exactly a princely remuneration, but I also managed to land the Lawrence correspondence of the St. Louis *Globe-Democrat* and, best of all, fell into the carrier's route for that paper and got also the correspondence for the Kansas City *News*. . . .

My mother and I installed ourselves in a little five- or six-room house three blocks from the university, where we set up housekeeping and were most comfortable. She, with her leisure time and only one mouth to feed, took up my books and followed me with my classes and sometimes later, as in the case of German and Latin, helped me with my lessons. . . .

The Kansas State University in 1886 was an epitome of its environment. It was like a dozen other state universities in the Mississippi Valley. There went the sons and daughters of the squires of the manor, of the gentry and nobility, and of the high lords of politics and business. In their blood was the struggle of the hour—the tremendous desire to make a material world out of raw material, God's great wilderness stretching up from the Mississippi River to the Rocky Mountains. We had been bred in politics and we took university politics into the academic cloister—not party politics, of course, but student affairs. There we conducted our business under a boss system, with all its chicane, with its terrors and its spoils, much after the manner and methods used by our fathers to rule their little local satrapies and fiefs.

Into university politics I plunged with Christian zeal. But I found quickly that unless I expected to be a leader of the nonfraternity world, known as the Barbs, I was barred from leadership in the college political activities which I understood instinctively and loved. So Vernon Kellogg and I renewed his efforts to get me into his fraternity. . . . As he tolled off my supporters inside the fraternity, we took the doubtful ones home to Sunday dinner, and my mother certainly put the big pot in the little one. . . . We wore down their natural objections to me as a fraternity brother. And in February 1887 I was initiated into the Phi Delta Theta and had crossed the first river in my university career.

A week or so before my initiation another belated initiate came into the fraternity. His name was Fred Funston—a congressman's son. Fred Funston was later Major General of the American Army. But at that time he was a pudgy, apple-cheeked young fellow, just under five feet five, who seemed to have decided in his cradle to overcome his runty size by laughing at himself, clowning in short. . . . Everyone in the fraternity loved him, and I clave to him like a brother. We made three—Vernon, Funston, and I. . . .

My grades were only fair. My extracurricular activities should have given me a Phi Beta Kappa pin, for I poked my nose into everything on the Hill except athletics. . . . As I look back at it, classroom pictures blur in my memory of the university. Fraternity meetings are clear; political excursions are etched deeply; parties, little dances, picnics, and what, in the student nomenclature of the time, was called "girling," I recall vividly. Also, I was downtown much of the time writing my news items for the Lawrence *Journal*, taking my copy for the *Weekly University Courier* to the printer, covering local events for the St. Louis and Kansas City papers. Though I sold at a small profit my *Globe-Democrat* route early in my university career, I became business manager of the *University Review*, a literary monthly. Thus I came to know the merchants whom I solicited for advertising. Indeed, downtown Massachusetts Street in Lawrence I knew better than I knew many a classroom, and certain businessmen better than some of my professors. . . .

Three or four men in the university faculty meant much to me. Their guidance and their influence have held through all my life. First of all came James H. Canfield, under whom I took more work than under anyone else. He taught me economics, sociology, political science, and history. He sat at the head of a long U-shaped table and around him ranged his students. . . . Canfield asked practically no questions. He promoted discussion. His classroom sometimes was a babble of clamoring voices. He laughed with the boys (only a few girls took his course). . . . He set us to reading books and loving him. He was an exceptional teacher, and until he died, twenty years after I left school, Canfield was my political mentor and my dear friend. I transferred my friendship to his daughter Dorothy and so lived happily all my life.

Another teacher who stimulated me greatly was Arthur Richmond Marsh, who taught English literature and composition. He also asked few questions. His classes were small and we read—that is to say, he read to us. He had a mellow, modulated voice with a Harvard accent. . . . Marsh was the kind of teacher who invited his class to his house, where we had tall talk. I became his willing slave and really tried to make decent grades in his class, but I never got much better than a B or B-plus. But he did chart my path into reading good English and American writers. He taught me to read the New York *Nation*, which I have read steadily since I first crossed his classroom threshold in 1886. . . .

Most of all, there at the university I met William Herbert Carruth, head of the German Department. My class there was taught by his wife Frances. And with Carruth, who was perhaps ten years my senior, I began a friendship which again only death severed. Finally, the other university professor who helped me greatly was Francis H. Snow, who taught the biological subjects—biology, zoology, entomology, comparative anatomy—and afterwards became chancellor. I had few classes under him, but he stimulated my reading, and because he was Vernon Kellogg's guide and friend, I often met him. Professor Snow certainly gave me a great respect for the sciences and made it easy for Vernon in later years to keep me reading along lines which otherwise I should have abandoned.

But what with the fraternity, the girls, the parties, Massachusetts Street and the businessmen, the Lawrence *Journal*, the university papers and the incidental university politics which controlled the university papers, and occasionally, by way of diversion, the classes, I took on a heavy load for a western student in the eighties of what passed for a sort of culture. At least, in my four years there, I got the habit of trained attention to the printed page . . . [which] is about the best that any man gets out of a college education. Given that capacity, if he will, any man or woman may keep abreast of his times and know how the world is put together and what makes it click and tick. Without it, the going in the modern world is tough! . . .

It was in the Christmas holidays in 1886 that I made my first literary pilgrimage. It was to visit Atchison, the home of E. W. Howe. Several years before he had written *The Story of a Country Town*, a Kansas story that had been acceptably received all over the English-speaking world. . . . William Dean Howells, my favorite novelist, and Mark Twain, my favorite humorist, had covered the book with warm praise. . . . [Howe] was running the Atchison *Globe*, a local paper, and I can remember that I spent an hour in the *Globe* office with his star reporter, Joe Rank, talking of Mr. Howe and preparing myself for the visit. His family lived in a large brick house with wide porches in an oak and elm grove at the edge of town. Because his family irked him or bothered him when he wanted to write, he was living in a little house, a two-room affair in the north part of the yard. When I came to Atchison the three children were with him in that little house and his wife sat sewing or knitting by the stove. Little good it did him to try to find peace outside his domicile.

Possibly he was used to visitors bringing the frankincense and myrrh of flattery, and maybe he liked it, for he was more than kind and we talked much longer than I should have stayed. I came back to Lawrence walking on the clouds, for I had seen my first literary hero, . . . and found a lot of books of James Whitcomb Riley which I had ordered from Indianapolis.

Then a new horizon opened—the poetry of common things. Emerson made me ready for it, and Mark Twain, I suppose, and Howells with his realism. But when the realism of Howells and the gaiety of Mark Twain and the homely philosophy of Emerson's transcendentalism were fused in the lilting rhyme of Riley, I felt a new thrill. I accepted poetry with an added joy. I did not know it then but looking back now I realize that those exciting days of exultation which came to me as I read Riley's homely verses came because Riley's verse fitted into my experience, welded my own experience into man's common joy. I thrilled as I had been lifted up when I first looked upon the beauty of the Flint Hills and when I first, as a little child, heard the El Dorado silver cornet band discoursing its new melodies and its simple harmonies. . . .

In the summer of 1887 I went back to work for Mr. Murdock on the El Dorado *Republican*. And there I met for the first time and embraced in delight a friend who has been steadily with me during all these years, a guide and ever-present help in trouble, the writer's friend and companion, Roget's *Thesaurus*. A few years later, Bartlett's *Familiar Quotations* came rolling across my sky and then Cruden's *Concordance of the Bible*. All these years there abideth with me these three—Cruden, Bartlett, and Roget—and the greatest of these is Roget. Where would I have been without the trinity? I still have Roget's *Thesaurus* before me as I write. The copy is inscribed in my adolescent writing, "Will A. White, El Dorado, 1887." I forget what I traded for it to another reporter, but it might as well have been gold and precious stones, for I was considerably interested that year in how I said things. I was consciously, perhaps with a certain smart-aleck fervor, trying to find new twists of language as I wrote the local stories of the little town. . . . Looking back over the files of that paper today, I can see how faint were the flickers of the great light that I thought I had within me. . . .

Mr. Murdock, who was preparing to run for state senator the next year, was building his fences, and he set them up with the economic and political nails which the system and the civilization in the United States in those times had made and provided. A county convention to nominate candidates for county offices was held, and it was my business as his employee, aged nineteen, to round up voters at the caucuses where the delegates were named. For it was necessary that his friends should control the courthouse the year before his nomination. Those were the days when the ins of any local politics were called the Courthouse Ring from one end of the United States to the other, and Mr. Murdock wanted to be an in. He had plenty of money—contributed, I learned later, by the Santa Fe Railroad. He put me on a hack and sent me out to a stone quarry to round up the boys. Santa Fe money had provided a tub of iced and bottled beer as a rallying point, and cigars were so lavishly plentiful that men grabbed in the box and took two and three and four. Other boxes appeared. And I learned my first lesson in politics under the boss system.

It was simple. A state boss collected money from the railroads, the packing houses, the insurance companies, and the banks in his state. This money he sent to his henchmen in the counties, who distributed the largess to their followers, who controlled the county conventions. The object and aim of all county conventions was to control the nomination of those Republicans who would run for the legislature and the state senate. When they were elected, as all good Republicans were, they would follow the boss. On most matters they were free, but where legislation touched the banks, the railroads, the insurance companies, or the packing houses, they were bound in honor to vote with the boss, and [for] his candidate for United States senator and for the tie-up the boss made with a candidate for state printer. The two united made a winning majority. So, over the United States, our senators went to Washington obligated to the large corporate interests of their states. As the railroads were interstate corporations, the railroad lobbyists and bosses in Washington amalgamated their forces. Thus the plutocracy built its mighty fortress.

Looking back at the campaign which made [Mr. Murdock] a state senator, I can see that it was symptomatic of the economic and social change that had come into the country. He was supported in his candidacy by the Santa Fe Railroad and opposed by the Missouri Pacific. . . . Kansas was veined by railroads running for the most part east and west—the Union Pacific, the Rock Island, the Santa Fe, and the Missouri Pacific. And each railroad had become, in its own territory, a political overlord. When two railroads crossed a county, often in those days the railway overlords struggled for domination. . . . The Missouri Pacific backed the Republican newspaper which opposed Mr. Murdock. The opposition attacked Mr. Murdock personally as a plutocrat and put up a farmer against him for the Republican nomination. The fact that he bought his clothes from Brooks Brothers in New York was advertised and used heavily against him. The truth—that he was the candidate of the Santa Fe and was opposed by the Missouri Pacific—did not come out in the campaign. If it had, it would have disclosed the fact that Kansas, along with the other American states, was no longer a republican democracy but part of a plutocratic republic.

I did not know those things in that day. Few people thought it through. I am sure, in El Dorado, Mr. Murdock's friends did not see the significance of the fact that he had plenty of money to help him control the conventions which nominated the county attorney, register of deeds, county clerk, sheriff, and the like—the Courthouse Ring! . . . It was an intricate system.

Money was easy. The farmers were borrowing up to their ears. The mortgage companies and trust companies had money to lend. No one cared what interest he paid—or promised to pay. Kansas was plastered with farm mortgages. Crops were good and prices reasonable; times [were] on the boom, and no one watched how the wheels of plutocracy went whirring and grinding, generating the power that ran the land. I was a part of it and never remotely dreamed its significance. . . .

It was in that summer that I got a pass from Mr. Murdock, who was the giver of all good and perfect passes, and headed out along the main line of the Santa Fe to Great Bend, where I took a work train and rode on a load of ties a long summer afternoon to Scott City. There was a busy, rough-board town, with board sidewalks and false fronts to the stores, and a courthouse looming out of the horizon. I went just at twilight to a real estate office. It was open. Real estate offices in those boom times in western Kansas towns were open until nine o'clock. There I located by section lines my destination. It was eighteen miles south and west of Scott City.

After loading in a big supper at a restaurant, I started forth with a plat of my destination that I made on a large sheet of note paper, marked and directed by section lines, fourteen miles south and four miles west, with a little oblong marked near the junction of the south and west where I would meet a depression of land called the White Woman's Bottom, one of those queer, dry, sunken prairie lakes which filled up in flood time. The government surveyor, a few years before, had plowed the section lines of all that part of western Kansas wilderness. The land was fuzzed with buffalo grass and nothing else. Only here and there and now and then had the farmer's plow furrowed a field. But the section lines, fourteen south and four west, were as well marked on the prairie as they were on the map of the real estate office. So I set out in the sunset glow, southward bound, full of food and full of romantic yearnings.

It was a silent journey. The August moon rose at the end of a long twilight and climbed the sky. As she rose she did more than shed the light that revealed the section lines that I crossed. She filled me with ineffable joy. I met no wayfarer, saw a few lights in a few cabins go out at bedtime, and was all alone with the moon and with a boy's desires and dreams on a journey that he thought would end in lovers meeting. So somewhere along about midnight, because I was very happy and too full of romance to be tired, I lifted up my voice in song, as I neared the White Woman's Bottom. Then a funny thing happened. Somewhere off in the distance a coyote, then another and another, awakened by my amorous outpouring, began to yell and yelp and howl. They understood me. After a little while I understood them. They had the same trouble that I had. We all belonged to the brotherhood! I had awakened them warbling my young man's fancies. So we all turn lightly to the thought of love.

I crossed the White Woman's Bottom a few hours after midnight and then turned west. At four o'clock, or maybe a little later, I came to the spot on my section line map which I knew was the journey's end. For near the barn I recognized the spring wagon that I could have told among a million. I had seen it come to El Dorado so many times and had watched its maneuvers like a hawk. So I lay me down under the wagon on the hard earth and slept like a child through the dawn to the sunrise, until the farmer's early rising brought the family out. And I wakened up with Agnes Riley's face bending over me and saying: "Why, Will! Why, Will, are you here? When did you come?"

And the family gathered around me, took me into breakfast after I had washed in the tin basin at the well. Then after the dishes were done, and maybe after I helped to wipe and put them away, for I did so at home, we walked out under the morning sky into the flat, endless plain, and there, as kindly as she could, she broke it to me that she was engaged to marry another man. So far as I can remember, I had no thought of marriage. I was nineteen and six months over, and she was just nineteen. Marriage had come naturally into her horizon, whereas I, being a boy and a male with other things around me—an education to get, a profession to cultivate, a living to earn—was just tramping on the clouds of pink romance without path or goal. I understood and she knew that I understood; and so, without kissing her goodbye, for the family was assembled, and anyway I really was hard hit and emotionally numb, they loaded me in that old spring wagon and the hired man took me southward to the railroad at Garden City. I caught the night train home.

As I walked through that plain in western Kansas—so different from the rolling Flint Hills, really another country from the wide valley of the Walnut—it was photographed in my memory that night under the moon. Years later when I was writing stories of the plains of western Kansas, the things I saw and felt under that August moon on that long and lovely night came out of the etching on my memory. Often I have reached into the etched mirror of that lonely land of the high plains three thousand feet above the sea and brought out images and have tried vainly to reproduce details of the weird and exquisite beauty which came to me that night, as the coyotes and I lifted our voices in amorous song. . . .

In the autumn of 1887 I went back to the university, a fraternity man, a budding college politician with the beginnings of a profession. . . . I continued to be a library hound, and Carrie Watson, the librarian, guided me in my major course, uncharted in the curriculum, through the poets and essayists of England. De Quincey was behind me, and Steele, Addison, and Johnson engaged me, and Carlyle set me afire. Goldsmith, Gray, and, for a few weeks, Pope charmed me.

But as to Shakespeare, not until I heard his poetry read on the stage did I realize the beauty and grandeur, the deep and lovely clarity of his language, the truth of his grasp of human nature. The stage was seriously beginning to interest me. Railroad rates were low, and traveling theatrical companies could move about in the United States so cheaply that every town over ten thousand had a considerable taste of what now would pass for first-class theatrical performances. . . . At Emporia, indeed even at El Dorado in the boom days, and at Lawrence I could see good shows. Stars of national reputation came to all of these towns. . . . They brought the current plays and the old standard plays to little towns where the theaters were well patronized. I and my generation received them gladly. That traveling drama was a part of our education. Vernon Kellogg and I often used to stag it together, and in the year 1888 we were both working on the Lawrence *Journal* and occasionally could wangle a complimentary ticket to the Opera House. . . .

I was also bootlegging music. I used to cut classes to go to the fourth floor of the main building of the university to listen to lectures on musical theory, on harmony, and on musical history. And, as a reward for letting me carry her books my second year at the university, I took Helen Sutliffe to all the concerts of the university course, heard for the first time really good piano music, and was learning to enjoy what we ivory-pounders and catgut squeezers used to scorn as classical music. . . .

Incidentally, in those days, I was supposed to be a rather hardboiled, ruthless college politician in glamorous and exciting contests wherein Kellogg furnished the brains and I got the glory. He was a senior and secretary to Chancellor Snow. He was admitted to faculty meetings and was as smug as the cat that swallowed the canary about university politics. Because he had an inside view, I had inside knowledge, and he pulled strings that gave me more distinction than I deserved.

So came the summer of 1888, and Kellogg and I found ourselves working downtown in Lawrence for Colonel Oscar E. Learnard, who owned two papers: a morning paper called the Lawrence *Journal* and an evening paper called the Lawrence *Tribune*. The Colonel was an old-fashioned, black radical Republican—radical in the sense that he would go any length for his party. He was a rich man, as the term went in Lawrence. His printing office did all the commercial printing for a railroad. So he had plenty of loose ready money. For some reason of high politics, he bought the *Tribune*. Perhaps he bought it because it had been abusing him and the Republican courthouse ring for a year or so. But at any rate, when he bought it he kept it running as a Democratic paper, though the milk of the word was heavily watered! . . . He made me editor of the evening *Tribune*, which was supporting Grover Cleveland and the Democratic ticket in Kansas, while Kellogg became editor of the rock-ribbed, staunch Republican morning *Journal*, supporting Benjamin Harrison and the Kansas Republican ticket.

No eight-hour day bothered us. To even things up, the Colonel made me reporter on the morning paper and Kellogg reporter on the evening paper. We began work at eight o'clock in the morning. We left the office after the proofs were read, somewhere around midnight, and often used to go home together with enough gimp and ginger to warble "Larboard Watch" as a duet while we ambled through the night. Our editorial work was light. Sometimes I wrote a ponderous leader, advocating free trade in the world, or a resubmission of the prohibitory law in Kansas. And sometimes Kellogg wrote oracularly about protection or the danger of turning the country over to the southern rebels, emphasizing the fact that Cleveland had traitorously offered to return the southern battle flags to the states that were in the rebellion. The only editorials the Colonel ever wrote himself were in support of the railroads in general, and because his handwriting was poor, his grammar worse, and his construction verbless and impossible, we had to recast his editorials. But most of our time and energy was devoted to gathering local items. . . .

Jim Dennis, the foreman . . . was our only editor. He revised our copy, corrected our spelling, put in the right initials, and above all he wanted the paper to make money. He had a theory maybe that his salary depended on such a remote contingency. . . . Kellogg and I had aspirations, noble ideals about the profession, that amused Jim. We tried to stop the habit of printing, at the end of her wedding notice, a list of all the gifts that the bride received. The bride's family and friends liked to see it in print, but Vernon and I thought it was unethical. Jim, because the list of bridal presents came in early and helped him get up the morning paper in time to quit shortly after midnight, loved them, and we had to fight with him to keep them out.

One evening the Houses, who ran the clothing store, put on a big wedding for their daughter. They were Jewish people, and to them a wedding was a great ceremonial. Vernon and I . . . heard for three days about that dinner from the grocery boys and their hired girlfriends and from the expressman who was bringing delicacies from Kansas City to the home: a crate of lobsters, for instance, and venison and molded ice cream—a new confection in the eighties—and a wedding cake four feet high. . . .

The Houses were good advertisers in the Lawrence *Journal*. They turned in their list of wedding presents and, with Spartan determination and Puritan resolve not to be bribed by advertisers, we carefully omitted the list of wedding presents from our wedding notice, which we sent to Jim, the foreman. When we showed up at the [reception at the] Odd Fellows Hall we were hungrier than she-wolves with cubs, ready for the lobster and the venison and the molded ice cream, little thinking that the devil was lurking in the dark windows of the Odd Fellows Hall waiting to bring us to shame.

By the time we had got to the dinner, the bridal party and the guests from all over that part of Kansas were seated at two long tables running the length of the room. We had two end seats down near the front doors of the hall. Just beyond those front doors were our good friends, the Lawrence hack drivers. . . .

Socially we were innocent youngsters. . . . It was hard to believe, but having grown up in prohibition Kansas and in families devoted to that cause, we hardly knew beer from whiskey, had not yet identified brandy, knew no difference between the various kinds of wine. We noticed that the waitresses poured into our tumblers some new kind of soda water, which went tingling up our noses and was not so very good. But we were tired and thirsty after a day's work, as well as hungry. And the waitress filled our glasses again with that belchy stuff. Also, we noticed that the third time our glasses were emptied, the hack drivers in the hall signaled to the waitress to fill them up again, which we felt was mighty decent of the hack drivers. Again, as we stoked away the venison and the lobster and the cakes and the exotic fruits that loaded the table, we drank that new soda water—clear and sparkling.

As the meal grew old I noticed that Kellogg, ordinarily a gentle soul with a soft ingratiating voice, was talking raucously, and it seemed to me perhaps a bit bawdily, to the bride at the other end of the hall, making great merriment. I don't know whether or not he noticed any symptoms in me, but that soda water was taking hold of both of us. I wanted to play the piano and was restrained by Kellogg, who always had a maternal influence upon me.

The next thing I recall, after these more than fifty years, is that the tables were gone and the orchestra from Kansas City, which included a harp, a flute, two violins, a cello, and a bass viol, was playing what seemed to me the most exquisite waltz music I had ever heard. And I wanted to dance. But because I had always played for dances, I had not learned to waltz. I could not, but I saw Kellogg floating down the long hall and in his arms rested Mrs. House, the bride's mother—a large lady whom Kellogg's arms only partially encircled. She was having the time of her life, and Kellogg was struggling nobly to do the honors.

It was a great occasion. I believe I made a short speech and I know that I tried to get to the rattletrap old piano on the platform where the orchestra stood and was persuaded by Kellogg, and perhaps by the bride's father, to join a square dance at which I was good. I took the bride out and the bride's cousins and a very pretty, black-eyed girl from Kansas City—a veritable sylph, a wood nymph—and I danced on air with her two or three times.

At least Kellogg and I were having an altogether deliriously happy time. Only Kellogg, whose sense of duty was always keener than mine, seemed to have a seven-devil lust to do the right thing by the Houses, who were good advertisers. So he took the bride's two aunts, one after another, and each one more ponderous than her sister, down the hall in a schottische—a military schottische where you ran two steps, clinched, turned around a couple of times and ran two steps more. And Kellogg was the belle of the ball, and the hack drivers, still standing in the door, laughed noisily, even rudely it seemed to me, at Kellogg, who obviously was doing the honors of the Lawrence *Journal*. . . . It was long after midnight when Kellogg and I, realizing that we had a day's work ahead of us beginning at eight o'clock, withdrew from the merry party, parted the wall of hack drivers in the hall as Moses smote the waters in the Red Sea, and started down Massachusetts Street for home.

It was a moonlight night and the street was deserted. I wanted to sing, and Kellogg said, "Hell, yes, let's sing!" We walked for half a block, arm in arm, singing "Larboard Watch, Ahoy," and then turned out into the street and lifted our voices in another duet, "Oh, Alice, Where Art Thou?" and then "Bye, Baby Bye, Oh, Why Do You Cry, Oh!" and then yodeled at the moon. And as we turned west to leave the street, old man Phillips, the town night marshal, in his blue army uniform, came running to catch up with us and said, tapping each of us on the shoulder: "Oh, my dear young gentlemen, don't you think you could sing as well if you stayed on the sidewalk?" And then he added, deprecatingly, under his breath: "Don't you boys know you're drunk?"

We had been drinking champagne and, God help us, we thought it was soda water! So we went home and to bed, only to wake up in shame and sorrow. For the wages of sin are death.[1] Old Jim Dennis had slipped down to the reporter's room, fished the bride's list of presents out of the wastebasket, and run it in spite of us, knowing from the hack drivers late in the evening that we were too happy to return to see the proof. In my shame at seeing the list of the bride's presents follow the wedding notice of an advertiser—certainly a special privilege flaunted before the town—in the dejection of a raging headache, it was borne into my heart's core that there is a moral government of the universe.

As the campaign deepened that year, our energies doubled and our enthusiasm grew in the contests for local county officers. My impression is that the Colonel, our boss, was more interested in electing the Republican ticket than he was in overthrowing Grover Cleveland. I seem to remember that we treacherously supported the Republican county ticket in both papers.

Anyway, Kellogg and I were forever in hot water, partly because we were young folks without conviction about the matters that seemed serious to the Colonel and partly because all the world seemed very funny to us. We were incorrigibly flippant. So life that summer was just one heat-lightning glow of hectic excitement.

I remember one night the Democrats had a great meeting, and the committee, not being able to get enough flag-printed bunting to decorate the speaker's stand, draped it with red, white, and blue bunting and scattered the stars from a

[1]According to St. Paul, "The wages of sin is death" (Romans 6:23).

few torn flags in and through the bunting. The heading that morning in the Republican *Journal* on the account of the meeting was "Under the Stars and Bars," meaning, of course, the Confederate flag. Lord, how hot that made the Democrats! The United States was only twenty-three years from the Civil War. . . . And that inference that the Democratic meeting was held under the Confederate flag stirred up such a stink as the town had not known for many years. When we came to the office early that morning, before the Colonel got down, the Democrats were waiting for us—not in squads but in serried ranks! Kellogg and I quietly slid out on the street. An hour later we came back to the office and a great crowd of wrathful Democrats, some of them leading advertisers, which really counted, had the old Colonel backed in the corner while they demanded that he make amends. When we hove in sight—young innocents grinning like the Cheshire cat—the old Colonel called across the throng: "Boys, boys, Goddammit, come here and tell these men how it happened!"

And he slid out through a back door, throwing us to the lions. I got behind a railing that marked off the lobby, and I can still feel the impact of air from Jack Watts' fist, Jack being a great husky blacksmith of a man—the impact of the air from his fist on my nose as I ducked just a decimal part of an inch away from it. We tried to laugh it off. The Colonel had tried to cuss it off. But after stopping subscriptions and discontinuing their advertising while we talked, the mob dispersed.

At another time, in trying to defeat the Democratic candidate for sheriff, we dug up the fact that he had been deputy sheriff ten or a dozen years before when three or four Negroes were lynched from the bridge across the Kaw at Lawrence. Then, indeed, there was trouble. In the seventies, at the time of the mob, a man named Jerry Gladheart had been accused of being ring leader. Jerry resented any discussion of the issue, though his name had not been mentioned. The rehash of the old story drove him temporarily to drink. Being in high spirits above his rum, he made the rounds of the town and threatened to kill me on sight. Why Kellogg was exempted I forget now, but I was the target of his wrath. So, like a fool, the next morning after Jerry's bloodthirsty pilgrimage, I borrowed two revolvers, a .22 and a .32, and, putting one in each coat pocket, sailed down Massachusetts Street to meet death.

Jerry had a way of sitting in front of his harness shop in the mornings, on the east side of Massachusetts, the only business thoroughfare in Lawrence in those days. He used to sit with his chair tipped back, greeting all and sundry in a jovial, democratic way. He had a voice that resounded up and down the street like Gabriel's trumpet.[2] As I came within a block of him on the other side of the street, I saw him sitting there. I tried to screw up my courage to turn from the

[2]It is believed that the archangel Gabriel will blow the trumpet on Judgment Day.

west side to his side. I could not do it. I walked a half a block further to a crossing. Then, with superhuman effort, I made myself turn and walk across the street, straight into Jerry in his chair. It was an ordeal. Physically I do not think I have ever known more terror. I gripped my two pistols in my coat pockets tightly, and with my eyes fixed on Jerry like a dying calf I finally came to the curbing. I must have walked slowly. He could have seen my terror—anyone could! He was sober then and grinning—a man in his late forties or middle fifties, and I just turning twenty. The ridiculousness of it all overcame him. His chair . . . came down with a terrific click, and I jumped like a scared deer straight up in the air. I have since thanked all the gods at once that I did not begin shooting like a fool. As Jerry came on his feet, he was laughing a great guffaw and I had turned past him, walking perhaps like Shadrach, Meshach, and Abednego[3] of the fiery furnace, slowly up the street to the office. The clerks on Massachusetts Street who stood in their doors awaiting my slaughter when I passed old Jerry echoed his laughter. Before I had gone the fifty yards between his harness shop and the *Journal* office, I was chattering with hysterical laughter along with the rest. I got those two guns in the desk drawer quicker than any bad man ever drew a bead and sat down to tell Kellogg all about it. We both whooped and hurrahed as my hysterical cackle died down, and I never was afraid after that to pass Jerry's shop. He did not mention the matter again. . . .

As I look back upon that summer, it seems one long act from a Gargantuan farce in which Kellogg was the walking gentleman and I the low comedian. . . . For we were twenty years old. We had hold of a lever, an Archimedean lever,[4] the same being the control of two newspapers which served a town of ten thousand in a hot campaign. . . . When it came to naming delegates to the state convention and nominating a county ticket at Lawrence, Kellogg and I, being on the paper, took a hand. I had had some experience in El Dorado. I helped to round up in the ward caucus a dozen or twenty university boys who were living in Lawrence that summer and, under the guidance of Charley Tucker, who bought chickens and eggs in a small way and had many dealings with the colored people in short-time loans and who was a ward boss, Kellogg and I were put on the delegation. . . . If we sloshed around in our glory going home that night, it was because we were somebody. We were young. Life was full of happy surprises and we laughed easily. . . .

It was in those days and under those circumstances that I decided to be a Republican. I had been talking it over for a year. When I sat in the Republican

[3]Shadrach, Meshach, and Abednego were young Hebrews who, though they were cast into a fiery furnace because they refused to worship a golden image, emerged unharmed (Daniel 3:12–30).

[4]Archimedes, an ancient Syracusan mathematician, was mistakenly believed to have said, referring to the power of the lever, "Give me a place to stand and I will move the Earth."

Douglas County convention as a delegate that year, my mother saw my name in the list distributed on slips at the convention. She was puzzled. She must have been torn between pride and duty. She said to me sternly: "What would your father say!"

Then we talked it out as Kellogg and I had talked it out, as Dr. Canfield . . . and I had talked it out, and even as the old Colonel at the office, who really loved me when he was not swearing at me, had talked it out. I told them all the cold truth—that I did not care particularly for either the Democratic or the Republican party, but I had to make a choice. Canfield agreed with that. I remember he said: "Well, White, I don't know. I have tried to be independent, and I have got nowhere politically. I know you dislike and distrust the protective tariff, which ought to make you a Democrat. But in Kansas, as a Democrat, it is hopeless for you. You probably can do more harm to the protective tariff by going into the Republican party and fighting it there."

That seemed sensible. . . . I knew even then I did not want office. In El Dorado I had seen men hanging around the courthouse because they had taken county jobs and it had removed them from their first business of earning a living by their trades or professions and spoiled them for normal usefulness. Even then I had a low opinion of politics as a means of livelihood. . . .

Then one day, perhaps it was the day after the county convention, I talked to my German professor, William Herbert Carruth. . . . He said this in a long and serious talk: "White, your job in life, so far as politics is concerned, is to make your private sentiment public opinion. You are going to be a newspaperman. You will have a great opportunity. Remember, that is what you are here on earth for."

Professor Carruth was in the city council fighting for all sorts of local phases of righteousness and the Will of God, like honest city scales and the proper location of the city library, and macadamed streets. . . . He gave me this other pearl of wisdom which was good for the 1880's and shone with luster through the nineties and into the first decade of this century: "You know it's vastly more important than many pious prayers and tons of highfalutin aspirations, to get a street in a country town made wide enough so that two loads of hay going in opposite directions still leave it possible for a woman to drive a horse and buggy between them without getting hay wisps on her buggy top. There is righteousness and the Will of God incarnate for any man in town politics.". . .

[So] I crossed the Rubicon and became a Republican without deep conviction, purely as a means to an end: to make my private sentiment public opinion and to see that all the various kinds of streets in my journey through life were wide enough. . . . Now at the end of nigh onto sixty years, in which I have consistently voted for Republican presidents and Republican governors, I have about the same idea of party politics that I had back there when Ben Harrison was defeating Cleveland, and Vernon Kellogg and I were wielding the Archimedean lever that moves the world. . . .

I entered the university again the autumn of 1888. It was to be my last year. I carried a heavy load of history, sociology, political science, English and American literature, the physical sciences, stressing biology because that was Kellogg's field, German which I disliked, and French which gave me delight. I dropped mathematics entirely. I had failed in sophomore mathematics somewhere between spherical geometry and trigonometry—failed signally and ignominiously. . . .

Athletics did not interest me remotely in the intramural contests of the various university fraternities. . . . I was not interested in university poker, which was a flourishing diversion. Not that I thought it immoral, but I was naturally tight and did not get enough excitement out of penny ante to pay for my losses. I had the same attitude toward the small doses of beer or wine that seeped into the college life. . . . I liked parties. I consumed gallons of convivial oyster soup with the boys and with Helen and her sorority sisters, indulging in the talk and the gay hyperbole of youth, blowing bubbles of great visions, also forever clowning. I had a stunt—an imitation drunk—that was popular in student societies and got me in bad with the faculty who sometimes took the imitation for reality. . . .

I acquired a mandolin and achieved some skill with it. We had a fraternity guitar, banjo, and mandolin outfit, and six or eight of us used to sing in the moonlight on the steps of the fraternity boardinghouse and serenade our girls. I suppose I might be called a leader in these activities. . . . The Phi Delts allied themselves politically with the Barbs (the nonfraternity men) and I was the fraternity figurehead—a conspicuous young rascal who delighted to foment political trouble on the Hill. We once had a riot in front of the chancellor's office when the regents were in session, roaring, clamoring, and hooting because they were trying to suspend or expel the editor of the college paper for criticizing a professor. We had a big college contest and college lawsuit, with the faculty for judges, over an election in the oratorical society, and I was rather too conspicuous in the ruckamuction. At the end of the year I had the most important political place on the campus. I was editor of the university annual, a rowdy college publication that rounded up the year's events in the college.

Incidentally, during that year I had become "Billie." . . . In the university publications I was Will A. White. That name was signed to the verses I wrote, the pieces I submitted for publication, and that should have been my name in the catalogue if they could have classified me. But I was "Billie," wore the best clothes I could afford and studied neckties in clothing store windows. I was careful to see that my collars were properly moded. . . . I debated a little, wrote essays for the literary societies, liked to lead in all kinds of pranks or capers. . . .

But the strange thing is that a boy so sentient of his surroundings should have been so entirely insensible to the real world about him. I knew in a general way that Kansas and the West in general were living on borrowed money, but I did not understand that I was living in a debtor land nor what that signified. . . . But we were all insensible, all of us over the western Mississippi Valley, of the fact that what goes up must come down. And while I sat in my political economy class, my sociology class, my history class, making fairly good grades, I did not relate what I was studying to the realities around me. It was strange. But I suppose I was like all the rest of that world—hypnotized by its shimmering surface of false prosperity. . . .

In the spring and early summer of 1889 I worked for a month for Colonel Learnard in order to get a round-trip pass to Loveland, Colorado. My job for the Colonel was to get in a rattletrap buggy with a sway-backed old horse which he furnished (trading advertising to a livery stable) and go up and down the countryside in Douglas County, Kansas, soliciting subscribers to the daily and weekly of the Lawrence *Journal*; also to sell job printing, letterheads, billheads, handbills, and the like in the various little towns and incidentally to write pleasant things about each neighborhood in which I worked. As I remember it, he gave me five or six dollars a week for expenses. But my mother put up my lunch and I managed to get the horse into the Lawrence livery stable every night, and so kept my expense money. . . .

I spent that summer in Colorado. Vernon Kellogg . . . went with me. There in Estes Park, thirty miles from the railroad, we joined a group of university boys . . . who were camped in a cabin by the Big Thompson River in Moraine Park, a valley above Estes. It was the most notable summer I had ever had, notable for the fact that I was associating every hour of the day with men who were intellectually my superiors. . . . We were not a serious crowd. We lived simply, gaily. We had two rules, only two, as the laws of our republic: Every man must clean his own fish, and no razor would be allowed in the camp. So we grew whiskers. Mine were red and upturned from under the chin—an Irish moustache. We cooked what [Ed and Will Franklin] told us to cook, for they were our elders, and washed dishes without rancor or friction. Every man made his own bed, which was on the floor of the one-room log cabin, for we all slept in a row over spruce boughs and under our own blankets. And every man looked after his own kit—a change of underwear, his store clothes which he never wore in the park, a book or two or three or half a dozen which he brought, and his gun if he had one, which I did not, and his fishing tackle, also ditto with me. . . .

Vernon and Funston and I were an inseparable trio. I went with them when they hunted, sometimes. I often loafed along behind them within yelling distance. I liked to gather the wild red raspberries and strawberries in the canyon, which the Franklins put into delectable shortcakes. I was willing to cook and wash dishes. I made a passable flapjack, fried fish with reasonable skill, helped to cut up the contraband mountain sheep which Funston shot, took my turn and probably had more than my turn in hauling down wood from the mountain for our cabin. I made a curious hammock out of fence wire and barrel staves and hung it in the woods above our cabin and went up there many an afternoon to read.

I should define life that summer as hilarious. It was a roar of laughter at me, somewhat as a pokey fool, or at Funston, who could not walk a log across a creek and had to coon it. But once he took his rifle and marched all alone down the road to where some advertising painters were smearing huge boulders with admonishings to use somebody's sarsaparilla. Literally Funston chased them down the road, largely by his unique and convincing profanity, supported somewhat by his cocked rifle. . . . The summer passed—certainly the most profitable two months I had ever spent in my life, for I learned to live with others. Proteus,[5] who changes us from decade to decade, with some kind of a transmigration of souls as the years pass with their ceaseless mutations, worked his miracle on me. If I ever grew up and became a man, it was in the summer of 1889, in Colorado, in a little log cabin filled with a dozen boys on the Big Thompson River.

[5]In Greek legend, Proteus possessed the power to assume different shapes at will.

6

I Become a Blind Leader of the Blind

I went back to the university in the fall of 1889 and tried to hold my job as a reporter for the *Journal* and do my class work. It was unsuccessful. Some way I had ceased to be a student and had become a reporter. . . . I tried again the mathematics examination that would take the academic skeleton out of my class record. It was no good.

In December of that year I had an offer from Mr. Murdock of the El Dorado *Republican*—eighteen dollars a week to take charge of his paper, hire and fire, write the locals and editorials, run the bank account and get out the paper. Said he to me, when we talked it over: "Now, Bill Allen, I am on a Senate committee to codify the laws of Kansas. We are on per diem and expenses. I am going to be away a long time. I want someone to take charge of this shop."

The eighteen dollars he offered me seemed to be beyond the dreams of avarice. . . . In the university the requirements for mathematics were strict, immutable. I never could graduate. I figured it out that I might as well quit when the quitting was good. . . . My mother and I put our little household traps into a freight car and went back to El Dorado. We moved into one of our smaller houses, ousting the tenant who had been there more than ten years. It was a small house—six or seven rooms—on a tree-shaded street, in the best residential part of town. She liked that part of it, did my mother. And I think while we were there she was happy, barring her moody moments when she remembered that I had missed my degree. She did not realize that since I walked out of the high school in June 1884, I had been for the better part of five years and a half in and around college, reading when I was not studying, playing the college game every vacant hour in my academic career that was not occupied by reciting, writing, or reporting. If ever a young man was exposed to an education, I

81

was—even though I did not carry an academic degree. Books and reading had become a major part of my interests and habits. . . .

In that day and time I began my real life, in January 1890, as a responsible head of a country weekly with a circulation of something under three thousand in a town of two thousand five hundred and in a county of twenty-five or thirty thousand people. Here I was at home. When I moved into the *Republican* office, I took Mr. Murdock's desk. He came down the first morning and saw me there and began to laugh: "Well, Bill Allen, you are a chip off the old block. Your father never hesitated to boss things. Where do you think I am going to sit?" After that, whenever I heard his footsteps upon the stairs, I sneaked over to another desk. . . .

That first morning, Mr. Murdock pulled from his vest pocket a leather case and threw down an engraved card—very nifty. . . . He was going to Topeka on the noon train. He was arrayed in his Brooks Brothers suit, had on an expensive but subdued necktie and his stylish, sawed-off, semi-plug hat. He saw me invoicing his sartorial outfit and he laughed softly.

"I'm going to the Coates House tonight, and tomorrow I'm going to send that card with a note to Ogden Armour. And by Godfrey's diamonds, he'll come and see *me!*" Then, squinting up his eyes and puckering his face, he said: "And he'll pay for it!"

At this point I should have been shocked, but I was not. He well knew I would not be. We lived in the age where the sort of thing he was explaining needed no defense, required no apology, was accepted as the way life was. . . . When he went forth, up and down the earth on his railroad passes, to the packing houses, to the insurance companies, and to the Kansas City banks and mortgage companies, seeking whom he might devour, that was a matter of common knowledge among the governing class, and I was born into that governing class. . . .

As solicitor of advertising, along with my other duties as local editor, editorial writer, business manager, once in a while I had to use strong-arm methods with reluctant advertisers. In that day there were three ways to get advertising for a newspaper: to sell it as a legitimate commodity; to beg for it as help for the paper which was booming the town; or to hold a more or less obvious gun in the ribs of the advertiser while a salesman, politely if possible but firmly if necessary, explained why it was to the intelligent self-interest of the advertiser to put an advertisement in the salesman's medium. So I got business from the merchants. So Mr. Murdock got business from Mr. Armour *et al.* Probably he had no more qualms about his task than I had about my job. As an Episcopalian vestryman, he came home every other Sunday. Certainly he was not a pious fraud in his own view, but a good solid citizen upholding the church as a pillar of a rather felicitous society—the Republican plutocracy, giver of every good and perfect gift, distributor of justice to the rich and benefices to the poor. And if sometimes Mr. Murdock, whose wife still was an invalid, had an eye for a pretty girl with a well-turned ankle and a come-hither smile—well, God was just and, after all, you could not expect perfection out of weak flesh and blood. . . .

The year 1890 opened God's perfect world, so far as the ruling classes were concerned, in the western Mississippi Valley and in the South. The Republicans two years before had swept everything north of the Indian territory. The Democrats in the South had returned to Congress and put into the governors' mansions the Confederate veterans from the big houses or their sons. It seemed to the people in the towns and to the better class of farmers all over the two regions west and south that life would go on about as it was for those whom hard work, good luck, and God's mercy had assigned to places in the upper social stratifications of a classless democratic society. Obviously, the distribution of wealth which nature and nature's God had written in tablets of stone would be undisturbed through all future ages. Revolt, reform, progress, change—all were unthinkable. . . .

Then out of the nowhere into the here came trouble. We laughed at it, of course. I remember one day in the midst of spring, when Senator Murdock came home from one of his predatory excursions to Topeka and Kansas City, I told him with glee about a meeting in the courthouse of the county committee of the Farmers' Alliance. They were arranging to call a mass convention to put out a county ticket. It was funny. I listed the leaders of the meeting. Among them were all the town and county malcontents who had been blowing off since the days of the Grangers and the Greenbackers,[1] and who had supported Ben Butler in '84 and the Union Labor party[2] in '88, which polled less than 10 percent of the vote. We knew that the Farmers' Alliance had been organizing in the county, and we presumed it was another of those farmer cooperatives which would start a store and maybe build an elevator, last two or three years, and then dry up and blow away. Such things had been happening since the beginning of the settlement of the county. Mr. Murdock listened to my story, grinned complacently, and pretty soon lit out for the bank, to talk it over with his cronies. . . . It was his opinion that it was another of those fly-by-night political disturbances which was of no great consequence, and of course I felt the same way. How could a group of incompetents that were not able to get into a county convention of either party, a group that for twenty years had been the laughingstock of the countryside for its visionary nonsense—how could they get anywhere in politics? We paid no attention to the platform upon which they had called the county convention. The Democratic paper printed it, but it was generally jeered at in the conclave that crowded the post-office lobby every evening after arrival of the five o'clock train.

---

[1]These were agrarian movements protesting economic conditions—including high transportation costs, low grain prices, and the long-term deflation of the money supply—that hurt farmers in the later nineteenth century. The Grangers grew out of a farmers' fraternal order, the Husbands of Industry; their influence peaked in the mid-1870s. The Greenback movement in the 1880s advocated returning to the paper currency (greenbacks) that had been legal during the Civil War.

[2]The Union Labor party attempted in the election of 1888 to unite former members of the Greenback party with organized labor.

If one of the group came in, he was assailed with good-natured raillery. He fired back as good as he got from the banker, or the lawyer, or the judge, or the old doctor, or the leading merchant, and the crowd had some good laughs. . . . I laughed with the crowd. . . . I wrote gay, ribald, and possibly subtly Rabelaisian editorials directed at the whole fly-up-the-creek, ragtag, and bobtail movement.

When they had their convention, it filled the courthouse. The size of the convention, symbolized by a dado of backsides sticking out of the courtroom windows, bothered for a moment the Olympians who ruled the county. I told Mr. Murdock about it. As a news item, we printed the county ticket which the rabble-rousers had chosen, and made supercilious and obliquely scurrilous reference to the kind of candidates they had chosen. . . . Naturally, because the editorials were pretty mean, I acquired some distinction with the ruling class. . . .

As the summer deepened, the Farmers' Alliance began to assume serious proportions. We who followed politics professionally with anything like sensitive ears knew its county ticket was amazingly gathering strength. Mr. Murdock would come to the office from the bank and caution me about the intolerance of my editorials. Sometimes he wrote an editorial himself. He astonished me one day by attacking the Republican leadership of the state. It was a sacrilege, but he owned the paper. I apologized for Mr. Murdock under my breath to the bankers and the post-office moguls when the paper was out and he was gone out of town on his codifying trips. His idea in attacking the Republican leadership was to placate the rebels. The word "appeasement" had not come to prominence, but he was an appeaser.[3]

I remember that during this first summer of what became the Populist uprising, he used to go about town in seersucker trousers, a spotless white shirt, red suspenders and a Panama hat out of George Tolle's stock on Main Street. He was a great hand to go through the stores of Saturdays when the farmers were in town, talking with everybody, particularly the rebellious farmers; maybe not about politics, maybe about crops, religion, business, or gossip. . . . He avoided controversy. He was just Old Bent to the farmers—Old Bent to his enemies, who always softened when he was around. He knew the names of their wives and their children, their dogs and their horses. And when he was electioneering, he carried fine-cut tobacco in his silver tobacco case which he chewed gingerly and passed freely among the farmers in the Saturday crowd. And so he came to me one Saturday in midsummer with the truth: "By Godfrey's diamonds," he said, "something's happening, young feller! These damn farmers are preparing to tear down the courthouse!"

It was about this time that he and his brother Marshall, who edited the Wichita *Eagle*, . . . started a counterrevolution known as "the Murdock rebellion."

---

[3]White is referring to those who, in the late 1930s, attempted to placate Hitler and thereby forestall his threatened aggression by conceding to his demands for restoration of territories that had been taken from Germany after World War I.

Its chief demand was that the Republican party in Kansas clean house. How the crowd at the post office hooted the day the paper was out, about the phrase "cleaning house," considering the past record and position of Mr. Murdock. . . .

Nonetheless and howsoever, "the situation"—which in political jargon means the environing developments—was getting serious. The Farmers' Alliance in midsummer put out a state ticket. . . . And in Butler County and all over Kansas, townspeople riding out at night noticed that once or twice a week the schoolhouses were all lit up. In Kansas, schoolhouses are used for political meetings. The Republicans had not begun their campaign. But the Alliance people had. And right square in mid-July, almost without notice, certainly without any clamor in the Republican papers, a procession two miles long moved down Main Street in El Dorado. It was made up of protesting farmers, their wives and their children. There were floats on hayracks filled with singers crying political protest to Gospel tunes. There were mottoes: "Special Privileges for None; Equal Rights for All," "Down with Wall Street," "Kill the Great Dragon of Lombard Street,"[4] "Let Us Pay the Kind of Dollar We Borrowed."

That was the core of the issue which had crystallized the political strength of the Farmers' Alliance. Said they, "We borrowed money in the seventies before the resumption of specie payment and the return to a gold basis for currency.[5] Now we are asked to pay in a gold dollar which is worth much more in crops and cattle and farm produce than the dollar we borrowed." It was the free-silver issue, a form of fiat money. . . .

I was satisfied, being what I was, that the whole Alliance movement was demagogic rabble-rousing, having no basis in sound economics. How intellectually snobbish I was about "sound economics"! Alack and alas, I took no account, absolutely no account, of the tremendous fact staring me in the face, that the short shimmering day of mass borrowing which had built a civilization in the West and the South, from Appomattox[6] to the nineties, was done. Its sun had set. The railroads were all built. Sound economics should have warned me that another day had dawned. . . .

The day of the great boom of the seventies and eighties—a day which had seen railroad pirates rise and become captains of industry; a day which had seen all the great industries organizing with capital gathered more or less by the same

[4]In the book of Revelation 12:3, the devil appears in the form of "a great red dragon, having seven heads and ten horns, and seven crowns upon his heads." Populists often used apocalyptic biblical language and here referred to London's financial center.

[5]During the Civil War, specie payment, which allowed money to be exchanged for gold, was suspended and the federal government issued its own notes, or greenbacks. After the war these notes were gradually withdrawn from circulation and the gold standard was reestablished.

[6]Appomattox was the scene of the surrender on April 9, 1865, of General Robert E. Lee's Confederate Army of Northern Virginia to the Union Army of the Potomac, which effectively ended the Civil War.

proud captains of industry, the packers, the steel men, the oil men, the railroads; a day which had seen the play of free, competitive industrial capital—that day was at its sunset. Those rumps of seedy farmers sticking out of the courthouse window in El Dorado, Butler County, Kansas, as the Farmers' Alliance county convention met, cast the shadows of a great twilight. In another three years came the night—the collapse and the depression of '93. But I was a fool. I sat at night in the office of the El Dorado *Republican*, writing reactionary editorials about sound economics which I had learned from Francis Walker's college text-book,[7] just one of ten thousand other fools across the land who thought that classic economics could be fitted into the social and political upheaval that was closing a brilliant era in our national history. . . . Being what I was, a child of the governing classes, I was blinded by my birthright!

In the last paragraph I wrote, "Being what I was." Well, what was I? Among my contemporaries . . . I was "Billie" as I had been in college. I read voraciously, loved formal society in the town, organized dances, took delight in serenading the girls and in rowing them up and down the three- or four-mile mill dam of the Walnut. I was given to conspicuous clothing, was not afraid to wear the first pongee silk shirt that came to town. Before I had been back from the university six months, I had bought, at a price, a statesman's double-breasted Prince Albert coat with mouse-gray trousers—hand-me-down! . . . There was a funny figure for a man aged twenty-four or twenty-five, who was writing editorials in the El Dorado *Republican* that goaded the Populists to wrath. That kind of dude was foreordained and predestined to hang in effigy in the Populist parade with the title "Silly Willie" painted across his capacious cartooned posterior.

How that effigy amused Mr. Murdock! We stood together watching the parade. And when the wagon containing my dangling effigy passed, Mr. Murdock looked at me over his glasses and, probably remembering my father's effigy figure as it floated in the breezes in Augusta nearly twenty years before, laughed his soft, ingratiating laugh: "Old Doc White, by Godfrey's diamonds! It's Old Doc White! Eh, Bill Allen!" and was proud. . . .

The hanging effigy gave me leadership among the young Republicans of the town and county. . . . I used my talent for verse-making to write rhymes for the Republican Glee Club: ribald rhymes, hooting at the Farmers' Alliance, deriding its leaders, jeering at the ragged nobodies who were its followers—silly rhymes which we Republicans in those days thought were grape and canister in the entrails of our adversaries. We who had eyes and saw not, and ears and heard not![8] . . .

[7]*Political Economy*, a widely used economics text, was first published in 1883.

[8]White paraphrases Jesus' description of those who "seeing see not; and hearing they hear not" (Matthew 13:3).

Through it all, there at Senator Murdock's desk, I was writing all sorts of things. I had become the El Dorado correspondent of the Associated Press, of the Kansas City *Star*, and of St. Louis, Chicago, and New York papers. I was writing syndicated articles for the American Press Association, a concern which sold stereotyped features to small dailies and weekly newspapers, and I was forever writing verse which appeared in the *Republican* and then was scattered like leaves upon the wind. It was imitation, of course, imitation of James Whitcomb Riley, or Will Carleton, or Eugene Field. But I did not realize that it was imitation. . . .

Also, as I was by way of being a poet, I courted other poets. Fort Scott had two: Eugene Ware, whose *Rhymes of Ironquill* have been more widely read than those of any other Kansan, and Albert Bigelow Paine, who had come there as an itinerant tintype photographer in a van, married a rich girl, started up in the wholesale photographer's supply business—the while writing verse which he sold to magazines in New York. . . . Ware, whom I idolized, was a Civil War veteran who learned the saddlemaker's trade to support him while he studied law, married a Vassar graduate, became a state senator, was defeated for Congress because his verse was not regarded as orthodox in that far-off day of the seventies and early eighties. He was one of the most distinguished lawyers in the Middle West and in the early part of the first decade of this century was appointed United States Pensions Commissioner by Theodore Roosevelt. . . . To me, those two—Ware and Paine—were persons of much consequence. Their careers represented to me, as I wrote in the office over the post office in El Dorado, realizable ideals.

So summer slipped by and the November election came. . . . In those days United States Senators were elected by the legislature. The state senate was a holdover body chosen in the Republican triumphal election of 1888, while the members of the house of representatives were overwhelmingly, almost unanimously, Farmers' Alliance, elected with just one purpose, to defeat John J. Ingalls.

He was the shining figure of western Republicanism—a national figure too for he was a polished orator, a graduate of Williams College and had helped write the Kansas Constitution and had designed its seal. He was elected to the United States Senate in the seventies. . . . He never discussed economic issues, leaving that for demagogues. Consideration of patronage irked him. . . . It was inconceivable to [him] that the people of Kansas should be seriously interested in issues touching on the realities of the economic situation. When he realized, late in his campaign, that the Farmers' Alliance was serious, he got up in the Senate and made a speech for free silver—a scholarly, futile, rhetorical performance. He could not realize how tragically real to the Kansas people, and especially the farmers, was the deflation of the currency. He could not understand why mortgage foreclosures got into politics; how ten-cent corn could affect Republican majorities; why deflation was scattering devastation across an agricultural state like Kansas.

He was set by nature and polished by circumstances as a shining mark for political death in 1890. And about that time he preened his political plumage and declared impudently that "the purification of politics is an iridescent dream." That bright saying—erudite, arrogant, cynical—deeply offended hundreds of thousands of Kansans who were struggling against debt, taxes, and a shrinking dollar to maintain their homes and uphold their self-respect. Was it coincidence that erected for the people of his state a man so exactly personifying all that they hated, or was it some impish prescience in the times that made Ingalls' defeat symbolic of all the anguished yearnings of a distressed electorate? Chance or fatal circumstance dramatizing the issue—whichever it was, like a lightning flash the fall of Ingalls revealed the political realities of the hour in understandable terms.

When it was found that the joint session of the legislature would defeat Ingalls by half a dozen votes, the Republicans, without consulting him too carefully, set Cy Leland—the local boss who handled the details of Kansas politics for George R. Peck of the Santa Fe Railroad and the financial interests thereunto appertaining—to buying the votes necessary to rescue Ingalls. Mr. Murdock, at the time it happened, told me this story; Mr. Leland afterwards verified it: It would take ten thousand dollars to buy the ten men necessary to Ingalls' election. They, of course, were a scabby lot. Their reputation in the state as mercenaries and worse was known to those who dabbled in Kansas politics; Leland knew it and Ingalls had to know it.

Leland called on him in his hotel bedroom and handed him the list. Ingalls rose and paced the bedroom floor like a caged panther, snarling, as he looked over the list, up and down. Finally, he burst out with imprecations, curses, and such profanity as a scholastic vocabulary could readily improvise. . . . Leland stood it for a while. He was a practical, little sawed-off cavalry officer, with chin whiskers and no nonsense, who faced the realities of the situation. He grew tired of Ingalls' vituperations.

"Ah, shut up!" said he. "Do you want to do it, or don't you want to do it?"

Again Ingalls began attacking the maternal genealogy of his mercenary supporters.

"Damn your stinking Massachusetts pride—hush!" cried Leland. "Of course that's exactly what they are. But do you expect me to take ten thousand dollars and go out and buy you a lot of Goddamn Sunday school superintendents?"

Ingalls stopped before Leland and dramatically handed back his list. "No, Cy, no! I have my family and my name, and I won't take the risk of disgracing them to hold this job." And buttoning his long gray coat, he strolled out of the room into oblivion. . . .

The fall of Ingalls, the rise of the Farmers' Alliance, the first wave of the shock troops of a revolution that was to gather force as the years went by—all this did not disturb either the Spring Chickens or their parents at the high-five clubs, the formal dances at the opera house given for the firemen, and the town charities. . . . We were conscious of some disturbance and quoted Tennyson's lines[9] at it:

> An infant crying in the night;
> An infant crying for the light:
> And with no language but a cry!

and let the little misbegotten creature bawl his lungs out on our doorstep. He was no concern of ours—but we were rather proud of that quotation.

I had that line first from Professor Canfield when I wrote him a letter after the Farmers' Alliance state convention—a bewildered letter asking him what was causing the upheaval. He sent to me or at least referred me to Richard T. Ely's book on *The Labor Movement in America* and a treatise on American Socialism, which I read—still more bewildered than I had been. In his letter he used the Tennysonian lines. Later, George R. Peck, our state satrap, who probably next to Ingalls was our most scholarly politician, used the line in a speech. . . . The quotation epitomized our general attitude toward the farmers' rebellion.

Vernon Kellogg came down to El Dorado to see me in the winter of 1891 and we had long talks about this agrarian rebellion. . . . [We] tried to make heads or tails of the whole mess, but vainly. Ewing Herbert's idea was simple: These men were traitors. They should be treated as such. They were in rebellion against the United States. Ewing's idea was the Republican idea, and the best they could do was to yell "Socialism" at the Populists and predict a recurrence of the French Revolution.

The charge against the Populists that they were Socialists had more basis in fact than we Republicans understood, for, after all, Populism stemmed back to the creed of the Grangers and the Greenbackers, who were led by the old abolitionists, those who proclaimed the rights of men—Greeley, Garrison, Wendell Phillips. All that the Populists were doing and saying boiled down to this: By their clamor against the trusts, by their demand that the railroads be regulated and that the currency be inflated, that an income tax be established more for justice than for income perhaps, that inheritances be broken up, again for justice rather than for income, that a score of minor irritations against the com-

---

[9]These lines from Tennyson's poem *In Memoriam* (1850) are, however, preceded by the line "But what am I?"

mon man be removed, these reformers were trying to use government as an agency of human welfare. They were trying to establish economic as well as political equality, to help the underdog, to cut down some of the privileges that wealth carried by reason of its size and inherent power. It was all Karl Marx, highly diluted, and the Republicans, who did not realize how true their indictment was, continued to cry "Socialism" at the top of their lungs without really believing it.

In the spring of 1891 I bought *Leaves of Grass* and became for the time inebriated with Walt Whitman's philosophy. . . . But the amazing thing about my madness was that I did not in any way connect the Whitman democracy with the Farmers' Alliance. For here, parading down Main Street, was a barbaric yawp[10] if ever there was one—a pure Whitmanesque picture! I was ten years making it all out! In those ten years two poets, entirely different, almost antagonistic, held me enthralled—Walt Whitman and Rudyard Kipling. I fear that Kipling's philosophy, rather than Whitman's, colored my mind in its practical attitudes toward life. But the two must have jangled and left me disturbed and uncertain. . . .

That year, well into the summer, I first met a young prince whose life was to be linked with mine fairly closely for more than two score years. He was Charley Curtis. He came down from Topeka to campaign the county, sent down by the Republican state central committee. His job was to fight the Farmers' Alliance. He had a rabble-rousing speech with a good deal of Civil War in it, a lot of protective tariff, and a very carefully poised straddle on the currency question (which I was satisfied then—and still think—that he knew little about and cared absolutely nothing for). For his politics were always purely personal. Issues never bothered him. He was a handsome fellow, five feet ten, straight as his Kaw Indian grandfather must have been, with an olive skin that looked like old ivory, a silky, flowing, handlebar moustache, dark shoe-button eyes, beady, and in those days always gay, a mop of crow's wing hair, a gentle ingratiating voice, and what a smile! . . .

Butler County is larger than the state of Rhode Island, and he and I, with a buggy hired by the county Republican committee, rode over the county together for three days. He made the speeches; I introduced him. A glee club went with us and sang ribald doggerel, lambasting the Farmers' Alliance. In those three days when we were together most of the time, we explored each other's minds. He must have thought me a silly, sentimental person, and I felt that he was a wonder with his winning ways. I never saw a man who could go into a hostile

---

[10]In his "Song of Myself," Whitman said, "I sound my barbaric yawp over the roofs of the world."

audience, smile, shake hands, and talk before and after the meeting so plausibly that what he said on his feet as an orator was completely eclipsed by what he was as a human being. We got on a "Will" and "Charley" basis which would last through our lives. . . .

In Kansas the young Republicans have a way of organizing. In the process of organization, youth gets acquainted. Youth pretends that it is organizing to re-form the world. As a matter of fact, it is organizing politically to get jobs. After the Republicans were defeated by the Populists in 1890, we young Republicans hustled into an organization. We were going to do big things, and did. In the next decade we got elected to a lot of offices. But in the state organization I met other young men whom I had known from the other Kansas colleges, whom I had met in the political battles of the State Oratorical Association, also many K.U. alumni of my own day and of the decade before. So I was at home in the organization of the Young Republicans.

I did not make speeches. I took no office. I knew enough even then to realize that he who seeks honors loses power. To help an up-and-coming young fellow get to be chairman of a committee gave me more power on the committee than he had, if he was grateful. And I suppose most of a man's luck in politics de-pends on his ability to keep away from ingrates. . . .

By that time I had become a full-fledged Republican with some enthusiasm—if not for my faith, at least for my friends! The more the local Populists denounced me, the surer I was that this was the best possible world, and that any attempt to remake or reform it was folly bordering on treason. So I wrote for Senator Mur-dock's paper with ardor, with force, and with considerable plausibility. Because he taught me more than anyone before him to write short sentences, to use sim-ple common words, to say exactly what I meant in the vernacular, and because I was young and full of youth's vigor, I carried conviction and attained some little fame.

After returning from the convention I sat down at the big desk in the *Republi-can* office one afternoon and wrote my first piece of fiction. It was the story of an old soldier Republican who returned to the Republican fold for purely personal reasons. It was all emotion, all sentiment, and probably all nonsense. It was called "The Regeneration of Colonel Hucks." . . . The Kansas City *Star* copied it. So did the Kansas City *Journal*. All the Kansas daily papers published it within a week after it appeared in El Dorado. The Republican state central com-mittee saw it, and Senator Plumb, who had been my father's friend, read it. I am sure he was telling me the truth when he said it brought tears to his eyes, for he was a good politician and his tear ducts were loosely valved. Anyway, he saw to it that the Republican state committee issued the story in sterotype plates the next week and sent it to every Republican paper in the state, credited to me, "Will A. White, in the El Dorado *Republican*." It fitted into the other western states where Populism was rampant—Nebraska, the Dakotas, Colorado, Iowa, Minnesota—and the Republican state committees there used it. For a month, perhaps, straggling letters, four or five a week from all over the region, came in thanking me for it. I have no doubt that my head swelled. . . .

Before the summer was over my good opinion of myself was strengthened by two offers of editorial jobs in Kansas City. One was a letter from Colonel William R. Nelson, editor of the Kansas City *Star*, offering me twenty-five dollars a week to come to Kansas City. . . . The other was from Charles S. Gleed, whom I had known in my Lawrence days, for he was an alumnus not only of the university but of the Lawrence *Journal*. . . . He was the receiver, or something like that, of the Kansas City *Journal*, representing the Santa Fe Railroad . . . which had in some way taken over the ownership and managership of that paper. Gleed offered me the same salary that Colonel Nelson offered me. Taking my Republicanism seriously, I chose the Kansas City *Journal*, thinking I should be happier writing for the Republican organ than for a mugwump[11] Independent newspaper that had supported President Cleveland.

Between the time I decided to go to the *Journal* and my departure from El Dorado, I had nearly a month. I was afraid I could not hold the job, and my mother and I decided that she would stay in El Dorado while I adventured. She was proud that I chose the Republican *Journal* and not so doubtful as I was about my holding the job. I gave myself one final farewell social toot in a dance in the Fraternal Insurance Hall. I went fishing with two visiting Kansas editors all day one Sunday and wrote a piece about it for the El Dorado *Republican*.

Whenever I wrote anything which I regarded as particularly flossy, my laurel wreath crowned my brow. Now Mr. Murdock came shuffling up to the desk and looked over his glasses to say: "Well, Bill Allen, I see you've spread yourself and writ a piece! . . . Well, young feller," he said, "that'll be your last piece. They'll tie you up there like a mule to the treadmill, and you'll grow old and gray in the city, a hired man, a nobody." He paused. "When you get your belly full, come back." Another pause. "Gawd, what a life! Your father wanted always to push West where he could be free." He half turned away, then said sadly: "Old Doc White, good Old Doc White!" Then he grinned and chuckled: "Well, go it while you're young, Bill Allen. When you're old you can't!" . . .

One other thing I remember—a strange thing and quite mad. The August harvest moon, under which a few nights before I had come home feeling most poetical from my day's fishing with my visiting editors, was still shining high in the sky when I walked home another night, . . . not unconscious of the night's splendor. I turned in and slept deeply. Then I remember waking up, when the

[11]"Mugwump" was a derisive name first given to those Republicans who refused to support their party's nominee, James G. Blaine, in 1884 and used during the rest of the nineteenth century to refer to anyone who remained independent of political parties.

moon's beams were slanting and the dawn must have been but two or three hours away. Now this is sure: I did wake up. Something—it seemed to me the sound of distant music—came to my ear. The head of my bed was near a south window and I looked out. And I will swear across the years during which I have held the picture, that there under a tree—a spreading elm tree—I saw the Little People, the fairies. I was not dreaming; at least I did not think so then and I cannot think so now. They were making a curious buzzing noise, white little people, or gray, three or four inches high. And I got up out of bed and went to another window and still saw them. Then I lay on my belly on my bed and kicked my heels and put my chin in my hands, to be sure I was not sleeping, and still I saw them.

For a long time, maybe five minutes, they were buzzing about, busy at something, I could not make out what. Then I turned away a moment, maybe to roll over on my side or to get up on my knees, and they began to fade away; an instant later they were gone. And there I was, like a fool, gawking at the bluegrass under the elm. I got up and sat in a chair. I was deeply upset, bemused, troubled. I thought, "Maybe I am going crazy!" I knew well enough of course even then that what I saw I did not see, but when you are cold sober and have the conviction spread over you that you are mad, you are bothered—and I have been bothered ever since. It is not impossible. Nothing is impossible. Many years later I heard of transparent fish—with other eyes, other creatures see other things; with other ears they hear much that escapes our human ears. Perhaps in our very presence are other beings like the transparent fish, which we may not feel with our bodies attuned to rather insentient nerves. Heaven knows! For an hour I thought I was crazy. And when I recall that hour and am so sure that I was awake, I think maybe I am still crazy.

Still, the marvel, or the hallucination, or whatever it was there in the moonlight before the dawn, was no more puzzling than the thing that actually happened to me a week later when I left El Dorado on the morning train for Kansas City, to make my fame and fortune in the big world beyond. . . . When I shook hands with my friends there at the station platform and climbed aboard the little plug train that took me out of my home town to what seemed to me the great city—a town over a hundred thousand then—I stepped as it were out of one body and one environment and one old chain of circumstances into a new world, a new body of thinking and feeling, a new life.

When the train stopped at Kansas City that evening, a young man whom I seemed to know but who some way was strange to me got off. He was a bit ashamed of his clothes. He was not sure how to get around or what to do. He went, at first bashfully, through the crowds of clanging cablecars to the heart of the great city, to the tall six-story building where the *Journal* was published, a countryman, probably quite as scared as young St. George when he first lifted his spear to the dragon. . . .

And so Will White, who was sometimes "Billie" in his late teens and early twenties, became rather definitely Will A. White of the Kansas City *Journal*, with his nervous, trembling hands tightly squeezing, more in fear than pride, the shaft of the spear that would slay the city dragon. It was as though he had burst from the cocoon of childhood and youth and had suddenly become a man!

7

A Gilded
Metropolis

The Kansas City of 1891, to which I came as
Childe Roland to the Dark Tower,[1] was an overgrown country town of a hundred thousand people. It was consciously citified, like a country jake in his first
store clothes. It had one ten-story building and a score of buildings from five to
seven stories. Its business area comprised a dozen blocks in something like the
center of the town. To the west of the business area were the packing houses. . . .
Around them were the small industries of the city and the stockyards, which
smelled to high heaven. And of course fringing these were the shabby, unpainted homes of the workers. North of the business district was the red-light
area, segregated and properly policed. South of the business area lived the ruling
class in lovely homes surrounded by green lawns and with spreading elms,
massive oaks, a few walnut trees and young evergreens. There, in great ten- or
fifteen-room houses, surrounded by hundreds of feet of deep porches, in wooden
houses that bulged with tumors and warts of the ornamental architecture of the
jigsaw period, lived the bankers, the merchants, the lawyers, the doctors, the
teachers, the preachers, now and then a prosperous gambler or a corrupt politician. These worthies were generally boycotted by the respectables, who were too
nice to accept socially those whose business they tolerated and whose immorali-
ties were acknowledged as a part of the necessary social order of a boom town.

But in 1891 the Kansas City boom was deflated. That year saw the collapse
that had begun on the farms of the Missouri Valley [swell] until it reached the
city. Mortgage companies in Kansas City were tottering. Several banks were un-
stable, and everyone knew it. The merchants were having a hard time making
their collections. It was rough going for young lawyers and young doctors. The

[1]Childe Roland rescued his sister from the fairies in an old Scottish ballad; the phrase "Childe
Roland to the Dark Tower came" appears both in *The Bride of Triermain* by Sir Walter Scott and in
Shakespeare's *King Lear*.

fat pickings had vanished, and only the stark white bones of many a financial and mercantile structure, of many a small industry were left for the young cubs. So life in Kansas City . . . instead of being hectic and regal, as I expected it, was beginning to be a bit drab.

But I was too green really to know it except as I saw it in retrospect at the end of a decade. Probably no young professional man who had been exposed to six years in college was ever so raw and unsophisticated in a city as I. I had visited Kansas City but a few times. The cable cars that ran up and down the hills around the Missouri River where the town was staked out were marvels to me. The electric lights still had a novel dazzle for my eyes. I had used the telephone a little at Lawrence and at El Dorado but always with the consciousness that I was tampering with a miracle.

I got off the train and went to the *Journal* Building, where they were expecting me. The managing editor had arranged that I should board out a defunct advertising due bill and led me to the Centropolis Hotel, a third-rate hostelry down near the edge of the red-light district but still the haunt of old Missouri cattlemen who remembered it in the days of its royal prime. We walked south from the *Journal* office and passed the Keith-Perry Building, which loomed above me seven or eight stories. I knew that Keith and Perry were coal operators, and when the managing editor said, "Mr. White, that building is made of coal!" I took him literally and touched my finger to its cyclopean dark, smoke-grimed sandstone masonry. Then I looked down and away quickly so that the managing editor would not detect my ignorance.

Along other lines I was not so innocent as I looked. I had not been in Kansas City a month before I discovered that, by working it right, you could get a streetcar pass, and I worked it right and the managing editor did not know it. But he would not have cared—much!

Mr. Gleed had put me in as editorial writer after he had discharged my predecessor for drinking too much. He, like many men who drink too much, was a charming fellow, much beloved by the reporters and the executives of the *Journal*. They had done his work for him to shield his negligence. So I was not popular. But I sensed the trouble. One night when I had been on the paper for two or three months, the managing editor, an old boy in his sixties, the telegraph editor in his fifties, and the dramatic critic who for some reason had really become fond of me knocked off at midnight after the paper was up and started out casually to roam down Grand Avenue, drinking as we went from bar to bar during the midnight hours. Early the dramatic critic left the party, and we three prowled around the saloons until it must have been three or four o'clock. My drinking experience was slight. It did not occur to me that I was taking on much. I knew I was talkative, but so were the others, and I stood up with the nerves of youth and no experience behind me.

I noticed as the night grew old that the other two were wilting. We chartered a hack somewhere over on lower Main Street, and I helped the managing editor to his door, rang the bell, and held him until it was opened. I took the telegraph editor to his boarding house, put him to bed, and went home and turned up the next afternoon fresh as a daisy. Dean, the dramatic critic, who heard the story, greeted me with cheers. It seems it had been agreed in the office that I was to be taken out and gotten wildly drunk so that the story should be told around that I was worse than my predecessor. It was my first bacchanalian triumph, and probably my last, for liquor never interested me. I acquired much face in the office by my prowess that night, for of course Dean whispered the story about, and the managing editor after that night felt kindly toward me, perhaps as he felt my arms about him climbing the stone steps to the terrace and the wooden steps to the front door of his home. . . .

For some strange reason I attracted the attention, and was honored with the friendship, of Colonel Robert T. Van Horn who was nominally editor-in-chief of the paper—but only nominally, poor fellow. If ever our profession knew a scholar and a gentleman, it was Colonel Van Horn. He had been a brave soldier in the Civil War. He had come to Kansas City before the Civil War and had started a Republican paper when it took courage in that pro-slavery stronghold. He had served a term or two in Congress and—being an old-fashioned man chary of his intimacies and proud to be called "Colonel"—he disliked and distrusted James G. Blaine, who had called him "Bob" the second time he met him. He seemed to me to be an old, old man, though he was only in his late sixties. He had a scraggly, snow-white beard, and a pink complexion which shone through it, and kind, wide blue eyes.

The *Journal*, in his heyday, was of course a political organ that depended somewhat for its patronage and prestige upon the Republican party. The tide had turned, and newspapers in the larger cities were becoming business enterprises, with their politics quite incidental to their prosperity. The old Colonel probably could not sell gold eagles for tin dimes. He had no salesmanship. He had little business sense. He was a stalwart, wool-dyed, black radical Republican who still was fighting the battles of the Civil War, so his circulation shrank. The advertisers, even the Republicans, were leaving him for the *Star*. The mortgage on his paper grew. As he could not pay the interest, his equity wore thin. Santa Fe Railroad interests bought the mortgage and kept the old Colonel in his rather stately editorial room—an exhibition piece without power, though he did not know it; with no authority, though he would not have used it if he had had it; and with only the privilege of seeing his name at the paper's masthead and occasionally contributing an editorial in highly involved sentences, and what to him was the precious boon, a Sunday editorial.

That Sunday editorial was the town joke and the office mystery. Every Saturday morning, promptly at ten o'clock, Colonel Van Horn appeared in the office where I sat writing the editorial for the next day. He generally chatted for a moment with me about some episode of the Civil War, or perhaps of the border war around old Kansas City, then went into his office, pulled down all the blinds, turned out all the lights, made the office as nearly pitch dark as he could, and there, with his eyes closed, he took his pencil and wrote his editorial. He told me, in that self-deprecatory, apologetic voice of old people who know they are eccentric, that his son guided his pencil. He adored his son, who had died in his youth. And the old Colonel some way or other, who wore heavy bifocal glasses to see when he wrote in the brightest light, managed by some automatic writing to get out that Sunday editorial. . . . His son may have been controlling the pencil, but the long and involved sentences were in the Colonel's own. To me and to most of the readers of the *Journal*, the editorials did not make sense. They were mystic and seemed mildly mad. I used to see the copy and always the proof. Sometimes I chopped them into short sentences or did what I could without telling the Colonel to make his stuff "read sense."

But he liked me and we established a kind of camaraderie. He was such a gentle man, so unworldly in his estimates of men and his judgment of events, so kindly and sweet withal, that I could not laugh at him. I could not even smile at him. And as he took me to his heart, as some sort of link perhaps with his dead son, I grew fond of him and have held him always in affectionate remembrance. . . .

He had a way of patting me very gently on the shoulder when I came into the office in the morning, perhaps in lieu of a word of greeting. When I had been in town less than a month, I was taken out of the Centropolis and promoted to the Midland Hotel, a first-class caravansary. He . . . stopped one day at my desk to say that the proper appreciation of food was a part of a gentleman's education. Looking me over, perhaps observing the youthful rotundity of my torsal curves, he added: "You like food, don't you? Well, learn to know about it."

So I did. At the Midland Hotel I took my Master's degree in the gentle art of consuming groceries. . . . My due bill limited me to the table d'hôte meals, but limited is a grotesque word to use. In the eighties and nineties, the table d'hôte menu of a first-class hotel in a town of a hundred thousand or over was a labyrinth of delight. And every dish that I had never heard of, I took. More than that, I asked the head waiter about it. His name was Willie—a large, double-jowled, good-natured colored man, who quickly discovered that I was good for a tip. Because I came in late, he used to stand by my table and talk to me about the food, tell me what it was, how it was prepared, where it came from. He loved to serve me and watch me eat. I think he got a vicarious thrill out of it for I certainly was a sincere and competent eater in those days. On the breakfast menu were baked oysters and broiled oysters with strange sauces. I learned to like them even for breakfast, along with pancakes, fried potatoes, and fruit. At lunch and at dinner I wandered through the bill of fare as a sultan might stroll through his harem. . . .

At the Midland, which was the headquarters of traveling salesmen and visiting capitalists, I also learned about clothes. For I had the quick eye of youth in looking at well-dressed men. I remember that I had three casual ambitions: to own a typewriter, to have a swallow-tailed evening suit, and to own a soft-spring, tufted, leather couch in my office. That was the acme of my physical desires. The week after I came to town I got the typewriter, also on a due bill, paying a dollar a week on a secondhand machine. I ordered a suit of clothes on tick by taking the managing editor to the tailor to vouch for my credit. And when I was fitted for this first tailored suit, the tailor showed me a gorgeous suit of evening clothes which had been left unpaid for by a customer of somewhat my figure—taller, but the coat and vest fitted with a few alterations. So I blazed out in evening clothes before I had any place to wear them. The leather couch remained an iridescent dream for ten long years. But it did not fade.

Thus went my first three months in Kansas City. In addition to writing editorials, I started a column. Every young newspaperman in the last sixty years has wanted to write a column before he could write a three-line item, and my column was probably as bad as any of them. I filled it with Kansas politics, my own verse, literary allusions, and personal gossip. Probably it did not amount to much, but it got my initials and sometimes my name, Will A. White, on the *Journal's* editorial page. . . .

I had little time for reading. Magazines? Probably an armful every month. And newspaper exchanges from all over the country I literally wallowed in, seeing for the first time papers I had read about for years—New York papers, Philadelphia papers, Boston, Atlanta, New Orleans, Los Angeles. I wolfed them down. I would glance casually at the news pages, carefully scan the editorial pages, looking for editorial ideas, glance at their poetry, and take account of the current books in capsule by reading book reviews. I read carefully the New York *Nation*, first because in classrooms at the university I had been taught to consider its style, and secondly because I liked its editorials. It barked so circumspectly at the status quo in this world, with which in a high and mighty way, as a youth of twenty-three, I was not entirely satisfied, even though I was a Republican and proud of it.

I had three roommates that year. I managed to get a room over on McGee Street, north of Twelfth, with two double beds. Frederick Funston had come back from Central America, where Charley Gleed had staked him for a share in a sugar and coffee plantation, and was on the paper as a police reporter. He had part of my bed. Lew Schmucker, of El Dorado, who was my dearest friend after high school days, shared a bed with Fred Vandergrift, a city editor of the *Star*—a man ten years our senior. . . . So I was never lonesome, and in that company of rollicking hellions I was never homesick nor sad. . . . We three roamed the city like sheep-killing dogs after my work was done. I was generally finished by half-past ten, my proofs read and my troubles over. Whereupon I made a bee line for the north-end police station where Funston was on dogwatch. We would sit around there or wander about, seeing the wicked life of what to me was a great city, making friends with the cops and the dopes and the toughs, male and female, who ranged the streets at midnight. Generally at one o'clock Funston called it a day and we two, because street cars ran infrequently and our legs were easier to use than our nickels to get, walked a mile home, indulging in tall talk, sometimes lifting our voices in ribald song. . . .

But I had two tremendous toots, jags, emotional outbursts. The first was when I heard Pat Gilmore's band, the first professional band of any competence that I had ever listened to. He played a concert program in the Warder Grand Theatre. The music overwhelmed me. I had not realized before what man could do with instrumental music, and a sixty-piece band was like something from another world, created by other creatures than the human beings I had known. I reveled in its memory for days. The clarion notes entwined in the harmonics from the various instruments kept calling in my heart—for the first time—tunes that I could not whistle, airs that I could not even hum. After that, while I worked on the *Journal*, I heard good music wherever I could, and Dean, who covered the theatres as well as the concerts, was forever taking me around with him to see good plays and hear good music. . . .

The second emotional rousement I had came when I heard James Whitcomb Riley. He packed the old Warder Grand chuck-full and recited his verse. He was an actor first and a poet incidentally. He had a flexible voice and his whole body—hands, head, arms, and legs—was synchronized in the song that he sang, the rhythm, rhyme, and cadence of his homely verse. It got me. I went raving mad. I kept saying over and over and with variations the whole long way home: "I can do that! I'm going to do that, I tell you! I know I can do that!" So I bent to the oar myself for some time after that night, writing dialect verse with all my might and main. . . . My dialect verse was supposed to reflect the colloquial idiom of mid-western middle-class people, presumably well-to-do and substantial farmers, out of New England by the Ohio Valley. In my rhymes was no touch of the wide sense of rancor in the hearts of those people which was flashing out in the conventions that I attended and manifesting itself in the elections of the day. One would have thought from reading that verse that the Kansas people were all prosperous, contented, emotional, smug, and fundamentally happy.

It was in those days that Walter Armstrong, whom I had known in college as a brother Phi Delt, told me he had a mighty pretty girl who would like to meet me. His suggestion did not interest me greatly, for in college I had noticed that his idea of a mighty pretty girl was a rattlehead. But he was a persistent cuss and one November evening we went over to Kansas City, Kansas, which was then Wyandotte, to see this mighty pretty girl. The girl proposition at that stage in my life was not so important as it had been in Lawrence and El Dorado, but Walter's girl made me bat my eyes. I agreed with him that she was a knockout. For she had brains—something that Walter accounted as of little consequence in young females. My surprise at his girl and my admiration for her made a dent in my self-sufficiency. And, as if to set a dent permanently, she served us cake and maybe coffee. Anyway it was nice food.

Her name was Sallie Lindsay. And as we left the Lindsay portal, I hit Walter a grateful wallop on the chest and made noises of delight. Within a month I went back. She wore, I remember, a red dress. A contemporary magazine story called "Miss Devilette," which we both had read, started us off. She produced a volume of Kipling's poetry which we read together, and then a book of Richard Harding Davis' stories. And then again, food—good food in man-sized lots, on a tray in front of an open grate fire.

Deep in my heart, though I did not know it because I did not want it, something was happening. If there was anything decent in me at that time beneath the vast complacency of the silly senility of my adolescence, Sallie Lindsay hailed it, and it spoke to her as a lovely ship in passing. I did not go back for another month, but I went carrying a book, which was a sign of surrender. I did not know even that. But the picture of "Miss Devilette" by the fire glowed in my heart and kept shining out at odd and most inopportune times, and so late in the winter I went back again, and maybe again. With each visit the dent that she made when Walter took me deepened and strengthened and became a part of my life and destiny.

It was in the late winter, maybe in February or in early March of 1892, that I persuaded Charley Gleed . . . to let me go to Topeka and fill a vacancy as Topeka correspondent of the *Journal*—a job that was quite as dignified as that of editorial writer. For a Topeka correspondent of the leading Republican newspaper organ of the Southwest made me practically an ambassador to the Republicans of Kansas. And I strutted in my job. That winter of '92 Ewing Herbert, Harry Frost, who edited a little society newspaper in Topeka, and Charley Harger of the Abilene *Reflector*, all young fellows in their mid-twenties, and I formed what afterwards became a potent political society, the Kansas Day Club. We issued the first invitations. We guaranteed the hotel for the first fifty guests. Eighty came and paid two dollars for a tenderloin beefsteak, fresh mushrooms, *au gratin* potatoes, ice cream and cake. The speakers at our dinner became the Kansas roster for Congress, for we were the young crowd. We were ostensibly hostile to the old soldiers, who were then at the apex of their political power in Kansas but soon to cross over to the sunset side. But we did not know that. We were just greedy for power—young buffaloes horning the old bulls out of the old herd.

It was a presidential year. Cleveland and Harrison were facing each other, each running for a second term. The Populists were sweeping over the Missouri Valley and through the South. There was talk of Populist fusion with the Democrats in Kansas. As in every fusion, respectable minorities of both parties were fighting it; but, on the other hand, those in both parties who wanted the flesh-pots[2] favored fusion. It was the business of a Republican ambassador to Topeka to stop the fusion so that the Republicans might defeat the divided forces. That was part of my job. For that I colored the news but did not realize that I was doing so. . . . For no one had taught me the modern ethics of sophisticated journalism.

I had to attend political conventions of the Populists, of the Republicans, of the Democrats in every one of the seven congressional districts. I had to attend state conventions. I knew what was going on in all three party councils, and of course sat in the councils of the conspirators in each of the minority parties who were opposing fusion. The Republicans naturally took me in as the *Journal's* vicegerent. So that year I left the blue lodge of county politics and learned to put on the work from the grand lodge of state politics, with a touch now and then of national affairs. I was going to school, taking a course in practical politics as it was played in the last quarter of the nineteenth century in the United States. I saw the game as one who watches the cards from back of the player. And, curiously enough, I did not know the stakes on the table. . . .

When I took the Topeka job my mother moved up from El Dorado and we established a home there. . . . I was virtually a traveling man that summer. Often I would be absent from home from Monday until Saturday night, attending district conventions of the Populists, Democrats, or the Republicans in various parts of Kansas. The automobile had not come to shorten distances. So to get from one convention seat to another I might have to travel a hundred miles east and west to reach a town fifty miles away. I rode on passes, of course. Sometimes I had Pullman passes, as befitted an ambassador from the Kansas City *Journal* to the Kansas Republicans. . . . I was seeing Kansas as I never had seen it before, from one end to the other, up and down and crisscross, on slow trains and fast, in miserable little hotels, or sometimes as the guest of "the best people" in the community. I did not see it again in such a way for many years. I found out from trial and error what in Kansas politics was regarded honest and what dishonest. The code was something like this:

In politics a man may take money if he earns it.

[2]In the Old Testament, "fleshpots" frequently referred to luxurious satisfactions, usually connected with spiritual corruption.

He is dishonest if he takes money from both sides or if, taking money from one side, he deserts for any cause to the other.

A man must be as good as his word and go down with his fellows, take a licking with his gang, and wait.

If, in a convention, a leader makes a slate and his favorite candidate wins, he must help to victory the other minor candidates who agreed to support his losing candidates.

If a man really has principles, he must not take money even to do what he was going to do anyway.

If a man takes money, he must keep his mouth shut. Otherwise, the pay-master will have to buy others whom he could easily fool.

A scoundrel is a man who swindles his friends. It is, however, permissible to cheat your enemies.

It was in the spring or early summer of 1892 that I formed my admiration for Cy Leland, a local factional boss, and established a friendship that lasted for twenty years until his death. In the Republican state convention he was supporting for governor a candidate named E. N. Morrill, a congressman. The game to nominate a governor was to tie up enough votes in a combination by getting the delegates, friends of candidates for minor state offices—secretary of state, treasurer, attorney general, and auditor—pledged to a slate in which all would combine to make a majority and nominate a state ticket. Leland formed his slate. He apparently had a majority, but some of the slate's candidates for state offices could not hold their supporters, for Morrill lost the nomination. The other crowd had its slate, but as soon as their man Smith was nominated for governor, its leaders disappeared from the convention hall. They had too many promises out which they could not keep.

I watched Leland in his defeat. All the afternoon he moved about the convention, guarding the Morrill slate. He nominated the entire state ticket below governor without a miss. He even stayed to nominate state superintendent of schools, generally a consolation prize that the convention often was left to choose without let or hindrance. I was reporting the convention, making a running story as the events unfolded. When the last nomination was made and Leland's candidate for state superintendent was nominated, not even one-fourth—perhaps not one-fifth—of the delegates were there. But Leland was there. The other reporters were gone. I was there. After the convention ad-journed, he stopped for a moment or two to console or comfort a few of his more intimate defeated followers. He saw me sitting alone at the reporter's desk when he turned to leave the hall. It was absolutely empty. The janitor was lock-ing the doors. Leland and I walked out together. And so down the primrose path of politics we strolled to the end. I gave my heart to a man who would stay in the game, protect his ante, and play his cards even after he had lost his major stake. I was a Leland man after that.

Cy Leland was a little, gray-brown, hickory nut of a man, five feet six, with graying hair, ruddy brown skin, and brown chin whiskers and moustache neatly trimmed, always meticulously dressed, always stingy of language, monosyllabic, who never loafed, rarely laughed except with his eyes, walked straight along some invisible crack, loved the mystery with which he surrounded his movements, was given to Indian feints, sorties, and ambushes, liked to fool his enemies almost as much as he loved to best them, and had an elephant's memory, of which more later.

In those days I met and formed a casual acquaintance that became a lifetime attachment—my first literary man—Hamlin Garland. I had read his *Main Travelled Roads* and other slight books describing the farm people. I had accepted his political heresies, his sympathies with the farmers' wrongs, yet I accepted these heresies in a rather highty-tighty mood. But when I talked to Garland for two hours on a train, as we were going to a Populist meeting some place in Kansas where he spoke, his passion for his cause disturbed me. It did not quite upset me. But it was strange, I thought, that a man with such competent literary powers should be so deeply touched with the political insanity of the hour. Also in that year I met and talked to Ignatius Donnelly, a Populist from Minnesota, a scholarly man who had written a most elaborate thesis to prove that Bacon was the author of Shakespeare's plays. . . . And when he, with burning eloquence, defended the Populist cause, again I was bothered that one I had come to respect should have such a soft place in his brain.

Of course I made friends with the Populist leaders in Kansas. I was a friendly dog by training and by breeding. Jerry Simpson, a self-educated man ten years or so my senior, I came to respect deeply. He was smart. He had read more widely than I, and often quoted Carlyle in our conversations, and the poets and essayists of the seventeenth century. His talk, as we rode together on trains, or sat in hotel lobbies, or loafed in hotel bedrooms, was full of Dickensian allusions, and he persuaded me to try Thackeray whom I had rejected until then. Jerry Simpson was not a sockless clown. He accepted the portrait which the Republicans made of him as an ignorant fool because it helped him to talk to the crowds that gathered to hear him. . . . When he went to Congress, his natural capacity for debate and his wide reading gained for him the friendship of the most sophisticated and erudite man in Congress at that time—Speaker Tom Reed. Years later, because the young man Jerry Simpson regarded me kindly and accepted me as a sort of Nicodemus,[3] the rich young man who turned away

---

[3]Nicodemus was a powerful Jew who came to learn from Jesus, but only under cover of night. After Jesus' crucifixion, however, Nicodemus helped to bury him (John 3:1–14 and Matthew 27:57–60).

sadly, Tom Reed was ready to talk with me at odd times and take me into the sanctuary of an old man's admiration for an acolyte. Jerry Simpson was that much of a person. He was intelligent enough to know that the more his silk-stocking opponents portrayed him as "Sockless Jerry," the quicker the discontented and the underprivileged citizens of Kansas would give him their vote. . . .

Another, perhaps the only other, really strong and conspicuous figure in the Populist movement was "Mary Ellen" Lease. Her real name was Mary Elizabeth Lease but the nickname "Mary Ellen" stuck. She was the complete antithesis of Jerry Simpson, a woman with a voice. I have never heard a lovelier voice than Mrs. Lease's. It was a golden voice—a deep, rich contralto, a singing voice that had hypnotic qualities. She put into her oratory something which the printed copies of her speech did not reveal. They were dull enough often, but she could recite the multiplication table and set a crowd hooting or hurrahing at her will. . . .

She was not so quick and intelligent as Jerry Simpson. She knew much less than he about the fundamental causes of the uprising, but she knew it was an uprising and she rode the waves. After the tide washed out, she left Kansas and made an honest and honorable living in New York and died a respected citizen. But she flashed across Kansas in that day of turmoil, a harridan in the eyes of her enemies, a goddess to her friends. Looking back across a generation, I think she was a little of both.

The other Populist leaders were mostly incompetents of one sort or another, sometimes moral misfits but more often just plain ne'er-do-wells, with here and there a visionary staring at his utopia, wandering in a dream with the marching hordes of the discontented, the disinherited, the poor. And we, the Republicans, knowing they were poor and maybe consciously realizing that they had a grievance, hid behind the words of Jesus, "The poor ye have always with you!"[4] and so went on with our business of guiding the Republic in the profitable ways of a ruling plutocracy.

It was late in that spring of 1892 that I began to be more than vaguely conscious that Sallie Lindsay was something more than an awfully nice girl. Our letters had become more than fortnightly, and probably in her circle over in Kansas City, Kansas, I was known as Sallie Lindsay's new beau. Wishing to show off, I invited her and a group of her girlfriends for lunch at the Midland one day. Before the luncheon I consulted Willie, the headwaiter, told him that I could not afford to go more than seventy-five cents a head for those girls; and we picked out what we thought was an elegant luncheon—elegant in its simplicity. It was built around chicken gelatin, and Willie without extra charge got me a private dining room on the mezzanine floor. He dropped in himself to take the

---

[4]"For the poor always ye have with you; but me ye have not always" (John 12:8).

order when the girls came in. I can still remember the show-off flourish with which I looked down the card most casually and repeated the menu that Willie and I had so carefully decided upon. Willie, for the tip which he knew was coming, put on a few frills and trimmings. It was really something in the way of a luncheon. When Sallie told me the next time we met that I had knocked the girls cold and stiff, I had to confess the truth that Willie had coached me. I am good as a show-off up to a point, after which I always have to laugh.

It was not long after that that Sallie and I had our first and really only tragic experience. We were scheduled by letter to meet at the gathering of the Western Artists and Authors at the Midland at Kansas City, late in the spring. The Western Artists and Authors Society was just what its name would indicate—a lot of us who were trying to be artists and authors, maybe a hundred from Kansas, Missouri, and possibly Iowa and Nebraska—newspaper poets, newspaper artists, painters of china dishes, writers of unplayed plays, but nonetheless striving nobly and hoping wistfully to rise. . . .

As I swung into the Midland Hotel that morning of the meeting, I ran into Albert Bigelow Paine . . . and Eugene Ware. . . . Passing the door of the bar, [Ware] suggested a drink and I, to show my sophistication, took a sloe gin rickey. The other two took highballs. Then after ten minutes or so, as we stood at a table near the bar, Paine ordered a round and, again to show my worldly wisdom, I ordered what I called a "calico drink". . . . Then as the talk was good for that first half hour, I bought a round of drinks and counted the cost like a Scotchman. I remember, to save myself, I took beer. And we lingered over that round, tearing the world apart and regluing it to suit ourselves. I had no sense of having too much under my belt. I felt good as I always did. I was going to see Sallie Lindsay, and that made me feel a lot better. . . .

Anyway, through the lobby we went, arm in arm, Paine and Ware on either side of me. We stepped gaily into the elevator and came out in the mezzanine parlor of the Midland, where the Western Artists and Authors had assembled in chairs well down the spacious rooms. I remember that I had about twenty feet of clear space to go and, feeling good, I did an old trick that I had learned from a circus clown sometime in my boyhood. I twirled my hat . . . high in the air and poked my head into it as it came down. This I did twice, and the Western Artists and Authors applauded. It was a neat stunt, and I was proud of myself. I sought out Sallie with my eyes and rushed over to see her. She was cool. When I sat down, she moved. I was amazed and bewildered. I could not imagine what had happened. After the session I tried to take her to the dinner, called a banquet, which was part of the Western Artists and Authors program. She eluded me. I pressed. She refused me. I was paralyzed. At the end of the dinner I followed her and asked if I might take her home. She probably maneuvered so that we were out of earshot of the others and said: "Now listen, Mr. Will White! I am not going home with a man in your condition!"

The liquor, whatever it did to me, had had two or three hours and a big dinner to tromp it down. I was cold sober and I gasped at the words "in your condition," realizing quickly that the exuberance of my entrance and maybe idiocy of my stunt might have deceived her. Also I realized that maybe I was just a bit high. She saw my questioning astonishment and went on: "If you are ever going to see me again, we must understand each other." There was no love light in her eyes, but cold, implacable reason, as she went on: "Unless you are willing to quit, absolutely stop, drinking, let's understand it now and quit."

Whereupon she turned quickly and went down the stairs with the elderly woman who was taking her home, leaving me with the whole universe sinking below the pit of my stomach. I stood there an instant; watched her at the turn of the stairs. She did not look back. I followed her quickly from the mezzanine floor to the lobby, followed her to the carriage, and, as she got in, I said: "All right, all right!" She smiled and the world went on rolling again.

That must have been in late May, for I took a night train from Kansas City to a convention and did not get back to Topeka for three or four days. Somewhere I must have written her a letter trying to square myself and somewhere I must have had an answer, and it was good. But after all, no words of pledged affection had passed between us. We were just "going together," rather more than casually but not quite anything else.

In early June, out in western Kansas, three conventions came. I left home Saturday night with my mail unread. . . . There was a two weeks' pile when I came home and on Sunday sat down and began to go through the letters and papers. There I found two unanswered letters from Sallie Lindsay, one telling me that she might have to go to the hospital for a major operation, the other written in the hospital a few hours before her operation. It was a sweet, gentle goodbye and the thing grabbed my heart. It was five days old. Without waiting for the meal that was on the table, I hurried to the railroad station, went to Kansas City, and thence to the hospital, where I was allowed to stand for a moment and smile, at the door of her room. And she smiled back.

God was in His Heaven, all was right with the world.[5] I hurried back to Topeka and returned at a date when the nurse said I might see her. . . . It was a week before they would let me call and during that week the seed of a great passion that was in my heart grew and blossomed, rooted and consumed my life, and made it part of something fine, something different, something I think divine.

I mooned around the bookstores of Topeka, trying to find a book to take to

[5]From *Pippa Passes* by English poet Robert Browning (1812–1889).

her. I finally bought four books with blue bindings and silver lettering, French short stories. . . . So, when the day came and I could visit her, armed with those four books, I hurried to Kansas City, went straight to the hospital, found her waiting for me with my telegram on her bed, and she smiled as I went in and I kneeled and kissed her and it was all over. I read the stories to her for a little while and the nurse, when I came again, said she kept them under her pillow. And so, August 13, 1892, we began our long life's happy journey.

I do not know how it happened. Perhaps she was telling the very truth when she said: "You were ripe for some girl. I only had to spread out my apron and shake the tree and you fell in it."

8

I Cross
the Rubicon

In 1892 the Kansas Populists for some reason de-
layed their state convention to nominate state officers until August and held it
at Wichita. The date, nearly three months after the Republicans had put out
their state ticket, made the Populist convention big news for the Kansas City
Journal, and indeed all of the Kansas papers. The question of fusion with the
Democrats was to be settled. The convention was to nominate or refuse to nominate, as it chose, the Democratic presidential electors who were to vote for
Grover Cleveland.

But Cleveland was not Populist. He loathed and publicly spat upon the whole
fiat money and reform programs of the Populists. The Democrats and the Populists had nothing in common except the desire to beat the Republicans. But the
fusion was not a fact accomplished when the convention met and much significance was attached to the Populists' nominee for governor. The Democrats had
not put out a state ticket. The left-wing Populists had a candidate whose name
would be an offense to the Democrats, a rabid advocate of fiat money and social
reform. The right-wing candidate would not hold even the Populist vote,
though he might get the Democrats'.

It was a dramatic convention. All day they balloted on governor and adjourned
until night. Of course, reporters were there from all the region, from as far east as Chicago and St. Louis. The other Kansas City and Topeka papers were represented by
men with whom I had been working for three or four months. The *Journal* had sent
as my associate one of Mr. Gleed's friends, Tom Norton, who was studying law in
Gleed's office after having edited the Newton *Republican* as I had edited the El Dorado *Republican* for the owners. Apparently Mr. Gleed regarded the convention as
most important for he asked Tom and me to do a good job and not to spare the wire if
we needed it. The night session was our big second act. It was in the Toler Opera
House, a big barn of a place that was crowded from pit to dome when the chairman's
gavel clicked. I went back of the stage just before the convention opened and there I

ran into Jerry Simpson, leaning against the wall and whittling. He looked up from his whittling, caught my eye with his shrewd Yankee quizzical glance, and said: "Well, mister, she's settled."

Like a trout, I leaped at the bait. To my question he replied: "It will happen after the third ballot tonight. We are going to give the old rabble-rouser his chance"—meaning the militant, anti-fusion Populist—"and then we are going to nominate Lewelling."

Lewelling was in the balloting, but far down the list. He was a Populist state senator from Wichita. Simpson's news floored me for a minute. I knew that he was a man of few words. I knew that he was honest. I knew that he was my friend and would not deceive me. Moreover, I knew that he was one of less than half a dozen leaders who would have decided upon the way to break the deadlock. So I asked: "Am I safe to use it? I mean, to begin filing now Lewelling's biography and an interview with you, telling how and why it happened? I can wire in the lead the moment the nomination is made, and have the story out for the first edition." Jerry whittled for a minute a long, curving sliver, and said: "All right!"

Then he told me the story of the combination that released the deadlock. I hurried to Tom, told him my news, then rushed to the telegraph office while Tom stayed in the convention and filed, first, the story of the combination; second, the biography of Lewelling, who was an utterly unknown man; and finally some comment on the significance of the combination and the nomination of Lewelling. It was then nearly nine o'clock. Two ballots had been taken, but I had filed enough to hold the wire, the only Western Union night wire into Kansas City, while the ballot slowly ground along. Then I went back to the hall.

Tom Norton had his running account of the ballot ready and he left the reporters' desk and went to the Western Union office to file it ahead of my background story. I continued the story of the ballot where Tom left off, and when finally, just before ten o'clock, Lewelling was nominated, I had the story of the ballot finished and a short, possibly fifty-word, lead concerning the result of the final ballot. I filed that while the man at the wire was still on our stuff. Tom and I were happy, for we had caught the first edition of the morning *Journal*. And by the time our story, a matter of fifteen hundred words, was cleared from the wire, it was too late for our rivals. They knew we had beat them. We were smug and wrapped the mantle of our couch about us and lay down to pleasant dreams.[1]

The next morning Tom and I and the other newspaper correspondents took the morning train at Wichita, eager to get to the main line at Newton and see our story. No newspaperman is so case hardened that he does not like to read his own stories in print. At Newton we bought the copies of the *Journal*. So did

---

[1]From William Cullen Bryant's poem "Thanatopsis" (1817): "By an unfaltering trust, approach thy grave, / Like one that wraps the drapery of his couch / About him, and lies down to pleasant dreams."

our rivals. Quickly we glanced at the first page. The story was not there. Up and down the passenger coach, half a dozen other reporters were opening to the second page, glancing quickly on the third, the fourth, and the fifth for editorial and departmental pages. We all turned to the seventh and eighth—no story. Finally, on the tenth or twelfth page, tucked in with the markets, we found our story mauled down to six or seven hundred words, hidden and, we felt, deliberately played down. Whereupon our rivals and contemporary reporters hooted, jeered, mocked, and Tom and I set our jaws.

We rode eastward from Newton to Emporia, through Topeka on to Kansas City—he and I getting madder and madder, nursing our wrongs. At Lawrence we bought the *Evening Star*, with a long story on Lewelling's victory and how it came about—the story that we had written nearly twenty-four hours earlier. We went from the train right to the *Journal* office. It was then around seven o'clock. We knew the telegraph editor would be on his job. We walked into his office, turned the latch on his door, and began on him. Each of us had a fairly good livery stable vocabulary. We poured it on him; dared him to fight; promised that he could have either one of us, and that the other would get out of the room. We bent over his desk jawing him, roughing his hair, slapping his jaws, but there was no fight in him. We left the room, hurried down to the business office, and then and there I quit my job, drew my pay, and hurried to Sallie Lindsay to tell her what I had done. . . .

She had just learned that Roswell Field, brother of Eugene Field, an editorial writer on the *Star*, was going to New York to work for the New York *World*. And the next morning I showed up in the *Star* office, found the man who had offered me a job a year before, told him my story and particularized about our defiance of the telegraph editor, who was unpopular in newspaper circles in town. By ten o'clock I had a job at twenty-five dollars a week, all that I was getting on the *Journal* and a good salary for 1892.

I was to write what was known as minion editorials. That phrase meant gay editorials—stuff about literature, the stage, frivolous comment on unimportant events of froth and foam on the daily newspaper's editorial tide. In addition, I was supposed to turn in a serious editorial every day or two, write the Kansas notes, and also to mark over from the daily paper the material that went into the *Weekly Star*. It never occurred to me that it was a heavy assignment, and I was so happy to have a job and at the same time to have my full free say to that telegraph editor that I went back to Sallie Lindsay, rejoicing as a strong man to run a race.[2] Also I wanted her to be proud of me, and I believed she was.

My mother moved down to Kansas City, and my real life began as a working newspaperman on a first-class paper. The Kansas City *Star*, twelve years old in

---

[2]In King David's Psalm 19, the sun is compared to "a bridegroom coming out of his chamber" who "rejoiceth as a strong man to run a race" (Psalm 19:5).

1892, even then was rated one of a dozen best and most influential newspapers in the country. . . . It was the daily expression of William R. Nelson, to the office sometimes "the Colonel"—because he looked coloneliferous, without any reference to a war record—but generally "the Old Man," though he was barely in his fifties. He was a great hulking two-hundred-sixty pounder, six feet tall, smooth-shaven, with a hard, dominating mouth and a mean jaw, high brown, and wonderful eyes, jade in color, which opened with wide frank cordiality or squinted like the lightning of Job. He became my idol. . . . After I had been in the office five or six months, I came in almost daily contact with Colonel Nelson, who was the directing force of the paper. I never saw his handwriting more than two or three times, and then only a dozen words. He wrote nothing for the paper. We men around the office understood he could not write, could not put ten words together on paper. Yet he bought writing talent and directed it.

In the *Star* office, for the first time in my life, I was learning practical ethics. For the *Star* was an honest newspaper. Politically, it was independent. Every man on the paper, from top to bottom—in the advertising department, the circulation department, the news department, the editorial room—was convinced of his own absolute freedom, his right to express himself unhampered save by the truth as he saw it. Which did not mean that any nonsense I wrote went through unscathed. But it did mean that when it was nonsense, the managing editor, Tommy Johnson, to whom I submitted my copy, or the editor-in-chief under Nelson, Mr. Runyon, carefully explained why it was nonsense, and I had a right to talk back and defend myself. In a newspaper that is heaven.

I wrote my head off and from the men who chopped my copy—competent, free, honest editors—I learned every day much that helped me. I was seriously writing. I turned in verses once or twice a week. I was growing away from dialect rhymes. Sallie and I were reading the New England poets—Whittier, Aldrich, Lowell—and of course the verse I wrote was colored by their minds and manners. Poor stuff it was, but I was proud of it and in a year became a sort of office laureate, was called upon even by the Old Man to celebrate this or that gay and festal occasion or funny local episode. I remember that on the birth of Kipling's first baby I wrote a rhyme that went the rounds of the United States, with a refrain: "They are walking baby Kipling in the morning."[3] Rudyard himself, through a mutual friend, sent back some word of approval.

After I had been there six months or so, [Nelson] called me into his office one day and asked: "Billie, what do you know about gas?"

I told him gaily that I knew absolutely nothing.

---

[3]The line is a parody of the refrain of Kipling's poem "Danny Deever": "An' they're hangin' Danny Deever in the mornin'."

"Well, by God, you are the man I am looking for. You have a virgin mind. I have an idea—maybe I am wrong—that this town is entitled to dollar gas." The price then was much higher. "I'll tell you what I wish you would do: read up on gas. Here's a lot of stuff."

He handed me some publications of various associations and researchers, mostly loaded heavily in favor of the gas companies.

"Read this, and then go down and look over the gas plant and see how they make it and where the stuff comes from, and see if you can get some kind of a squint at the cost of the stuff in the storage tanks and delivered at the outlets. Don't write anything about it for three or four weeks and then come back and talk to me."

When I had learned all I could of gas, I went in and talked to him. He said: "All right! Now write a local story, write a series of articles about gas in Kansas City, and we will see where we get. Don't editorialize about it. You don't know enough yet. I don't either."

So we studied gas again. And I wrote my stories. They did not amount to much, but they did set folks talking, and from then on for five years, the *Star* kept hammering away for dollar gas. It made no difference that Colonel Nelson's friends owned the gas stock. It made no difference that the bankers who were financing the gas company were his dear friends. He was absolutely incorruptible on his social side and one of the few publishers I have ever known who did not yield to the lure of the country club. He was making money in real estate as well as with the *Star*. He bought tracts of farm land, laid them out in subdivisions, walled off in stone from rock picked up on the premises, large plats, acre plats, planted the stone walls to honeysuckles, constructed six- or seven-room houses beautifully designed, built by the day and not by the contract, with no skimping and jerry-carpentering, and sold them at a decent profit. He started a love of beauty in Kansas City suburbs.

On another occasion he called me into his office and assigned me to write an article about a series of slums, called the McClure flats, terrible places. I made a horror story which pleased the Colonel, though his friends—the owners of the slum property—were boiling hot. But the hotter they got, the more he pounded on his desk and Goddamned them around and made them ashamed of themselves. The tenements were either improved or torn down to be replaced by better buildings. He tackled the corrupt elections that were conducted by the local Democratic city machine and gave me the job of bedeviling a poor election crook, named Pinky Blitz, whom we sent to the penitentiary later, and we pounded a county officer named Owsley rather mercilessly for what we felt was his responsibility in the election corruption. . . .

One spring we conducted a mayoralty campaign, and not long afterwards the victorious opposition candidate, Joseph J. Davenport, whom we had treated rather roughly, came stomping into the office. The Colonel's room and the rooms occupied by the editorial writers were on the second floor. My room was directly opposite the Colonel's. The second floor was reached by a grand stairway sweeping upward out of the lobby on the first floor and branching north and south, left and right, into the telegraph room and the editorial offices. I saw the double-breasted, Prince Albert coat of the aggrieved statesman sweeping past my door and saw Tommy Johnson, the managing editor, and Ralph Stout, the city editor, follow the raging people's tribune into the Colonel's office. I was writing with my face to the door. I heard the loud voices and in a minute, maybe two, I heard that unmistakable thud of fist on flesh and looked up to see the Colonel lying on his back and the mayor bending over him. Phillips, the telegraph editor, who chewed gum in his front teeth and wore a dark green celluloid shade over his eyes, came mousing out of the telegraph room as I looked up. He too had heard the voices and identified the swat. In an instant Stout and Johnson, both good-sized six footers, had hold of the assailant. While the Old Man was getting up, they rushed the mayor out of the room and into the hallway, where they kicked his feet out from under him. Phillips grabbed a leg. I grabbed a leg. Johnson and Stout took an arm each, and we literally threw the mayor down the first flight of that grand staircase to the landing. I was located so that I was the first man to reach him after he fell. As he got up, I started to rush him. He pulled a revolver from under his Prince Albert coat and stuck it in my face. It was the largest, most terrible-looking circular aperture I ever beheld. His eyes were glaring. I put my hand over the banister, and God knows why I said it, but I cried, half in hysteria and half because it was funny: "Excuse me!"

And I vaulted over the stairs and landed on a circular desk below where a white-haired Danish boy named Siested, brother of the business manager, was working on a row of circulation figures. He did not know of the row above and as I landed on his papers he nearly passed out from fright. This also was a funny thing: As I went over the banister I saw down in the newsroom a thing that greatly heartened me. Old Campbell, the stockyards reporter, with one arm resting on the top of a tall desk, had a dead bead on Davenport and a mean glint in his hard old eye. I do not know whether Davenport saw that bead or not, but as I landed I saw Davenport begin to walk slowly down the grand staircase to the first floor with his pistol drawn and cocked, bellowing something. But he made his exit and all hands began telling the story of the assault. It was in time for the first edition and we had it on the streets in no time. The Colonel was proud to omit no detail.

Now don't get an idea that the Old Man . . . was an angel. His clay foot was Grover Cleveland, who could do no wrong. We who wrote the editorials—Alex Butts, who had owned the Emporia *News* just before I came to Emporia as a student, and Noble Prentis, a Civil War veteran who wrote like an angel and seemed to have reincarnated Oliver Goldsmith, and I—all hated Grover Cleveland. And when Cleveland did something that required incense, we took our turns at swinging the incense pot and gagged behind the Old Man's back. Once when I had been there over a year, Grover Cleveland did something, Heaven knows what, that required heavy buttering and, in our disgust, we three decided to go the distance on the Old Man. Alex Butts . . . wrote an encomium of Cleveland, comparing him to Washington. The next time we had to write on bended knee about Cleveland, Noble Prentis compared him to Lincoln. And I in turn wrote a veiled editorial indicating that Cleveland had many Christlike qualities. When even that got by, we felt better. By *reductio ad absurdum*[4] we purged our hearts of sin. The Old Man was mad and let it go at that. But, otherwise, we were happy.

I mingled with the reporters in the downstairs because they were my age, but I was deeply fond of the older men I worked with. They read my copy and cut it wisely. They taught me much about editorializing. They were men of books, all self-educated—Mr. Runyon, the editor-in-chief, was the only college man in the lot. But I never mingled with a more cultivated group of gentlemen. . . .

Prentis loved James G. Blaine as all Union veterans of the Civil War loved him, though Blaine had never been a soldier. Prentis followed him with an abject devotion. When Blaine died, I remember Tommy Johnson came in gently and said: "Mr. Prentis, will you give me something for the telegraph page about Blaine, and then maybe an editorial?"

That was in the afternoon. For three hours Noble sat writing that biography of Blaine. Then he straightened up with a sigh and wrote the editorial obituary, a beautiful tribute. When he had finished, he straightened up again, and I remember seeing his face begin to twitch. He buried his face in his arms on his desk and began to sob and sob, shaking his pudgy little body with his racking grief and coming up in two or three or four minutes swearing like a pirate at his weakness. He did not speak to me, but toddled over, took his hat and coat from the hook behind the door, and shuffled down the hall, down the stairs into the street, and I saw him trudging homeward—plodding under the burden of his grief.

The *Star*, printed in Missouri but really for Kansas circulation in those days, was top-heavy with Kansas affairs. It was a Kansas daily newspaper, the leading Kansas daily. And living in Kansas City, somewhat aloof from the contemporary battle, I had better standing in Kansas on the editorial page of the *Star* than I had when I lived in Topeka. . . . When I visited Topeka, or any considerable

---

[4]As commonly used (although not the proper meaning of the term), an extreme argument that brings out the absurdity of a belief.

Kansas town, as an editorial writer on the *Star* and the author of its Kansas notes, I was treated with something of the royal acclaim of a visiting statesman. But my vanity was cloying fast. I had pretty nearly enough of it, the sense of political distinction.

I went to Kansas fairly often, but I did not sense the change that was coming into Kansas politics. George R. Peck . . . was moving his office to the Santa Fe general offices in Chicago, where he would take charge of the region along the Santa Fe Railroad from Illinois through Missouri, Kansas, Colorado, and New Mexico to Albuquerque. From that point the general counsel of the Santa Fe at Los Angeles controlled politics for the Santa Fe in California and Arizona. But in Kansas the other railroads, with Peck gone, were setting up rival satraps. M. A. Low, of the Rock Island, represented Rock Island territory. Major Richards of Fort Scott and Balie Waggener of Atchison controlled politics along the Missouri Pacific lines. Loomis, the attorney for the Union Pacific, directed Union Pacific political activities in Kansas. These rival railroad attorneys clashed. They sometimes battled in a convention to control the nomination of a governor, or fought with one another for the right to name a United States Senator. Of course, it made scandal. In the *Star* we knew what was going on at Topeka. The same thing was going on at Jefferson City, the capital of Missouri. . . .

It was the twilight of the gods for the railroads. Competition and skulduggery in rate-making were reflected in corruption and shenanigans in state politics, all directed from railroad offices—sometimes in St. Louis, sometimes in Omaha or Chicago, often in Wall Street. The day of competition in American industry was doomed to close because it was clumsy, scandalous, and indecent. Yet when I went to Topeka, as I often did, to cast an appraising eye for the *Star* over the political landscape, I did not realize what was happening at the heart of things political and economic. . . . Wealth in those days of the early nineties, when the Populists were clamoring across the land, was learning that the fear of the Lord was the beginning of wisdom. So the forces of economic privilege were amalgamating the great banking houses, were consolidating ownership of the bickering railroads in a pool of railroad capital. In other industries, the steel trust was being welded under Carnegie, oil was flowing into one vast tank under Rockefeller, the copper interests were forming interrelated corporations. The day of the trusts was dawning.

Kansas politics was reflecting the iridescent colors of the dawn. I saw the gorgeous picture. I wrote about it. But I had no idea of its meaning, of its real significance, and for those who were aware of some vague shadow of the truth—men like Jerry Simpson, Ignatius Donnelly, Thorstein Veblen, and Edward W. Bemis, a Chicago economist who was to come to Kansas State Agricultural College—for all those astrologists and seers who were trying to give some account of the forces that were moving the world, I had the deepest scorn.

It seemed to me then that honesty and good government—that is to say, tax saving, the purification of politics and personal integrity—were enough to save the world. I fancy Colonel Nelson had somewhat the same idea, except that the Colonel held in profane contempt those men around him and near him who were assembling fortunes by what he regarded as shady methods. . . . But neither he nor any of us around the paper in those days had any idea of the deeper currents of life that were shaping events and directing the destiny of our country. It was enough for the Old Man on the *Star* to Goddamn the protective tariff, suspect the gas company, look at the street railway company and the light company with a baleful eye, trust in God and Grover Cleveland. The rest of us around the office . . . were willing to draw our salaries, hate old Cleveland, regret the frigid ineptitude of Benjamin Harrison, hoot at the Populists, and sputter for the relief of our frustrated spirits.

A perfect example of our attitude in those days was revealed by Fred Vandergrift, then city editor, my roommate the year before. One afternoon when the national ball games were closing in climax and an important local story was gathering on the horizon, the telephones from all over town began piling up on his desk. We had no central telephone system in our office then. Fred was trying to edit the big local story. The telephone bells jangled and jangled. Finally he got up, red-faced in wrath, went to the basement, came back with a hatchet and chopped off all the telephone wires that connected with the office, and went on calmly with his work. All of us on the *Star* were using that hatchet more or less to shut out the warning voices that were clamoring to know the truth or to tell it to us. Old Van at the city desk might well have been the god of our machine.

But my chief source of education and delight was Sallie Lindsay. Together we saw the pageant of the theatre. Every Saturday afternoon we went to a matinee. I managed either to wangle complimentary tickets or to raise the necessary cash. And we saw the best of the contemporary American theatre there in Kansas City in those years of the early nineties. . . . Together we heard our first symphony orchestra, conducted by Walter Damrosch. It was to both of us a momentous experience. It was as far above Pat Gilmore's band, which had set my spirit aquiver, as Pat Gilmore's band was above the El Dorado silver cornet band. That night with Damrosch, I heard for the first time Wagner with a full-throated orchestra. And Sallie and I nearly squeezed our hands off with delight as we listened. We read books together, the novels of the day, and browsed in bookstores at odd times before and after Saturday matinees. . . .

Vernon Kellogg came down to stay with me the night before the wedding, which was April 27, 1893, and he went over to the Lindsays with my mother and me. He was shocked to know that I had not bought roses for the bride, and so we stopped in at the florist's and bought a dozen white rosebuds. He was my only guest. . . .

Ours was not a formal wedding. Kellogg was not my best man. Sallie's friends, perhaps a dozen or fifteen, gathered in the little parlor of an eight-room frame house at 330 Waverly in Kansas City, Kansas. Kellogg's step-uncle, the Reverend Charles B. Mitchell, a fashionable Methodist preacher over in Kansas City, whom Kellogg had persuaded to come and take the five dollars that I could afford to pay the preacher, performed the ceremony. Sallie, the eldest of ten children, had risen at dawn, scrubbed and bathed the three little ones, helped her mother with the breakfast dishes, seen that her four brothers were dressed in their Sunday best, helped her father with his necktie, and made herself useful that morning before her girlfriends of the neighborhood came to dress her in a simple gown. Then we all sat to a lap breakfast, and we two—in a blaze of splendor—went away to the station in a hack which cost a dollar and a half, quite a hole in our gross savings. . . .

It was nearly noon when Sally Lindsay and I stood on the wooden station platform of the old Kansas City Union Depot waiting to take Train Number One to Santa Fe. After a bright sunrise, it had clouded up in the mid-morning. We were quite alone—we had forbidden our families to come to the station—she in a modest tailored outfit and I in my best Sunday suit, when three old bachelors from the *Star* office appeared: Alex Butts, . . . Tommy Johnson, . . . and Ralph Stout. . . . They brought with them as a wedding gift a brown alligator traveling bag, quite scrumptious. And as they came toward us under the train-shed, the sun suddenly burst out of the clouds, and they formed a little ring around us and sang, "Happy Is the Bride That the Sun Shines on," in high glee. And so we went away, waving to our friends in the trainshed, on a journey whereon we have truly lived happily ever after.

The train . . . rolled out of Kansas City at midday of April 27 with the buds a little more than green-brown on the elm trees, with the bluestem staining the hills and pastures of eastern Kansas, with the wheat finger-high and the alfalfa a deep, lovely green, the meadow larks all singing on the barbed-wire fences, and the first Johnny-jump-ups showing on the south banks of the railroad cuts. . . . At Florence we stopped at the Harvey House for dinner at twilight. The Harvey Houses in that day, and for thirty years after, were famous for their food. They were Santa Fe Railroad eating places of great distinction. That evening they passed great platters of meat, beef, spring lamb,[5] and roast pork. I took the lamb, being rather sophisticated with my Midland Hotel palate, and Sallie reached for beef, a conventional pink sliced roast. I cried: "No, try this lamb, you'll find it gorgeous with the mint sauce," as it was.

---

[5]Throughout the manuscript version of this anecdote, White used the word "mutton," which each time Sallie White replaced with the word "lamb." The latter makes more sense in context, but it would seem that the controversy continued even in death.

"No, thank you, I don't eat lamb. I never eat lamb," said Sallie in her gusta-tory simplicity.

I turned and looked at her with amazement, shaded perhaps, but just a glint of dis-appointment. "You don't eat lamb?" I repeated it with ill-concealed amazement.

"No, no, I don't care for lamb."

It was a trying moment—do or dare, then or never. I knew the kind that "never eat lamb." With rare presence of mind, taking our life's happiness in hand, I answered as sweetly as I could: "Oh, yes, you do, yes, you do, dear," and helped her to the lamb.

And so, on the 27th of April, now for forty-nine long and lovely years we have had lamb on our dinner table, to celebrate that triumph of mind over matter.

Of course, we were riding on railroad passes. We were in the privileged class. I had made it my business, even on the Lawrence *Journal*, to know the passenger agent and the advertising manager of the Santa Fe. When they heard I was to be married, they wrote asking where we would like to go on a wedding trip and sent us passes to Santa Fe, New Mexico. More than that, the Santa Fe had an interest in a hotel called the Montezuma, at a mountain resort at Las Vegas where there were sulphur springs and a great barn of a hotel with roomy porches, nearly a quarter of a mile of them, which we walked as upon the deck of a ship. And they gave us rates at that hotel—I think ten dollars a week for two weeks for the two of us, with a lovely room and board in-cluded, which we could afford. . . . We hired a burro and walked over the hills. Sallie, still convalescing from her operation the summer before, rode. I was engineer and fire-man to the burro. We drank, at least I drank, quantities of the terrible sulphur water, and other guests at the hotel sometimes invited us in their carriages and we rode through the irrigated fields of that lovely region. But, best of all we enjoyed the table d'hôte meals. We acquired a waiter, by reason of modest tips, and he led us in the green pastures of that great menu, great even for breakfast where there were steaks and mackerel and bacon and eggs and ham and eggs and—even as at the Midland—baked oysters—a cornucopia of canned fruits and pancakes and waffles. . . .

No one ever was happier on a honeymoon. I wrote pieces, one or two a week, back to the *Star* about the country. I had never seen an irrigated country before, nor an ancient land where now and then a church, an old watermill, or a deep irrigation ditch dated back two hundred years and more to the Spanish occupa-tion. The Mexicans squatting against the sunny sides of buildings at noonday, sleeping with their sombreros pulled over their eyes, sometimes wrapped in gaudy serapes, sometimes just clad in blue overalls and shoes without socks, seemed to us denizens of another day and time—ambassadors from another world. We were seeing foreign parts and were gravely impressed with our privileges.

After two weeks of that we went to Santa Fe, where my mother was visiting old El Dorado friends. We stayed with them in what was known then as the Bishop's Garden, the home of the Archbishop made famous by Willa Cather's story.[6] It was altogether lovely, an ancient adobe house surrounded by a formal garden which was bordered with high cottonwoods with shining, shimmering leaves and willows nearly a hundred years old. A mountain brook ran through it, with flowers neatly bedded along its banks, and the vegetable garden was bearing even in May. The low, one-story adobe palace of the governor of New Mexico, occupied by General Lew Wallace when he wrote *Ben Hur*, and the great curio store where we saw for the first time Indian blankets, Indian jewelry, and Indian pottery and baskets, gave us a sense that we were far from home, from the middle western, middle-class America that we had known all our lives.

When we left for Manitou, Colorado, my mother went with us. It was the first honeymoon I ever knew where a mother-in-law tagged. But she was a strong-minded woman, had her own income, and paid her own way. And at Manitou, Sallie's little brother Milton, aged thirteen, who was frail and needed a summer's outing, joined us, and after a week or ten days we went in June to Estes Park—a bridal party of four. There we rented for five dollars for the season a log cabin on the banks of the Big Thompson River, far up in the canyon a mile and a half from any human habitation, in the heart of what became, many years later, Rocky Mountain National Park. We bedded on spruce boughs, cooked over an open fire, and Milton furnished the fish. He was a wonderful fisherman. We picked red raspberries and wild strawberries and had watercress unlimited for salads, brought fresh beef from the ranch house when they butchered, and fared sumptuously, if roughly.

I had been sending editorials back to the *Star* every day. But sometimes they arrived rather late and were cold potatoes and could not always be used. They were paying me my salary, which was generous of them; now they wrote to me to come back. But Sallie was getting so strong and life was so beautiful that I stayed on. Then one day, by wire, they fired me, and the next day the bank at Denver, which held all of our money, one hundred twenty-five dollars, failed. That was a dark day. I got ready to go to Denver to look for a job as a printer, a reporter, an editorial writer, or an advertising salesman, all of which I had done, or even as a solicitor of subscriptions. I knew I could land a job, one way or another, even in the midst of the devastating panic that was sweeping over Denver, as other banks went down in the national depression.[7] Some way, being penniless and fired at twenty-five did not seem to bother me, since I had a trade and one or two professions. And then Providence was good to me, for it gave Mr. Prentis . . . a light stroke, and the *Star* wired me to come home and help. So I took the

---

[6]Cather set her novel *Death Comes for the Archbishop* (1927) in early nineteenth-century Santa Fe.

[7]A wave of bank and business failures in the spring and summer of 1893 triggered a severe depression throughout the United States that lasted into 1897.

stage two days after I had been fired, and two days later was at work. The rest of the bridal party trailed in later in the summer. On the whole, even if the wedding journey became a caravan, even if calamity came upon us in its direct form this side of death, we were happy. . . .

It was about that time that Colonel Nelson decided to establish the *Sunday Star*. Being a good general who knew what his troops could do, he decided to establish it without hiring much extra help. Moreover, he decided that most newspaper features were made for sale rather than for reading. So he put the men who were working on the *Daily Star* to writing features—chiefly local features in which they were interested—for the *Sunday Star*. We editorial writers had to get up Sunday editorials which would avoid politics. The old Colonel made that much of a concession to a religion which generally he ignored in his cosmos. In addition to the Sunday extra editorial, the managing editor assigned a feature article every week about some phase of Kansas City—the stockyards, a gypsy colony, the Greek neighborhood, and so on. . . . Sometimes I wrote interviews with prominent citizens, not political interviews but interesting stories of their lives. Maybe I was too realistic. I put this down because often my feature stories made trouble in the office.

A story I wrote about the Kansas City stockyards made a lot of trouble. The *Weekly Star* was being sent under a stockyard subsidy to ten thousand Kansans and my article was so flippant and so generally highty-tighty that the stockyards threatened to cancel the subscription. Tommy Johnson, who loved me but knew my weakness, said after the stockyards delegation had been mollified: "Bill, you can conceal more dynamite in three or four innocent lines than any man I know. How do you do it? Just tell me that."

So I began to learn a new trade. For feature articles I began to write fiction, short stories with the background of Kansas City and Kansas. Most of these stories appeared two or three years later in a little book called *The Real Issue*. Before they appeared I read some of them at a rather unique institution in Kansas City known as the East Side Literary. It was a fairly authentic revival of the old country literary society, except that all of us, something like a hundred, participated. We thought we were pretty smart. I read short stories and poems. The town's newspaper dramatic and musical critics wrote and read comments on plays and concerts. Our local fiddlers fiddled and our sopranos and tenors sang their prettiest, and the town's pianists played Chopin, Liszt, and Rubinstein with here and there a jigger of Beethoven or Debussy. And the wealth, beauty, and fashion of Kansas City's smart neighborhoods came out to grace the occasion. The East Side Literary in Kansas City was a shadowy ghost of an institution that passed with Hayes and Garfield.

I do not recall that the young people of Kansas City, who mingled in the society of the nobility and gentry, showed any consciousness of the economic storm that was passing over the Missouri Valley and America. Occasionally a bank failed in the business district and we heard from a reporter in the *Star* office the story of the long queues, during the runs which smashed the banks, and the tragedies that these queues revealed. Once in a while a suicide, with a financial angle, splattered over the first pages of the papers. I was conscious of many vacant store buildings and of cloth signs fluttering outside of bankrupt establishments. But the White household had a hard time finding a detached house in what we regarded as a decent neighborhood for the twenty-five dollars that we could pay, and a year later we had to pay thirty dollars. Groceries were cheap, and we managed to live on our income and without debt. . . .

Through 1893 and 1894 and on for a year or so further, the depression held its blighting hand over the country and especially over the Missouri Valley. Railroads were going through bankruptcy, the big ones swallowing the little ones. Financial institutions were reorganizing after failure, or to avoid it. The whole structure of American business and finance was being recast before our eyes. Yet I doubt if any of us in the *Star* office, which should have been a watchtower, knew even in rough approximate what was going on. The merchants advertised the growing literacy of the population coming out of the Kansas schoolhouses under compulsory education, which was furnishing the *Star* more and more subscribers. The advertisers found these literate subscribers good customers. The paper grew and prospered. As a side line, I began to write advertising for the Jenkins Music House, adding a few dollars a week to my salary, and felt most important.

I kept my connection with Kansas politics vital. Often I saw Cy Leland, the local Republican boss. He had plans for Kansas politics, and because I was in a place of power where I could further his plans, he talked with some candor to me. The Colonel, who distrusted all politicians, listened while I unfolded Leland's plans and, as they seemed a decent way to overwhelm the Populist state administration, he let me play Leland's game. The Republicans nominated Congressman Morrill for governor. We supported Morrill during the campaign and shared his triumph in the election of 1894.

That year another gubernatorial election marked the rise of the Ohio politician who was to dominate the close of the century in national politics—William McKinley, a friend of Cyrus Leland. Leland undertook to see that the Kansas delegation in the [1896] national Republican convention was for McKinley. After the [1894] election, McKinley set forth under the tutelage and with the financial support of Mark Hanna, fronting for Wall Street, to tour certain Republican states.

When he came to Kansas City, he had a private car attached to one of the Sunday trains, and the *Star* sent me again as its ambassador on the train. I was to report the doings of the Kansas statesmen and to send a running account of

McKinley's speeches by wire to the *Star* as he proceeded in his double-breasted, Prince Albert coat and white vest up the Kaw River, over the ridge into the Neosho and Cottonwood valleys and along to the Arkansas River Valley at Hutchinson—a long day's journey. It was the best reportorial assignment I had ever had, and was a part of Colonel Nelson's idea about an editorial writer. He must, first of all, be a good reporter and, so far as possible, make his editorials news.

Here is the story of how, in the middle of the last decade of the nineteenth century, a leading candidate for the nomination of a major party proceeded to woo his way to place and power. The royal train left Kansas City about eight o'clock in the morning. We were scheduled to stop for short speeches a minute or two at Holliday, ten minutes at Lawrence, a quarter of an hour at Topeka, three or four minutes in Osage County, ten minutes in Emporia—and so on through the afternoon to Hutchinson, where a great meeting had been arranged in an agricultural hall at the fair grounds, with McKinley as the speaker of the evening.

Mr. Leland was in charge of the train. His political friends were invited to come on at certain stations and get off at certain other stations, so that the private car never would be crowded but always would be comfortably filled. McKinley was the looming candidate of the Republican party. He was a high-tariff man. . . . On that train only Republicans of the strictest high-tariff cult were accepted as Mr. Leland's guests. Half a dozen reporters from as far away as New York and Chicago and reporters from the St. Louis, Kansas City, Topeka, and Wichita papers had a baggage car. Here we set our typewriters on mail racks, chairs, and boxes and hammered out our stories of the regal triumph as it made its way across Kansas. We were always welcomed in the throne room—an observation parlor at the rear of the private car.

It was interesting to see how craftily, during that long jaunt through Kansas, McKinley handled the Kansas statesmen. He sat most of the time in a large, cushioned wicker armchair in the rear of the observation car and back of the door where the swing of the rear doorknob would catch anyone who was standing up before him right between the back suspender buttons. As that door was swinging frequently, it was unprofitable to stand long before the Presence in the chair, and of course no chair could wedge into the door side of McKinley's corner. He carefully kept any chair from his right-hand side. The politicians who drifted in and out of the car and on and off of the train had to be satisfied with an introduction and a few formal words. The great man rose for the introduction, stepped into the midst of the arriving pilgrims, shook hands, pleasantly chatted for a few moments, most formally, and then retired to his inaccessible throne. Cy Leland, during the journey, explained to me with great pride that this was McKinley's strategy: He did not want to talk to any man personally before a crowd. No man could say on that journey that McKinley had made any deal with him, that any man had his confidence. It was written on the wall that Leland, and only Leland, was McKinley's vicegerent. And with the rise of McKinley's power, Leland waxed stronger and stronger in Kansas.

One of the more purple moments of the day came as we stopped at Florence, a railroad division point, for a short talk. There, when the train started after McKinley's deliverance, standing in the midst of the little lobby of the private car, was my old boss, Bent Murdock, adorned in a brand-new Brooks Brothers cutaway coat with diplomatic braid binding, gray trousers, a purple Ascot tie most fashionably arranged, and a shiny, brand-new, bell-crowned plug hat styled down to the split second of the day. He made the other grass-fed statesmen look like rustics, and I caught McKinley's eye going over him, appraising everything—for McKinley was a master politician and given to those hunches which are the result of keen, quick, accurate observation through eye and ear. I was standing in the appropriate niche at McKinley's right hand after he had greeted Mr. Murdock and looked through those double-lensed, bifocal, gold-rimmed glasses into the old man's gray-blue smiling eyes—the ingratiating eyes of one who lives by his own charms. McKinley, who knew that I was a reporter and Leland's friend, asked, under the roar of the train, who was our Ward McAllister friend. I told him and, in telling him, buttered it on pretty thick for I loved old Bent. McKinley smiled complacently and put a period to my remarks, closing the interview with an "Ah!" And in that "Ah!" let me know that he had catalogued the specimen, pasted him in the golden book of memory for life. As a postgraduate education in Kansas politics, the McKinley train was most valuable to me.

I worked like a horse between Kansas City and Emporia, and at eleven o'clock filed three thousand words with the telegraph operator when the train stopped at Emporia. It did not show up in the *Star* office until after six o'clock. . . . The Western Union took the blame for mislaying my story, but that did not make it any better for me at the office. I filed another good three-thousand-word story that night at Hutchinson, but the next day it was cold potatoes. And, being an editorial writer in my mid-twenties among reporters who were generally older, I knew what they were saying, and it was true. I should have done or said something to that telegraph agent to make it impossible to mislay or misread the instructions on my story.

So, the net of my journey was to watch two master mechanics of American politics—McKinley and Leland—handle the procession of Kansas statesmen faultlessly. Each of the statesmen wished to have an inside rating with McKinley. . . . But because his bread and butter depended on knowing how to reach men, size men up, and handle each according to his worth and not his outer invoice, McKinley had been able to survive twenty years in Ohio politics, where survival values combined the virtues of the serpent, the shark, and the cooing dove.

McKinley, for my taste, had a little too much of the cooing dove in his cosmos. He was too polite, too meticulous in his observation of the formalities of the political Sanhedrin.[8] He used too many hackneyed phrases, too many stereotyped forms. He shook hands with exactly the amount of cordiality and with precisely the lack of intimacy that deceived men into thinking well of him, too well of him. His Prince Albert coat was never wrinkled, his white vest front never broken. His black string tie, or a dark four-in-hand, was always properly tied but never attractively. He was well tailored but not fashionably dressed. His smooth fat face made the casual observer feel that it was a strong face. It was not. It was a wise face, wise with the ancient lore of politics, crafty with the ways that win men and hold them. He had a sweet, but not cloying, manner; gentle but always, it seemed to me, carefully calculated. He weighed out his saccharine on apothecary scales, just enough and no more for the dose that cheers but does not inebriate.

I came home to Sallie Lindsay the next day and poured out my heart about this statesman—the first of a major size that I had met with any degree of familiarity. And I made her see why I rejected him. He was unreal. McKinley was to influence my life in the years to come rather definitely, and I saw him often. But I never changed my opinion of him—the one I formed that first sunny day riding on his train through Kansas. . . .

As I look back on those years in Kansas City when I was on the *Star*, and try to patch together some picture of that youth in his mid-twenties, his chief characteristic seems to have been an eager ardor—like that of a friendly pup. Probably that is why the old Colonel sent him to represent the paper on one of those chamber of commerce goodwill excursions which cities used to give in those days. The chamber of commerce hired a special train and sent it south to the Ozarks and east almost to St. Louis, skirting eastern Kansas, northern Arkansas, west and central Missouri. We were on a train a week or ten days and I came to know some of the businessmen of Kansas City as I knew them in Lawrence and El Dorado. We had our dining car, and because the train was fairly hilarious, some one of the twoscore passengers was tight most of the time, giving us a continual source of uproarious delight. And we ate where chambers of commerce in other towns would invite us.

The businessmen made speeches and contacts with prospective customers. . . . We organized a chorus, sang a good deal, and got to know one another's favorite stories and what our orators would say at every dinner in the towns where

---

[8]The Sanhedrin was the chief judicial council of the Jews from the third century B.C. until A.D. 70.

we were dated. And the eager pup that I was, was accepted so heartily that later when the chamber of commerce gave a minstrel show in Kansas City to raise funds, I was made an end man; did a turn of buck-and-wing dancing, sang a song, and thought myself quite a figure in Kansas City affairs. I have a notion that it amused the Colonel to have this monkey on the string—such an amiable monkey with so many tricks. For sometime along the line I got a five-dollar raise without asking, which Sallie and I saved for the most part.

It was in those years that Albert Bigelow Paine and I put together a volume of our verses and Ewing Herbert wrote the introduction. It was printed in Fort Scott and rather festively decorated with drawings by two Fort Scott artists. Paine and I had no definite understanding about the publication. The publishers sent me ten copies. Paine took upon himself without my authority the task of distributing the press copies, and left off many of my friends. I felt that I had the right to send as many press copies as he. We quarreled. The book sold out quickly. We could have had another edition, and maybe a third, if I could have resumed relations that would justify the title *Rhymes by Two Friends*. But it was impossible. Eager and ardent as I was, I had my pride and after the publication of the book I saw little of Paine. He went Fast, kept on writing, became editor of *St. Nicholas Magazine* and, through his connection with Harper & Brothers, became Mark Twain's official biographer and did an exceptional job, for he had real ability and great energy. When he became famous twenty years later, *Rhymes by Two Friends* became a collector's item. . . . The book got pleasant notices, only pleasant in the proper places. In the East, where it was a curious visitor to the editorial desks of critical magazines, their pleasant reaction toward the book was probably, in part, surprise that such a book should come out of Kansas. . . .

I liked to think in those days that I was quite somebody downtown. At the office I was what in the vernacular was called "a hell of a fellow.". . . On the streets of Kansas City I spoke to many people. It pleased me to dress as well as I could afford to. Sallie and I liked to go out always to the Saturday matinees, sometimes to dinner and to public gatherings, but I had no nonsense in my head about going downtown at night. The happiest place I knew was home. . . . For I had always homework to do and it bound me with golden chains. . . . I wrote on the dining-room table the stories for the Sunday paper that brought me praise in the office and some little fame outside. Then, of course, I was always tinkering at verse and Sallie was always reading to me the books of the hour and the magazines of the day. There were hours of tall talk before I wrote, and afterwards while we were revising what I wrote.

I went to Kansas maybe once or twice a month, spent hours in smoky bedrooms with politicians going over that interminable, intangible, and eternally changing thing which politicians call "the situation." When I came back to

Kansas City the Colonel let me talk over "the situation" with him, much as a fat Buddha hears the prayers of the temple acolytes. Occasionally he would let out a crashing, thunderlike, jovial laugh or an indignant "Bigod," but otherwise he was as a god should be—a bit detached, self-contained, imperturbable. But I wrote largely what I pleased about Kansas, . . . which brought me again into the councils of Cy Leland, who had many of Colonel Nelson's qualities except that they were pickled in vinegar. Cy never had a belly laugh. His "Bigods" were staccato, pianissimo—not fortissimo or crescendo. And I think he liked me. I know he trusted me and I am sure I served him well. But I am sure of this: If I served Cy, I knew that this service was at the Colonel's pleasure, and that irked me.

Other things around the *Star* were beginning to gall me. I had to submit my Sunday stories to a Sunday editor named Richardson. He was a major cross. Also, Saturday matinee tickets were becoming harder and harder to get, and they had meant much to me. And then probably, in the core of my heart, I was a countryman. Ever since I had touched that Keith-Perry Building and looked at my fingers to see if it really was built with coal, the city had disturbed me. I rejected city ways. I subscribed. I bent the knee. I played with the chamber of commerce. We went to the East Side Literary. I wrote about gas and Pinky Blitz. But my heart was in Kansas and I wanted to be my own master. Most likely, what I really wanted more than any other spiritual thing was independence. I could not be happy as a hired man. . . .

It was in those days, and for these reasons, that I began to hunt for a Kansas newspaper, one that I could afford to buy. We talked it over at home—Sallie and I—and, at the proper time, with my mother. She had a little property at El Dorado. . . . With that capital in the back of my head, Sallie and I began to talk over various locations. And we were this smart: We knew we had to live in a college town. Whatever talent we had, whatever freedom I yearned for, could thrive and take root only in a town where there was a considerable dependable minority of intelligent people, intellectually upper middle class. These I could write for. These, I felt, understood what I was trying to do. These people, being in the leadership in a college community, would afford me an insurance which instinctively, even then, I felt that I must have. So I tried to buy the Lawrence *Journal*. It cost too much. I tried the Manhattan *Mercury*. It was not for sale. I tried an Ottawa paper. It was making too much money and was beyond my reach. So it narrowed down to Emporia.

Two papers were slowly starving to death in Emporia in the hard times of the middle nineties, the *Daily Republican*, which had absorbed the *Daily News*, and the *Gazette*. . . . The *Republican* [founded in 1880], . . . was a staunch, rock-ribbed party paper. Its rival—the *Gazette*—had been established in 1890 by the Populists, who could not get advertising support nor much cash from circulation. So they sold it to W. Y. Morgan, who helped me with my first job on the

Lawrence *Journal* as he was retiring from the university. Morgan was financed by Major Calvin Hood of the Emporia National Bank, and after much dickering we agreed on a price of three thousand dollars. Offering my mother's property as security, I borrowed a thousand from Governor Morrill, who was a banker, and a thousand dollars from the Plumb estate—somewhat because my father and Senator Plumb had been friends, and somewhat because his oldest son, A. H. Plumb, and I had been fraternity brothers. . . . George Plumb, a brother of the senator, lent me two hundred fifty dollars on my personal note, and Major Hood transferred to me a seven-hundred-fifty-dollar note which Morgan had carried. I was three months making the deal, at odd times when I could get away from the *Star*. Cy Leland helped me persuade Morrill to lend me the money, though the security was ample. Ewing Herbert helped me with Hood. And I had no serious trouble persuading the Plumbs. . . .

Sallie and I had a hundred dollars or so in the bank, which was spent mostly on moving and the thousand little incidentals that come at such times. I only know this: Sallie and my mother did not come with me when I went to Emporia to take charge of the *Gazette*, and when I bought my ticket on the afternoon train, the Saturday before June 1, I had a dollar and twenty-five cents in my pocket. It seemed ample at the time.

I was happy. I still can remember with what delight I rode across Kansas into the sunset and through the long twilight. The train came by way of Ottawa, and I still retain the picture of the ride through the Marais des Cygnes Valley. The grass was lush. The trees were in first foliage. The prairie flowers were abloom in the pastures and in the wood lots. Mostly blue flowers, they were. The streams were full. The ponds were full. The hour filled me with a delight that I have held through nearly fifty years. I have forgotten what visions of conquest I had; they were probably lively enough. I only remember that the road across eastern Kansas into the sunset and through the twilight was ineffably beautiful and gave me a deep joy. This also I remember: When I stepped off the train at Emporia, it was into a considerable crowd of idlers who in that day came to the station to see the two plug trains come in from Kansas City. The announcement had been made that I had bought the *Gazette*. I was a fairly familiar figure on the streets of Emporia. . . . I knew many of the faces that greeted me. I had a moment's indecision: Should I lug my heavy baggage uptown to the boarding house where I was expected and establish a reputation as a frugal, thrifty young publisher, or should I establish my credit in the community by going in a hack? The hack was a quarter. I decided, as a credit-strengthening act, to take the hack. I piled in. I never regretted it. I was never the kind who could have made my money by saving it. But if the crowd had known that when I paid the hackman I had just a dollar left (a fact which was nobody's business), the opinion of the town would have been divided about me. As it was, no question arose in the mind of the town about my financial ability. A good front is rather to be chosen than great riches.

I was twenty-seven years old. Just ten years before that May evening that landed me in Emporia, I had left Emporia to take a job in a printing office. In those ten years I had . . . fitted myself to do everything, from sweeping out to writing the editorials and keeping the bank account, that I could ask any other man to do. So I was not afraid to plank down twenty-five cents to the hackman and go on a dollar over Sunday until the money from the *Gazette* began to come in. Which is another way of saying that I was a brash young man with a lot of assurance, who took considerable satisfaction, even pleasurable delight, in getting in a tight place and wiggling out. I never played poker but I did enjoy throwing dice with fate that May evening as I rode regally through Emporia with the top of the hack down, a dollar in my pocket, and in my heart the sense that I had the world by the tail with a downhill pull.

9

The New Editor
and His Town

I had crossed the Rubicon—that border line in this world between the hired man and the boss. I waked the next morning, which was Sunday, scared. I had the key to the office in my pocket. After breakfast I went to look at it all alone.

Here's what I saw: a room twenty-five by sixty with a smaller cubbyhole ten by fifteen subtracted from that floor space. In the cubbyhole were three chairs and a pineboard table built into the wall. There I and the two reporters were supposed to do our writing, to keep the books, and get out the copy generally for the paper. It opened into the street. The walls of the cubbyhole were covered with theatrical posters, campaign pictures of statesmen pasted on the wall paper, and a few photographs of local celebrities and crooks tacked above the desk. There was a swivel chair, presumably mine. A second chair had a large cane bottom and arms, and the third was a common kitchen chair. The old oil cloth on the floor had been scuffed into holes beneath each chair. So much for the editorial department.

The rest of the sixty-by-twenty-five floor space was the composing room and printing office. In the middle stood the cylinder press on which the *Gazette* was printed: a Cottrell equipped with a water motor which in drouthy seasons was disconnected and replaced by a colored man who turned a crank. Half a dozen racks for type cases were strung along the walls of the room, and three composing stones stood in the center of the floor. A heavy lead roller weighing seventy-five pounds stood on one end of the largest composing stone. That was the proof press and that was all of the machinery that went with the Emporia *Gazette*.

And I wonder if God has yet forgiven me for my sinful pride in it all. I knew what everything was—how good it was, or how bad from misuse or wear or tear. As a printer, I looked over the various cases and was pleased to find they were full. . . . The foreman, Jack McGinley, a six-foot, two-hundred-forty-pound, curly-headed, black-eyed Irishman with a goatee and moustache, showed up in mid-morning, and he and I talked until noon about the paper, the payroll, and business prospects generally. The paper was supposed to have between seven and eight hundred subscribers. . . . Jack told me that there were only four hundred and eighty-five in the town of Emporia and fewer than a hundred more in the county, and that the county collections were far in arrears.

Jack was a dozen years older than I, and was a good printer who had at one time owned his own paper. I did not know it then, but he was a periodical drinker and sacrificed his position on the right-hand bank of the Rubicon to his lip for liquor. He took me in hand like a father, and I have never had a wiser, more loyal friend than he. . . . He and I, being somewhat of the same blood and of an ardent nature, dropped our guards in that hour alone in the office, and when noon came, we stood at the front door. I offered him my hand. He looked me over from head to foot, quite formally . . . then smiled a beaming, possessive fatherly smile and said: "You'll do. I guess we'll make it!" . . .

Sunday afternoon I wrote my salutatory editorial. Reading it the other day, after nearly half a century, I am amazed to find that it stands up. It still represents my ideals, realized with such a sad and heavy discount in approximate. But what I wrote I tried to do.

ENTIRELY PERSONAL

June 3, 1895

To the gentle reader who may, through the coming years during which we are spared to one another, follow the course of this paper, a word of personal address from the new editor of the *Gazette* is due. In the first place, the new editor hopes to live here until he is the old editor, until some of the visions which rise before him as he dreams shall have come true. He hopes always to sign "from Emporia" after his name when he is abroad, and he trusts that he may so endear himself to the people that they will be as proud of the first words of the signature as he is of the last words. He expects to perform all the kind offices of the country editor in this community for a generation to come. It is likely that he will write the wedding notices of the boys and girls in the schools; that he will announce the birth of the children who will someday honor Emporia, and that he will say the final words over those of middle age who read these lines.

His relations with the people of this town and country are to be close and personal. He hopes that they may be kindly and just. The new editor of the *Gazette* is a young man now, full of high purposes and high ideals. But he needs the close touch of older hands. His endeavor will be to make a paper for the best people of the city. But to do that he must have their help. They must counsel with him, be his friends, often show him what their sentiment is. On them rests the responsibility somewhat. The "other fellows" will be around. They will give advice. They will attempt to show what the public sentiment is. They will try to work their schemes, which might dishonor the town. If the best people stay away from the editor's office, if they neglect to stand by the editor, they must not blame him for mistakes. An editor is not all wise. He judges only by what he sees and hears. Public sentiment is the only sentiment that prevails. Good sentiment, so long as it does not assert itself, so long as it is a silent majority, is only private sentiment. If the good, honest, upright, God-fearing, law-abiding people of any community desire to be reflected to the world, they must see that their private opinion is public opinion. They must stand by the editors who believe as they do.[1]

It is a plain business proposition. The new editor of the *Gazette* desires to make a clean, honest local paper. He is a Republican and will support Republican nominees first, last, and all the time. There will be no bolting, no sulking, no "holier than thou" business about his politics, but politics is so little. Not one man in ten cares for politics more than two weeks in a year. In this paper while the politics will be straight, it will not be obtrusive. It will be confined to the editorial page where the gentle reader may venture at his peril. The main thing is to have this paper represent the average thought of the best people of Emporia and Lyon County in all their varied interests. The editor will do his best. He has no axes to grind. He is not running the paper for a political pull. If he could get an office he wouldn't have it. He is in the newspaper business as he would be in the dry-goods business to make an honest living and to leave an honest name behind. If the good people care for a fair, honest home paper that will stand for the best that is in the town, here it is.

In the meantime, I shall hustle advertising, job work, and subscriptions, and write editorials and "telegraph" twelve hours a day in spite of my ideals. The path of glory is barred hog tight for the man who does not labor while he waits.

William A. White

I slammed that editorial on the copy hook when I left the office that Sunday night and the next morning came down to take charge. Nothing new confronted me except the sense that I was actually boss, not a sub-boss for someone else, which was more frightening than exhilarating. But I had this comfort that first day. I met scores of my father's old friends who had known him twenty-five years before in Emporia. They were mostly substantial citizens, many of them old-line anti-Populist, silk-stocking Democrats. And they heartened me. Mr.

---

[1] I have lost some faith in this lot; but I have gained some faith in just plain folks.—W.A.W. [Added in *Autobiography*.]

Morgan, my predecessor, took me up and down Commercial Street, introduced me to all the merchants and most of the lawyers and some of the doctors. I picked up local items as I went, talked advertising to advertisers, and did a good day's work. . . .

I did not realize during those first days in Emporia why the town was divided, as were most towns in the western world, into bank factions, deeply divided, bitterly feudal. But now I see across the years that those two factions in Emporia—the faction gathered about Major Hood and his bank and the faction gathered around Charley Cross and William Martindale and their banks—arose and thrived as local clans bound by purely monetary interests, and somewhat made necessary by the fact that storekeepers, professional people, and the owners of the little industries around the town could not live without credit. This, the banks furnished. . . . Factions, feuds, internal bitternesses, wicked and sometimes bloody rivalries were fostered at the front doors of the banks in towns and cities across the land—at least across our western land. I only knew about that.

So when Mr. Morgan took me up and down Commercial Street and Fifth and Sixth Avenues, calling on our friends and customers, I went unwittingly wearing the collar of the Emporia National Bank, Major Hood's bank. . . . Let me paste in a picture here of Major Calvin Hood, our banker friend, known in the town as the Little Major. He was in his late fifties then, a slight little figure beginning to bend just a bit at the shoulders. He had sharp brown eyes, a clear skin, gray hair thinning at the brow and gray whiskers always immaculately trimmed. Behind the barrier of those whiskers he kept a hard cruel mouth, rapacious and hungry. Yet he smiled easily, laughed gently, very gently, when he smiled, the refinement of his face appearing. He was another man. It was this man who always headed the subscription for every good thing. It was this man who lent students money, who bought lovely pictures for his home when he went to New York, and good ones too, who patronized the arts in Emporia, gave generously to the library, kept a box at the Emporia Opera House until he fell out with the owner of the theater, had a spanking team of well-matched sorrels hitched to a rather magnificent Phaeton which adorned the streets. Compared with all other carriages in the town, the Little Major's equipage was a Rolls-Royce beside a T Model. He was generous to his friends and ruthless to his enemies. . . . He was a type, a product of his day, the banker who was a free man, who ran his own bank in his own way, deferring only slightly to the nonsense of the federal bank inspectors. In his town and county, that typical banker was the sheik. . . . He and his kind have disappeared as have the Mound Builders.

The Little Major, there in the backroom of his bank, spinning his web (his enemies used to call him the Old Spider), dominating the politics, controlling the business, bossing his church, financing and directing the local college, was my friend, loyal, generous, and understanding. I had no sense that he was corrupting our newspaper. When we talked over local or state politics, I had the feeling that we were two free men. He never gave orders, and in many minor matters, I suppose he took advice. It was years before a major matter appeared to threaten a division between us. I just happened to think his way most of the time in those first years as a young editor, and maybe sometimes, because I was young and he was old, he deferred to me. Certainly he was an easy boss. I doubt not that they all were easy bosses in the big world which he symbolized.

That night,[2] in the Emporia *Republican*, "our loathed but esteemed contemporary," a two-line item appeared thus: "Will A. White, of Kansas City, has bought the *Gazette* from W. Y. Morgan. Next!"

The editor of the *Republican* was [Charles V. Eskridge], a man in his sixties who [had been lieutenant governor, who] had served the town in the legislature, who had secured the location of the State Teachers College in Emporia, who was an acknowledged leader of the Republican party in Kansas, and vice-gerent of the Santa Fe Railroad, which named a town for him on one of its branches in an adjoining county. . . . He was of the samurai caste[3] in Kansas Republicanism, receiving remuneration as needed for his paper's payroll from the Santa Fe, and was a spokesman of the other bank, the Cross Martindale bank. When it was closed, a few years later, a sheaf of the old editor's blank notes, accommodation paper, was found in the bank which they slipped into the note case to polish up the record for the national bank inspector. He did not realize it, but I was the young bull who had come to horn the old one out of the herd. Toward the end of his career, as was the fashion of the day, he devoted much space to abusing me. The *Gazette* never replied. Not a line in our paper indicated that we even knew he was on earth, and that, his reporters told ours, galled him more deeply than anything we could say. He was used to every form of abuse but contempt.

Sallie and my mother came to Emporia the weekend after I arrived. Sallie came down to the office daily, and we worked together—she on society items and other local items, I writing the editorial, soliciting advertising, taking care of the bank account. Soon we invited Lew Schmucker to quit his job as a railway postal clerk and come to the *Gazette* as bookkeeper, reporter, and advertising salesman. To him it was a dream come true, for he had always wanted to be a newspaperman.

The total payroll of the office was forty-five dollars. Jack, the foreman, got twelve dollars; later a raise to fifteen. The best printer got eight dollars a week,

---

[2]This announcement had in fact appeared in the Emporia *Republican* of May 21, 1895.

[3]In traditional Japan a samurai was a warrior, a lower-ranking member of the military caste, who was generally the retainer of a high-ranking caste member.

and four girls set type at from two fifty to four dollars a week, according to their skill. The office devil got two fifty and Mr. Morgan told me he was due for a raise to three dollars the first of July. The reporters got eight and ten dollars each.

But living costs were low. A frying chicken cost fifteen cents, steak ten cents a pound, bacon eight and nine cents, flour two dollars a hundred, sugar twenty pounds for a dollar. Sallie and I paid eighteen dollars a month for a six-room house. It did not have a sign of a pipe or a wire in it. . . . We laid aside five dollars and no more for our grocery and incidental budget and lived within it. We kept no maid, but we could have gotten one for from a dollar and a half to three dollars a week.

So we jogged along six months or so, with nothing more serious to cloud our happy lives than a weekly overdraft at the bank Monday morning, which was wiped out by Wednesday evening. Then one Saturday night we rocked the town with laughter in one of those sheer accidents which the devil in his ingenuity sometimes contrives for newspapers alone. Sallie had made the announcement in the society column of the wedding of Hortense Kelly, daughter of a Methodist elder and a man of great political power in the state, and George Crawford, son of a former governor and brother-in-law of Arthur Capper, of the Topeka *Capital.* . . . Saturday morning she wrote a funny story about John Martin, the laundryman, who had taken his son Charley to Kansas City. Charley came home saying that his father had given him a dollar to call him Uncle instead of Papa when the girls were around. She had prefaced her story about John Martin with a Kipling quatrain:

> This is the sorrowful story
> Told as the twilight fails,
> When the monkeys walk together
> Holding their neighbors' tails![4]

And then, the devil only knows why, the make-up man on the paper put a separating dash between that quatrain and the John Martin item and tacked the verses on at the end of the Kelly-Crawford wedding which concluded thus: "This marriage unites two of the oldest and most important families in Kansas, the Crawfords and the Kellys." Then followed: "And this is the sorrowful story . . . ."

When old Jack saw it after the last paper was out and the carrier boys were gone, he began to roar with laughter, and within ten minutes the barbershops of the town were churning with hilarity. In an hour the town was giggling its head off. In three hours the town was divided. Nine-tenths of the burghers thought

---

[4]This is the first stanza of Kipling's poem "The Legends of Evil" (1890).

we did it on purpose and that it was a dirty shame. The other tenth realized that it was one of those devil's accidents which come to newspapers in spite of all their care. But on the whole it was good medicine for the *Gazette*. It had never made such a deep and widespread impression on the town as that which came in that item. As for Sallie, she went to bed in tears, and when she tried to explain to the Kellys she was greeted by cold, rebuking unbelief. If the *Gazette* gained circulation and attention, it was the woman who paid, and paid, and paid. . . .

The first real knock-down-and-drag-out fight I had in Emporia was with the Grand Army of the Republic. The Union veterans literally packed and controlled the courthouse. They had majorities in the city council and on the school board. The Republican county convention and the Kansas state Republican convention were their private parade grounds. When I came to town, I determined to cut down extra words in the *Gazette* and boil down the items to the bare bone. The G.A.R. had two posts in Emporia, and every week their notices came to the newspaper office in the form of a military order. It took twelve lines to say that the P. B. Plumb Post of the G.A.R. would meet in its hall as usual Wednesday night. I cut the twelve lines down to exactly that many words, eliminating all the military phraseology, the names of the commander and the adjutant and the corporal—and the G.A.R. blew its head off and boycotted the *Gazette*. I explained to the people that I was not refusing to give the news of the G.A.R. meeting but was refusing to clutter up the paper and take the space that real news would occupy by printing every week a lot of military jargon. And the boycott dissolved impotently after a few weeks. Governor Eskridge faunched wildly because I was insulting the men who had saved the Union and struck the shackles from four million slaves, but little good it did him.

We stressed local news and printed a number of items that ordinarily would not have been printed in a strictly conventional newspaper. We were chatty, colloquial, incisive, impertinent, ribald, and enterprising in our treatment of local events. Looking back over it now, I can see that much of it was based upon a smart-aleck attitude, but the people liked it. Circulation grew. The *Gazette* was generally abused in conservative households. A few prudish people sighed that they could not allow the *Gazette* in their homes on account of their children, which I felt was silly. So did Sallie. It was that year and the year after that I traded space with the man who owned the billboards. Whenever one was vacant, the town read in flaring red type: "All right! Cuss the *Gazette*, but read it!"

Editorially, from the very first week, the *Gazette* was a conservative Republican newspaper. . . . But I set no great store by the editorial page. I believed that local news, if honestly and energetically presented, would do more for subscriptions and more for the *Gazette*'s standing in the community than its editorial page. Indeed I believed then and believe now that a newspaper that prints the news—all of it that is fit to print—can take any editorial position it desires without loss of prestige or patronage. People choose their paper not because of its politics but because of its integrity, its enterprise, and its intelligence. They want an honest paper, well written, where they can find all the news to which they are entitled.

Except for occasional boycotts, which were noisy but highly incompetent, our editorials never got us in trouble. It was the news items that brought in irate subscribers. Our policy, for instance, was to drop the word "lady" and substitute the word "woman." A lady who had paid a fine for streetwalking came in to protest not the publication of the news of her fine, but the fact that we called her a woman and she assured us that she was as much of a lady as any of the other girls in this town. And from that hour to this, the *Gazette* has referred to all females as women except that police-court characters are always to be designated as "ladies." . . .

Whatever figure I may have cut on Commercial Street . . . at home our lives were simple and gentle and sweet. At night we read or Sallie read to me. I remember that about that time we read *The Crowd* by Gustave Le Bon,[5] which impressed me. We were reading the current Howells novels as they appeared in the magazines, and of course Kipling, every line of him; and were taking excursions into the English minor poets like Henley and Andrew Lang. . . . Even with our scanty means we had *Scribner's, Harper's,* the *Century,* the *Atlantic,* the *Nation,* the *Outlook,* and the *Independent.* Some of them we got by swapping advertising. The others we paid for. We had no time for bridge. We seemed to be out of the dancing zone. Probably we did not go out to parties more than two or three times a month, for we were an extra couple at cards and had to work too hard in the daytime to dance very much at night. It was not that we were pious. The Lord knows it was not that. We were just busy. What a strange couple we must have made in those dear and dizzy 1890s in Emporia, when, even though a depression was blighting the land, the townsfolk, with their social diversions— with Colonel Whitley's Opera House filled three nights a week with passably good plays, the lecture course at the Normal crowding them in to hear the year's celebrities in lecture or song, and all the gaieties of the Feast of Belshazzar[6] were making the night merry through those sad, drab days. . . .

It was about this time that Sallie told me that any of a thousand men in America could write as good verse as I, but that I had a chance to do something with prose which might really carry me. And I knew she was right. I had an idea for a novel in those days which was to deal with a county-seat fight in western

---

[5]Le Bon argued in *The Crowd* (1895) that human beings behaved differently in large groups than they did as individuals, being governed by emotion rather than intellect.

[6]During the Israelites' captivity in Babylon, King Belshazzar gave a sumptuous feast for a thousand of his followers, who drank from sacred vessels stolen from the Jewish temple in Jerusalem (Daniel 5:1–4). The term was therefore used to connote excessive and sinful pleasures.

Kansas, full of the beat of horses' hooves, the crack of revolvers, the tense rivalries of towns, massacres, and sudden death. It never came off, but many is the hour I sat in the dining room at the table at night writing page after page of that story while Sallie sat by, reading a book or a magazine.

I printed two stories in the *Gazette* for filler which Richardson, the Sunday editor, had rejected on the *Star*. One story was called "The Court of Boyville," the other was the story of "Aqua Pura.". . . From the *Gazette* they were copied and got around the country. So, in the winter or early spring of 1896, we had two offers from legitimate book publishers asking if we had any other stories like that, enough to make a book. We had! We chose Way and Williams, Chicago publishers, largely because they were western, and we turned down Henry Holt & Company chiefly because they were eastern. We were loyal westerners without much sense. So we began gathering up our stories for The Book. We had entitled [it] *The Real Issue*—a bad title, as it afterward appeared, a confusing one. Over and over we revised those stories, boiling them down, recasting the sentences for clarity. But when we sent the book off . . . we were proud and happy. We had sense enough to know that *Rhymes by Two Friends* was a most amateurish enterprise, but we felt some way that *The Real Issue* was in a way professional.

In the meantime, the campaign of 1896 was opening. Mr. Leland was selecting the delegates to the national convention from Kansas, instructed for William McKinley for president. . . . I had a chance to report that convention for the Kansas City *World*. I went to St. Louis, where the convention met [in June 1896], in a crash suit that cost me five dollars, and I was proud of myself. I filed a story every day, a thousand or fifteen hundred words which I wrote in an hour or so, and had the other twenty-two hours for sightseeing, for hobnobbing with other reporters, and for running about with Ed Howe, who, being an old stager, knew the good places to eat. We discovered Tony Faust's restaurant, then famous all over the Midwest, and went to comic opera in an outdoor beer garden. I remember I saw *The Bohemian Girl*[7] for the first time. Though I knew all the tunes taken from that old opera, it gave me an added thrill to hear them in their proper setting. . . .

I was interested in Mark Hanna, a human sort of a man in his late fifties with a barrel chest, slim legs, a fleshy mobile face that looked Irish, with a way of twitching his upper lip and nose sideways like a horse that was most expressive. I saw him, asked him a few questions which he answered politely but with great discretion, and got a fine impression of him as an earnest, honest, courageous, though somewhat hotheaded and impulsive man, not like the politicians who hid behind the mask of imperturbability and veiled their designs like Florentine conspirators. . . . Hanna sputtered on, even Goddamned. He was forthright.

[7]*The Bohemian Girl* (1843) was a popular opera by British musician Michael W. Balfe.

But holding him up beside my own ideal politician of that day, Mr. Leland, Hanna talked too much.

I reported the superficialities of the convention, chronicled the events without real knowledge of what was going on. . . . Here in St. Louis, the issues of the new times first appeared. The battle was over the inclusion of a straight, unequivocal stand on the currency. The East, and particularly the eastern bankers who supported [Thomas] Reed, had no faith in McKinley; they demanded that in the platform the currency plank should declare, "We favor the single gold standard.". . . Most of the western Republicans were for free silver. The Rocky Mountain states were rampant for it. The economics of the depression of the nineties found their expression in the politics of the times. The debtors who had borrowed to build a trans-Mississippi civilization believed that an inflationary measure would relieve them. In the East lived the creditors, the holders of western farm mortgages, the owners of railroad stocks and bonds who also had in their strong boxes the state, municipal, and county bonds of those western communities which had borrowed to build their cities, to make state improvements, and to enjoy those new, shiny gadgets of American civilization introduced by the public utilities—light, gas, and water. . . .

It was apparent early that Hanna, by controlling the southern delegates and by hard work in the Ohio Valley and Great Lakes commonwealths, had a majority for McKinley. Tom Reed made a sorry showing in delegates, but his friends and supporters dominated the platform committee and forced upon Hanna a plank that was at first odious to him, then became more and more acceptable. Finally he surrendered. The Republican party was committed then and there to the doctrine that prosperity in a land is the first requisite for justice. The Hanna-McKinley surrender on the currency plank wrought deep, widespread turmoil among the delegates in St. Louis. A bolt was organized. Leland had trouble to keep the Kansas delegation from joining the mountain states in revolt. . . . The plank, as the New York bankers wrote it, came out of the platform committee into the convention.

Between the publication of the committee report and its adoption, rumors of the silver rebellion in the party swept through the hotel lobbies. I reported those rumors, but I did not know essentially why the western Mississippi Valley and the mountain states were raising their outcry against gold. Only vaguely did I sense the fact that the drama I was to see in the convention when it met to adopt the platform was the opening scene of a great political morality play which would hold the boards for more than fifty years—a play of which the long procession of Populists winding through the Kansas streets, hanging me in effigy in Butler County and rising in wrath in Emporia, was but the prelude. It was a revolt of the man with one talent or with five talents against the man with ten, who was hoarding his gains in unfair privileges.[8]

Wednesday morning of the convention, we knew that Senator Teller, of Colorado, was to lead a bolt after the adoption of the gold-standard plank. No one knew how many delegates he could call around him in the march out of the convention. The moment was tense because of the uncertainty. . . . When the reporters tried to interview Mark Hanna that morning he was gruff and wrathy. I wanted to see how he would take it when the big scene was staged with Senator Teller as the hero, so I quietly slipped a dollar to a colored delegate from North Carolina and occupied his seat immediately in front of Hanna and the Ohio delegation. . . .

When the Republican platform had been reported by the committee on resolutions and the clause endorsing the gold standard had been read, Senator Teller, advocating the free and unlimited coinage of silver at the ratio of sixteen to one, made a speech favoring the adoption of a minority report of the resolutions committee which report eliminated the gold-standard declaration. . . . The loose muscles about Hanna's mouth twitched irritably as Teller's silver swan song rose and fell. Occasionally he lifted a broad hand to a large, bumpy cranium, as if to scratch. Instead, he rubbed the rich, healthy, terra-cotta hide on his full, firm neck. His bright brown eyes took the orator's mental and moral measure with merciless precision. But with the rise of passion in Teller's oratory Hanna's expression changed from a mobile smile to a vicious iron glare. When Teller sat down weeping, Hanna grunted his relief; but he was nervous. He kept rubbing his jaw. His long upper lip twitched from side to side. The muscles under his eyes quivered. Others spoke in favor of the Teller resolution. . . . Then a dapper young chap, with a boutonniere on his perfectly fitting frock coat, came sashaying down the aisle, and received Chairman Thurston's recognition. "Who's that?" asked Hanna of Congressman Grosvenor of Ohio.

"Cannon."

"Who's Cannon?"

Mind you, it was Mark Hanna who was asking these questions—Hanna, who was popularly supposed to be omniscient and omnipotent at St. Louis that day. Yet here was a United States Senator whom Hanna did not know—Hanna, who really held the convention in the hollow of his hand.

"How did he break in?" growled Hanna.

"Senator—Utah," replied Congressman Grosvenor of Ohio.

The westerner opened his mouth to read his address.

---

[8]In his "Parable of the Talents," Jesus told of a man who, before leaving on a long journey, gave his three servants five, two, and one talents (coins), respectively. The first two invested their talents and doubled them, but the third merely hid his in the ground and was punished when the master returned (Matthew 5:14–29).

"Well, for heaven's sake, goin' to read it! Lookee there!" And Hanna's broad, fat head waved toward the orator. "Perty, ain't he?" His eyes slitted, and he sneered: "Looks like a cigar drummer!"

The orator soon abandoned his manuscript.

Hanna showed a wise serpentine tongue between his thin lips and snapped, "So that's Cannon!" After appraising the dapper young man, he jeered to Governor Bushnell beside him: "Why, it's a regular stump speech. Listen there!"

The man on the rostrum made an acrid reference to the gold standard.

A small-boned, fat leg flopped across its mate, and Hanna changed his weight from one hunker to the other. "They ought to admit a lot more of those little sand patches and coyote ranges out West as states. We need 'em!" said Hanna by way of sarcastic persiflage to Grosvenor.

Cannon's remarks were growing more and more luminous. As the orator proceeded, Hanna's brown eyes, which had been twinkling merrily at his own humor, began to glow in heat lightning. His mouth twitched two or three times, as if to cut off the tail of a truant smile, then spilled its rage in grunting imprecations. The rhetoric of the Utah man was telling. He referred to the Republican party as the party of oppression and began to threaten to leave the party.

Then Hanna's harsh voice blurted out across the multitude. "Go, go!" He stopped, then renewed his courage and grumbled in a lower voice: "It's an insult. It oughtn't to go on in the proceedings of the convention."

Grosvenor swore a couple of bars. Bushnell carried the bass. Finally Cannon, shaking a flamboyant head of hair, put the threat to bolt in a rococo period of rhetoric, declaring that the Republican party had seceded from the truth. Hanna, uncoupling his short, fat legs from behind his chair, stretched out in nervous wrath. A steel sneer wired its way across his face as he groaned in a flat, harsh snarl: "Oh, my God!"

There was a tragic half second's silence. Ten thousand eyes turned toward Hanna. Evidently he could feel their glances hailing on his back for his flinty auburn head bobbed down like a cork. He was still the businessman in 1896, and this blab was unbusinesslike. It was political. Hanna, the ironmaster, ducked. The orator on the rostrum had used the phrase: "The parting of the ways"—famous through the whole campaign to follow. It was Hanna's voice that cried out "Goodbye," an instant later. The whole convention was firing the word "Go" at the rostrum. Then Hanna, the politician, rose proudly from the small of his back and got on the firing line. After that the Utah man was in the hands of a mob. Hanna devoted himself to the pleasurable excitements of the chase. He stormed and roared with the mob; he guyed and he cheered with the mob. He was of it, led by it, enjoying it, whooping it up.

Then when it was all over, when an hour or so later the gold-standard platform had been adopted, Hanna climbed into his chair, clasped his hands composedly behind him, threw back his head, let out his voice, and sang "America" with the throng. Where he did not remember the words, his dah-dah-de-dah-de-dums rang out with patriotic felicity, and his smile of seraphic satisfaction was a good sight for sore eyes. For Mark Hanna was giving an excellent representation of a joyous American citizen with his wagon hitched to a bucking but conquered star, jogging peacefully down the Milky Way of victory.

When I came home from the convention Sallie was ill, and the doctors had told her that there was a spot on her lungs. Passes being easy to get, we went to Colorado, where my Aunt Kate was running a hotel. She took Sallie in.

I came back to Emporia and sat at a telegraph desk while the story was going through of that great day in Chicago when William Jennings Bryan was nominated by the Democratic party as its Presidential candidate. That story, even on the wire, thrilled the nation. Here was a new figure. Here was a young man. Here was an intrepid advocate of a cause which he proclaimed as that of the downtrodden. It was the first time in my life and in the life of a generation in which any man large enough to lead a national party had boldly and unashamedly made his cause that of the poor and oppressed. The story coming through in bulletins, even detached and sometimes overlapping and out of chronological order, pictured a scene that some day will be a part of a great drama. It was the emergence into middle-class respectability of the revolution that had been smoldering for a quarter of a century in American politics.

I saw the story in no such perspective as I do today. I was moved by fear and rage as the story came in. I had never heard of Bryan. To me, he was an incarnation of demagogy, the apotheosis of riot, destruction, and carnage. A little group of us were standing around the ticker as the story came in, and I can remember someone . . . cried out as the drama climaxed in Bryan's nomination: "Marat, Marat, Marat has won!"[9]

It was with those words echoing in my heart that I entered the campaign of 1896, full of wrath and inspired with a fear that became consternation as the campaign deepened. It seemed to me that rude hands were trying to tear down the tabernacle of our national life, to taint our currency with fiat. So, swallowing protection as a necessary evil and McKinley's candidacy as the price of national security, I went into the campaign with more zeal than intelligence, with more ardor than wisdom.

The ardor of Kansas was more than a fever. It was a consuming flame. After the nomination of Bryan, which seemed like the swinging of a firebrand in a powder mill, people argued on the streets. The Republicans cried "Socialists," which would have been a reasonable indictment if they had not immediately

[9]Jean Paul Marat was a leader in the French Revolution.

followed by calling the Democrats nihilists and anarchists. In offices, on the front porches of the town homes, everywhere the clamor of politics filled the air.

I remember one day in July going to Topeka, and in Eugene Ware's office I sat with delight and heard him deliver a diatribe which rang the changes of what ails Kansas or what's wrong with our state. I sat chuckling at his poetic eloquence and told him that I was going to use that in an editorial sometime. He waved his hand and cried: "Go to it, young man, with my blessing!"

At home I could not walk up Commercial Street without being pulled and hauled by the Populists. I hated wrangling. I never debated anything orally. My answer to argument all my life has been a grin or a giggle or a cocked eye, anything to avoid an acrimonious discussion. Anyway, I have always had to work too hard to bother with the futilities of debate for its own sake. . . .

In mid-August the proofs came to me for the book of short stories, *The Real Issue.* When I opened the package, I was inordinately proud. I remember that I stopped in the midst of my work to look at the type and examine the make-up and form of the title page. It was most exciting. Being what I was, there was no alternative. I must take those proofs right out to Sallie Lindsay and we must read them together. So came Saturday, August 13.[10] I had decided to take the evening train to Colorado with the proof sheets. I hurried through my morning work. I got up some editorial for Monday, clipped out some editorials from other Republican papers, wrote the day's local stories, and broke it to Lew Schmucker that he would have to run the paper for four or five days.

Early that afternoon I went to the post office for the mail. . . . I was dressed to go to Sallie in my best bib and tucker, and I probably looked like a large white egg as I waddled down the street to the post office and came back with my arms full of newspaper exchanges. A block from the office a crowd of Populists tackled me. I was impatient and wanted to be on the way. They surrounded me. . . . They were shabbily dressed, and it was no pose with them. They were struggling with poverty and I was rather spic-and-span, particularly offensive in the gaudy neckties for which I have had an unfortunate weakness. Anyway, they ganged me—hooting, jeering, nagging me about some editorial utterances I had made. I was froggy in the meadow and couldn't get out, and they were taking a little stick and poking me about. And my wrath must have flamed through my face. Finally I broke through the cordon and stalked, as well as a fat man who toddles can stalk, down the street to the office. I slapped the bundle of mail on Lew Schmucker's desk and sat down to write for Monday's paper an editorial, and I headed it, "What's the Matter with Kansas?" And I remembered what Eugene

[10]August 13 fell on a Thursday in 1896; "What's the Matter with Kansas?" appeared in the *Gazette* for Saturday, August 15, 1896.

Ware said and added frill for frill to his ironic diatribe, and it came out pure vitriol:

WHAT'S THE MATTER WITH KANSAS?

Today the Kansas Department of Agriculture sent out a statement which indicates that Kansas has gained less than two thousand people in the past year. There are about two hundred and twenty-five thousand families in this state, and there were ten thousand babies born in Kansas, and yet so many people have left the state that the natural increase is cut down to less than two thousand net.

This has been going on for eight years.

If there had been a high brick wall around the state eight years ago, and not a soul had been admitted or permitted to leave, Kansas would be a half million souls better off than she is today. And yet the nation has increased in population. In five years ten million people have been added to the national population, yet instead of gaining a share of this—say, half a million—Kansas has apparently been a plague spot and, in the very garden of the world, has lost population by ten thousands every year.

Not only has she lost population, but she has lost money. Every moneyed man in the state who could get out without loss has gone. Every month in every community sees someone who has a little money pack up and leave the state. This has been going on for eight years. Money has been drained out all the time. In towns where ten years ago there were three or four or half a dozen money-lending concerns, stimulating industry by furnishing capital, there is now none, or one or two that are looking after the interests and principal already outstanding.

No one brings any money into Kansas any more. What community knows over one or two men who have moved in with more than $5,000 in the past three years? And what community cannot count half a score of men in that time who have left, taking all the money they could scrape together?

Yet the nation has grown rich; other states have increased in population and wealth—other neighboring states. Missouri has gained over two million, while Kansas has been losing half a million. Nebraska has gained in wealth and population while Kansas has gone downhill. Colorado has gained every way, while Kansas has lost every way since 1888.

What's the matter with Kansas?

There is no substantial city in the state. Every big town save one has lost in population. Yet Kansas City, Omaha, Lincoln, St. Louis, Denver, Colorado Springs, Sedalia, the cities of the Dakotas, St. Paul and Minneapolis, and Des Moines—all cities and towns in the West—have steadily grown.

Take up the government blue book and you will see that Kansas is virtually off the map. Two or three little scrubby consular places in yellow-fever-stricken communities that do not aggregate ten thousand dollars a year is all the recognition that Kansas has. Nebraska draws about one hundred thousand dollars; little old North Dakota draws about fifty thousand dollars; Oklahoma doubles Kansas; Missouri leaves her a thousand miles behind; Colorado is almost seven times greater than Kansas—the whole west is ahead of Kansas.

Take it by any standard you please, Kansas is not in it.

Go east and you hear them laugh at Kansas; go west and they sneer at her; go south and they "cuss" her; go north and they have forgotten her. Go into any crowd of intelligent people gathered anywhere on the globe, and you will find the Kansas man on the defensive. The newspaper columns and magazines once devoted to praise of her, to boastful facts and startling figures concerning her resources, are now filled with cartoons, jibes and Pefferian[11] speeches. Kansas just naturally isn't in it. She has traded places with Arkansas and Timbuctoo.

What's the matter with Kansas?

We all know; yet here we are at it again. We have an old mossback Jacksonian who snorts and howls because there is a bathtub in the State House; we are running that old jay for governor. We have another shabby, wild-eyed, rattle-brained fanatic who has said openly in a dozen speeches that "the rights of the user are paramount to the rights of the owner"; we are running him for chief justice, so that capital will come tumbling over itself to get into the state. We have raked the old ash heap of failure in the state and found an old human hoop skirt who has failed as a businessman, who has failed as an editor, who has failed as a preacher, and we are going to run him for congressman-at-large. He will help the looks of the Kansas delegation at Washington. Then we have discovered a kid without a law practice and have decided to run him for attorney general. Then, for fear some hint that the state had become respectable might percolate through the civilized portions of the nation, we have decided to send three or four harpies out lecturing, telling the people that Kansas is raising hell and letting the corn go to weed.

Oh, this is a state to be proud of! We are a people who can hold up our heads! What we need is not more money, but less capital, fewer white shirts and brains, fewer men with business judgment, and more of those fellows who boast that they are "just ordinary clodhoppers, but they know more in

---

[11]Populist U.S. Senator William A. Peffer was known for his eccentric appearance and dry, statistic-laden speeches.

a minute about finance than John Sherman"[12]; we need more men who are "posted," who can bellow about the crime of '73, who hate prosperity, and who think because a man believes in national honor, he is a tool of Wall Street. We have had a few of them—some hundred fifty thousand—but we need more.

We need several thousand gibbering idiots to scream about the "Great Red Dragon" of Lombard Street. We don't need population, we don't need wealth, we don't need well-dressed men on the streets, we don't need cities on the fertile prairies; you bet we don't! What we are after is the money power. Because we have become poorer and ornerier and meaner than a spavined, distempered mule, we, the people of Kansas, propose to kick; we don't care to build up, we wish to tear down.

"There are two ideas of government," said our noble Bryan at Chicago. "There are those who believe that if you legislate to make the well-to-do prosperous, this prosperity will leak through on those below. The Democratic idea has been that if you legislate to make the masses prosperous their prosperity will find its way up and through every class and rest upon them."

That's the stuff! Give the prosperous man the dickens! Legislate the thriftless man into ease, whack the stuffing out of the creditors, and tell the debtors who borrowed the money five years ago when money "per capita" was greater than it is now, that the contraction of currency gives him a right to repudiate.

Whoop it up for the ragged trousers; put the lazy, greasy fizzle, who can't pay his debts, on the altar, and bow down and worship him. Let the state ideal be high. What we need is not the respect of our fellow men, but the chance to get something for nothing.

Oh, yes, Kansas is a great state. Here are people fleeing from it by the score every day, capital going out of the state by the hundreds of dollars; and every industry but farming paralyzed, and that crippled, because its products have to go across the ocean before they can find a laboring man at work who can afford to buy them. Let's don't stop this year. Let's drive all the decent, self-respecting men out of the state. Let's keep the old clodhoppers who know it all. Let's encourage the man who is "posted." He can talk, and what we need is not mill hands to eat our meat, nor factory hands to eat our wheat, nor cities to oppress the farmer by consuming his butter and eggs and chickens and produce. What Kansas needs is men who can talk, who have large leisure to argue the currency question while their wives wait at home for that nickel's worth of bluing.

What's the matter with Kansas?

---

[12]Republican politician John Sherman was responsible for securing passage in 1873 of a bill ending the coinage of silver dollars, which was denounced by silver advocates as the "crime of '73."

Nothing under the shining sun. She is losing her wealth, population and standing. She has got her statesmen, and the money power is afraid of her. Kansas is all right. She has started in to raise hell, as Mrs. Lease advised, and she seems to have an over-production. But that doesn't matter. Kansas never did believe in diversified crops. Kansas is all right. There is absolutely nothing wrong with Kansas. "Every prospect pleases and only man is vile."[13]

I remember even across these years that I slammed that editorial on the copy spike with a passionate satisfaction that I had answered those farmer hooligans. I was happy and turned to something else for the afternoon. Before I left I had read the proof on it, which meant that I probably revised it two or three or four times, as I always do even now when I have for the paper an editorial that I am proud of. And so, late that afternoon I gathered up my proofs, a book or two that had come, the magazines of the week, and took the train for Colorado to lay my treasures before the feet of my lady love, fancying myself a romantic figure. . . . And so there at the little red stone depot of Manitou, where she came running down the platform eagerly to meet me, and I hurried with all my treasures for her, the book of our pride, the papers and magazines which would bring us together so happily, a journey ended in lovers' meeting.

[13]From "Missionary Hymn" by Reginald Heber.

10

I Awaken
to Fame

Sallie and I began that very Sunday morning reading the proofs of *The Real Issue*. . . . On Tuesday, the Monday *Gazette* came with the editorial "What's the Matter with Kansas?" in it. Sallie was shocked. She feared I had gone too far; that it would make enemies, and enemies would make trouble in Lyon County. So now I was scared . . . The next Sunday I took the train for home. Lew Schmucker wrote during the week that there was quite a lot of mail there for me about "What's the Matter with Kansas?" and I was frightened.

When I came in the *Gazette* office there was a fat stack of letters from all over the country about the editorial. A few of the letters were abusive. Most of them were laudatory and asked for extra copies. One which pleased me most was from Thomas B. Reed, Speaker of the House of Representatives, who declared: "I haven't seen as much sense in one column in a dozen years." I have kept that framed in my office over my desk now for forty-six years—my proudest trophy. Reed did not then even know my name. In his even handwriting, he had addressed it to "the Editor of the *Gazette*."

Day after day those letters kept coming. We reset the editorial and printed it by the thousands. The Republican national committee reprinted it as a circular, and state Republican committees reprinted it in many forms. Mark Hanna told me a few months later that he had used it more widely than any other circular in the campaign.

Suddenly, I—the editor of the Emporia *Gazette*—a country paper with little more than five hundred circulation, was a somebody. The dimensions of my world were enlarged. Papers from all over the country asked for exchanges. Charles Curtis, now a member of Congress, came into the office early in September, two or three weeks after "What's the Matter with Kansas?" had struck the world, and offered to get me the Associated Press franchise and to buy two or three thousand copies of the paper to circulate in his district. It was done, though a little while after the election, of course, I stopped taking the telegraphic press news. I had to hire a part-time stenographer to handle my correspondence, and Lew Schmucker used to hoot and jibe at me as I dictated letters. . . .

The Bryan-McKinley campaign came to a noisy highly emotionalized climax on election day. Bryan carried Kansas. The Democrats swept the state house and the Lyon County courthouse. But McKinley won in the nation. I do not believe, as the academicians have said, that McKinley won because Hanna spent so much money. Few votes were actually purchased in that campaign. McKinley won because the Republicans had persuaded the middle class, almost to a man, that a threat to the gold standard was a threat to their property. Incidentally, labor as a class was persuaded to the point of coercion that if McKinley was defeated industry would shut down, and that if McKinley won, prosperity would return because capital had confidence in the Republican party. . . .

In Emporia, the day after election, the Populists and Democrats for all their county and state victories, were sad, disgruntled, and discouraged. I felt at once that the pressure of opposition to me, to which I was extremely sensitive for all the success of "What's the Matter with Kansas?" had been relieved overnight. It was then in their national victory that the Republicans of our town rallied to me. As a national figure, I had their respect, and my ancient competitor, Governor Eskridge, who had before McKinley's nomination been a free silver leader, could not quite claim a share in the Republican victory. . . .

In mid-autumn, after "What's the Matter with Kansas?" came the publication of *The Real Issue*, a book of Kansas stories. It had the tremendous lift of the campaign editorial. But the campaign editorial could not have given the book the kinds of reviews that it had from the kinds of reviewers who praised it. For the book had nothing to do with the politics of the campaign of '96. . . . The stories were modeled on Kipling, Davis, and Frank Stockton—on an American last with a little of the French influence, Maupassant, Coppée, and Daudet—tearjerkers most of them, though some were just ebullient Kansas spirits. Before the book had been out a month, a letter came from *McClure's Magazine*, asking for the right to publish the story called "The King of Boyville" and ordering half a dozen others at five hundred dollars each. It was enough to lift one's hair and fit one's head into the dimensions of something approaching success. But the real thrill came in the late autumn. I went into the corner bookstore where Vernon Parrington and Frank Miller, who drove the oil wagon, and John Van Schaick, a young college professor, were loafing in the "Amen Corner." They yelled at me: "Hey, Bill, did you see the review of your book in *Life*?" And "My God, man, you've hit it!" And "How did you wangle that out of them?"

I bought *Life*, which was then a critical journal with a humorous slant, and hurried with the magazine unread to Sallie, who was in the office. We walked out, to be free of the slings and arrows of Lew Schmucker and the other reporter, and read it as we walked home on the sidewalk. It was a beautiful review written by Robert Bridges, who for years was one of the editors of *Scribner's Magazine* in its best days. He was the top-ranking literary critic of the country. Even a pleasant notice from Mr. Howells did not go so far nor mean so much as the review by "Droch," which was Bridge's nom de plume. Our eyes filled with tears and our hands met in a passionate grip as we walked along under the falling leaves of the elm trees, along Sixth Avenue toward home. It was a moment in life never to be forgotten. It was indeed the journey's end of our struggles and hardships. We had entered into a new life. We were breathing another atmosphere. The printer, the reporter, the editorial writer on the *Star*, the country editor wrestling three days a week with his payroll, with his petty cares and troubles—all these skins which I had worn were cast aside. I was a young author. . . .

That fall, amid great preparations at home which included a new suit of clothes, I crossed the Missouri River, headed eastward for the first time. I went to Chicago. Waiting at the station was a man who for ten or twenty years meant much in my life: Chauncey Williams of the firm of Way & Williams, publishers of *The Real Issue*. . . . He was twenty-six years old. His father had left him a hundred thousand dollars. He was of the University of Wisconsin and he had found a book collector who loved rare books and first editions—Irving Way, who had been Secretary to the President of the Santa Fe Railroad. . . . And with an earnest, honest patience they were spending Chauncey's inheritance on publishing fine books. Another publishing house in Chicago, Stone & Kimball, was engaged in the same artistic task, though Stone & Kimball had a wider list of books, which were more imaginative. . . .

Around those two Chicago publishing houses a group of authors had grown up, George Ade, Finley Peter Dunne ("Mr. Dooley"), Maurice Thompson, Elia W. Peattie, (mother of Donald Culcross Peattie), Hamlin Garland, and Henry B. Fuller. These people were found often in the big living room with a wide, hospitable hearth at one end of Chauncey Williams' house. It was built by Frank Lloyd Wright, a young architect still, who was just pursuing the harlot goddess—Fame.[1] And we used to sit around that hearth of his own envisioning, with Chauncey and Helen, his lively wife who looked like a creature out of Rossetti's poems,[2] and there was tall talk there, and sometimes a gaunt, loose-skinned, fiery-eyed rebel, Clarence Darrow, sat in the fireside circle, and sometimes Hamlin Garland came, always serious, always a rebuke to our ribaldry.

---

[1]William James referred to "the bitch-goddess SUCCESS" as "our national disease."

[2]Dante Gabriel Rossetti created idealized, mystical poems and paintings that often featured ethereal-looking young women with flowing hair.

And once in a while "Octave Thanet," a short-story teller from Iowa, a huge two-hundred-pound, human marshmallow of a woman who smiled easily and had a twinkling mind, was in that fireside group at Chauncey's.

It was all new to me that November 1896, a new world with a brand-new set of angels, rather different on the whole from the Imperial Club, the Pan-Hellenic group at Lawrence, and the Pi Phi girls, and the Trundle Bed Trash at El Dorado. I was moving in a rarefied atmosphere and my toes were just barely touching the insubstantial clouds beneath my feet. I used to pinch myself sitting there, or perhaps lunching with Chauncey and the literary nobility of some Chicago club which was rich and sumptuous beyond my imagining, and ask myself how that bellyful of Walnut Creek water, which had started the steam in my engine, had sent me so far! But I was always conscious of the Walnut Creek water and never pretended I had any other kind of steam in my pipes. The Chicago experience into which Sallie soon came was a definite step up in our lives to a place where we could see wider horizons and lovely visions. Chauncey's prodigality—and it was princely—brought us much that was dear and lovely in our lives. It seems, looking back at it now, that it was really a loftier rise, as indeed it was, from Emporia to Chicago than from Chicago to New York, or London, or Paris, or Moscow, or Rome, or Peking, where our journeys led us. The Chicago of the late nineties, provincially conscious of its new literary aspirations, was much more than New York a center of eager, earnest artists.

Even then, I led a double life. I had to speak at the Marquette Club, the official Republican organization of the Middle West. And, best of all, that winter I went to a feast at Zanesville, Ohio, whereat Mark Hanna was the host. It was given for those who, he had publicly announced, had helped to win the battle of 1896. . . .

Hanna was the first national political boss the country had ever seen—a man who at that time held national power in a victorious party by reason of his control of its organization. We had had congressional bosses who dominated Congress. We had had local bosses who dominated states and who, through the horse-trading power of states in conventions, sometimes for a day or a week or a month or season, rose to national eminence. Hanna, garbed by his cartoonist enemies in a dollar-marked checked suit, represented—with full authority and power to act—the amalgamated wealth, the merged and associated fears of the American middle class and its allied plutocracy.

When I came to him across the tiled lobby of the Zanesville Hotel, . . . he turned upon me his glowing brown eyes, reached for my hand, put his left hand on my shoulder, looked at me steadily from top to toe for a moment, twitched his loose lips and his nose in a funny grimace of pleasure, and said confidently: "Well, my boy, I am mighty glad to see you." Then quickly he added: "I owe a lot to you." Then, after a second's deliberation, he said: "Come on up to my room, I want to talk to you."

And so I met the most powerful man on the American continent. We went to his bedroom. In that day and time the political bedroom was the throneroom of American politics, and this of Hanna's was typical. . . . Under the washstand drawer, the occupant of the room generally kept his whiskey or, if he was sophisticated, a flask of brandy. When the doors opened into the bottom of the washstand, the political ritual of the meeting had begun. Hanna affected to open the washstand doors and said: "Want something?" I shook my head. He said: "I thought so." He made me sit in the big chair. He took the little one. A third man would have sat on the bed, or a fourth. But there was no third; just he and I were there. Hanna began: "Well, young man, I suppose you know now that I used your 'What's the Matter with Kansas?' all over the country. I suppose we must have printed more than a million copies."

I do not remember how I replied. . . . Then he went abruptly at it: "Well, what do you want?"

I did not parry. That I remember well. And I came back at him as bluntly as he came to me: "Nothing, absolutely nothing. You couldn't give me an office if you wanted to, and I guess you do."

Hanna looked straight into my eyes for a second or two and then began to laugh. "That's all right, young man; that's all right. You'll come to it." Then he said quickly: "Is your paper making any money?"

I answered: "A little. Enough."

"All right, all right. When you change your mind, just come around to me. I'm kinda glad you take it as you do. Have you been down to see the Governor yet?" (He meant, of course, McKinley.)

I answered: "No."

He snapped back: "Well, you've got to go. He'll be glad to see you."

I had not planned to visit McKinley, probably because he didn't interest me. . . . I hesitated for a moment and Hanna looked straight at me and said: "Nevertheless, you must go!" and sat there at the washstand where he had pen and paper, and with his own hand wrote a letter beginning: "My dear Governor," then identifying me with "What's the Matter with Kansas" and adding and underscoring, "He wants no office!" He read it, then showed it to me, then put it in an envelope with the proper inscription.

He then began to ask me about Kansas politics. . . . And then after he had assembled a little information, he rose and steered me out of the room. Probably five minutes was all the time he gave to me. But in that five minutes he convinced me that, personally, Mark Hanna was an honest, just, even generous man who had no frills, no side, no nonsense about him, a man with a sense of humor and a sense of loyalty, and I have not changed that opinion in nearly fifty years.

I remember little about the dinner except the Democrats called it the Feast of Belshazzar. . . . I remember that I sat beside Booker Washington, the Negro president of Tuskegee Institute. I sat there by choice. . . . I saw the man who was placed there did not sit down and I landed at Booker Washington's side. He may have seen the maneuver. He said nothing about it. . . .

The day after . . . Chauncey [Williams] and I went to Canton armed with my letter. We sat in the anteroom, ten or fifteen minutes, then I went in, taking Chauncey. My letter was lying on McKinley's worktable. Our interview was short. McKinley sat in his chair. I sat at his side. And while we were talking, I picked up the letter and had it in my pocket. I do not think he saw me, for I stood where he could not see my hand. I treasured the letter more than I valued the audience he gave me. The audience was most perfunctory, cordial enough but I felt the heat was regulated by a thermostat. He gave me just the degree of warmth I deserved. He thanked me for "What's the Matter with Kansas?" but even though Mark Hanna told him that I wanted no office, he had that inner shrewdness, that bland cynicism which distrusted human nature, and he left no opportunity for me to change my mind, then or ever. . . . When we got out of his presence, we hurried into our coats in the anteroom, and on the front porch Chauncey reached down and got a handful of snow and rubbed the hand that had clasped the hand that held the scepter of his country. And then we both ran roaring down the steps to the hack that was waiting for us.

That day Chauncey and I visited "the trade" in Ohio, to stimulate the sale of *The Real Issue,* . . . and then went down and spent a day with James Whitcomb Riley. We invited him to lunch at our hotel. He dined us at his club. And that day also I met for the first time off his presidential pedestal, Benjamin Harrison, and chatted with him for half an hour. He left me with profound respect for him—a man of erudition, of real culture, a wise and kindly gentleman who never could wear the courtesan's scarlet mantle, and so in his Quaker gray of reserved sincerity seemed cold and repellent to the politicians who were used to those manners which the second oldest profession in the world—the ruler's cult—learned from the oldest profession many thousands of years ago. . . .

As 1897 opened and as the Republicans came back to power nationally, a post-office row arose in Emporia, and patronage rows arose all over the state. Mr. Leland's leadership was being challenged by his factional opponents, the followers of J. R. Burton. Our congressman, Charles Curtis, in the local post-office fight arrayed himself with the Emporia faction that opposed Major Hood. Curtis recommended a candidate for postmaster, and Major Hood's ally—United States Senator Baker—recommended another. It was a bitter fight. I favored a third man who had no chance and, finally, I supported the Major's candidate. By June, even with Leland's support and the senator's endorsement, our candidate was having a tough time at the White House because after all the postmaster is congressional, not senatorial, patronage and the gentle McKinley was playing the game according to the rules.

A letter came from Senator Baker to the Major saying that Curtis would com-promise on my appointment as postmaster at Emporia. I had just one card in my hand, Mark Hanna's promise to stand by me. So I got passes for Sallie and for me, and the Major came tiptoeing into the office before I went and handed me a hundred dollars, for which I afterwards gave him a note and later paid it. At the train, as we passed through Topeka, Cy Leland came in, handed me an envelope and said, "This ought to help you out a little," turned quickly and went away. . . .

So Sallie and I made our first trip across the Alleghenies. She was twenty-six and I was twenty-nine. We were young and scared. We had railway passes; we probably had a shoebox full of fried chicken and deviled eggs, which lasted us two days for meals. We went to a little hotel known as the Normandie, infested with congressmen, judges, and statesmen, some of high degree. Across McPher-son Park was the Arlington, where Senator Hanna was housed in regal splen-dor. . . . We had arrived early in the morning and by half past eight we had had breakfast and I was in the lobby of the Arlington and the boy who was paging Senator Hanna led me into the dining room where he was at breakfast with his secretary and some Ohio politicians. He saw me and knew me as I came across the room and rose with his napkin in his hand, to meet me half way to his table. He turned his fine, glowing brown Irish eyes on me and his nose and loose lips twitching in mischievous gaiety, called out: "I knew it. I knew you would be back. I knew you would change your mind. Well, I'm as good as my word."

And he sat me down among the statesmen and told them who I was.

I blurted out my story, the object of my journey. I wanted his help, I said, to keep out of office and told him about the Curtis-Baker compromise. When I had finished he asked quickly, almost abruptly: "What can I do?"

I told him that I wanted him to take me to the president and wanted him to ask the president in my presence to promise never to sign my commission. I must have spoken awkwardly and with some emotion for the crowd at the breakfast table laughed and Hanna threw back his head, put his hands on the table and said: "Gentlemen, witness this marvel. I have had all kinds of requests from all kinds of people in the last six months, but this beats them all. This boy puts me on the griddle and wants me to promise to keep him out of office. Well, I'll be damned."

Half an hour later, Hanna and I were in the White House. . . . As we ap-proached, the senator, with his arms in fatherly affection around my shoulders, . . . the president at his desk looked up and saw us. It was clearly ob-

vious to me that all Hanna's gaiety and the obvious turning on of charm, which
was a bit conscious, bespoke a surprising relation. McKinley, not Hanna, was
dominant in their friendship. Hanna . . . was just a shade obsequious in the
presence of the bronze statue, the double-breasted Prince Albert coat, and in
the unwrinkled mask of a face. His greeting, whatever words he used, amounted
to: "Well, what can I do for you two?"

And Hanna waggishly began: "Mr. President, this is my boy."

A shocked, humorless batting of an eye showed Hanna that the president did
not understand. McKinley looked at the two of us. We were the same shape,
about the same height, and had much the same moon faces. And Hanna, who
was quick, perceived the question in McKinley's heart. "Oh, no, Governor, no,
no! I mean he's my spiritual son."

McKinley was not too sensitive to show his relief, and Hanna went on: "The
only promise I have out is to help this young man, and I ask you to heed his request for we are both indebted to him."

The president withheld any assent to Hanna's question. His eyebrows raised
in interrogation and I cut in: "Mr. President, I want you to keep me out of office.
I do not want to be postmaster at Emporia."

There the president was on solid ground. He knew then what I wanted. It was
plain that the Curtis-Baker compromise had been presented to him. With conspicuous judicial poise, he said: "Well, I don't see what I can do if the congressman and the senator agree to it and the commission comes up from the postmaster general."

Hanna cut in rather sharply: "Well, you can refuse to sign the commission.
Mr. White is in earnest about this, Governor, and I think we owe it to him."

The president looked up slowly to see if Hanna was really in earnest and
caught unmistakably the true ring in his voice and the sincerity stamped on his
countenance. The president paused a moment, fingered his desk, shut his jaw,
registering judicial composure, probably counted five or maybe ten to save himself, then replied: "Well, Mr. White, so long as Mr. Hanna insists, I see no reason
why I should not grant your request."

I then presented Mr. Leland's compliments to the president, got exactly to the
pennyweight the return of cordiality which a national committeeman is entitled
to for his message, and after a few most perfunctory remarks, Senator Hanna led
me away. He saw by my face, when we were in the anteroom, just what I
thought had been revealed in those few moments there at the president's desk
about the attitude of the two friends. Hanna, looking at me askance, grinned
and said: "When you know the governor better, you'll understand him." . . .

We stayed around Washington, doing various chores which I knew Mr. Leland
wanted and which I could do easily. . . . It was on that trip to Washington that
Congressman Charles Curtis introduced me to the man who, more than any

other in my twenties, thirties, and forties, dominated my life. Curtis said one day: . . . "Will, there's a man down in the Navy Department that has been asking for you. He knows you are my constit—a young fellow named Roosevelt. He read 'What's the Matter with Kansas?' He knows about your book. He heard you were in town, and he wants to meet you."

So we arranged an appointment. I met Theodore Roosevelt. He sounded in my heart the first trumpet call of the new time that was to be. I went hurrying home from our first casual meeting, in the office of an assistant of the Navy Department, to tell Sallie of the marvel of the meeting. I was afire with the splendor of the personality that I had met, and I walked up and down our little bedroom at the Normandie trying to impart to her some of the marvel that I saw in this young man. We were to lunch together the next day at the Army and Navy Club, where I went stepping on air, as one goes to meet an apparition. It was a rather somber old barn in those days, that club, and we sat there for an hour after lunch and talked our jaws loose about everything. I had never known such a man as he, and never shall again. He overcame me. And in the hour or two we spent that day at lunch and in a walk down F Street, he poured into my heart such visions, such ideals, such hopes, such a new attitude toward life and patriotism and the meaning of things as I had never dreamed men had.

We had this in common: Neither of us could work up any enthusiasm for McKinley. I remember the first shock of pain with which he revealed not only his scorn for McKinley and his kind, but his disgust with the plutocracy that Hanna was establishing in the land. For Hanna, he had a certain large, joyous tolerance as a man, but for the government he was maintaining, for the reign of privilege he was constructing, for the whole deep and damnable alliance between business and politics for the good of business, Roosevelt was full of vocal eloquence and ironic rage. That was the order which I had upheld, to which I was committed, to which I had commended my soul. Yet so strong was this young Roosevelt—hard-muscled, hard-voiced even when the voice cracked in falsetto, with hard, wriggling jaw muscles, and snapping teeth, even when he cackled in raucous glee, so completely did the personality of this man overcome me that I made no protest and accepted his dictum as my creed. Presently we launched out into Heaven knows what seas of speculation, what excursions of delight, into books and men and manners, poetry and philosophy—"cabbages and kings!"[3] After that I was his man.

It was not the ten years between us. It was more than the background of his achievements in politics. It was something besides his social status which itself might have influenced me in those days, something greater even than his erudi-

---

[3]From Lewis Carroll's poem "The Walrus and the Carpenter" in *Through the Looking-Glass and What Alice Found There* (1871): " 'The time has come' the Walrus said, / 'To talk of many things: / Of shoes—and ships—and sealing-wax— / Of cabbages—and kings.'. . ."

tion and his cultural equipment, that overcame me. It was out of the spirit of the man, the undefinable equation of his identity, body, mind, emotion, the soul of him, that grappled with me and, quite apart from reason, brought me into his train. It was youth and the new order calling youth away from the old order. It was the inexorable coming of change into life, the passing of the old into the new. . . . Theodore Roosevelt and I, walking that summer day under the elms on F Street in Washington, going from the lunch at the Army and Navy Club, visioned a vast amount of justice to come in the cruel world. Much that we visioned has come. . . .

All of this I poured into Sallie's ear that summer afternoon, and the next day or so she bundled me up and sent me on my pass to New York City—my first trip to the great metropolis. I had seen cities, Kansas City, St. Louis, Denver, Chicago, but even in 1897 the New York skyline as I ferried across to the Twenty-third Street slip, made my country eyes bug out with excitement. . . . I hurried downtown to the office of *McClure's Magazine*, somewhere around Twenty-third Street and Fourth Avenue. There, for the first time, I met in the flesh real magazine editors—Sam McClure, John Phillips, his guardian angel, Auguste F. Jaccaci, the art editor of the magazine, and Ida M. Tarbell. They had bought my "Boyville" stories. They were gracious beyond words to me. . . . The McClure group became for ten or fifteen years my New York fortress, spiritual, literary, and, because they paid me well, financial. They were at heart midwestern. They talked the Mississippi vernacular. They thought as we thought in Emporia about men and things. They were making a magazine for our kind—the literate middle class. This group had real influence upon the times from McKinley to Wilson.

That night John Phillips, Jaccaci and Ida Tarbell took me far uptown on a street car amid an unbelievable squirming army of bicycles to Grant's Tomb, where we had a gorgeous dinner and much tall talk about the magazine business and current literature. . . . During the day they had made an appointment for me to see William Dean Howells, who had written pleasantly about my book. He was living somewhere south of Twentieth Street between Third Avenue and Broadway in an apartment, and I remember that they were all packed up to leave for the summer. He was a gentle, sweet-voiced, keen-eyed, stoop-shouldered, stocky man, then, I should say, about sixty years old, and I remember that he sat on a trunk and tattooed his heels against it as we talked quite informally. He poured honey into my ears about my book and a "Boyville" story that he had read, and his sparrowlike wife kept flitting in and out of the room, perhaps to remind him that he was holding me too long. At least I thought so. And after a few minutes, maybe twenty or perhaps a half an hour, I hurried away and and, as Jacob must have left the Angel after the wrestle,[4] quite out of breath spiritually and greatly exalted. I became a literary acolyte in his Temple. Many times afterwards we met but looking back on that day, I am still proud and happy when I think that amidst the crowded hours of packing for a journey, this kindly man who meant so much to American letters . . . was so patient with me, so altogether lovely and forbearing. He tolerated fools gladly, which I suppose is a test of human kindness.

To be fathered by Mark Hanna as a son; . . . to have met Theodore Roosevelt and to have walked with him under the young maple trees of F Street between his club and his office; to have met even casually, as a part of my errands for Mr. Leland, a dozen congressmen and senators; and to have shaken hands and had the glowing brown eyes of Tom Reed beaming upon me from his height, a great hulking blubber of a human figure; to have seen the skyline of New York from the ferry at early morning; then to have seen William Dean Howells sitting on a trunk and scuffing his heels on it as he talked so greatly and so wisely to me; and then to have walked with the high gods that sat as a Jovian rabble around Sam McClure, surely that eastern trip for a young couple in their late twenties was enough glamor for one year. "Mine eyes have seen the glory"[5] of the seven hills of Olympus. . . .

[4]In the Old Testament the patriarch Jacob wrestles with a stranger, refusing to stop until he blesses Jacob. The stranger, an emissary from God, blesses Jacob and names him Israel (Genesis 32:24–32).

[5]The first line of the "Battle Hymn of the Republic," the Civil War poem by Julia Ward Howe, was "Mine eyes have seen the glory of the coming of the Lord."

11

At the Century's Turn

For me, 1898 brought my thirtieth year. I felt that there was something irrevocably sad in being thirty—middle aged. I felt impatient at the futility of my life, that I had done so little and now it was about over. . . . Sallie and I were in Cloverbend, Arkansas, in mid-February, visiting "Octave Thanet"—the pen name of Alice French. . . . She was from Iowa but lived in the winter on this southern plantation. . . . We sat after dinner before her great log fire and talked far into the night about everything in God's wide lovely world. It was one of those nights, I think the night after my birthday, when the news came upon us suddenly, I don't know how, of the sinking of the *Maine*. And we realized that sooner or later it meant war.

What we did not comprehend was that the war would lead into an imperial realm where the Monroe Doctrine would become virtually a protectorate over this hemisphere, and where we should take an excursion into the Far East and find ourselves established in the Philippines as one of the great world powers. We did not realize that as we talked on and on by the smoldering log fire that night. But we did know, all of us, that the explosion of the *Maine* had jarred something fundamental in our own way of life. We were afraid, dreading what the war would reveal. Probably millions of our countrymen in those days, who had accepted the vain, glorious vision of America's manifest destiny and all its pompous nonsense, were sobered when they saw the anchors of the *Maine* clipped as though they were part of our ship of state, "the Union strong and great,"[1] setting forth under sealed order to do combat for only God knew what. . . .

In those days I was of two minds about the rising issue of imperialism. My editorials revealed my uncertainty of purpose—not so much that, as an uncertainty

[1]Longfellow compared the American nation to a ship in his poem, "The Building of the Ship": "Sail on, O Ship of State! / Sail on, O Union, strong and great! / Humanity with all its fears, / With all the hopes of future years, / Is hanging breathless on thy fate!"

159

of those I saw in my daily walks. . . . [But once we were in the war,] Emporia was thrilled to the core. We celebrated the fall of Santiago with a big public meeting outdoors at the corner of Fifth and Commercial, and Ike Lambert, our leading lawyer and most accomplished orator, spoke to the multitude. He rang the changes of noble patriotism, the band played "The Star Spangled Banner," and we sang "Hail Columbia" and threw out a full-throated hymn to imperialism with the verses of "America" and were most pleased with ourselves. We had two companies in the war—one from the state normal school and the college, and one from the town and county. When the Spaniards surrendered in Cuba and gave us Puerto Rico and the Philippines to conquer, America had turned down that fork of the road which led to world domination. American imperialism was planted on this globe. We were committed to a new way of life. . . .

We thought in those days that the glory we had won and the lands we had taken over had come to us because of the valor of our soldiers and the blessings of liberty which we were showering upon the dark places of the earth. We did not know that America, our United States, was just a guinea pig in the vast planetary experiment that the spirit of man was making with the many inventions springing out of the human heart and the human mind. Ike Lambert's oratory told us of the glories of Bunker Hill, the triumph of Appomattox, the victory of Dewey in Manila Bay, our naval prowess at Santiago. And we patted ourselves on the shoulders here in Emporia as our citizens were congratulating themselves across the land. We were the chosen people; imperialists always were—from Moses to McKinley. The Emporia *Gazette* was just as crazy as any of the newspapers, no better. . . .

Robert Bridges, who was then an editor of *Scribner's*, wrote to me asking me to write some political stories, and George Lorimer, editor of the *Saturday Evening Post*, commissioned me to do an article or two. I was like Shakespeare's Thane of Cawdor, "a prosperous gentleman,"[2] no longer conscious of the payroll until Saturday morning and then only mildly fidgety about it. . . . Cy Leland, the state boss, had been appointed pension commissioner for thirty-four states, including Kansas, Missouri, and Nebraska. The pension blanks sent to him from Washington had to be partially reprinted, and he gave me the job. I bought a Gordon press, later two, started a small job office, and the income from printing the pension blanks amounted to nearly three thousand dollars a year—all velvet. The mortgage faded in a year or two and prosperity around the *Gazette* office was a reality. I paid all the notes at the Major's bank.

Our daily subscription list already had doubled and was more than a thousand. Our weekly was growing in the county. A new dry-goods store had come

---

[2]Unaware that the Thane of Cawdor has just been killed in battle and that he has been awarded the title, Macbeth says to the witches, "The Thane of Cawdor lives, a prosperous gentleman" (*Macbeth*, Act I, scene iii).

to town. It was buying page advertisements, putting on special sales. The hardware dealers were realizing that advertising would bring results, so they told about their buggies, farm implements, kitchen gadgets, and paint in quarter-page and half-page lots. The newspaper business in country towns passed definitely in those latter years of the nineteenth century out of its character as beggar and blackmailer, and became one of the major industries of every little town. . . .

That summer I had occasion to borrow two or three hundred dollars for thirty days or so, and because I was conspicuously on my feet in the town financially I strolled into the other bank, the Major's rival, where I had two good friends. My two good friends in the bank were Charley Cross, the cashier,[3] and D. M. Davis, the vice president. . . . [Cross] had lived in the town thirty years—since his boyhood. He was then a man in his early forties. As a boy he had had the first Shetland pony the town had known. He went away to an expensive military boarding school which set him apart from the common run of boys. He was the town beau in the early eighties, married the prettiest girl in Kansas, and took her to a beautiful home which he had built and around which he had planted elms. He was the glamor man of Emporia. I met him in Kansas City sometimes, loafed around at the clubs with him, enjoyed him, for he was a good fellow, an easy spender. He owned the finest Hereford cattle-breeding ranch in Kansas and entertained cattle kings from Texas and editors of the great livestock papers from the East. Also he bought my book, *The Real Issue* in large lots and sent it away to his friends in pride. When bank examiners came to town Charley Cross telephoned for me to come over to the bank. I was his prize exhibit, next to his famous bull, Wild Tom, a national character in the breeding world. And I talked to the examiner, told them all my best Kansas stories. . . . Charley mixed up drinks for the examiner, which I did not care for. And I know now, which I did not know then, that too often the examination of the bank was made rather perfunctorily. . . .

In the autumn of 1898 the Major . . . confided to me that the First National was in grave difficulties with the federal comptroller of the currency. [Major Hood] was in politics, owning a considerable interest in a United States senator and being himself a candidate for governor that year before the Republican convention. He was a first-class power in Kansas. The bank examiners leaped to the Major, in fact were sent to him as their advisor. Now when bank examiners came to town they were special examiners from Washington, stern men whom Charley Cross could not wheedle into slackening their duties. I learned afterwards that [Cross] dictated letters to the department which were signed by all

---

[3]Cross was in fact the president, William Martindale the vice president, and Davis the cashier of the First National Bank.

the directors, with only the last page, where the signatures were, genuine. He re-wrote the other pages, which presented an entirely different set of facts from that to which the directors attested. But he was fighting for his life.

This is fairly axiomatic: that no banker whose bank has failed should be held to strict moral accountability for anything he does in the last sixty days before the failure. His motives are mixed. He wants to save his bank. He desires to save the depositors and stockholders from loss. And perhaps more keenly than that, he feels that he must save himself. So he lapses into crime and justifies his crime by the danger he is running, the responsibility that burdens him.

The stories that the Major told me about the Cross bank were confidential. I could not warn my friends. . . . One day when November was a week or ten days old, he came to me, took me into the back room of the bank, closed the door, sat down, spread his arms on his desk, began drumming with his fingers on its glass top, and said: "Will, you can save the First National. You can keep Charley Cross out of jail. He is in a tight place. He cannot escape. They have pinned a criminal shortage on him of about seventy-five thousand dollars. I want you to go to him. He's friendly with you. Tell him that I will buy his bogus notes and free him of criminal responsibility for a majority of his stock in the bank. I can swing it for fifty thousand dollars."

He was not that direct, but that was the substance of a ten-minute talk. I was frightened. I felt the job was too big for me. Charley Cross was ten or a dozen years older than I. He was a man of substance, and I still trembled a little in the presence of money. But I went out on that errand. I could not go into the bank—perhaps because I did not have quite the courage, but also because I was afraid that the other bankers there would see me and suspect my errand. It was necessary to deal with Cross alone. His criminal shortage was unmistakable, and he knew it.

So I loafed around the outside of the bank, in stores and offices, until I saw him come out. I hailed him on the north side of Sixth Avenue, headed toward Commercial Street. I stopped him casually and tried (Lord how I tried!) to make my lips say what the Major had told me to say. I started in to talk about the bank examiners. Charley gaily threw off that grappling hook. And I started to talk about the bank, and he had some flippant and ribald remark to make about the bank and the times. He was a proud man. . . . We started to walk east to-gether, and I could not get my nerve up to deliver the message. I was a coward and knew it and went to the Major in humiliation and told him I just could not do it, that I had tried and it would not come. The next day, early in the morn-ing, I saw the Major. He said: "Well, Will, they'll be closing in on Charley today. Jobes, the bank examiner, has wired to Washington for authority to shut up the bank."

After a few words I left and went on my rounds through the stores and offices, gathering news. I saw my friends taking their deposits to the bank that morning. I could not stop them. To have stopped them would have caused the run that would have closed the bank even if Washington had delayed. . . .

About half past eleven I saw Jobes, the bank examiner, coming across the street from the Western Union office to the bank. I could not bear to look at the bank as he went in, and a few minutes later I crossed the street to the bank, expecting to see it closed. Instead, I saw Charley Cross standing by the front window of the bank. What a handsome figure he was! He had his hands in his pockets and as I came across, he waved his hand gaily at me. He was looking at the street—his street, his town. He had a quizzical smile on his face. . . . Five minutes later, [the bank] was closed, and Charley Cross went out the back door of the bank, never to return. I think the quizzical smile on his face as he waved his hand to me was his way of saying: "Well, Will, in another hour you'll have such an item for your paper as it has never printed before."

For he went directly to his home, harnessed his trotting horse to his red-wheeled trap, hurried across the town, out through the fields of his stock farm—and within twenty minutes of the time when I saw him, I picked up the telephone at the *Gazette* office and learned from Sunnyslope Farm that Charley Cross lay there dead, a suicide.

The two stories, the story of the suicide and the story of the closing of the bank, swamped us in the *Gazette* office that day. Sallie came from the house. Everyone around the *Gazette* office worked on the story. At four o'clock we had two pages full of it, fairly well written too, it was—a good story, the biggest story the town had ever seen. In my heart as I wrote, and I certainly worked hard with it, was that agonizing self-reproach that I, through my weakness, had brought death to my dear friend and misery to hundreds of our citizens. The Major would have saved Charley. He would have had the bank and have paid the depositors in due time. Even in a year, while the bank was going into receivership, the tide of the times changed and the depositors received about as much as the Major would have given them. It was not the financial loss but the shame of it in my own heart—the death of my friend.

After the bank closed, one day the receiver showed me the wreck there, where thousands of dollars were wasted in stock of boom enterprises—a big barn of a hotel in Cascade, Colorado, an electric light company in Salina, stock in an interurban railway, mortgage bonds, and little jerkwater railways that were never built. Then accommodation notes, pads of them, signed by the bank's satellites—cattlemen to whom the bank granted credit, old Governor Eskridge, editor of the *Republican*, merchants whom the bank held in its power. These blank notes were slipped into the note case when examiners came along and the books were tampered to indicate that the notes were bearing interest; so for a year, perhaps for two or three years, the bank had remained open—a fraud and a swindle.

Charley Cross, a night or two before he died, had written a pathetic letter taking the blame for the bank's failure and explaining that he had inherited a criminal shortage from his father, who died suddenly—a suspected suicide—a dozen years before. He had shouldered the criminal shortage and then had gone in deeper and deeper, kiting checks, appropriating deposits, tampering with accounts. It was all terrible, but it was a typical picture of one side of America's gay, careless journey out of the day of the self-sufficient economy into the corridors of the machine age. . . .

If the Little Major, in his spider hole at the Emporia National thought that the bank fight would end when his rival bank was closed and its surviving officers indicted, he was sadly fooled. The town row warmed up. The indicted officers had their liberty to fight for, and nothing much else to do, so that the air was thick with lawsuits and countersuits. Lyon County politics was conducted largely with affidavits and lie-nailers, anything from libel to mayhem.

I was in the thick of it. Indeed I took the brunt. I became precinct committeeman in my ward. It was my job to return a delegation that would stand by my side in the county convention. Legally we held a caucus. Let me describe this one so future historians may know how a party caucus worked in a highly literate state like Kansas, with 95 percent of the voters American born and 85 percent American born of American-born grandparents; how these people ran their politics in the interest of the prevailing plutocracy. The night before the caucus my cohorts met. We agreed on our ticket. I assigned one man to nominate a certain other man on the ticket until I had enough men who would stand up and nominate other men as delegates to fill the delegation. Then I gave my nominators their order from one to, say, twenty-eight, the number of delegates we had in the convention. I then proceeded to memorize in their order the men whom I would recognize the next evening. The next night, the little room where the caucus was held was packed full. My men, by order, were standing as far front as possible. I opened the caucus on the tick of the clock, stated the purpose of the meeting, and set the chairs ready to receive nominations for delegates to the Republican county convention. Then I shut my eyes and recognized Number One amid the clamor of voices. Number One put the name he presented, which generally received an overwhelming viva voce vote, with scattering negatives, and so went down the line to Number Twenty-eight. At about Number Ten, the crowd saw what was up and the row began. But we went through with the program. The delegation to the county convention was elected—my crowd. I remember that Mort Albaugh, the chairman of the state committee and sub-boss under Cy Leland, also being at the time receiver of the First National Bank, stood in the back of the room and watched me perform.

He came forward after the meeting and looked at me for a moment or two and said: "Well, you fooled me. I thought you was one of them long-haired, literary fellows. God!" He paused in awe and reverence: "You pretty nearly got away with murder."

In the county convention, of course, the big prizes were the nomination of members of the legislature, for they elected United States senators. For these legislative offices, we who controlled a convention swapped anything that would make a majority slate. Generally we could combine the delegates who were eager to name, let us say, sheriff, county attorney, county treasurer, and one other county officer in the convention to make a majority. We put our slate through in order to control the nominees to the legislature. And generally the organization succeeded. That is why I was in the organization in those years of the late nineties. I ran with the machine. . . .

But in 1899, in the town of Emporia, I took my first long step forward in public affairs by putting on a street fair. Ed Howe had been doing the same thing in Atchison for a year or two and, copycatting him, I went into the street fair business in Emporia. It was a three-day festival. We had booths in the main street and also a flower parade, a mile long, wherein buggies covered with gorgeous paper flowers and harness similarly adorned drove up and down the street, parading for prizes amounting to something over a hundred dollars. Then we had a lot of little colored boys in G-strings, or less, carrying stalks of kaffir corn, brown-tipped with the ripened corn—gorgeously colored stalks that looked like spears—and we put a band at their head, playing the jungle jazz of that day; they did look splendidly barbarous until their mothers, catching sight of them parading down the street in their shiny skins, raided the procession and spanked the kids out of it, to the delight of the multitude.

We had a tribe of Indians from the Pottawatomie Reservation giving Indian dances. The highlight of the fair was the first automobile that ever crossed the Missouri River. It came from Chicago from a friend of Chauncey Williams' friend, Sam Clover, of the Chicago *Evening Post*, who persuaded his friend—a rich, young mechanical engineer named Ed Brown—to send it. The Santa Fe gave him a freight car free from Chicago to Emporia and back. And what a crowd that first horseless carriage drew! It was the marvel of the fair. People came for a hundred miles around to see it. And then we rented a big circus tent and had all sorts of shows and entertainment going there. The first colored photography that had been seen in Kansas appeared one evening. And another evening we put on a baby show. We had a colored section and appointed three old bachelors as judges. If anyone ever saw a pretty sight, it was those colored babies competing for prizes. They were dressed to kill, and their mothers stood bursting with pride near the platform when the exhibit began. And Lew Schmucker, the old devil, who had a sense of humor, told the band—we had six bands from neighboring towns on duty in that street fair—to play "All Coons Look Alike to Me" as the judges filed by in solemn plug hats; and you can bet the colored mamas knew what that tune was and grabbed their offspring and marched out of the tent in wrath and broke up one of the finest features of the street fair.

But the fair gave me prestige. I collected the money, most of it at least. Mit Wilhite, owner of the hotel, George Newman, owner of the dry-goods store, and I collected it together and paid for everything. It cost nearly four thousand dollars. I stood for it, hiring the bands, paying the prizes, taking care of the payroll day by day, guaranteeing the attractions. People knew that I was responsible for the show. It was called "Will White's Street Fair." And Emporia also began to realize that the editor of the *Gazette* was not one of them damn, long-haired literary fellows. . . . That first street fair, which made the merchants a lot of money, did more for me in the town than "What's the Matter with Kansas?" did for Mark Hanna. . . .

The years at the turn of the twentieth century were vintage years if I ever had any. In those five years from 1898 to 1903 I stepped out into the big wide world. . . . I was awakening to the deep spiritual truths in the Christian Bible. Its theology did not interest me, but the wisdom of the ages there moved me deeply. . . . I had been buying for several years separately bound books of the Old Testament, with notes and commentaries. I loved its English. I was moved by its mystic wisdom. Job, the Psalms, Proverbs, and Ecclesiastes seemed written on purpose for me. But it was not until the turn of the century that I began to understand the New Testament.

I have no recollection that I ever travelled on the road to Damascus. But Theodore Roosevelt and his attitude toward the powers that be, the status quo, the economic, social and political order, certainly did begin to penetrate my heart. And when I came to the New Testament and saw Jesus not as a figure in theology—the only begotten son who saved by his blood a sinful world—but a statesman and philosopher who dramatized his creed by giving his life for it, then gradually the underpinning of my Pharisaic[4] philosophy was knocked out.

Slowly as the new century came into its first decade, I saw the Great Light. Around me in that day scores of young leaders in American politics and public affairs were seeing what I saw, feeling what I felt. Probably they too were converted Pharisees with the zeal of the new faith upon them. All over the land in a score of states and more, young men in both parties were taking leadership by attacking things as they were in that day—notably Mark Hanna's plutocracy and the political machinery that kept it moving. And literature was rising. Novelists were making fictional exposés of plutocratic iniquity. Magazines were full

---

[4]The Pharisees were members of an ascetic Jewish sect that self-righteously refused contact with nonmembers.

of what later was to be called muckraking, uncovering cesspools in the cities and the states, denouncing the centralization of power in the United States Senate which assembled there through the dominance in the states of the great commodity industries—railroads, copper, oil, textiles, and the like. So I, opening my New Testament and reading wide-eyed the new truths that I found revealed there, began to relate my reading to my life. . . . The better-known works of Herbert Spencer also stirred me up. When Herbert Spencer died, I wrote for the *Saturday Evening Post* an account of his life and works, one of the few things I ever asked George Lorimer, its editor, to print. Herbert Spencer, along with Whitman, Emerson, and Dickens, became at the turn of the century one of my spiritual ancestors. . . .

It was in 1900 that I met William Jennings Bryan for the first time. *McClure's Magazine* asked me to write a character sketch of him, and I journeyed to Lincoln, Nebraska, where he lived, to see him. We spent the greater part of a day together. The picture I held of him in that day is still with me. He was a tall, at least a tallish, young man who was, as I was, beginning to get too opulent a crescent on his vest. He had a mop of black hair and a tawny complexion. His eyes were large, expressive, kindly. In all things he was a gentle person, I felt. He was kind to me, though I could see that he suspected me of no good motives because I was a Republican and because he knew I had written "What's the Matter with Kansas?" which he thought had been rather devastating to his presidential career. Nevertheless we were both extroverts and got along gaily.

Bryan, even in that day, was too much of a professional politician to suit my tastes. He was getting what all politicians get, a lively sense of his capacity to influence people individually and in the mass by charming manners, meaningless courtesies, pleasant words, outworn phrases. A politician who is professionally trying his lures on the people, seeking to gain their confidence and thus secure their votes, gets into bad habits. He develops a technique—the fatal ability to so assemble and spread his particular charms that they will attract the admiration of his fellows. I suppose a courtesan falls into the same routine of bad habits and becomes a professional charmer. I felt that Bryan, who in 1900 was about forty, was too definitely conscious that he was an extraordinary personality, that he knew too well that he had many graces. In short, he was dramatizing himself with a skillful art as William Jennings Bryan. This did not offend me, but it did steel me a little against him.

So when he left me for an hour in his library and told me to look around and I would find there the foundation of his faith, I was saddened to find it was founded not upon a wide reading in general economics of accepted credibility. I found instead that most of the books dealing with the currency and with the tariff were written by partisans of a theory and published by groups interested in propaganda. The Bimetallic League published many of the volumes that I saw on his library shelves; the various free trade associations put out books on the tariff; and so on down the line—books written not by scholars but by partisans of the creeds that Mr. Bryan preached. It was a shabby library and, to me, revealed much. . . . The article which I wrote about him was coldly subjective but not deeply critical. . . . But [it] for some strange reason pleased Theodore Roosevelt immensely and he seemed to take me more closely into his heart because of it.

When Theodore Roosevelt returned from Cuba, after the Spanish-American War, I saw him several times and, because each of us was a rather voluminous letter writer, we exchanged our views and he gave me some confidences about his intentions. He did not want to be governor of New York. He wanted to be president of the United States. Of course, I hoped he would be president, and I saw the New York politicians take him up in 1898 and make him governor rather against his will. But he surrendered coyly, and even then when we met I was consulting him about the way to capture the delegates to the Republican national convention when his time should come. He knew that McKinley was entitled to his second term, but even in 1899 we were planning for 1904. I knew something of the factional Republican line-up in each of a group of midwestern, trans-Mississippi states bordering upon Kansas and Colorado. . . .

He [tried] earnestly and I think absolutely honestly in the spring of 1900 to avoid nomination as the Republican candidate for vice president. He wanted a second term as governor of New York and felt that he could get into the White House more easily from Albany than from the vice president's chair. . . . He received the nomination with considerable inner disturbance. . . .

After the election Roosevelt began definitely to organize the Republicans of the country to nominate him in 1904. I was torn between two obligations. I admired Hanna . . . but my heart was with Theodore Roosevelt, and I joined his camp. Hanna knew it and was appreciative of my position. And he let me know it once or twice when I saw him in a gay, half-rueful way, after he had spit out his protest. All of this, of course, was behind the scenes and under cover, as politicians ply their trade. As vice president, Roosevelt sat presiding over the Senate with a reasonable amount of dignity for him, and went on trying with what small power he had in the Senate to gain the friendship and support of various senators, and so capture state delegations to the Republican presidential convention three years ahead of him.

In the summer of 1901, a number of Roosevelt's friends in the Middle West . . . began meeting with him and discussing ways and means to organize that part of the country in his behalf. He came to Colorado Springs in mid-summer and, at the house of his friend Phil Stewart, a Harvard man, Roosevelt held a conference of leaders. I was there representing Kansas. In those days Roosevelt had to do business with the local political machine in each state. It was before the primary was widespread, and so the Republican machine in the various states had power of life and death over a presidential candidate. So the politicians gathered in Colorado Springs—as fine an assemblage of political gangsters as you would meet on a journey through a long summer day. I sat with men who, ten or a dozen years later, were to be denounced by name by Roosevelt as enemies of the Republic because they stood by Taft in 1912. But we did make proper plans and we did give due pledges, with our political lives as hostages for those promises, to return Roosevelt delegations to the Republican presidential convention of 1904 from Colorado, Wyoming, Kansas, Nebraska, and Missouri—and, we hoped, Iowa if Senators Dolliver and Allison could be rounded up.

I was tremendously swelled up, of course. Teddy Roosevelt was the vice president. I rode on the train with him and brought to the train half a dozen Kansas politicians. The train stopped at various stations and Teddy made speeches from the rear platform. And I stood by him, swelling like a poisoned pup, and was proud and happy. When we came to Emporia, he got off the train and there were Sallie and little Bill, and Roosevelt kissed them both and visited with us a moment in the midst of the crowd assembled. It was honey in the comb for us.

We parted with a promise that I should come to Oyster Bay in early September with reports on Iowa and Missouri and, when the train moved out with him standing on the platform waving at us and a good-sized Emporia crowd, I was somebody, or thought I was, and beamed on my fellow citizens with pride and complacence. When I got back to my desk I found there a letter from *McClure's Magazine*, asking me to write a character sketch of President McKinley. The Bryan sketch had pleased the editors of the magazine. They had also asked me to prepare a sketch on Senator Platt. With those two orders in my pocket and my appointment with Roosevelt in the back of my head, I left Emporia in late August with an appointment to see both President McKinley and Senator Platt. . . .

It was in late August that I met William McKinley for the last time. I had met him three times before. . . . I was familiar with his political record and his political views and attitudes and public methods and manners. I had read everything biographically about him that was available in books and magazines before I went to see him to prepare the article about him for *McClure's*. I took the order reluctantly after one or two letters of mild protest. . . . We were two human beings who could not develop any intimacy founded upon anything like mutual respect. . . .

The time I entered his home at Canton I had one purpose: to find out if the man was entirely a public mask or if he had any private life whatever. I wanted to find the real man back of that plaster cast which was his public mask. I can remember that I wished if I could only see this man in his shirt sleeves, with his suspenders down, in slippers, with unkempt, tously, really friendly hair and a two-day beard, what would he be like? So as we walked through his modest home that hot August day, I kept an appraising eye upon him all the time. A photographer came along from *McClure's Magazine* to make a portrait, and I wondered if the story was true that he always laid aside his cigar before the camera. It was true. He smiled and said, as he always said, quietly, sweetly, and gently: "We must not let the young men of this country see their president smoking!"

When the photographer had gone, we took chairs on a side porch opening into a little garden, a pleasant, shady spot, and began to talk. I explained that I was not seeking an interview, did not desire to quote him, but merely wished to get his views and understand his position on certain passing public questions without in any way presenting these views as officially his. He was wily. He had heard reporters say that before. . . . I tried him on reminiscences and his reminiscences were as intimate as a newspaper biography, not pompous of course but consciously conventional. He had no stories of his boyhood or youth that would not fit into the Fourth Reader. In our hour's talk, he was completely guarded. Other reporters had told me what I would find, confirming what I had seen at the other times I had met him. I knew that somewhere behind the bastions of his fortress of reserve a real man was hidden. Again and again I charged the fortress only to find myself most engagingly and, I felt, almost unconsciously on his part, repulsed.

He sat there in a large cane veranda chair in a light-weight, dark alpaca coat and trousers, with a double-breasted immaculate white vest adorned only by his watch chain, with a dark purple fore-in-hand necktie meticulously arranged . . . without spot, blemish, wrinkle or sign of care or sorrow upon the smooth, sculptured contour of his countenance. I was sweating, for it was a hot day. He was stainless, spotless, apparently inwardly cool and outwardly unruffled. I thought then, and I think now, that he sensed what I was seeking and guarded it from me, maybe consciously. I also thought that his bland and amiable manner, his array of a politician's tricks—to enchant acquaintances and to hold friends—was somewhat consciously used upon me as we talked. As the first hour closed and he could see that through my mushy affability I was not caught, he was not exactly worried or irritated but puzzled that the spell did not work, and I caught his slight bewilderment as we chatted. Finally, as I knew my time must soon be up, though his body gave no signs of restlessness or anxiety, I said as gaily as I could: "Now, Mr. President, there is just one thing I really want to know."

He smiled pleasantly and said: "Well?"

"It is this: Your strongest quality, the characteristic which I think has been the source of your strength, has been your capacity, your ability, sure and instinctively certain, to pick honest men for important places. How do you do it? What is your method of testing and balancing human characteristics? . . ."

McKinley rose and stood before me as I sat there with a leg over an arm of my veranda chair. He smiled down at me as he would to an audience which he was about to address. . . . Our eyes must have conveyed the inner antagonism of our hearts, though we were both most polite, even warmly cordial. The president put one hand under his buttoned alpaca coat and in the other he held his cigar and began to make a speech. . . . His speech had no answer to my question. It was the thing he might have told the Canton High School at commencement. He stood there—a public man on an occasion. I do not remember what he said. After he had spoken a minute or two, I closed my memory. He was saying nothing that interested me. Perhaps he knew it. Probably he did. If he knew it he could not help it or perhaps feared to loosen his spiritual collar, feared to reveal the real McKinley, even the strongest lineaments of the man imprisoned in the fortress of his public life. When he had finished he said: "Is that what you wanted?"

And I said: "Yes." And thanked him. A moment later we were out on the front steps of his house. He was most cordial. His handshake was genuine. His hand on my shoulder was kindly, I should say simulating and probably approaching an affectionate warmth. He told me that if any other questions occurred to me, to let him know and he would answer them as best he could, which I think was an honest affirmation—"as best he could." He had somewhere back in his youth or young manhood, possibly as a soldier in the war, buttoned himself up and had become almost unconsciously the figure that stands now in Canton not far from his front door—William McKinley in bronze. . . .

I hurried on to New York where I had appointments which would give me the material for the Senator Platt story. Colonel Roosevelt had made these appointments with some ancient and some recent enemies of Platt who had once been his intimates. . . . Platt was a typical Republican state boss. He deserved attention only because he was the Republican boss in the greatest Republican state in the Union, and the story of intrigue, corruption, and the sordid amalgamation of plutocratic self-interest and political power was typical of American politics in the North at that time. . . . To make my picture intimate and personal, I saw Senator Platt in his office downtown, a frowzy little cubbyhole that had not been readied up for years. Papers, books, pamphlets, records—mildewed junk— lay around it everywhere; on top of his desk, on tables, beside his desk, along the walls. And when I went in and saw him, he looked to me like a little, old, mangy rat in his nest.

He was not so old as I am now, but his face was blotched with brown spots, his bleary eyes were rheumy, his jaw was uncertain. Yet there was a power behind his eyes, and a curious electric quality in his rather noncommittal handshake, that I cannot describe. It was the deep personal source of his power and he impressed

pressed me, even in the adolescence of his senility, as a powerful man. He did not hold his power by chance but by conquest, and it was held by an indomitable spirit. What he must have been in the days of Conkling and Garfield and Arthur and Blaine explains what he was that day I saw him in his rat's nest in New York—a little, old, frightened man who saw death around every corner and who blinked at it a rather cowardly defiance. I wrote the Platt story on that basis.

It was in the midst of my work on that story that William McKinley received the assassin's bullet at the Buffalo fair.[5] I had seen him in all his strength and physical pride. . . . When he was stricken down, I was shocked. I read in the papers that the vice president, Theodore Roosevelt, was hunting, or fishing, or roughing it in the Adirondacks, and I wondered how the attack on McKinley would leave our appointment.

For a day or two McKinley seemed to rally from Czolgosz's bullet. Then he suddenly sank, and the newspapers carrying the story of his death described it as curiously like a stage deathbed. They said that as he sank out of consciousness, he was humming: "Nearer My God to Thee," and that he reached an affectionate hand to Mark Hanna and parted with him in a well-set, school reader deathbed scene. I wondered then if that was the truth—if the tremendous force of a lifetime of conscious dramatics, stage-play, and character-acting had really persisted thus in death—or whether the power of his life's drama had written the story as the reporters unconsciously tried to round out the heroic figure that he had envisioned in his heart and carried into his career. Certainly McKinley died—in truth or in accepted fiction—in character; the statue in the park was expiring.

The day of his funeral I had a most astounding experience. I sat in the Century Club with Thomas B. Reed, former Speaker of the House of Representatives in Congress. We ate lunch together. He was the first national character who wrote to me about "What's the Matter with Kansas?" and we had built up a friendship in those six years. I saw him often. (I suppose, in parentheses, the reader has begun to realize I made the most of every toehold I had among men of power and circumstance.) It was decreed that for five minutes in the afternoon during the McKinley service in Buffalo, that the whole nation should pause. Every wheel in every factory stopped. All across the land, workmen stood at rest. Trains paused. The nation held a session of silent prayer. It was in the early afternoon in New York when Reed and I, sitting at the dining-room window on the third floor, looked down and saw the cabs and drays suddenly halt. We realized that this was the hour of prayer for the spirit of McKinley, which also was as he would have written the script for his funeral. McKinley and

---

[5]McKinley was shot on September 6, 1901, in Buffalo, New York, by Leon Czolgosz, an anarchist, and died eight days later.

Hanna had ousted Reed as Speaker of the House when it held an overwhelming Republican majority. It was done behind the scenes, and anyone knew it who was at all familiar with the inside workings of the party. . . .

Reed was a great porpoise of a man. He must have weighed three hundred pounds. He stood six feet of blubber, and yet power exuded from his excess adipose, his triple chin, his big, jowled countenance, like visible electricity. He was a man of wide erudition and exceptional culture—New England Brahminism blowing a hundred miles an hour.

As the cabs and drays pulled up and stopped in the street below our window, Reed literally hauled off, smacked his flapperlike hands heavily on the table, stiffened up, and began—not a prayer but a diatribe. He cursed McKinley and Hanna for what they were. I have never heard such exquisitely brutal, meticulously refined malediction in all my life. It was an experience out of the bitterness of a life that had been thwarted, for Reed, under the rules of the political game, had deserved the presidency in '96 and had been deposed as Speaker behind the scenes because he did not believe in the divine alliance between business and politics which was cemented by the protective tariff, because Reed cried out for the gold standard when McKinley was wobbling. Reed had reason for his bitterness, and justification for his contempt. He poured it out in a torrent of wrath, a cold, repressed New England cascade of icicles.

I was a fairly good reporter in those days. I tried to reproduce it. I could not. It was rage, chilled into sarcasm and frigid contempt. The man's bleak glacial passion—New England understatement freezing in invective—flowed in that icy Yankee drawl across that histrionic moment, shattering the drama of the hour. For Reed spoke as a man who knew for a fact and in deep truth what a terrible thing was happening to his country. And, as a patriot but mostly as a wronged man, he spoke for ten minutes, even after the clatter in the street had resumed, with such force and in such beautiful language of power, and with such chaste, simple diction, that I realized that I was the witness of a great occasion. Alas, the only witness! If I could have only reproduced those words! But there was a great figure, a huge, angry face livid with petrified rage, and there was the quiet of the club and the deserted dining-room tables, and the melodramatic pause below the window which set the scene. I could never regain that moment or recapture words that would reproduce that mood. It was a philippic. If only it could have been reported, what a speech it would have made for the school reader, on the opposite page from the story of McKinley's stage deathbed and stage funeral.

12

I Discover Reform

In New York I had received word from Theodore Roosevelt that he would be in Washington the night but one after McKinley's funeral. We were to meet, according to his suggestion, at the home of his Navy brother-in-law, Captain Cowles. So in the morning after McKinley's funeral, I went to Washington and at seven o'clock, in my tux and black tie, hurried over to the Cowles residence. . . .

Another young man was there—perhaps six or eight years my senior, a rather handsome young fellow with black hair, keen, searching eyes, and a strong, full, eager face. I was introduced to him and thus first met Nicholas Murray Butler. We dined with the Cowleses . . . . and Mrs. Cowles and her brother, the young president, kept the conversation rippling brightly through half an hour. He was to go to the White House the next morning. I was filled with curious excitement to know a president as well as I knew Theodore Roosevelt, to hear him talk about the McKinley funeral, to know in my heart how low an opinion he had of the things McKinley stood for. These things kept stirring in my mind as I listened to the dinner table conversation, the best I had ever heard. . . .

After dinner . . . I heard the young president, who was in his very early forties, tell of his plans and his hopes, his dangers and his fears. Theodore Roosevelt was a most candid man and I was shocked at the casual way in which he considered affairs of state. I could not get used to it. What he said I do not remember except that he feared Hanna and was frankly out to beat him for the nomination in 1904. That would stick in my memory. And one other thing which [Mr. Butler] and I both recall through forty years: He was worried about what he would do when he left the White House. He would be barely fifty, a strong and vigorous man who had had every political ambition satisfied yet was wedded to the political life. He said: "I don't want to be the old cannon loose on the deck in the storm." He knew himself so well. No man who could make himself the butt of his own jokes could fail to see himself after he had left the White House, still in the midst of American politics.

As I sat on the edge of my chair and Nicholas Murray Butler, with more dignity and aplomb, sat back in his chair, I noticed early in the evening that the old captain's eyes were drooping. He was not much interested in the talk, chiefly his young brother-in-law's gabble. He was used to it. He refused to be excited about the young man coming to the White House. He had heard many times Theodore Roosevelt rattle on, and the good dinner had lulled him to rest as we young fellows sat with wonder, awe, and praise in front of our prophet and ruler. And in the midst of one of Roosevelt's more dramatic sallies into the intimate affairs of the nation, I glanced at the captain. His hands were linked across his paunch. His eyes were closed, and he was gently snoring through it all.

Undoubtedly Nicholas Murray Butler discounted the young man and his enthusiasm more heavily than I did, for always in Dr. Butler's veins ran a few drops of the blood of doubting Thomas. But I swallowed it all, and it was a heady wine. I walked back to my hotel, the old Normandie on McPherson Square, on clouds of moonshine and amazement that I could see such things as I had seen and hear such tall talk as I had heard. I did not go to the White House the next day, I remember that. I hurried home and wrote my piece about Senator Platt.

Platt had scorned my hero. Unconsciously, or perhaps consciously, I used my best and most burning adjectives in that article expressing my scorn of Senator Platt and his machine, and contempt for the things it represented. It was a bitter piece. I could not write that way now. I realize that Platt was a senile old man who held his power because those about him had to keep him as a symbol and use his name and fame to hold his machine together. But I was proud of the job, and the editors of *McClure's* seemed to like it, and we put it into the hopper in mid-September for publication in the early winter.

I came back to Emporia to be a country editor. We were trying about this time to promote a railroad from Emporia to Omaha, a north-and-south interstate line that would use a branch of the M.K. & T. to connect with that road going south to the Gulf. It was a pretty dream. We were in the midst of a boom then, an upward spiraling wave of business activity that began early in McKinley's administration and for five years rose lustily and spread out over the land before the tide went out a year or so later. Our railroad dream seemed all but reality. When the receding wave of depression came, it washed away. But I was busy with it after the Platt article was finished and also was taking a part in Kansas politics. The election of 1902 was not so far away but that we who were somewhat on the inside of Republican politics were busy setting up the pegs to control the state conventions of that year and so to elect a governor and a United States senator. . . .

In the late autumn of 1901 I came back to Washington—I think it was at

Roosevelt's suggestion—to talk over his candidacy for 1904 as it had been going since he became president. The Roosevelts had moved into the White House, bag and baggage. I remember that Roosevelt said: "You know, Will, Edie[1] says it's like living over the store!"

I ate a meal or so with them, luncheon, and I remember a breakfast at this time, at which half a dozen senators, after devouring scrambled eggs and buckwheat cakes, discussed the Platt amendment[2] which concerned the government of Cuba and the attitude of this country. The Platt amendment was introduced by Senator Platt, of Connecticut, no kin to the New York boss. The discussion was good. Roosevelt had assembled men on both sides of the controversy, and he really let them talk—though at the last he took the floor and set forth his views with great positiveness and clarity.

The Roosevelts lived in middle-class simplicity. At family meals the children came to the table. The president, of course, was served first and in the early years of his office he used to apologize for it, indicating that he did not see any sense in the formality, but declaring that he could not overrule the servants. . . . At dinner he ran the table—not that he talked all the time but he primed others and pumped them to talk about what they knew best. I remember once, when John Sargent was painting Roosevelt's portrait and we three were at lunch together, the Colonel made me talk about club women in the Middle West and how they read papers on John Sargent's work, and I gave a picture of western town culture that I am sure John Sargent never imagined and could scarcely believe for, having been Anglicized, he thought that the West was a bleak, windswept semidesert where the best white men still married squaws. Roosevelt sat chuckling and prodding me on, and I don't think John Sargent much cared for the picture I was making. It was too homely, too folksy, too civilized for his idea of the Middle West. . . .

But the Roosevelts' meals and the Roosevelt household were always riotous. And he gave them their rambunctious character and keenly enjoyed it. Mrs. Roosevelt once said to Sallie: "How Theodore loves a party!" It was beautiful to see him with half a dozen guests at his table, with the children there cutting in, for they were never repressed children, and once—in a lull during the meal, perhaps before the main course—someone asked the youngsters: "Who are your father's favorite Cabinet members?"

As if they were trained to it—and maybe they were—they took their knives and forks by the handles and drummed on the table and piped in something like unison: "Mr. Root and Mr. Knox." Which made a great hit in the Capitol

[1]Theodore Roosevelt, Jr., the president's eldest son, was known as "Edie."

[2]Platt's amendment, among other things, provided for American intervention in Cuba in cases of internal unrest.

after the story got around; indeed the Capitol was scandalized at the Roosevelt children. . . . But the atmosphere of the White House, which bewildered diplomatic circles by its general informality and occasional disregard of usage, was nevertheless typically middle-class American—sincere, wholesome, a bit boisterous, but always well-bred in the deep sense of the word, which makes kindness the soul of manners.

Now to go back to the autumn of 1901. In our Kansas politics we had elected [Joseph R. Burton], a crooked senator whom Roosevelt afterwards sent to jail. He was my particular black beast in the politics of Kansas. He was a flashy dresser, flashily equipped intellectually, full of flashy demagogic works in politics. He had reason to hate my guts and did. At that time he was trying to get my old friend and boss, Cy Leland, deposed as pension commissioner for the Missouri Valley district. When I saw McKinley, a few days before his death, he told me that he was going to reappoint Leland, which was natural. . . . Leland headed the Kansas Republican faction that fought the crooked Kansas senator, and Leland was implacable in his hatreds. The first thing that the new senator from Kansas asked the new president for was Leland's head on a platter, and I, recounting McKinley's promise, asked that Leland be saved from the senatorial fury. The other Kansas senator was a Democrat and a decent man. Two or three other national politicians, including Hanna, told President Roosevelt that McKinley had plainly indicated his desire to reappoint Leland.

But the senator had much power. He was not to be checked. He had National Committeeman Mulvane back of him, and half of the congressional delegation followed the senator. The fight was publicly staged. I was fighting the senator. Kansas knew it. The Civil War veterans generally lined up with Leland. He was one of them, and they felt deeply the senator's attack on Leland. The senator picked a Spanish War veteran as Leland's opponent and that also galled the Civil War veterans, who regarded the Spanish-American War as mere fly-swatting and its veterans as upstarts.

Those Civil War veterans had passed the peak of their power and, in their hearts, they knew it. The knowledge was bitter medicine. They were beginning to huddle together, gathering in their old blue coats and brass buttons in reunions and in politics, like bluebirds preparing for flight. The day that Roosevelt yielded and appointed the young Spanish War veteran to Leland's job, the members of the G.A.R. in Emporia came out on Commercial Street like a swarm of bees, buzzing their anger. I remember Tom Fleming, city marshal for years, a kindly, gentle person who mothered the drunks and roisterers of Commercial Street, picked them up, brushed the flies from them, took them to the cooler, locked them up, bathed them, sent them out to their families refurbished; he always warned the evil-doers for the first offense and arrested them for the second. Tom was getting old and walked with a cane, but like a grenadier. And when the news came that our crooked senator had triumphed, old Tom met me on the street, led me two blocks aside and into his livery stable, took me into the boxstall where he kept his prize hearse horses, pulled the door to, and hissed into my ear: "Well, Bill White, what do you think of your Goddam Jew president now?" and stalked out, beating his cane on the dirt floor; and, like Pontius Pilate, he would not wait for an answer,[3] but left me standing speechless in the encircling gloom. . . .

I was working hard at the *Gazette* office every day from eight until six. At night I worked until midnight on magazine articles and stories and on the proofs of books I had written. . . . In December of 1901, *McClure's Magazine* printed my article on Thomas Platt. He read it. His friends read it. The enemies of Theodore Roosevelt in the Senate read it. They all raged. It was fairly obvious that I, who had been a familiar spirit around Roosevelt for four years, must have garnered much of the information from the article from Roosevelt or from his friends. This was true, though I was cautious enough never to print any story that Roosevelt gave me without getting the story from another source. Generally he told me where to find the other source. For he loved intrigue. So when the story of Platt infuriated its hero, he went to the White House and made a scene there, accused Roosevelt of abetting the article and demanded, as a senator from New York, that I be barred from the White House. He came out of the president's office and told the reporters that I had been barred, which made a fine story. It helped the sale of the magazine. It boosted the market value of my writing. For a few days it revived the author of "What's the Matter with Kansas?" as a national figure, which was fine.

But Platt started, or threatened to start, a libel suit for six figures against *McClure's Magazine*. Also against me. It scared me to death, and by Christmastime I was going into nervous exhaustion. One day in the *Gazette* office I was dictating a letter ordering a carload of paper. I began to sweat and tremble. The order was a formal one, routine in its nature, but I just could not finish the dictation, and came home and went to bed. The doctors hustled me out of town. I went to Colorado, then to California, and did not come back until May.

For hours together, [Sallie] and I sat on the beach on Catalina Island off Los Angeles, I lying down speechless, dozing in and out of sleep with my hat over my eyes, she beside me watching me, shooing off the children who might disturb me, reading and sewing. . . . By mid-April I was well on the mend. We had left Billy, our baby, at home with his two grandmothers. One grandmother will spoil a baby. Two working together will bring him up in the way he should go, for

---

[3]Francis Bacon began his essay "Of Truth" (1597) with the words "What is truth? said jesting Pilate; and would not stay for an answer."

each will suspect the other of spoiling him and will check it. This should be put somewhere in a book of advice to parents.

While I was gone the papers controlled by Senator Burton, Mulvane, and Curtis, my factional enemies in Kansas, printed a story that I had gone mad. So when I returned to offset the story, dear old Major Hood, the Little Major, God bless him, hired the Emporia silver cornet band, rounded up a congregation of my friends who crowded the depot platform, and as the train came in the band began to play "See the Conquering Hero Comes." Sallie and I got off the train, and what did we care for the band and what did we care for the crowd, for little Billy in his grandmother's arms came to us and spoke his first two words very slowly and astutely—"band boys." Our cup ran over. I was well.

Of course the newspapers carried the story of my return and told about the band and the crowd, and swiftly a letter came from the White House congratulating me upon my return. The president had sent word by mutual friends before I left for California, to pay no attention to the rumors that Platt was spreading. The editors of *McClure's* wrote even before I left not to let the Platt lawsuit worry me. And when I was in California I saw a story in a New York paper that *McClure's* had hired Tom Reed to defend them. They said afterwards that the story was without foundation, but it had frightened Platt so that he abandoned his libel suit. It was never filed.

Sometime in early June 1902, I went to Washington and, for want of a better time for a talk, the president invited me to breakfast with a number of statesmen who were wrangling with him about some bill before the Congress. I think he wanted these Republican politicians to see me in the White House, whence Platt had banned me six months before, and of course I was happy. . . .

A funny thing happened that was most characteristic of Theodore Roosevelt's love of danger and intrigue. Following this breakfast . . . he maneuvered me away from the retiring statesmen and said: "Did you meet Platt when you were writing your story?"

I said "Yep!"—snapped it out just like that.

He said: "How long did you talk to him?"

I replied, consideringly: "Let me see, probably ten, possibly fifteen or twenty minutes."

"All right, he won't remember you. Come along with me if you want to have a good time."

I had no idea what he was up to. We went into his private office. He put me in a chair just back of his. He looked at his clock. It was nine-thirty. The office doorman announced Senator Platt of New York. I started to go. The president with his hand made an almost mandatory gesture and said: "Stay where you are!"

In tottered old Platt on some minor errand about New York patronage. He glanced at me. I meant nothing to him. He was an old man, and my twenty-minute interview with him ten months before had not registered in his memory. He supposed I might be some Harvard friend of the president and went on with his errand. He and Roosevelt talked for ten minutes. Roosevelt walked with him to the door. It shut. He turned to me, beaming with delight, and squeaked in the falsetto that indicated his pride in himself and his keen love of danger: "Didn't I tell you? I knew he wouldn't remember you. Did you enjoy it?"

And then he burst into high, happy, nervous laughter and we both giggled. I went out of his office, following Platt. The reporters were there. They saw us coming out of the White House only a few moments apart. They made a good story. Platt was too old to protest. When he read the story, his friends did not care to take the matter up. My stock advanced. And then, to give me still more prestige on Commercial Street, the president named my candidate for the Emporia post office, ignoring the recommendation of the congressman. . . .

During the winter of 1903, I learned how states elected their United States senators under the old plan which made senators elective by legislators. . . . The legislature of 1903 was overwhelmingly Republican. . . . Senators were elected by a joint ballot of the legislature. Under ancient precedent, the nominee of the Republican caucus was made the nominee of the party, so the struggle in the election of the United States senators was to control the Republican legislative caucus. . . . On one side were friends and forces of Charles Curtis, a member of the national House of Representatives. Opposing him was a coalition between the friends of Representative Chester I. Long and Governor Stanley, each seeking to control what was obviously a majority anti-Curtis faction in the legislature. Curtis' tactics were to break the Long-Stanley alliance.

The railroads of the state, represented by their political attorneys, had great power. But they could not agree. The Rock Island Railroad was supposed to be for Curtis. The Santa Fe was neutral, with leanings toward the anti-Curtis crowd and in particular toward Chester Long. The Missouri Pacific was divided but finally swung into the anti-Curtis crowd. These railroad attorneys had great power to negotiate on their own, but they were nevertheless controlled by the railroad managers and owners in Chicago, St. Louis, and New York. The switch of the Missouri Pacific from Curtis to Long was made in St. Louis.

The power of state railroad attorneys lay in the fact that they could issue passes. Practically every member of the legislature came to Topeka on a pass. Generally the pass included members of their families, and if the legislators had any power, they could demand passes to and from Topeka for their friends at home. Imagine how the railroad passes controlled state politics in the last quarter of the nineteenth century and in the first decade of this century! Little money passed in the election of the United States senator, but passes talked the same language that money talks.

Yet scores of legislators were influenced more by personal friends than by rail-road attorneys. I was among the supporters of Stanley, and I worked on my friends to support him. I was one of half a dozen of Stanley's friends who worked upon the legislature. Long had as many friends, and Curtis had more. And we all descended like wolves on the foe. Cy Leland was in charge of the anti-Curtis forces. He said frankly that in the end he would support the man who could get the most votes to beat Curtis. Both sides had faith in him, and probably with reason. Both Long's friends and organizers and Stanley's reported to him, and the friends of both Long and Stanley united on a candidate for speaker and a candidate for state printer. . . . When we lined up the friends of the speaker and the friends of the state printer, who were more interested in them than in the United States senator, and then lined up the friends of two United States senators, who were more interested in the Senate than they were in the election of the speaker or the state printer, we easily elected a speaker and quickly elected the state printer. After that the patronage of the speaker was ours, a powerful weapon, for it meant the appointment of committees in the house, of doorkeepers, postmasters, janitors, and the like. I remember one day going with Henry Allen to round up a member of the legislature from Rooks, or maybe it was Decatur, County who had come down to the legislature with just one aim and ambition. He was a Civil War veteran. He wanted a job as janitor for a broken comrade, a one-legged man, to whom the three dollars a day for three or four months made quite a little nest egg, and the legislator was willing to swap a speaker and a state printer to be assured that his old bunkmate could have that little contact with the public tit. Of course Henry and I promised him, as we were authorized to do, what he wanted and we brought him into the campaign, triumphantly. He chose Stanley rather than Long, but we knew he would go with Long if it was necessary. At the end of the day, I walked into Mr. Leland's room, a Holy of Holies, and told him about my conquest.

"What did you have to pay?" snapped Leland.

"Assistant janitor, and we have got it. Assistant janitor," I repeated, "for Old Jim Higginbotham, the representative's comrade."

Leland looked up quickly and snapped: "Jim who?"

"Jim Higginbotham," I repeated.

"No, by God, no, by God!" he shouted. "Jim Higginbotham double-crossed me in the Osborne Convention (convention of 1876) when I needed him. No, by God!"

The Osborne Convention had been thirty years before, but the elephant remembered the man who had given him the red-pepper peanut. When I broke into a laugh, Leland looked at me for a second with flashing anger, which cooled, and he smiled grimly: "Nevertheless, we won't do it!" and turned away.

So Leland let the member from Rooks or Decatur County go to Curtis, badly as we needed him.

That's the way the game was played. The Republican caucus deadlocked for a week. Finally the Missouri Pacific moved its cohorts from Curtis to Long, on the promise that Long would support Curtis in the next senatorial campaign, with all the railroad attorneys concurring and affirming the bargain, so that the next senatorial election was decided in advance. The people had nothing to do with it. In order to get the support which elected him, Long went to the office of J. Pierpont Morgan in New York and pleaded his case. Morgan's railroad connection gave Long the backbone of his strength. And Long in the Senate was known as a railroad senator.

The rank and file of the Kansas people had no way to break up the plutocratic control of their state except to join the other states and change the federal Constitution to provide for the direct election of United States senators. Those senators elected in that way in the days when machines and the ownership of machines were passing into the hands of a class-conscious, organized plutocracy had no obligations to the people of their state. They were obligated to the machine owners in other states. In Kansas, it was the railroads. In western Massachusetts, it was textiles. In eastern Massachusetts, it was the banks. In New York, it was amalgamated industry. In Montana, it was copper. But the power which developed and controlled any state went to New York for its borrowed capital and New York controlled the United States Senate. Mark Hanna's plutocracy seemed unbeatable. The grade of senators, as far as intelligence went, was higher than the grade which the people selected, but on the whole and by and large it was not representative government. Only a minority of the people of the United States had any control over the United States Senate. And that minority was interested in its own predatory designs.

I saw it work in Topeka. I ran with the machine and I realized at the end of that session what a tin-cornice front for organized wealth our sham election of United States senators was. The day after Long's election my dear little friend, the old Major, came walking on his toes into the *Gazette* office, and after a gentle cough clearing his throat, said: "By the way, Will, I loaned Stanley and Long fifteen hundred dollars each to pay their own personal expenses at Topeka this month. I wish you would go to Long and ask him to take care of Stanley's note. Long will understand."

And he did, for the note was paid. The Major was playing safe. He was a good banker. But that, my dear posterity, in another day, is the way we chose United States senators when the state legislature elected our senators. The organizing capacity of keen, selfish minds in this country cannot be trusted to organize except in their own self-interest. . . .

I was in Washington a year or so later. I was sitting by the fire one evening in the White House with the president, talking over some casual matter, when he said: "By the way, what do you know about Judge Blub Blub (which, of course, was not his name)[4] . . . of St. Louis? I have decided to make him a federal circuit judge. He comes highly recommended by all the senators in the district and seems to be a man of parts and consequence, though he is a Democrat."

I knew Judge Blub Blub. He was a man to whom the Long forces appealed when they took the Union Pacific from Curtis. Judge Blub Blub always came to our state conventions in a private car and participated in Republican and Democratic politics with equal keenness and perspicacity. He was Jay Gould's political fixer for the upper Mississippi Valley—the very type of man who represented that "predatory wealth" which the president was denouncing. He knew the game—did Theodore Roosevelt—as well as I. So I told him the truth: that Judge Blub Blub had not appeared in a courtroom as an attorney for twenty years; that he handled the money for Gould in all the shady political transactions that Gould needed to perpetuate his empire. Then I explained, and Roosevelt got it before I was through explaining, why all the senators in that federal circuit came clamoring for Judge Blub Blub. Roosevelt snapped his jaws, showed his teeth and cried: "Well, by George, I almost bought a gold brick."

My answer to that was to advise him to talk to some of the honest congressmen of that circuit district. . . . I saw the president the next day. He had scratched Judge Blub Blub's name off the available list. However, later I ran into the Magnificent Chester I. Long, whom I had known for a dozen years, and I said: "Well, Chester, Judge Blub Blub is out of the running."

The senator smiled patronizingly, "So?"

And I said: "Yes, I saw the president scratch his name with my own eyes. Go talk to him."

Long literally jumped into the air with amazement. He cried out in sudden wrath: "Why, you, you, you—!"

He couldn't quite use the name. I grinned, and he whirled around and headed for the White House. And the next day when I saw the president, he said: "I had a lot of fun with Long."

And then someone came in and interrupted him. But Judge Blub Blub was out.

It is easy to see, when a system of corruption begins to mildew any section of government, how hard it is to check the blight. The nomination of Judge Blub Blub would have been secure and he would have held the rights of property in

---

[4]This refers to Alexander G. Cochrane, who was at this time the general counsel of the Missouri Pacific Railroad. Perhaps to avoid a possible libel suit, Cochrane's name was replaced in the 1946 edition of the *Autobiography* by the pseudonym "Judge Blub Blub."

that federal court like Leonidas at Thermopylae.[5] But Theodore Roosevelt, when he had the truth, was not afraid to defy senators, nor to discredit his party when it was wrong. He had courage and knew the game. . . .

But one must not presume that this was an unhappy country, oppressed by special privilege and extra-legal power. It was indeed a prosperous country, and the prosperity filtered down pretty well toward the bottom of the middle class. Millions of foreigners, coming into the country to take the rough, hard jobs, probably depressed wages and made the living standards of workers too low. But those foreigners who came in during one decade, either by their wits or by their strength rose out of the lower ranks, and their children had something approaching equal opportunity with the children of the better-placed parents in their community. Caste lines were not set. The flow up and down was unimpeded, from the top to the bottom of the scale. . . .

I saw a lot of the American continent in the decade of my thirties. Writing, of course, took me East. But I went into North Dakota once to write about wheat. Illness took me to California and brought me back by way of Portland and Seattle through the Northwest. Of course Sallie and I were riding on passes and occasionally we rode in private cars with railroad officials. I remember in those days meeting Senator William A. Clark of Montana, a curiously little dried-up, shriveled man . . . with a mean little voice and more arrogance than I had ever met assembled under one hat. I rode in his car for an hour or two with some other western railroad officials.

The mountain states were opening up in those days. Irrigation projects, mostly financed by private capital, were appearing on the great rivers of the West. And one afternoon, riding on the Oregon Short Line across Idaho with some officials of the road in their private car, we cooked up a scheme to buy some desert land which in a year or so would be under irrigation, and to start there a cantaloupe farm. We made a jackpot. The ante was low—less than a thousand dollars, as I remember. And the first thing I knew, I was in Boise and with the others was buying an entry-right for one hundred sixty acres of desert land. A former governor of Idaho transacted the business, and I was puzzled to learn when I offered my check that the money must be paid in gold. Now about that time Theodore Roosevelt began prosecuting the western timber thieves . . . who had bought these entry-rights from unimportant people. And suddenly my hair raised in amazement and genuine fear when I found they were sending men to the penitentiary for doing exactly what I had done.

I had my moments of anxious pause and was scared stiff. Here I was, fighting the United States senator from Kansas as a crook. Here I was, working with the

---

[5]Leonidas, king of Sparta in the early fifth century B.C., died with all his men, resisting the Persians at the Thermopylae Pass.

forces of righteousness in New York state—attacking Platt and Croker—and I myself had certainly violated a federal law and was liable to go to the penitentiary myself as a dirty corruptor of morals who had illegally acquired a quarter section of Uncle Sam's good rich land almost under the irrigation dam.

I did not know what to do. But finally I wrote to Senator William E. Borah, whom I had known in my student days at Kansas University. He knew Idaho laws and federal laws, and I told him the whole story as I have written it here and asked him what I could do to get out of the net. He replied quickly, seriously, and with affection that the best I could do was to deed the land back to the man who had deeded it to me, and he dictated a letter I was to send with the deed. I did it, and breathed below my collar button for the first time within a year. But I think I understood crooks better after that and lambasted them less cruelly. It was a great thing for me. Nothing is so good for an uptious person as a consciousness of guilt. It is the father of tolerance.

Also, in the middle of the first decade, I took my first real political licking. It came about with the election of Charles Curtis to the United States Senate. . . . Curtis was a Gould man, as I knew Chester Long was a Morgan man. But Chester was of my faction. Curtis was not. So my indignation boiled quickly at the subserviency of Curtis. I went to Topeka with the crowd that tried to defeat Charles Curtis. Two or three young congressmen—Dan Anthony, Phil Campbell, and Victor Murdock—were opposing him, but our crowd was working against the promise of all the railroads to support Curtis. We were nothing but starry-eyed reformers. The railroads cleaned us up in short order. And along about that time, in the files of the *Gazette*, will be found my first reform editorial.

It was an editorial directed at the evil of railroad passes. I certainly knew what I was talking about, for when I wrote that editorial I carried a system pass on the Santa Fe, a state pass on the Missouri Pacific, the Rock Island, and the Union Pacific, a telegraph frank and an express frank and, as a symbol of my thirty-third degree in the Sanhedrin of the boss's temple, a visiting card from Fred Harvey directing all Harvey hotels on the Santa Fe System to give me of its flamboyant nourishment. But I knew that the system was wrong, and for all that I had that hump on my back like a camel made from the big book of passes in my hip pocket, I sailed into that reform with fine indignation.

About this time I had another shock. I had gone into the Thunder Mountain region of Idaho to write a series of articles on the new gold boom that was rising there. . . . But I was cautious enough in my *Post* articles, though I told the truth about the unsolved difficulties. Then one day along came an offer from what looked to me like a reputable mining journal in New York for two thousand dollars for another article about Thunder Mountain. I wrote it and was amazed and ashamed—ashamed that I should have been such a sucker and ashamed of my profession when I read the article in that mining paper which had entirely distorted my viewpoint, which had even inserted puffs for certain mining enterprises that I did not believe in, and otherwise again mixed me up in scandalous proceedings. That men of wealth, if not of standing, could do such things, soured me on wealth, made me suspicious of the whole system which was institutionalized in the prestige and power of wealth. I narrowly escaped disgrace. Only luck and the fact that I answered scores of letters denouncing what the mining journal had done kept me from real trouble, but I was sore clear through at myself—largely at the social stupidity that was the foundation of many of my political views.

It was in [the] movement against railroad domination of politics that I came across the trail of the elder Robert M. La Follette. He had just gone through a successful fight in Wisconsin, leading it as governor, for the primary system, for the state control of railroads, for the reorganization of state government, for a state anti-pass law, and for reform taxation. And he was the hero of the young hopefuls of American politics.

It was curious that two men so entirely different as Theodore Roosevelt and Robert M. La Follette should hold the allegiance of hundreds of thousands of men of both parties—chiefly, however, young Republicans north of the Mason and Dixon line. They were mostly college men and they rejected Bryan. . . . They were thinking things through. Probably this was typical of the whole lot. They had grown up conservative and they had reaped in full measure the benefits of the conservative plutocratic democracy, with its convention system of nominations, its reactionary ballot laws which made it easy to vote a straight ticket and thus control city and state. They were a growing power in this democratic plutocracy, after they had come into it—and become a part of it—and tried its institutions and saw its evils.

But friendship, association with Theodore Roosevelt, and an intimate relationship with the governing powers in my state and, as my horizon widened, in the nation, gave me, as it gave hundreds of thousands of young men in their twenties, thirties, and early forties, a quickening sense of the inequities, injustices, and fundamental wrongs of the political and economic overlay in our democracy, which was keeping too large a percent of its citizens below average participation in the blessings of our democracy. It took a licking in the Curtis senatorial fight to open my eyes. The fact that from the private car I had walked straight to the threshold of the penitentiary also disturbed me deeply. . . .

When I went into that battle of insurgency, I knew full well that I had to walk circumspectly, that I was under the merciless eyes of a powerful enemy. And whatever virtue of word and deed I have developed in the last forty years of my life has not been, I fear, so much a deep and righteous conviction as it has been a lively sense that I had to walk straight or be tripped—and tripped to destruction. Time and again, in those first years, when I walked with the insurgents, I have caught myself withholding an itching hand. Time and again, I have painfully retracted a course that I began which might have brought quick gains but also might have cost more than it came to. I am not naturally a good man, but I have been scared to death so many times that I have learned regretfully but definitely that honesty is the best policy.

Kansas politics during those first years of Roosevelt's elective term were in a turmoil. A redheaded reformer, named Stubbs, was chairman of the state central committee. . . . A curious man was this Walter Roscoe Stubbs. He was a Quaker; had attended the state university a year or so, dropped out to go to work; had become a railroad contractor, amassed a fortune in his forties and appeared in his early fifties as chairman of the state central committee in the day of the Boss-Buster's victory over the Leland machine. He was a two-fisted slugger in politics. He introduced the long-distance telephone; spent thousands of dollars calling up leaders, organizing his progressive machine; and he was a good salesman and sold himself and his cause to young men. He talked an hour with me on the phone before I first surrendered. It was a Quaker exhortation to righteousness.

Under his leadership and that of Governor Hoch . . . Kansas abolished the [pass] system. . . . Kansas, after a desperate struggle, adopted the primary system. Kansas began to try to regulate interstate commerce and tried to establish a state oil refinery, but the courts checked that. Kansas gave her cities the commission form of government, with the initiative and referendum included. Kansas tried to do everything that La Follette had done in Wisconsin, as other states from New Jersey west to California were doing. And in those days I spent much time in Topeka, more than I have ever spent since, working for the Kansas reforms. I was the problem child of the state committee that was about four years behind the governor and the legislature. Political organization always is sluggard. I remember one day, sitting at a meeting in a committee, bubbling with carbonated ideas and getting set upon heavily by the chairman. It was in the days when Alice Roosevelt in the White House was going strong. Mort Albaugh, the chairman and regular to the core, looked over at me and said: "Bill White, sometimes I know just how your friend Roosevelt feels when he sees Alice coming his way!"

13

Happy Days

Alongside this turbulent, boiling stream of politics in the life of that young, fat, apple-cheeked political insurgent ran another current. . . . In Emporia we were rebuilding the town. We had been building square houses, two stories with rather wide eaves, sometimes square houses with brick or stone for the first story and wood for the second story. They were called shirtwaist houses and were right fancy. . . .

Our opera house was open three or four nights a week the year around. Generally the shows were cheap—ten, twenty, and thirty cents—[given by] traveling stock companies, and a good theatrical attraction appeared three or four times during the season. . . . The moving picture was a freak entertainment. It was installed in vacant store buildings twenty-five feet wide and maybe fifty or seventy-five feet long, with folding chairs for the spectators. It was a ten-cent show, often a five-cent show; the theater was called the Nickelodeon and the pictures were terrible. No one who amounted to very much liked to be caught in the Nickelodeon.

The automobile was just around the corner. Emporia had three in the first half of the first decade of the century. All the automobiles did in those days was to scare horses and provoke laughter. Major Hood's spanking sorrels, George Newman's big bays attached to their family carriages, and the scores and perhaps hundreds of one-horse phaetons, buggies, and traps rode around Emporia and went spinning along the dusty country road of a fine summer evening. When, at the end of the first half of the first decade, we put in a few blocks of paving in the town, the whole cavalcade rode up and down that paving in the summer twilight with relish and delight. There was even talk of good roads.

People played bridge, which then they called bridge whist, and the town supported several layers of whist clubs with naturally the Club, which rotated around the Hoods and the Newmans and the Warrens, at the top. And the news of their parties, indeed all in all the whist club parties of those days were chronicled in the *Gazette*, the names of the guests and prize-winners and sometimes we noted the prizes—chiefly cut glass and hand-painted china, most elegant and estimable.

In the summer the town's baseball team played the teams from other towns in Kansas in Soden's Grove. And of a late summer afternoon, the town gathered at these games with noisy loyalty and great excitement, the women in their best big hats and high sleeves and wide skirts, the men in what then were called shirtwaists, tailless shirts gathered with a rubber string under the waist just inside and below the trouser top—quite fashionable and exciting. The ballgame was the only public summer sport. We had a small swimming pool in a vacant building, for men only, who wore no bathing suits. As the summer closed, the horse races at the county fairs round about attracted the populace, and half a dozen men in Emporia owned fast-steppers which often they drove themselves—doctors, lawyers, merchants, railroad men. And the ownership of a good pacing horse gave a man distinction in the town.

We were ten thousand. We owned our light and water plants. We were beginning to use gas for cooking. The sewer was going down every alley. The old-fashioned privy was becoming extinct. Thus, another sign of social distinction was being wiped out. But the barn and the chicken house still survived in the town. The town herd still was gathered in the morning and brought home in the evening, and still old Tom Fleming, the city marshal, found most of his summer troubles rising from chickens that destroyed their neighbors' yards, flower-beds, and lawns.

It was curious how the turn of this century marked such a strange, quick change in our country. In those days the old machinery seemed to go with a rush. By 1901 the *Gazette* press was operated by the gasoline engine. We had six girl compositors in the new century, who were getting from three to five dollars a week, and we worked on an eight-hour schedule, sometimes overtime ran it to nine, rarely ten. Within a year or two after the century turned, we put in a linotype to save money. The girls married or found other jobs and we helped them relocate, and we set almost a third more type for about the same money we paid the girls.

The paper was growing. Our circulation at that time was around twenty-five hundred and we bought a new press—a web press—which cost seventy-five hundred dollars, printed papers five times as fast as on the old press, and the town and the country came in to see the wonder. Within three years after the first linotype, which I paid for by the month, we had bought a second linotype and were paying twice as much wages for setting up type as we were when the girls were doing it.

But a new thing was happening in the business world. Advertising was multiplying as fast as machinery was coming into the office, and Emporia merchants who ten years before had spent twenty-five or thirty dollars a month for an advertising card which remained standing often for a month, now were spending fifty, seventy-five, and a hundred dollars a month. They were proclaiming bargains. Page advertisements were frequently in the *Gazette* for special sales. Dry-goods men, hardware men offering new machinery and labor-saving gadgets but who were still advertising buggies and wagons, were our best customers.

The people of Emporia and Lyon County, our twenty-five hundred subscribers, someway were finding money to buy things which their fathers—the pioneers—did without and lived most comfortably. The milk separator on the farm was passing out. Milk, as a farm product, was coming to town in great cans to be distributed by milk dealers. The hen was helping the cow, and farmers were learning the value of breeds in all their livestock. Farming in Lyon County was becoming not a way of life but an industry. Hired men could no longer be had for ten or fifteen dollars a month and keep. Twenty dollars was the going price, and the farmers raged at the injustice of it. But the hired man demanded the keep of his horse and bought a buggy and came to town spruced up in store clothes.

The whole face of life in Emporia and in the world was changing. Nothing better illustrates the thing that happened in the world than what happened at the Emporia *Gazette*. When I walked into that office in 1895, I could do everything that I asked anyone else to do. . . . Ten years later, when I walked over the threshold of the mechanical room of the *Gazette*, I could not do one process that led from the copy desk to the printed page. The change had come that swiftly. But one thing I could do: I could take the heavy lead roller of the proof press, which weighed fifty pounds, and raise it above my head, straighten out my arms and repeat it ten times, which was more than any man in the office could do—and I had that much physical prowess to back my right to speak in that office. It was little, but it was something.

The gymnasium of the woods and fields and water that had hardened me in my youth held its strength during my manhood. All my life it has stood me in good stead. A man gets something from living near the earth, from running barefoot on the earth over the open field, and the waters of the creeks, and the sunlight on the prairie—something real yet something indefinable, which gives him a life inheritance in physical reserve. . . .

One day about this time, when I had cleaned up the last of my notes that paid for the *Gazette*'s new flat-bed web press and was rejoicing about it, in came W. T. Soden, an old-timer contemporary of my father in the fifties. He was a director of the Major's bank, a man of considerable means and substance, an Irishman with a long black beard and an ineradicable twinkle in his eye. . . . He came in, sat down, and evidently had brought his knitting. Something was on his mind. He came to it quickly. Said he:

"Well, Will, I have got a story to tell you, and I guess I can tell it now pretty freely. Listen: When I was a young man, just about the time of the outbreak of the Civil War, I was a young buck on the turf, and I had a little water flour mill here. (He was still the town miller, with flour dust on his clothes and in his black whiskers.) And your father, a man in his early forties, a dozen years older than I, lived here too. He kept store in addition to practicing medicine and used to go to Lawrence two or three times a year on a marketing trip. Well, one day, the federal soldiers, they were under Buchanan then and generally hated in Lawrence— were occupying the town, and either some soldier or some camp follower raped a girl in the ravine down back of what is now the Eldridge House, and the town was pretty mad about it. And by God, they thought I did it and they grabbed me. I expect they had some circumstantial evidence because, as I say, I was a young buck on the turf. But I didn't do it. I didn't have to in those days." And he smiled across forty years of not unpleasant memory. "Well, the crowd kept swelling and yelling: 'Hang him, hang him!' And I was scared pea-green. But I noticed at the edge of the crowd your father, in his white nankeen suit and his panama hat, elbowing straight through the crowd and coming straight to me with blood in his eye. He got on top of something, maybe it was a wagon, and began waving his hands, nodding his head, and cried: 'Hear ye, hear ye, hear ye!'

"And he took over the crowd. 'I know this man; he is a loyal Union man. He is a Republican and he runs a mill in Emporia and is a decent man. He didn't do this. He is not that kind. Let him alone. Give him time. Hear his story.' And after talking three or four minutes, I'll be damned if the crowd didn't break up."

Soden paused and looked at me and grinned: "You're doin' all right. I notice you got your notes all out of the bank; your account's in good shape."

I forget what I said in assent but I remember that, pounding my desk for emphasis, he said: "Well, by God, Will, I have watched you, and many's the time down there at the bank I have put my name on the back of your note, standing good for it. What less could I do? And now you don't need me, and I'm damn glad. You are your father's Yankee son. You've got money sense."

By that time he had put his hand on my shoulder as I sat at the desk and without another word said: "Well, I'll be going," and walked out. I had never heard of the episode he related. I had never dreamed that I had two friends in the Little Major's bank.

In the early part and middle of the first decade in this century, I became involved in the ancient Emporia town row. When I came here, and for twenty years before, it was a row between the banks. It made politics out of everything, bank politics. . . . It attached itself to things outside of politics. One of those things was a quarrel which was started by the county medical association against a doctor whose practice was irregular and whose personal and professional conduct offended them.

In this particular row, the doctors went to the preachers, the Ministerial Association. They also went to the state board in Topeka to demand a revocation of the enemy doctor's license to practice in Kansas. That, of course, threw the contention into state politics. The doctor involved deposited in one bank. The bank rallied its factional forces to him and the other bank wheeled into line and, before I knew it, I was the spearhead of the fight. I was supposed to take the matter to the governor and the state medical board, and did. The license was revoked. It took nearly two years. And that quarrel, which, of course, brought the doctor's patients rallying around, stirred the town to its foundations. Scandals were circulated in the form of affidavits. It was bitter and wicked on both sides. And because I had a lot of energy and no fear and a capacity for indignation which I called righteous, I was more or less the figurehead of the fight. And of course the little old Major and his bank stood by me.

The doctor appealed his case to the United States Supreme Court, trying in the meantime to spot machinery that would answer the appeal by getting dirty affidavits on his opponents. I was threatened but gave the doctor's friends the laugh. However, one day in the heat of it, I saw the Little Major and [Ike Lambert], one of my dearest friends in town, approaching the Gazette office from the south. I knew that my friend had been attacked with a blackmailing affidavit, rather terrible in its accusations. I felt in my bones they were coming to see me. When they appeared in the office, the Little Major sat down beside me, put his warm, hard, bony hand on my knee—a favorite gesture of his in the technique of his seduction of adversaries—cleared his throat and said, in his softest, most self-deprecatory voice: "Now, Will, here's a little matter in which you can help our friend." He nodded to his companion and went on: "Our good friend, the doctor" (which was bitter irony) "has got out an affidavit about our dear friend here and threatens to use it, and has told us that if we could just persuade you to drop the fight and let his appeal to the Supreme Court go unopposed, he would be glad to forget this affidavit!"

I had had just five minutes as I watched them through the window to make up my mind, to arrange my answer, and take my stand. It was the hardest thing I have ever done. I must have hesitated, moistened my lips, and managed to get out without much emphasis but feebly and finally so that the Major knew it was final: "Oh, Major, I just—I just can't! I mustn't do it!"

I looked at my dear friend. His face was distorted with fear and pain, but I shook my head. I did not dare trust myself to further language. I was tempted of the devil. The Major tried again: "You know, Will, you wouldn't have to do anything. All you would have to do is to do nothing more. You have done enough. You have shown the town and the state where you stand!"

He ended on a rising inflection like a question, and I knew all I had to do was just shake my head, and I did it—and finally got out a "No, no!" and I grasped the hand of my friend and said: "Old man, I just—I just—I just can't do it!"

And that ended the interview.

The United States Supreme Court finally, a year or so later, rejected the doctor's appeal; a rather important decision had been made that in matters of public health and public morals the state has a right to control finally the decisions of its boards and commissions. It was a fight worth making.

Then a funny thing happened. We printed the news of the court's decision in the *Gazette*. I tried to eliminate bitterness and thought I had done it. But probably the decision itself enraged the doctor and the sense of defeat angered his friends, for they persuaded the divorced wife of the doctor to lay in wait for me that afternoon with a rawhide. I saw her in a stairway about seventy-five feet from the *Gazette* office. I had the start of about twenty feet of her. She was handicapped by skirts. I grinned at her, giggled at her, waved at her, and ran like a whitehead. She never came within a rod of me. And the next day (November 18, 1904) I inserted this account of the episode in the *Gazette*:

Last evening at dusk as the editor of the *Gazette* was starting for home, a few yards from the office door he met Mrs. Delta Meffert, divorced wife of William Meffert, of whom mention was made in these columns recently. She was accompanied by a lady friend, and as the *Gazette* man started to pass, Mrs. Meffert pulled from her cloak a small but effective-looking whip. The editor of the paper side-stepped and did what every true gent would do; ran forty yards like a whitehead back to the office by the back door.

That calm dispassionate communion which a man holds with a situation in the sixteenth part of a second convinced the man in question that when a lady challenges a gent to an athletic contest of any kind, he cannot win a sparring match with any grace, nor be the victor in a wrestling match with a lady with any credit at all; but that a foot-race is the one event in the sporting calendar in which any gent may vie his prowess with any lady. And how he did run! Shooting the chutes, leaping the gap, or looping the loop are clumsy dilatory tactics, compared with the way that fat old codger hiked the hike around to the back door of his office.

That was the only way to handle the episode. But I must have made a funny figure covering those hundred-odd feet in three or four seconds flat, with the lady trying to take long steps in her hobbled skirt, waving her rawhide. When I got back to the office, a telephone call came from a lawyer friend telling me to watch out because he had just heard the lady was lying in wait for me, and he tried to warn me. Afterwards, though he was a Democrat, I did what I could to see that he had a term as county attorney, and later two or three terms as district judge. I tried to show the same degree of gratitude to my friends as I gave in indignation to those whom I made my enemies.

That episode and the uproarious ending I gave it strengthened me in the town. Of course, in a little town like that, everyone knew that the Major had failed to call me off from the fight and everyone knew how much it cost me to say "no" that day. And the attempt of the lady with the rawhide to avenge her friends of course advertised the victory over the doctor all over Kansas and even across the country, for of course the episode and my ribald editorial were used by the Associated Press. And I established a reputation for competent and determined righteousness in a local row that I probably would not have had except for the desire of the doctor's friends for revenge. . . .

The pleasant life in Emporia, at 927 Exchange, had produced in those days of the first Roosevelt three books and almost a hundred profitable magazine articles. . . . Our family was growing. Bill, the baby, was four years old when Mary was born. She was a frail baby. In those years of 1904 and '05 and '06, we lived all the summer months in Colorado, at Manitou near Pikes Peak. And of course I shuttled between Colorado Springs and Emporia many times. . . .

When I was alone in Emporia, I began writing a series of short stories reminiscent of my life around a newspaper shop. Each story was complete in form, yet they all strung together as an account of country newspapers in the eighties and nineties. As I was writing those stories and all the other articles, books, and such like word-carpentry, I wrote out the job and [Sallie and I] read it over and corrected it together, revised, rewrote, and revised again. When I sent two or three to George Lorimer of the *Saturday Evening Post*, he wrote eagerly for more and paid well for them, a thousand dollars each for most of them. . . .

After [their] publication . . . in a book entitled *In Our Town*, which had a considerable sale and more than passing vogue—Howells and all the critics reviewed it with some enthusiasm and Mark Twain wrote me a letter about it—[Sallie and I] decided rather formally, walking one day through the Garden of the Gods in Colorado in February 1905, to tackle a novel—a full-length, man-sized novel. For three or four months we talked about the mainspring, the central theme of this novel, for we knew then that the first need of a man who is writing fiction is to have something to write about—a story to tell with a meaning, a fundamental fable which has "hic fabula docet."[1] My favorite story of all . . . was the story of the prodigal son,[2] the young man who got too big for his breeches, who took his inheritance and went out into the big world and realized that he was not as

---

[1]A moral, or, roughly, "this story says."

[2]Luke 15:11–32.

smart as he thought he was, then got on his uppers, living among swine of various kinds, and finally arose and went back to his father's house. I suppose unconsciously that was the story of my own inner life. . . .

So our first novel became the story of the prodigal son. It was mainly set in the politics and economics of the last half of the nineteenth century. But it was more than a political novel. The hero was John Barclay, son of a pioneer Kansas mother; and her faith in some kind of moral law of gravitation toward righteousness was "his father's house." He went into life seeking money and power, and he got it. And in his prime, John Barclay saw that the money was husk and that the money-grubbers were swine, and he rose and returned to his father's house. That is the plot of *A Certain Rich Man*. We were four years working on it. . . .

In the summer of 1907, leaving the turmoil of politics, Sallie and I picked up the family—the two children and my mother—and set off for Manitou, Colorado, to finish our novel. . . . All day long I went into a little alcove on the porch that ran around our two-story cottage and hammered away on my Smith Premier typewriter, working on the story of my hero. . . . I knocked out over two hundred thousand words that summer. And to me it was a delight and a joy—all of it. Bill and Mary were little folks, one eight and the other four. They were good children and they and their mother and my mother shielded me and muched me. I had no physical cares or interruptions. I ate well and slept well and lived well and worked like a horse and was happy. "Heaven," says Thackeray somewhere, "is the place where all the parents are young and all the children are little!"

We went to New York in the early winter [of 1907] and spent nearly a month there seeing the shows, visiting friends, mostly among the writing people in the book and magazine world and absorbing the joy that comes to country people in a great city. I have seen New York grow from the little old town of the nineties to the imperial city that stands there now. It is a soul-shaking spectacle, this American metropolis—our capital in everything but politics and once the home of our ruling class. But I never saw it gloomier and shabbier, nor did I ever see the nation droop and wilt as we saw it wither under the panic of 1907. Factories that had been booming turned glassy-eyed windows to us. Inland towns in the Ohio Valley and Pennsylvania showed us crowds of idle workers on the streets as we whirled along. Cloth signs on store buildings in the little cities and villages advertised bankrupt sales. The banks were closed. Towns were issuing script in lieu of cash. Commerce and industry stopped dead-still. It was a terrible time. Before we left home, the town bankers called me into a meeting. They wanted the cooperation of the newspaper in establishing their script as temporary legal tender. Some way I feel that it was more dangerous while it lasted, which was but a few months, than the panic of 1933, or perhaps my eyes were keener and my heart more sensitive than they were nearly thirty years after this panic. . . .

When Sallie and I went to New York that autumn in the midst of the panic, we found no serious hindrance to our comfort and happiness. We went about the town as usual. The theaters were gay and the dinners were good. We knew many of the young reformers of the press and the magazines whom Roosevelt about that time was calling muckrakers, and they were busy and cheerful. One night on that trip Bob Collier, of *Collier's Weekly*, gave a dinner down at Martin's, a gay restaurant near Madison Square. There we had our first meeting with nobility, real British nobility—no one less than the Duchess of Sutherland—a famous beauty and a leader in high society in the England of that day. . . . Our first Duchess was a curious person. As we went home we wondered how she would fit into Emporia. We could not see her in the young bridge club. We certainly could not see her in the college faculty group. The bankers' wives would have rejected her—too much make-up! Her clothes were rather out of line for the best dressmakers in our town. . . .

We were glad to get home for Christmas where the stockings were hung over the fireplace in the workroom, where we gave everyone in the office a present and they all gave us presents and then all came out to the house and we had a big romping party and ended by gathering around the piano and singing. It was good indeed. They were our kind of people and I was entering the last year of my thirties. We both felt young—Sallie and I. At the holidays we always had a houseful of kin, and the panic, which had then passed its peak in Emporia, did not darken our doorway.

It was [during that trip to New York] that I met Mark Twain. John Phillips, one of the editors of *McClure's*, and Auguste F. Jaccaci invited Mark Twain to a luncheon and took me along, one autumn day in 1907. . . . The luncheon was at the Aldine Club on lower Fifth Avenue, an organization of publishers, writers, and master printers. And Mark Twain came in white flannel and a white hat. He wore a contrasting plain black bow tie. His hair was a fluffy halo of white around his head, and a heavy, drooping white moustache slightly colored by nicotine arched above a firm, strong mouth. During the meal sprightly talk went around the board. The table was set in a little private dining room fifteen by fifteen, near a window looking down on the avenue. After we had finished, Mark Twain lighted a cigar rather formally, with what seemed to me theatrical ceremony, puffed it a few times and then rose from his chair and began to talk.

Of course, I was a young man and did not quite comprehend what was going on. Our guest was putting on a performance for us. He paced the vacant area of the room in tracing rectangles and diagonals across the rectangles for two solid hours, and recited contemporary magazine articles which he had written and which heroized himself pretty strongly as a man who could not be imposed upon. He stuck closely to the text of his articles, which I had read and which I afterwards reread. It was an amazing thing to do—to give a two-hour humorous lecture about himself to three comparatively unimportant people. We had other appointments that afternoon. Phillips tried to stop Mark Twain, but he roared ahead like an engine on a track. His hands were behind him as he walked, slightly stooped, and he droned on—sometimes laughing at his own humor and sometimes indicating by facial grimaces a place for us to laugh. It was a conscious performance and greatly shocked me, though Phillips and Jaccaci had heard of our hero staging such acts before. But while we appreciated the distinction he was conferring upon us, we certainly were eager to get back to our afternoon's work. He did not realize that he had bored us. We parted pleasantly and I am sure he felt that he had greatly honored us and entertained us.

Men who knew Mark Twain—particularly Mr. Howells, whom I afterwards told of the incident—said that the oratorical habit was growing on him and declared that in his earlier days his sense of humor would have saved him from making such a spectacle. I am sorry, but that is the only memory I have of the greatest figure in American letters which the last quarter of our century produced. . . .

When Vernon Kellogg [wrote] to me about his bugs and biology, he put in a few purple lines now and then about a young woman author, Mary Austin, with whom he was enamored for the hour. She had written two books, *The Land of Little Rain* and *The Flock*, and he sent them autographed to us; we were greatly stirred by them. . . . She had written what I considered, and still hold, to be one of the great American novels—*A Woman of Genius*. I was excited about it and when I met her in New York at the National Arts Club down in Twentieth Street off Fourth Avenue, we ate together often, talked interminably, and I was convinced that she had a tough-fibered brain. She was vainer than a wilderness of gargantuan peacocks, a strong, overbearing woman. When she entered a group of friends, she at once took charge of the meeting and began to monologue. She was a mystic and believed a lot of interesting and uncanny, nonsensical things that were easy to discuss if one did not care to keep his feet on the ground.

For years after, when Sallie and I went to the National Arts Club, Mary Austin was there. She was addicted to gaudy shawls and the most God-awful hats that made her look like a battleship. . . . But Sallie and I loved her and took her to our hearts. Until the end of her days, nearly forty years later, Mary Austin was a familiar in our house and held a high dear place in our hearts. She was a thwarted spirit, a frustrated person who needed her man and her babies, and took it out in books and in many love dramas—some of which were written in her books and others graven with scarcely more reality than fiction upon her warm tender heart. But she talked well, lived honorably according to her code and thought strongly and as logically as a mystic can, was on the whole a most interesting, stimulating, and lovable person. Always we left her presence feeling that our minds and hearts had been kindled with new energy and refreshment. Some way her books, which gave out that same energy and delight, passed away when her body perished.

I was seeing more and more of William Dean Howells in those days. Once he gave a luncheon for me in his studio apartment on Fifty-seventh Street, and after lunch I remember that he took me down on Third Avenue to see little grocery and fruit stands there. He chatted amiably with the Italian keepers in their language and seemed to know them and understand them, and obviously they had great respect for him. He wanted me to see these gentle people and to know them. I wish he could have written a novel about them, but alas, they were beyond his depth and he was not enough of a reporter to learn about them and write about them superficially.

The book of mine which he liked the best was *In Our Town*. It was a newspaper story and it revived for him his newspaper days in Ohio before the Civil War. He used to tell me what fun he had writing editorials that would stir the rich southern blood across the Ohio in Kentucky. He was probably a homeopathic abolitionist, intellectually persuaded rather than emotionally, and that kind made the southerners rage perhaps more than emotional protagonists like Wendell Phillips or William Lloyd Garrison. He must have had an amazingly good time as an editor. He was graduated out of the printing office without much schooling, and his sense of humor was larded through his mind and heart so that he could not feel too deeply without a smile at his own rising intolerance.

As he moved about New York in the last ten years of his life, a struggling, bustling, raw, contemptuous place literally popping with the dynamic progress of the new century, he seemed to be detached and aloof from it all. He loved it but could not quite comprehend it; but was immensely pleased with it and hopeful about the picture. He was a Swedenborgian, a mystic, an addict of optimism, who could not take it or let it alone. . . . He had almost ceased writing novels when I met him, yet he has a fat sheaf of them to his credit, and they do portray American life east of the Mississippi and north of Mason and Dixon's line accurately, with solid, honest realism, even though they do not give much space to the short Saxon words which pass for realism now in the middle of the twentieth century. He discussed love in its rise, its glow, and its decay with a decent biological sense of the earthy texture of his subject. He was more, it seems to me, than a novelist of manner. He left a picture of the American scene that was revealing to his own generation and will be valuable to those who will return to his day and times. . . .

Often he put me up at the Century Club, and there I met many writing men of renown—men who had lingered over from another day and time. The distance was short in time and space from the Century Club, with its ancients and honorables, to the *Century Magazine* office on Union Square where Richard

Watson Gilder resided in a frowzy old office, book-lined, paper-strewn, charming, or to the office of *Harper's Magazine* far downtown, which seemed to be covered with the mold of *Harper's* antebellum antiquity, or to *Scribner's* . . . [which] in those fin de siècle days, was brighter, more alert, less covered with the hoarfrost of forgotten winters. But even so, those magazines—the staid old standbys of upper middle-class America in the middle 1910's—were still printing reminiscences of the Civil War, articles on archeology, stories of the old western ranchers and Indians, and novels by Mr. Barrie, Robert Louis Stevenson, and Hardy. Each magazine was produced after its own formula, discovered sometime in the seventies, edited by men in their fifties and sixties, and some who had reached their fourscore years and ten. . . .

I was fond of Mr. Gilder, and sometimes Sallie and I dined with him and his family down near Twelfth Street in a lovely museum of a house, furnished with rosewood furniture, rather scantily upholstered, and where we ate on heavy damask linen, with beautiful silver and exquisite china, all out of the reconstruction days. Gilder was a wraith of a man, one of the last living survivors of the New York mugwumps whom Theodore Roosevelt secretly adored and openly scorned. . . .

And when in my New York visits I left the sweet serenity of the Century Club and its literary hereditaments and I walked across Fifth Avenue and up into Twenty-third Street to go to the *McClure's Magazine* office, it was as though I had stepped out of some "ancient volume of forgotten lore"[3] into an unexpurgated dictionary of tomorrow. *McClure's* was housed much as a wholesale silk or hardware office would be housed. There were glass partitions reaching only half way to the center. There was clatter, noise, and bustle. There was method and every known gadget of managerial efficiency. There editors talked about new presses and new processes in printing. One saw blueprints. And if occasionally there were on the walls pictures of Mr. Kipling and other writers who were about to recede into the imperial past of a fading era, there also was Sam McClure.

Look at Sam McClure in his early fifties, a Swedish blond with a yellow moustache, big, sensitive but challenging eyes, and a sharp, hard but still ingratiating high voice snapping orders like a top sergeant, conscious—Heavens, how conscious—of his power and glory, yet concealing his complacency by self-deprecation. Sam McClure from 1900 to 1907, who was selling his magazine by the hundred thousands, who was a partner in a thriving book business that was conducted like a compromise between a broker's office and a textile mill—Sam McClure was among the ten first men who were important in the American scene. He was the pioneer of a reform that was to surge onward in American life

[3]In Poe's poem "The Raven," the narrator ponders "over many a quaint and curious volume of forgotten lore."

and run for forty years as the dominant note in our political, social, and economic thinking.

We used to say around the office . . . that Sam had three hundred ideas a minute, but J.S.P. was the only man around the shop who knew which one was not crazy. J.S.P. was John S. Phillips, a complete antithesis of Sam McClure. If Sam was a crackling motor, John Phillips was the governor and power belt that conveyed the force and drive of the motor to the manufacturing machine that turned out the finished product of the McClure corporation. John Phillips was perhaps half a head taller than Sam. Both were educated in Knox College at Galesburg, Illinois. John Phillips had gone on to Harvard. He and Sam formed a partnership, first at writing and selling advertising. Then they organized a literary syndicate and bought novels from the great figures of the nineties—from Howells, from Hardy, from Kipling, from Stevenson, from F. Marion Crawford, from Frank Stockton. Sam put them in a pack and peddled them personally to newspapers across the land. Sam was a born salesman, a fast talker, a go-getter. William Dean Howells, in his novel *A Hazard of New Fortunes*, put Sam like a bug on a pinpoint in the character of Fulkerson. John Phillips spoke softly but he carried a big stick, and the power of his club was his wisdom. Sam knew it; generally accepted it. But John was a man of books and vision and deep fundamental honesty of heart and soul and body, whereas Sam blew where he listed and had few restraints. He did not entirely realize where he was going nor know exactly what he was doing, but he was conscious of his hunches and that one in many was good. He had—and knew it—a spark of genius. John Phillips could blow on that spark and make it burn and set the land aflame with a strange new light, for John Phillips knew what it was and deeply respected it and consecrated his life and work to it. As McClure came into power he began to reject John's influence, to be irked by the bit and rein. When the rift between them came it was over what seemed to us, who followed John over to the *American Magazine*, a question of common honesty. Sam could not see it. That kind of insight was not his gift.

But in the middle of the decade we had left, John and a few of the others, with a little help from some of us, bought *Leslie's Monthly*, called it the *American Magazine*, and started out to carry the torch of an evolutionary revolution to the world. Around him, John Phillips gathered Ray Stannard Baker, Lincoln Steffens, Finley Peter Dunne ("Mr. Dooley"), Ida Tarbell, John Siddall, and what with the investments large and small of a few other eager souls with bank accounts like Charles R. Crane, Walter Roscoe Stubbs of Kansas, and a dozen others whose eyes saw the glory of the coming of the Lord, we had a magazine. It was an organ of propaganda wrapped in the tinfoil of a literary quality which at least reflected the temper of the times.

Among the centurions as Mr. Howells' guest . . . the Kansan who clipped his g's and was unashamed of his western brogue and lingo must have been an amusing exhibit. But with John Phillips and his crowd, or even with Sam Mc-Clure, the brusqueness, the breeziness, the colloquial metaphor and hyperbole of the brash young man . . . was not out of key or focus with his New York environment. For I had become in Kansas politics a bleeding reformer. . . . We were all fighting for a better world. We in Kansas were off the same piece of goods that Sam McClure was and John Phillips and two or three other monthly and weekly magazines—*Collier's*, for instance, and *Everybody's*, which was blazoning across the sky Tom Lawson's book on Wall Street.[4] We were all the inevitable products of our environment. We were doing what we had to do. . . .

It was in those years that I first met Albert J. Beveridge, a young United States senator from Indiana. He was an eager young man, so earnest that he could not smile easily and never giggled or tittered. His ambition was obvious and sometimes a bit ridiculous, but always innocent and shameless like a child's indecencies. His was a warm personality, gentle, kindly. He liked to talk sometimes sensuously and seemed to be stroking himself on the back with a pride in his oracular wisdom that was not offensive—at least not to me, for I knew that inside he was a noble soul. Sometimes he irritated President Roosevelt. The grand manner that Beveridge assumed so theatrically forced Roosevelt to swallow his risibles, and his regurgitated chuckles sometimes soured into annoyance.

One day in Beveridge's room I met a slim, handsome, silky-moustached, clear-eyed young man, a friend of Beveridge's, George W. Perkins, a young political representative of the House of Morgan in downtown New York. Beveridge told me in Perkins' presence that Perkins was his political godfather. The two of them had lived in Kansas in the middle eighties and Beveridge had tried to practice law at Dighton, Kansas, while Perkins had tried to sell life insurance at Wichita. A few weeks after that meeting I spent an hour or so with Perkins in Beveridge's apartment. Beveridge tackled me with: "White, why don't you go to the Senate? It can be arranged. Perkins likes you."

And I recall that Chester Long told me he had gone to J. Pierpont Morgan to make his senatorial "arrangements." I was scared. Whatever I was to be, I did not want to be in the United States Senate under "arrangements" made in Wall Street. There was no use saying this to Beveridge. It would only start an argument in which he would justify his suggestion. So I laughed at the absurdity of the idea and the matter dropped there. And in the end Beveridge said: "Well, don't ever forget what I have told you."

So I haven't, and here it is. I had come to Emporia for that self-respect, even bumptious self-respect, even for considerable conceit which comes with free-

---

[4]A former stockbroker, Lawson wrote "Frenzied Finance," a series of articles exposing Wall Street manipulations, which *Everybody's* published in 1904–05.

dom, and I knew enough to know that servitude to the House of Morgan, even with padded golden chains, would be servitude. Freedom is one of those things that is absolute or nothing. . . .

14

I Join
a Rebellion

In 1908 Kansas had her first statewide direct primary and had her first direct vote for a member of the United States Senate. There I entered the game of Kansas politics as a leader. United States Senator Chester I. Long was up for reelection. He and his friends represented the conservative faction in the Republican party. Governor Stubbs was the leader of the liberals, who in those days were called insurgents. Kansas rejected the word "Progressives," which La Follette had coined for his Wisconsin party. The Kansas insurgents were after Long's scalp and senatorial seat. Long had a friend named Joseph L. Bristow. Long's friends encouraged Bristow to enter the fight for the United States Senate. They felt sure that Governor Stubbs also would be a candidate. With two candidacies definitely against him, those of Bristow and Stubbs, Long could win easily.

It fell to my lot to eliminate Stubbs and to get him to run for governor—a job he did not care for. I knew Bristow could not be dislodged from his candidacy. Chief Justice Johnston, of the Kansas Supreme Court, was my patron saint. He called Stubbs to his office, and Stubbs and I, sitting on the leather sofa in the Chief Justice's room, went at it. We were there for an hour. I wore Stubbs down. It was one of the hardest things I have ever done. . . . Stubbs went out and announced to the reporters in his office that he would not run for the United States Senate but that he was a candidate for governor. It was a body blow to the Long forces. Henry Allen and I, a few hours later, saw Senator Long going out of a conference surrounded by his satellites—certainly a commanding-looking man, handsomer than a bird-dog pup but with an anxious face in that hour. They huddled together and trudged down the corridor and Henry giggled: "The retreat from Moscow."[1]

[1]When the French under Napoleon Bonaparte invaded Russia in 1812, they found Moscow abandoned and in flames. They were forced to retreat through the harsh Russian winter and more than two-thirds died on the way.

From that hour I made it my business to support Bristow.

Stubbs, in his gubernatorial fight, was fairly well assured of winning, for his opponent was on the wrong side and was the wrong man for the wrong side. But Senator Long was backed by federal patronage, so it was an uphill fight for Bristow.

That was 1908, but a similar fight was going on in a dozen northern states in that year in the Republican party. Nationally, La Follette rather than Roosevelt was the leader of the revolt against the Republicans in the United States Senate in 1908. . . . I went to La Follette and asked him to have his office compile the voting record of Chester Long in the House of Representatives and also in the Senate. It was a bulky document. There, by page and chapter, La Follette had recorded a long list of unbroken conservative votes which Representative Long, and later Senator Long, had cast in Congress. It was a black record in the eyes of the Kansas voters. I took it and tried to give it vitality. I explained the significance of each vote. I prepared the manuscript in triplicate, divided it into three sections, and sent it to the Kansas City *Star*, to the Topeka *Capital*, and to the Wichita *Eagle*. I wrote a stirring introduction and a rousing closing for each article, and ended every diatribe with an address to the voters, which closed with this paragraph:

"Will you help?"

I began publishing that record in the spring, and by June I had collected enough money to make boiler-plate stereotypes of my three articles and send them to friendly country daily and weekly papers. I covered the state. It cost three thousand dollars. Most of it I put up myself. Heaven knows I could not afford it, but I did.

Certainly it aroused Kansas. I had been Long's affectionate friend. When Stanley failed of election to the United States Senate in 1903, I was one of those who persuaded Stanley's men to go to Long. I had cautioned him against making too conservative a record. He thought I was mildly mad in those days; so when the record was made, my attack was savage, I suppose, and he felt its effect. Moreover, Bristow was going over the state, a lone figure, making speeches on street corners, in opera houses when his friends in a town would hire them, in schoolhouses at crossroads—covering one county after another. He also was reciting that record to the people. It was new tactics. It was winning.

Long came home from Washington. A rich banker at Wichita had lent him a big, black, shining, brass-bound automobile. He toured Kansas in it. Charley Knowles, the editor of the Leon *Indicator*, lent Bristow his old bay mare and a rattlety-bang buggy when he campaigned in those counties. A similar shabby equipage took Bristow from town to town. He was a tall, lean, gaunt Kentucky-bred creature, hungry-faced, fiery-eyed. He looked like an animated cadaver. He had a long arm and a long bony hand, with a point on it like Banquo's ghost.[2] When he directed it at the well-kept, well-tailored figure of Long as he orated, he challenged him to answer. That also was a new figure in Kansas. The contrast between that lean hungry figure and the fine, florid, broad-browed, deep-voiced, well-fed Senator Long was damning, for the Kansas people had just been through the panic of 1907.

The tide was turning against Long. He came to Emporia to meet me, and asked me to go on the stage and respond to his reply to my charges against him. Of course I accepted. The opera house was crowded. His defense mainly was that he had voted in line with the recommendations of the Republican party caucus—a defense that pleased only those who were ironclad Republicans. Senator Long could not conceive that the state was in the midst of an insurgency and with that defense was anathema itself.

La Follette had made three mistakes in compiling the record. They were Long's trump cards. He faced me with them. There was nothing for me to do but to rise and admit they were mistakes—three out of nearly fifty in the indictment. The others stuck. By my admitting my wrong and thereby apologizing for those three mistakes, Long's friends thought they had scored a triumph. They were exultant. Their papers said I had withdrawn my charges, which everyone knew was untrue. I was terribly cut up the next day to think that even three of the counts in my indictment had to be withdrawn. But with my humiliation came wrath, and I went at it hammer and tongs. I loaded the papers full of the general charges, withdrawing absolutely the three mistaken counts.

Roosevelt, in the White House, did not dare to give us encouragement. He had to get along with the Congress, and the Republican representatives and senators, many of them, were under attack. To join the foes of these congressmen would have precipitated a fight on the president in Congress. He gave me many a cheer behind his hand in Washington, but he did not say the word that would have helped me to defeat Long. But La Follette did.

I rented a circus tent in Kansas City, pitched it in our high school yard, brought La Follette to Emporia, gave him a great meeting there, took him to three other similar meetings in the state the week before the primary. Standing under the tent on a hot afternoon, La Follette held a chunk of ice in a towel to the back of his neck while he spoke, held the record in the other hand and waved it for gestures. He talked three hours. And certainly La Follette read Long's record and all the changes thereunto appertaining to an eager, serious, sweaty multitude.

Long, knowing of Bristow's raucous voice, his awkward manner, his halting

---

[2]In Shakespeare's play, Macbeth is haunted at a banquet by the ghost of the nobleman Banquo, whom he has had killed.

speech, challenged Bristow to a series of debates. That was a terrible mistake. The crowds were with Bristow. Long struggled to keep a front but his courage waned. The last debate was Bristow's from the start. The retreat from Moscow ended in calamity. In the primary, Long was defeated for United States senator; Stubbs was nominated for governor; and a number of Kansas papers hailed me as the new boss.

If I was a boss, I had no desire to be one; I was not in the least interested in patronage. I cared nothing and never have cared for organization. But I did believe in the mass appeal. Obviously, I could make it, and I took my place among those of the first rank in Kansas politics when the old convention horse-trading system went out and the new primary, with its direct vote for nominations, came in. I had functioned fairly well under the convention system, and with the legislative election of the United States Senate, but it all irked me. . . . The primary was a new boon in Kansas. I knew how to swing it, and I was of the younger generation.

We, who had begun as young rebels in 1890, two decades later in the prime of our manhood were in control of the state and we dominated the statehouse. We were in the majority in the House of Representatives in Washington. Now in 1908, we had the governor and the United States senator in Kansas. It was our day of triumph. I record this only because similar contests were going on at the latter part of the first decade of the 1900's in Iowa, in Illinois, in Indiana, in Michigan, in Pennsylvania, in Massachusetts, in New Hampshire, in Wisconsin, in the Dakotas, in Minnesota, in Colorado, in Wyoming, in Montana. The fight was spreading to the Democratic party where Bryan led the liberals. The primary system gave the liberals an effective weapon against their conservative opponents. Fights like our Kansas fight were being won in those years, everywhere. . . .

That year Jane Addams came to visit us—a large, wholesome, eager, earnest woman, with a real sense of humor and a deep purpose showing forth from her glowing eyes and kindly face. Presently, Sam McClure, editor of *McClure's Magazine*, came out for a visit and insulted our hired girl when he left by trying to slip a five dollar bill into her hand. She was not used to it, and indeed it was not the custom in the West to receive tips from guests. Sallie had trouble explaining to her that Mr. McClure's intentions were entirely honorable.

That year we travelled a long summer's day with Taft, when before his nomination he was out going through the rather empty forms of canvassing the country in his own behalf. If ever there was a folksy man in his ways and manners, it was William Howard Taft. He stood a good six feet two or three and must have weighed around three hundred pounds. . . . He was full of anecdotes that portrayed him as the common man. There was no Yale about him. One forgot he was the son of a federal circuit judge who had married a girl with a rather long upper-class lineage. Neither Sallie nor I realized at the end of the long day that this genial, chuckling, courteous, kindly gentleman was in his heart a deep-dyed political and economic conservative, and bull-headed at that. I wrote a piece about him for *McClure's Magazine*, portraying him as a sane liberal, and I really believed it.

In 1908, as a reporter, I attended the Republican national convention which named William Howard Taft for president. That was a curious convention and, in reporting it, I saw how little enthusiasm those delegates had for Mr. Taft. They cheered the reactionary leaders. Joe Cannon was their idol—not Taft. But they obeyed vox populi, which was the bidding of Theodore Roosevelt in the White House. I sat for several days at odd times during the convention beside Alice Roosevelt, and she knew what a hollow victory was Taft's in that convention. Two years before, she had married a rising young conservative congressman, Nicholas Longworth. She knew what was going on. She gave me the tip that gave me the beat over all other correspondents in that convention. So I was able to announce that James Sherman, the most reactionary of the Republican congressmen, would be nominated by the convention for vice president. It was the revolt of the conservative Republican party against the liberal leadership of Theodore Roosevelt, the young president. If ever a convention was cut and dried, it was that convention. If ever a convention showed its contempt for its master, that convention showed it for Theodore Roosevelt—and his daughter knew the truth. All of the world of change that was abroad in the land, all the new spirit of revolt and liberalism, the Republican party that year rejected in scorn, with the Sherman nomination. . . .

In the year 1908 William Jennings Bryan was nominated for the presidency by the Democratic party for the third time. It was his last race. He had no opposition of any consequence in the convention. His twelve years of leadership in the party, scarcely broken by the revolt against him in 1904, when Parker—a reactionary—was nominated, had a curious similarity to Roosevelt's leadership in the Republican convention. A section of the national Democratic convention was for Bryan—a noisy section. Obviously the sentiment of his party rank and file was for him. But, as a reporter in that convention, I felt a majority of the delegates accepted Bryan, even licked the spoon, but screwed up their faces in some disgust. The party was not yet liberalized. The people of the country and the leaders, Roosevelt and Bryan, were going faster than the party regulars approved. The political machines functioned without conviction. . . .

I had a pretty good opinion of myself after the defeat of Chester I. Long. . . . I was the cock of the walk, a young radical, but not so young—I was just out of my thirties, with something of a literary reputation and about to finish my first novel. It had been retyped for the third time and had gone to New York, where the elder George P. Brett, head of the Macmillan Company, had accepted it with what for him, a rather cold-blooded Englishman, was mad enthusiasm. . . . If I strutted a little, I should not be blamed too heavily. If I put a little too much complacency into my smile, that also would be granted to me, considering how blind I was. I was a bubble on a swiftly moving current. . . . All of my associates at home and everyone I knew or worked with in New York ranged in political opinion from liberal to radical. . . . We who were the leaders of that day, rejoicing as a bridegroom coming forth from his chamber, we were strong men running a race. How little did we realize that we were merely reflexes of deeper changes.

The rise of commercial credit in the world, made necessary by the introduction of machinery into industry, was remaking all relations between labor and capital. The farmer was beginning to realize that the farm was no longer a way of life but a part of a great agricultural industry. Consolidations were everywhere, great trusts were forming as the result on the one hand of manufacturing units and wider distribution across the land and over the globe of the products of industry, and on the other hand of the need for capital to finance these inevitable growing units of industry. The panic of 1907, the defeat of Chester Long, the rise of the radical magazines, the appearance of Socialists at reasonably respectable dinner parties, the tremendous vogue of Theodore Roosevelt and of my novel, *A Certain Rich Man*, which was an attack upon the commercial spirit of the age—all of that movement, politically called insurgence in America, was the response of a new stimulant to the life of the world-expanding capital in the form of growing credit. It was all the product of the machine age.

How could I, looking in pride that August night of 1908 when a great crowd gathered around the *Gazette* office to read the primary election returns, how could I know that my victory in Lyon County and in Kansas was not of my doings? If it had not been I, sitting on the cow-catcher flopping my wings inside and crowing in my heart while I assumed my sweet, modest, Christian attitude, it would have been someone else. For change was abroad in the world. Four linotypes in the Emporia *Gazette* office, doing the work of a dozen or fifteen printers, the new web press printing *Gazettes* three or four times as fast as we could print them on the old cylinder press were merely symptoms of what all the world was experiencing. . . . And I, in Emporia, a mere pip-squeak, singing a squawky little political and industrial radicalism, thought I was somebody; fancied I was a part of the chorus that the morning stars sang together.[3] I did not realize until many years later, that I had floated—a mere bubble—on the swift-moving current of the change that was coming over humanity and that was remaking the world.

[3]"The morning stars sang together, and all the sons of God shouted for joy" (Job 38:7).

15

The Europe
Which Has Vanished

The year 1909 was memorable in the life of the White family. It began with a letter from President Roosevelt asking us to come to what his letter declared would be his last and nicest party. This party was to be the White House reception for the Army and Navy. With the letter he sent a gold-embossed invitation, rather gaudy for the Roosevelt of that day. So we packed up and went to Washington. . . .

[It] was all that the president had promised. It was a gold braid occasion—the Army and Navy in full dress, the diplomatic corps in full regalia, and their wives dressed to kill. The cabinet was there, a few special members of the Supreme Court, and perhaps a dozen friends like us. As we passed by the Roosevelts on the reception line, the president pulled us out of it, turned us over to a young aide who took us upstairs into the private apartments of the Roosevelt family. There gradually assembled fifty—maybe a few more—special friends. When the line went past and the reception downstairs was done, the president came storming up into the parlor where we were gathered, and I can remember I was standing by a door which led into a toilet somewhere near. I tried to stop him to say something and he gave a great "Ugh!" and said: "I'll be back in a minute. I have got to wash my hands." And another "Ugh!" "Shaking hands with a thousand people! What a lot of bugs I have got on my hands and how dirty, filthy I am!" He came back a few minutes later and resumed where he had broken off: "Now I am clean. I always do this after a reception. You should remember it. It may save your life some time!"

In a few moments the company formed and went downstairs. There were a score of small tables. On the sideboard was a buffet supper—and a good one, for T.R. loved good, plain, palatable food and lots of it. . . . The talk was leisurely and good. In those last days, as in the last days of any outgoing president, the White House was fairly well deserted. The sycophants were gone, for the outgoing president has nothing to give. The Tafts were forming their own center. In

Congress, the president's recommendations were being kicked around and scorned. But he had delivered a scorching message to Congress blasting the idle rich, using the words "predatory wealth" and shocking the daylights out of the congressional conservatives, particularly Joe Cannon, who publicly damned the president, and Aldrich, who carefully sneered at him, much to the delight of the president. I can remember hearing him snort like an elk in his high falsetto about it across the tables to Justice Holmes.

The whole occasion was a gay one. It was indeed his nicest party. And as the supper guests were leaving, he put out his arm and called back Sallie and me and we went up to the White House living room. He stood by the fire and we sat on the lounge nearby. Mrs. Roosevelt came in, probably to warn her husband to bed, but we stood there reviewing the party, talking over the isolation of the White House and the scornful attitude that Congress had assumed toward him. He took it in glee. . . . In a few moments we left. It was our last White House reception for thirty years, and we were thrilled to the core. We were easily thrilled to the core in my earliest forties and Sallie's very latest thirties.

We hurried home to prepare for our first trip to Europe. We were all going— the children and my mother, aged seventy-nine and more vigorous than either of us. . . . The children were little. Mary was going on five and Bill was going on nine. But we felt they would get something out of the trip, and they did. It was high adventure for the White family. We had been saving for ten years in a building-and-loan and had scraped together three thousand dollars, with all our debts paid. It seemed like wealth beyond the dreams of avarice. . . .

In that far day, when we had less than two score blocks of paving in Emporia and were immensely proud of it, any Emporian's trip to Europe was a matter of townwide interest. So the week before we sailed our friends gave us a going-away party—a beefsteak dinner of considerable proportions at the Harvey House. All the automobile owners were there and many of the conservatives who still drove horses. But the drivers of the more spanking teams—merchants, princes, lawyers, bankers, and doctors, that also was a rather spacious group—made speeches at us. There was a lot of kissing at the end and a few tears as we left for the ends of the earth. . . .

Probably nothing on the trip impressed the children and their grandmother more than eating on the dining cars between Emporia and New York. My mother got her delight vicariously through the children. They ate a wide swath down the menu card and she insisted that we give them what they wanted, on the theory that naturally we were stingy, cruel parents who would starve our children but for her. Our boat, a dear old tub called the *Cretic*, which perished ten years later in the first World War, sailed [from New York] the latter part of March. On the dock, as we sailed, were our magazine friends—John Phillips, Ida Tarbell, Ray Stannard Baker; some flowers from Howells, some fruit from the

House of Macmillan, and a parting floral salvo from Emporia, I think—as I remember it, from the chamber of commerce.

How wonderful everything seemed to us on the *Cretic*! It went the southern route, stopping at Madeira and the Azores, going through Gibraltar, and landing us in Naples. Nothing seemed more romantic to us than this sea voyage. Our only ocean experience had been on the Fall River Line from New York to Cape Cod. I paced the deck and figured that it was as long as an Emporia block, and I was tremendously impressed by the size of the little tub. The passenger list was not large. After two days out I knew everybody. So did the children. And on the third day, Mrs. White and my mother had become oriented socially. I went below at the first gentle breeze. I always do. Until we got to Madeira I saw more of the pattern of the springs above me in Mary's berth than I saw of the bounding billows. I have always thought that the ocean was a mistake and that God should have fired the angel who made it. It has kept the world apart too long, and it is too wet anyway and a waste of space. Also, it turns my stomach and I hate it even now after having crossed the Atlantic ten times one way or another, and having traversed the Pacific to the Philippines and back, and again to Hawaii. . . .

In any account of my life this first trip to Europe deserves emphasis. It was a milepost. In the new environment of Europe, I saw myself in perspective. And, as Kipling puts it, "I stood beside and watched myself behaving like a blooming fool,"[1] and I enjoyed it. . . .

The civilization was different in Switzerland and more or less in western Europe from that we saw around the Mediterranean. . . . The air was full of hope, visions, plans for betterment. Politics, which we did not encounter on the Mediterranean, nor understand when we touched it in the north, became a struggle for economic advance. The Swiss were using their initiative and referendum to establish human welfare under government. When we came into Holland and Belgium, the Socialists were obviously taking charge of political leadership, though they were not in a majority. Often as we talked to people in hotels, on the streets, and in the stores and shops, and gossiped with our various guides in Amsterdam, Antwerp, the Hague, and Brussels, we remarked that the Kansas boss-buster movement which gave us Old Stubbs as our leader must have slopped over the Kansas boundaries into Holland and Belgium, and in Germany it was obvious that the Social Democrats, more or less with a wink and a nod from the Kaiser, were establishing all sorts of institutions to provide for social and industrial justice, and [upgrade] the living conditions of the workers. . . . The same energy and largely the same purpose that animated us

[1]The line is from "For to Admire," one of Kipling's "Barrack-Room Ballads" that draw upon British working-class dialect: "Oh, I 'ave come upon the books, / An' frequent broke a barrick rule, / An' stood beside an' watched myself / Be'avin' like a bloomin' fool."

was stirring in northern Europe between the British channel and Russia. . . . Over and over we remarked as we went through Western Europe that we were among our own kind of people. Italy and the Mediterranean were more fun, but northern Europe was more comfortable to us than life in the Mediterranean.

In Paris, we . . . [were] conscious of the fact that the Stubbs rebellion was on in France. Labor troubles often broke out. The waiters at the hotels, who spoke English, told us that the struggle for an eight-hour day was on. They also were beginning to realize that old-age pensions were a part of any just establishment of human relations. . . . It struck me as interesting and deeply significant that we found in continental Europe the people perhaps a decade ahead of Kansas and the United States in the matter of labor and agricultural legislation, and my faith was strengthened in the righteousness of the Kansas struggle by finding that it was a part of the world agitation. . . .

A few days before we left England, [we had one last adventure]. . . . For days the newspapers were talking about the great parade that Lloyd George was backing, to demonstrate for his budget bill. The budget bill was [revolutionary] . . . for it proposed a tax on land, a deep gouge in income tax on the rich. Moreover . . . Lloyd George's supporters were saying that if the House of Lords opposed the budget, the Commons would take away its power of veto. Revolution was in the air.

We were anxious to see the parade, so immediately after lunch one summer's day we hired a rattle-bang old taxi, all of us, and sallied forth. I never saw such a parade before. Organizations from all over England, Wales, and Scotland were on the march—laboring men, farmers, farm workers, miners, clerks, the little people of England. They were singing as they marched. Bands were blaring, drums rolling, and it was almost orderly. They even kept step, many thousands of them. Hundreds of thousands were in line. For an hour we rode up and down alongside the procession where the police would let us cruise.

I began to see old banners that I had seen in the Populist parade fluttering in the air. Among them were a lot of Jeffersonian mottoes that gripped at our hearts. Pretty soon, in the midst of a battalion of Welsh miners who had bands fore and aft, came, on a purple banner lettered in gold, the Jeffersonian slogan I had heard in the days of the Greenbackers and the Grangers and that I had seen coming down Main Street at El Dorado and Commercial Street in Emporia, when the Farmers' Alliance and the Populists appeared: " 'Equal rights to all; special privileges to none.'—Thomas Jefferson."

How often my father had quoted that when he talked politics on his hundred forty-four feet of porches around the old White house in El Dorado. It was too much for me. I tapped my taxi driver on the shoulder and said: "Wheel in there behind that banner if you can!"

He could, and did. And that taxi load of Kansans, old and young, rolled slowly into the line and followed the banner for half an hour. We had to stop sometimes. It was a slow pace for a taxi. But I thought of Stubbs and Bristow in Kansas, and of Roosevelt and his fight for seven years in Washington. And I knew that old Bob La Follette would have crowded into the taxi if he had been on the sidewalk. And we were all proud and happy to follow his Jeffersonian flag in the great British revolutionary parade. It was the high day of our trip thus far. . . . As we rode in the procession in a rattle-bang old hack, and as I closed my eyes and heard the same old tunes from the bands along St. James's Park that I heard in Kansas—"John Brown's Body," among others— . . . I was stirred to the very roots of my being. Sallie and I held hands and when I opened my eyes through my tears I saw hers. We felt that we were a part of something great and beautiful. We did not know exactly what, except that we knew the under-dog had slipped off his leash and this was his time to howl. So in our hearts we gave voice for him and with him. . . .

We picked up our ship, the *Cretic*, for the home voyage at Queenstown (now Cobh), [in Ireland], and our great adventure closed. . . . Sallie and I settled the children and their grandmother in their cabin and then after breakfast we came out on deck. We were parading up and down, arm in arm, and probably hand in hand, when my eye was caught by a New York *Times* in the hands of Franklin Hurd of Chicago. He was reading the paper, and on the side facing the deck I saw to my amazement—almost to my horror, so close are delight and fear—a half-page advertisement. I caught the words "A Certain Rich Man," and my own name in block type, and then the words "fourth large printing." I grabbed Sallie and we shamelessly stood trying to read the advertisement on the one side of the sheet while Mr. Hurd read the news on the other. He caught us at it. And, seeing our interest, offered us the paper. We tried to protest faintly but took the paper and there saw the solid evidence that *A Certain Rich Man* was making a hit in the United States. There were highly flattering excerpts from critics; the leading literary commentators of the United States were offering their praises. But that phrase, "fourth large printing," told the tale. Our eyes glistened. We took the paper, folding it almost reverently, and hurried to our cabin. There we sat on the side of the berth and read it all with mounting and mixed emotions. Then almost automatically we turned, because there was noth-ing else to do in God's wide world, and slipped on our knees and said a little prayer of thanks. That moment was a high moment in our lives. . . .

At the dock . . . a crowd of welcomers from the *American Magazine* met us, helped us through the customs, and took us to our hotel. That night, to end the journey in a blaze of glory, we went to Coney Island, and there the children and my mother really had the thrill of the journey. My mother wore us all down, tired out the children, doing everything, riding the Ferris wheel, buying taffy, eating the gala food in stands and cafés, slam-banging through the Crazy-Cat

House and riding on the roller coaster. Across one of the avenues of the Coney Island carnival was the great glittering sign "Ain't It Grand to Be Bughouse." We adopted it as the family motto for our coat-of-arms if we should ever get one, and went home limp and weary. . . .

In New York we had learned that the sales were moving along. We had a good contract with the publisher, and the royalties were coming in heavy and fast. In the end, what with various editions, . . . the book sold a quarter of a million copies.

As we came into Emporia, we ran into the town's surprise for us. There was the band. There was a crowd, and as we stood on the platform we began to see men and women in strange old-fashioned costumes. The town and half a dozen friends in the state had worked out some sort of a costume party of characters in *A Certain Rich Man*. The costumes were of the seventies and eighties. The characters gathered around us, picked us up—all of us, including the kids and their grandmother—and took us down to the grandstand in the park by the station, and the characters from *A Certain Rich Man* began to make speeches at us. Whereupon Sallie and I bolted. We just couldn't stand it. It was tragic, and funny, and pathetic, and absurd, and dear. So we ran to the phaeton where Old Tom was hitched nearby, climbed in with the multitude trailing behind us. Someone grabbed the hereditary appurtenances of the family, put them in a neighbor's buggy and some way the band got ahead of us and we sailed through the streets of Emporia to our home, trailing clouds of glory. There the crowd caught up with us, the band played, and they all sang "Home Sweet Home." And the children made a bolt for the barn and their playthings, and their grandmother went to her home next door and began cooking with all her might and main. And finally all the neighbors left the house and we were alone and happy. The great European adventure was over.

So in the procession of my life—which had seen Willie White come and fade into Will White; and Will White grow up and become Will A. White, the poet— in that journey across the sea, another—perhaps not a more dignified figure but one a little bit more self-important—William Allen White came to his own and began to merge into still another: a man called "Bill"—Bill White, who was taking more and more part in the politics of his state and his nation. He was somebody. And the struggle of his life in that day was to keep people about him from knowing how keenly he realized it. So I tried to make modesty a protective habit and a mask. . . .

16

The Battlelines Form

I set to work immediately writing a series of articles on the political changes that were in the air, afterwards published in a book called *The Old Order Changeth*. It was an attempt to define the issues of the day, new issues then in politics but now a generation old, and to chart the course of the new movement. . . . I worked hard on it and did what I thought was a research job, writing to official sources in every state, getting a list of the new measures passed there, and really outlining definite trends.

Politically the people were feeling for new weapons of democracy: the secret ballot, called "the Australian ballot"; the primary; the direct election of United States senators; the initiative, referendum, and recall; a commission form of government in the cities; and other laws amending the registration laws which brought down part of the control of the citizen. In the economic field the movement which Theodore Roosevelt was calling "a square deal" advocated an income tax amendment, postal savings banks, parcel post, regulation of the railroads, prosecution and breaking of the trusts, a pure-food-and-drug law with state laws to support it, extension of laws promoting public health and hygiene, shorter hours for labor, collective bargaining—and this was the catch phrase, "with representatives of their own choosing"—workingmen's compensation laws, state and national extension of the civil service, the movement for good roads, the regulation and control of insurance companies, banks, and savings institutions. . . . Along with this movement commencing at the beginning of the century was the sweep toward national prohibition. . . . In the West where the Puritan tradition still held, they believed that it would work for economic good. So it was a part of "the movement.". . . Along with *A Certain Rich Man*, *The Old Order Changeth* had its place and did its work in its time.

That decade which climaxed in 1912 was a time of tremendous change in our national life, particularly as it affected our national attitudes. The American people were melting down old heroes and recasting the mold in which heroes

215

were made. Newspapers, magazines, books—every representative outlet for public opinion in the United States—was turned definitely away from the scoundrels who had in the last third or quarter of the old century cast themselves in monumental brass as heroes. The muckrakers were melting it down. The people were questioning the way every rich man got his money. They were ready to believe—and too often they were justified in the belief—that he was a scamp who had pinched pennies out of the teacups of the poor by various shenanigans, who was distributing his largess to divert attention from his rascality. . . .

But the point of it all, as I look back upon it now after nearly forty years, is that the leaders . . . were the product of their times. If it had not been they who rose at the head of the procession in the red sash and gilded epaulet of political powers, others would have come along, for it was a people's movement. The mercy that permeated their hearts, their yearning for justice which sent them to the newsstands and bookstores buying by the tons newspapers, books, and magazines that told them how to be intelligently just and fair in their political aspirations—all published, edited, and written by men who took the coloring of their environment—sprang from a widening sense of duty, rather than of rights, moving in the hearts of the American people in that decade. . . .

Some way, into the hearts of the dominant middle class of this country had come a sense that their civilization needed recasting, that their government had fallen into the hands of self-seekers, that a new relation should be established between the haves and the have-nots, not primarily because the have-nots were loyal, humble, worthy, and oppressed—Heaven knows we knew that the underdog had fleas, mange, and a bad disposition—but rather because we felt that to bathe and feed the underdog would release the burden of injustice on our own conscience. We should do it even unto the least of these.[1] We were not maudlin, as I recollect it. We were joyous, eager, happily determined to make life more fair and lovely for ourselves by doing such approximate justice as we could to those who obviously were living in the swamps, morasses, deserts, and wildernesses of this world.

It was not religious—at least not pious—this progressive movement. It was profoundly spiritual. And the insurgents, who were later called progressives, had the crusader's ardor, and felt for one another the crusader's fellowship. They sang songs, carried banners, marched in parades, created heroes out of their own ideals. It was an evangelical uprising without an accredited Messiah.

What the people felt about the vast injustice that had come with the settlement of a continent, we, their servants—teachers, city councilors, legislators, governors, publishers, editors, writers, representatives in Congress, and

---

[1] Jesus predicted that at the Last Judgment God would say to the righteous who had given charity to the poor, "Inasmuch as ye have done it unto one of the least of these my brethren, ye have done it unto me" (Matthew 25:40).

senators—all made a part of our creed and so carried the banner of their cause. Because I wrote books and magazine articles, had my newspaper, and sometimes went around making progressive speeches, I was probably in the list of the first hundred leaders who were thrown into the public eye by this evangelical demonstration. . . .

I fear I have painted too smooth a picture. All this social and political change did not appear automatically in American politics; the spirit of change did not wave a wand and say, "Let there be light."[2] In every state, indeed in every county and city across the land, these progressive leaders in both parties rose only after bitter struggle. . . . And it was not all black or all white. The battles were in gray areas. Demagogues on both sides clamored for leadership. . . . Of course men had to change sides if the progressive minority became a majority in many states.

As a concrete example, consider the case of my old employer, Bent Murdock. In the seventies and eighties, Bent had been the righthand man of George R. Peck, the railroad representative of the states, who ruled it in those decades with an iron hand. . . . But even in the nineties, his chains were galling him. He tried to break away, and did, from the system which he had done his part to establish. In the early part of the century, in Kansas, he had joined a group known as the boss-busters. His group was composed of two kinds of politicians: those who wanted to unseat the Leland faction—for Old Cy was the boss—and those who really felt the need for political freedom. . . . In the middle of the century's first decade, Mr. Murdock stood valiantly with Stubbs for all the Stubbs reforms. The El Dorado *Republican* was one of a dozen Republican papers which supported Stubbs to the limit. And by 1908 when Stubbs was elected governor, Mr. Murdock—Old Bent to the rank and file of Kansas Republicans—was among the first score of Stubbs' trustworthy lieutenants.

I left Kansas in the first month of the Stubbs administration. I knew—for Mr. Murdock had told me, and I had told Stubbs, who received my message blinking hard and grinning rather stonily—that Mr. Murdock would like to be one of the three state railroad commissioners. I knew he had two motives, each struggling for supremacy in his heart, when he asked for that job. First, he wanted to show the railroad politicians who were waning and had seen their best days that he could be a railroad commissioner without their help and that he could be honest with the people. And second, I knew in my heart that he wanted to be a railroad commissioner because under the law and custom of the state, the railroad commission had its own private car. This car was carried over the state free by the railroads while the commission was assessing the railroad property. Its lar-

[2]"God said, let there be light, and there was light" (Genesis 1:3).

der was supplied by the railroads. Its porters were taken from the Pullman service. It was a magnificent equipage. . . .

When I left for Europe Mr. Murdock's candidacy was still on Stubbs' desk:
When I came back the first thing I inquired about was Mr. Murdock's status.
They told me this story. . . :

"God, Bill, it was awful. Stubbs couldn't do that. He couldn't make a man a
railroad commissioner who had been the railroad's footman. It wouldn't do.
Stubbs knew and I knew that the old man was earnest and honest and convinced. But it just wouldn't do. So I went to him in the National Hotel last
spring and broke it to him. I said: 'Bent, we just can't do it!'

"He asked: 'Why? What's the matter with me anyway? Don't you believe I
have served Stubbs faithfully, and well?'

"I said to him: 'Bent, can't you see? Can't you see?'

"And he shook his head: 'What have I done?' he cried. And repeated it. And
I told him: 'Bent, it's your long years with George R. Peck and his dynasty.'

"His face flushed and he cried out: 'Wasn't Stubbs a railroad contractor?
Didn't he make all his million dollars feeding moldy beans and wormy, dried ap-
ples and infected and condemned beef to the railroad construction gangs?
Wasn't he a pet of the railroads in his day?'

"And I said: 'Well, maybe so. I don't know. But anyway you know how Stubbs
feels about it, and I have told you.'

"And he asked: 'What did he say?'

"And I told him blunt; I said: 'Bent, Stubbs says he can't make a railroad commissioner out of a man who has been upstairs with every railroad in the state for
the last thirty-five or forty years.'

"He looked at me a moment. The tears came into his old rheumy eyes and he
cried out like a stuck hog: 'Did Stubbs say that? Did Stubbs say that of me, his
friend!' And then he put his arm on the table, lay his head on it, and his body
shook in sobs for a moment. Then when his grief and anger were spent, he
looked up piteously and said: 'Well, I suppose it's all right. Ask him what else he
has got.' "

It was a terrible story. I have often thought of it. But Stubbs was kind. He
made Uncle Bent fish and game commissioner. Stubbs sensed the enchantment
of a private car. The fish and game commissioner had a private car with a fish
tank in it which went about the state putting little catfish, bass, and carp into
the streams and lakes. Back of the fish tank were some berths, a kitchen, a dining room, and a club car. Uncle Bent took it, and his spirit was healed. It was his
car. He did not have to share it with two other commissioners. It was a bit
shabby compared with the shiny office car that the railroad commission had,
but it was a private car. It stopped at El Dorado and stood on the siding sometimes, receiving the worshipful homage of the multitude.

As soon as I returned home, I sent him *A Certain Rich Man*. I sent it in pride for he had believed in me since I was a child. . . . Hearing that he was sick, I went down to see him. I did not realize that it was his deathbed. In his active life he had spanned the chasm between the two worlds: the old world of the pioneers in the Missouri Valley and the new world of their restless, discontented, aspiring sons. In his own way, he had been a triumphant leader in both. In both worlds he had been somebody. He died a fortnight after I saw him.

I had more than an academic interest in politics. I had been chairman and Republican precinct committeeman in the Fourth Ward for a dozen years, had served on the state central committee and on the executive committee of my county and state organization. When I came home from Europe, I began consulting with other independent, progressive-minded Republicans over the country about President Taft's obvious decision to go with the conservatives. . . . In matters of patronage, he recognized the conservative senators, where a Republican insurgent senator had to be rebuked. Senator Bristow of Kansas was set aside and Senator Curtis was the president's Kansas mouthpiece. . . .

Excepting the congressmen in Washington, I probably knew more of the progressive leaders across the country than most men, and my letter files show that I was writing to them all, stirring up trouble for Taft. I went to the White House to see him before we started our campaign. I hoped I could show him that if he would give us fair treatment, we should be glad to work with him. We met at luncheon. Mrs. Taft was there, and his half-brother Charles P. Taft. . . . I tried to steer the conversation toward my mission. The president knew what I wanted to say. It would be disagreeable, and I could feel him edging away from any serious talk. We had a most amiable time. At one point I began, and said: "Here is what we want definitely: support for the income tax amendment, and for postal savings banks, for a railroad regulation law; and we want our senators to have a—"

And there the president began to chuckle and said: "Oh, White, if you mean Bristow, you know Bristow."

And I did. He was disagreeable and tactless and edgy and I could not help but grin. And the president grinned and said: "Go talk to Bristow!"

Which was a good answer. It turned away wrath. And either he or his brother or Mrs. Taft cut in with some irrelevant remark, and the significance of the conference was over—a futile journey, a fool's errand. . . .

That sunny day, as we sat for half an hour talking over everything under the sun but the thing he knew I wanted to say, I realized how hopeless was the job of weaning him from the reactionary crowd that was surrounding him. . . . I could not have asked more courtesy, more consideration, more cordial hospitality, yet occasionally when I referred to Cannon, or Aldrich, with the gentle malediction that was in my heart, I could see his eye behind his smile veiling with almost the hint of a serpentine glitter. The day we had spent together on the train in 1907 or '08 taught me to take warning when that glitter flashed across his sweet and gentle countenance. When I left the White House I knew that I and my kind, the whole progressive lot, were anathema—outlawed from his counsel. He would have none of us.

Outwardly it seemed that he did not want to be disturbed. Many progressives felt that his detachment from our group was a result of a lazy desire to avoid disagreeable encounters. It was not that. He was convinced that we were mad. He was a consistent, honest, courageous, most intelligent conservative. He believed in the existing order. He was nice about it, most felicitous, and could at times smile at it with indulgent condescension. But it was his world. He deeply resented the hands that would touch the Ark of his Covenant.[3]

Many times after we parted that day I tried by letter and by messenger to reach him, to make him understand how serious was the uprising against his creed and crowd. Possibly he knew, for he was sensitive. But if he knew, he was unmoved. He walked to his doom "a gentleman unafraid!"[4] . . .

For a dozen years following 1901, Theodore Roosevelt led the progressive movement in the Republican party. His leadership was challenged by that of Robert M. La Follette, . . . [who] represented the left wing of Republican insurgents, and an intransigent left wing it was. Roosevelt and La Follette wanted, on the whole, about the same things, but they were poles apart in their methods. Roosevelt would make a noisy fight and in the end would compromise when he had gone as far as he could. La Follette never compromised. He would prefer to dramatize his cause in failures and take it up later rather than to surrender one jot or tittle of his original bill of contention. La Follette was bitter in his controversies. He was merciless in his attacks. In all my life I have never seen a braver man in politics. Moreover, he made his bravery count. He had come up from the ranks in Wisconsin politics when those ranks were organized against him. When he came to the Senate he had a long line of Wisconsin achievements in his baggage, which afterwards went into the platforms and statutes of other states. And the principles for which La Follette fought were known later as the Roosevelt policies.

But Theodore Roosevelt kept pleasant associations with his political enemies where he could. He was bitter enough at times, but I never found him stubborn. He would listen to the populace for compromise. His success lay in a rather large stock of half loaves which were better than none. La Follette was a "lean and

[3]In the Bible the Ark of the Covenant was a holy shrine that Moses built to carry the stone tablets containing the Ten Commandments (Deuteronomy 10:5).

[4]From Kipling's poem "Barrack Room Ballads: Dedication": "And they rise to their feet as He passes by, gentlemen unafraid."

hungry" Cassius to Theodore Roosevelt's Caesar.[5] It was inevitable that they should clash and, clashing, it was written in the stars that they should never respect one another. And I think, as a friend of both, I am fairly safe and charitable in saying that they were jealous of one another constitutionally, temperamentally, inevitably.

I trusted both. I admired both. Probably "admired" is too cold a word; "adored" is too ardent. But between admiration and adoration, I gave each of them a warm heart and I hope an affectionate loyalty. I never was a go-between. I was too smart for that. I should have been ground between their suspicions and probably, in my instinctive desire not to give offense nor to bring pain to a friend, I should have betrayed them both. . . .

I found a letter the other day that I wrote to Colonel Roosevelt just after he had come back from Africa, in the spring of 1910. A paragraph or so from that letter will convey my feelings, my political attitude at that time. After explaining why I felt that Taft had failed as Roosevelt's successor, I wrote:

> I am against the movement that would make you a presidential candidate. I have said nothing unkind to President Taft and have not criticized his administration. Yet I may not be classed as an ardent supporter of it. Its intense materialism has saddened me. I have been unhappy many times at the way things have gone. But I believe sincerely that the country would be better off with Taft until 1916 than with you in the next presidential term. Of course, the country would be further along in 1916, with you in the presidency. You would take us a long way ahead. But as matters stand, the people are not looking to the presidential office for leadership now. They are beginning to walk alone. They are going ahead themselves in their own way. There is a distinctly growing, automatically organizing public opinion in America today that is the same in every section and corner of the Republic. It knows no class or occupation. It is national. It will triumph over every president, Congress or court that can be found. It is the outgrowth of necessity. With you in the White House, the people feel secure, so the necessity of a self-guarded sentiment is removed. If you were in the office in 1916, we would undoubtedly have better laws and a cleaner administration than we may have without you, but what we would have without you would be net gain, and we would be in a position to fight whatever devils are sent against us in the future with greater success, than if we did the ornamental standing-around for four years while you did the real work.

It seems to me that I expressed the sentiment of a considerable majority of the progressive leaders at that time. We had met often in small caucusing groups and

[5]Cassius Longinus was a Roman general who planned the assassination of Julius Caesar. In *Julius Caesar*, Shakespeare has Caesar comment, "Yon Cassius has a lean and hungry look."

conferences in Chicago, in New York, and in Washington. We felt that we could win with La Follette if Taft had to be overthrown. We were saving our ace. . . .

It was our job in Kansas, we who worked together politically around Governor Stubbs and Senator Bristow, Victor Murdock and Henry Allen, to bring out Republican candidates for Congress in every district not then represented by a progressive. I did much of the leg work on that job and in the August primaries we turned up with six progressive nominees out of eight for our congressional delegation. It took a lot of work, and as I remember it, I had a lot of fun with it, as I think the others of our group had also. For as I remember them, not only in Kansas but generally everywhere, those progressive leaders were a rollicking crowd—except La Follette. He was grim. So were his followers in the Northwest. But the rest of us on the wrecking crew of conservatism enjoyed our work. . . .

It fell to my lot when the state party council met in Kansas in August to write the Republican platform. It was regarded as most radical. It preceded the New Deal program by twenty years, and before I submitted it to the party council in Topeka, I sent a draft of it to Roosevelt, who gave us a green light. . . . It was what might well be called a forward-looking platform. Yet not one demand of the platform was out of line with the general tendency of the time. It was this platform which Colonel Roosevelt made the basis of his Osawatomie speech.

Shortly after the party council, he came West and spoke in Kansas at Osawatomie, the home of the Kansas saint, John Brown. In fact, he dedicated a monument to the old fanatic and in nearly an hour's speech devoted less than seven lines to our hero. But he did get squarely on the Kansas progressive platform, a position which shocked his friends in the East. They were much more conservative than we were in the West. And many of his old Harvard cronies, who were rallying about him and urging him to oppose Taft, seemed to us in the West to be using the Colonel rather than promoting our cause. Very likely these Harvard patriots had no deep sense of the issues of the hour. They wanted to shout, "To hell with Yale," and Roosevelt's candidacy afforded them a beautiful opening.

It is hard to bring back today the sense of excitement, almost of tumult, that was in the air over this land in the summer and autumn of 1910. It was revolutionary. Colonel Roosevelt joined it, and despite my qualms and cautions, became the leader of the revolution. He had not yet publicly broken with Taft. But when he endorsed the Kansas Republican platform which was aimed directly at all that Taft stood for, it was plain to the American people that a clash was ahead between the ex-president and the president. . . .

The Little Major, at the bank, was having a sad time with me. Of course he regarded my political activities as definitely insane. But they were successful. I had a little power at that time, more power in the state than he had. For his friends had been mown down by the rising tide of insurgency. If I had failed, I think our relations would have been different. But I carried a decent deposit in his bank. I owed no money there. So he looked upon me as something like a prodigal son, with sad but none the less genuine affection. One day I went into the bank on some errand and the Little Major, who by then was in his seventies and walked like a wiry skeleton with a soft and not very steady tread, came pattering out of his room, took me back and there sat me down opposite himself at his desk. He hemmed ominously as he always did when he was about to relieve his mind, opened a drawer carefully, pulled out a large manila envelope, dumped its contents on the glass top of his desk, again cleared his throat, and said: "I was going over my papers the other day, clearing up old documents, and I found this which I thought you would like to see."

He shoved it across the desk. It was a letter in longhand, written on the stationery of the United States Supreme Court, signed by an eminent justice, complaining to the Major, who at that time had been the political representative of Senator Plumb in all dubious matters—complaining that the two receivers of the Katy Railroad, whom the writer had appointed when he was a circuit judge, were not, since he had come to the Supreme Court, making their promised and agreed monthly payments to his sister. The justice complained that she was a poor woman and needed the money.

When I read this over and saw the name signed there, . . . I saw in a flash the whole system of American politics wherein wealth controlled government, exemplified perfectly with a dozen lines in longhand of that letter before me. There were the courts controlling the railroads through receiverships. There was the Senate controlling the courts through what, in that day, passed not for corruption but for the political amenities of the hour. All that I saw, except the payment of the money to the sister of the justice, I had known as well as one knows anything without the evidence. But to see it there in black and white made me bat my eyes. . . .

I knew the justice.[6] I had met him when he was a circuit judge. In Kansas he was known as our scholar in politics. He had been graduated from Yale. He was a man of wide reading and considerable culture. He believed in the divine right of the plutocracy to rule. He distrusted the people, and his decisions limited their power whenever the question of their power came before the court. It was only when the people themselves rose up, broke the lever which United States senators held over the federal courts, and by the primary smashed the machine through which the railroads controlled the legislatures and elected the senators; only then did the people erect the machinery by which they could set up free government. . . .

[6]Elsewhere in the *Autobiography*, White explained that this justice was David Josiah Brewer, a political ally of Plumb's who had been appointed to the Supreme Court in 1889.

I made some casual remark, but the Little Major could see that he had jarred me. I knew what he was thinking of—that all this progressive nonsense which was engaging me at the time was a passing phase and that my world of reform was built of cardboard, papier-mâché, and paste. . . .

He broke the silence, smiling amiably back in his well-trimmed gray beard, after moistening his lips: "Well, Will," he said almost behind his hand and with his soft, deprecating voice, "the world has changed a lot in thirty years, hasn't it!"

I could only nod my assent. I wanted to cry out: "God, how it has changed and how you and your kind have passed, let us hope forever, from American politics!"

A few months later we buried him. He was my dear friend. Without him I could not have survived the nineties. We saw eye to eye in those days. We were friends to the last. So we gave him nineteen guns in the *Gazette* and buried him with a page of obituary biography and with editorial heralding trumpets that should have gotten him well past the pearly gates. I set all of this down here to show what a strange world we have, how mixed and confused and baffling it all is. The Little Major, exactly as he was, Plumb's political fence, was one of the best citizens in Emporia, public-spirited, generous, essentially kind, and to those he loved he was sweet and gentle. And yet . . . .

In the election of 1910 Kansas went overwhelmingly progressive Republican. The conservative faction was decisively divided. The same thing happened generally over the country north of the Mason and Dixon line. The progressive Republicans did not have a majority in either house of Congress. But they had a balance of power; amalgamation with a similar but smaller group of progressive Democrats under Bryan's leadership gave the progressives a working majority upon most measures. . . . So in the legislatures and the Congress that met in 1911 a strange new thing was revealed in American politics. Party lines were breaking down. A bipartisan party was appearing in legislatures and in the Congress. It was an undeclared third party. But when the new party appeared on the left, the conservative Democrats and the conservative Republicans generally coalesced in legislative bodies on the right. For the most part the right-wing coalescents were in the minority. In Congress, on most measures, the left-wing liberals were able to command a majority. . . . But they were unable to unite in the passage of a tariff bill. Local interests in regional commodity industries like cotton, lumber, copper, wool, and textiles were able to form a conservative alliance which, under the leadership of President Taft in the White House, put through a tariff bill that was an offense to the nation. But otherwise the new party of reform which had grown up in ten years dominated politics in Washington and in the state legislatures north of the Ohio from New England to California.

I was happy following in the train of this new alliance. After the election of 1910 I spent considerable time in January and February of 1911 helping Governor Stubbs with his legislative program. . . . The regulars on the right did not give up their fight easily. So 1911, despite the progressive victory of 1910, was a year of stress and tumultuous hubbub all across the land in American politics. . . .

I went East many times in the early part of 1911, saw Colonel Roosevelt frequently, held prolonged and unimportant conferences in Washington with such progressive leaders as Victor Murdock, Borah, and Norris could assemble, and we were full of plots and counterplots. At that time most of the progressives I saw were rather for La Follette as our presidential candidate the next year than for Roosevelt. He also was undecided what he would do. I am sure that he was trying to make peace with Taft. And I am also certain Taft would have been glad indeed to make peace with Roosevelt. But the courtiers at the White House in those days made peace impossible. Though several conferences were arranged, the result was negligible.

It was heartbreaking to watch that gradual, apparently inevitable estrangement between two old friends, for Roosevelt and Taft had been dearly beloved companions. . . . A public gibe here from Roosevelt, a bitter private retort repeated over the grapevine of politics from Taft, the innocent recognition of some enemy of Roosevelt by the White House, the constant hammering upon Taft by men near Roosevelt—all the accumulating little jeers and slights slowly grew into the proportions of a cause and a quarrel. . . .

And so matters stood in June 1911 when Mrs. White and I picked up the family and went to Colorado for the summer. For more than a year in our hearts we had been mulling over the basic ideas for a second novel. We had talked a lot about it, were seeing glimpses of the characters, but above all had a sense of what might be called the fable of the novel—the backbone, the thing it was to say and be, the spiritual idea behind it. The theme of the novel which afterwards appeared under the title *In the Heart of a Fool* was that there are no material rewards for spiritual excellence and no material punishment for spiritual dereliction. So I had two characters: one a most prosperous sinner and the other a suffering saint. All that summer I wrestled with those two figures to make them human; to give the saint his peccadillos; to give the villain his decent moments. The plot of the book was intended to be not a struggle between black and white but between different shades of gray. Seven years we were working on that book.

So we rented a cottage in Estes Park from Professor Hodder of the state university and in early June cut loose from politics, forgot all about Stubbs and Bristow and set ourselves up on the side of a mountain, with the two children, their Grandma White and their Aunt Jessie Lindsay. I set up a tent a hundred feet up the hill, put my cot and a typewriter there, and every morning after breakfast went up to write. . . . In the evenings we gathered the children, seven and eleven, around the fireplace and read Dickens until Mary had to be lugged off dead asleep to bed, and Bill, who always wanted more, had to be dragged to his couch; then his mother and I sat up until all hours while she read aloud to me. That year, I think we read for the third time Dickens' *Hard Times*[7] which in many respects is his best novel. . . .

When I came home from Estes Park in mid-autumn, the tragic quarrel between the two major figures in the Republican party, Theodore Roosevelt and William Howard Taft, was opening a big second act. As a spectacle it had all America on the edge of their chairs. For after all it is not every day that a nation can see a popular hero (and Colonel Roosevelt had superseded Bryan as the political idol of the day) and his lifelong friend, who happened for the purposes of the hour to be president of the United States, coming to verbal blows over matters not of personal interest but of public policy. Neither of them wanted to fight, yet each of them was drawn into combat in spite of himself. Each was the center, or representative, or embodiment of what amounted to a political party. . . . There it was on the national stage, a battle of the giants for all the world to see. I could not enjoy it. . . .

In the meantime, in the autumn and early winter of 1911, we in Kansas were trying with all our might to line the state up for Senator La Follette as our progressive presidential candidate. We had three county conventions early in the winter, and La Follette was beaten in all three. It was jarring. Then a strange and terrible thing happened to Senator La Follette.

He was on the program for a speech at the annual dinner of the Periodical Publishers Association of America. Remember that these publishers were conducting magazines that were anywhere from liberal to radical. There were gathered all of the progressive leaders in Congress and on the eastern seaboard. It was a most important occasion. La Follette knew it. But he came to Philadelphia, where the convention was held, dead tired, dog tired after a terrible day's work in the Senate. He never spared himself. His place was late on the program. It was after ten at night when the toastmaster came to him. Just before he rose to speak, his secretary told me, he took a great gobletful of whiskey and swallowed it neat as a stimulant. He was not a drinking man. But, his secretary said, sometimes, to stoke up his machine, he used any stimulant that might be at hand and had no bad consequences, contracted no habits, but had kept his machine going when his normal strength was gone. He had his manuscript that night at the dinner, and for ten minutes or so, perhaps twenty, he read along fluently and well. Then he put his manuscript down for a moment to emphasize a point. The dinner guests noted that he wandered a bit, repeated himself. When he

---

[7]*Hard Times* (1845) contained Dickens's harshest treatment of the social hardships brought about in England by industrialization.

picked up his manuscript he had lost his place and read for five minutes or so paragraphs that he had already read. Then he laid it down again, and the second time he departed from his manuscript he began to lose control of his temper. He came out of his fury maudlin. No one at the table dreamed what was the matter. For nearly two hours, fumbling occasionally with his manuscript, he raged on and on, saying the same things over and over at the top of his voice. It was a terrible spectacle. The progressive leadership of the United States that night received such a shock as they had never had. . . .

From that hour in Philadelphia, La Follette's candidacy faded. The progressive leadership he had counted on was afraid of him. It never brought opportunity for the presidency again to La Follette. He lived on a decade and a half as a minority leader, but only that—a great leader, a brave, wise, uncompromising leader who deserved of his country much more fame than it gave him. No other left-wing leader ever impressed upon the laws and institutions of his country and upon the purposes and impulse of the American people in his time so strong, definite, and considerable an achievement as Robert La Follette, Sr.

As it seemed to me then, so it seems to me now, looking back a generation and considering all the men who might have been chosen president in 1912, that La Follette would have done more than any other man to guide the destiny of his country through the devastating second decade of this century. I say this realizing that he was a convinced and fanatical pacifist. But he was nonetheless a patriotic American; and in the crisis where Wilson seemed to fumble, to vacillate, to procrastinate and so let war come creeping upon us almost unawares, La Follette—who was a man of decision, a patriot, unafraid even of a majority of his people—would have been a stronger, wiser man. But the United States in that day was not ready to risk itself with a strong, determined, indomitable man. So LaFollette stepped aside and fate passed him by. . . .

In February 1912, I went to Boston to make a speech before the Progressive Club, a group of young left-wingers; and as I always kept Colonel Roosevelt posted about my whereabouts before I went to Boston, he asked me if I would dine with him, the evening after my speech. . . . By the time I got to Boston I knew what was in the air. The Colonel had determined to make a formal announcement, that night, of his candidacy. He knew that I still felt he should keep out of it. . . .

A small group of Colonel Roosevelt's New England friends were at the dinner. We read his statement. . . . I told him that I thought he was sacrificing himself unnecessarily, but that if he was going to make a mistake I would help him with all my heart to make it as terrible as possible. And we had a laugh and let it go at that. He accepted two or three verbal and rhetorical changes that I suggested, and the statement was given to the press fairly early in the evening.

I took the midnight train to New York and Washington, full of a bewildered

I took the midnight train to New York and Washington, full of a bewildered zeal for a cause that I did not then entirely approve. The next afternoon I was in Washington. The first man I went to see was Victor Murdock. He was amazed and not altogether delighted with the Colonel's statement, for he was no Roosevelt worshipper. Victor had fathered a congressional resolution which cut off several million dollars of graft from the American railroads in their mail-carrying contracts. The president, who did not quite understand it, felt that Murdock, Norris, and the midwestern anti-Cannon insurgents were not obeying the party signals and playing their own game. So when the Cannon crowd started to crucify Murdock, the president did not lift a hand to uphold him. But it was obvious that Murdock was going along with the progressives. He knew that La Follette was hopeless. He thought Roosevelt could win. I remember I greeted him with: "Victor, the Colonel thinks it's 1860 and it looks to me about like '56. He's not running against Douglas.[8] He's running against Buchanan."

Victor grinned and said: "Bill, he's running against Franklin Pierce. This rebellion has a long, long way to go before it wins."

Victor knew the powers of inertia in the House and the strength of an organized reactionary minority, well-financed, socially entrenched, politically arrogant. He was not afraid, but he was not deceived either. And I have always thought that Colonel Roosevelt fooled himself in that February statement. For the clamor in the country for him was maddening. No wonder it turned his head.

Naturally in Washington his statement had given much courage to the insurgents there. They rallied to Roosevelt and practically all of them left La Follette to drain his cup of bitterness alone. A few nights after, a dozen or twenty Rooseveltians met in downtown Washington—I think in the Willard Hotel—to discuss ways and means. I can remember only a few senators: Jonathan Bourne, Moses Clapp, Bristow, Johnson of California, Beveridge, Dixon of Montana, Dolliver, Borah, Victor Murdock. I believe George Norris brought in half a dozen or more members of the House of Representatives. We formed a loose organization without a name, devoted to the Roosevelt primary campaign, for by that time most of the northern states had presidential preference primaries.

In the discussion of attitudes, Senator Bourne stood up and said, after we had made Senator Dixon our chairman: "Gentlemen, the first thing we have got to decide is a matter of fundamental policy. If we lose, will we bolt? To get this thing before the house, I move that we agree, here and now, and not be too secretive about our agreement, that if we lose, we bolt."

He had consulted no one, apparently. The motion was a stunner. There was a

---

[8]Stephen A. Douglas was defeated by Abraham Lincoln, the nominee of the new Republican party, which had only been organized in 1854. Democrats Franklin Pierce and James Buchanan were elected in 1852 and 1856, respectively.

moment of silence when Bourne sat down, and the men around the table moistened their lips and batted their eyes. They were faced with a proposition which might seal their political doom and end their congressional careers.

I had no such career to end. I was thinking only of the Colonel's position if he should bolt the possible nomination of Taft. This nomination did not seem possible at that hour. We had forgotten the mercenary southern delegates. We were all hypnotized by the clamoring voices across the land.

As we stood there, with that motion before us, we realized we were at the near bank of the Rubicon. The discussion was louder than it was sincere, I thought. Too many men were thinking of themselves and not the cause. A precious few of them were thinking in terms of what it would do to their hero. In the end, without a vote, but because it seemed to be the consensus of opinion, the sense of the meeting was that we should bolt and make our campaign with that aim in our own hearts and with that threat hanging over the heads of our adversaries. After that we discussed ways and means, state organizations, appointed committees to raise funds, and did the usual things that political conspirators do who are organizing a raid on any political citadel.

But after that meeting, for a day or two I talked with various members of the conference and after they had slept on it the proposition to bolt did not appeal to them. I found no one except Bourne, and perhaps Beveridge, who was willing to admit that a threat to bolt was good policy. Yet because every political conference is a sign, the substance of that threat sifted into the minds and hearts of the friends of President Taft, and instead of terrifying them it gave them the purpose and direction of their campaign. It was to hold the Republican national organization as it was constituted in the Republican national committee and ride the storm even if Taft was defeated, and win for four years later.

A political organization is party-minded. Also it is set eternally in the heavens. Tomorrow is also a day with the national senatorial committee of either party. It functions not by quadrennial but by decades and generations. The threat to bolt gave the conservative Republicans their one hope to win—not with Taft, but with time. They planned their campaign along those lines. Because I sensed that, I redoubled my effort in Kansas to be elected to the national committee. I did not believe, until the deed was done, that Roosevelt would bolt then or ever. But I did feel, that spring of 1912, that on the Republican national committee I could be a troublemaker for the conservatives, and I took my own campaign rather seriously. . . .

Looking back into my life over the year 1912, I seem to be forever busy about something, stirring around in the midst of tumult and struggle, making decisions that seemed important in that hour, decisions that now seem so irrelevant to anything that persists in the world today. And for me, all this hurrying about, all this tumult, struggle, mental and spiritual pulling and hauling, was about and around Theodore Roosevelt.

I was drawn to him by personal loyalty. I disagreed with him on unimportant matters. I was often annoyed a little with things that he said or did. He made a speech in Columbus, a most radical and indefensible speech, advocating the recall of judicial decisions. I never knew who advised him to make that speech, though at the time I tried to find out. But it hurt him; probably it crippled him more than any other one thing that he did in his life. For the speech shocked millions of his countrymen whom he had gathered about him as followers, and it attracted only the radicals who are never dependable to follow in any man's train nor to pursue any consistent course. I tried to explain that he meant by recall and judicial decisions only the legislative enactments needed to amend the statutes upon which the decisions were made. Probably he meant something of that sort. But the phrase "the recall of judicial decisions" set the key of the marching song in the political combat that made the year such a time of clamor and alarm. It was a high key and too much in falsetto. Colonel Roosevelt . . . was forced in self-defense to a position much further to the left than he should have taken—indeed further to the left than he would have taken naturally if in the back of his head he was not always trying to justify "the recall of judicial decisions" to a public that challenged it.

My first job was in Kansas. . . . I travelled about Kansas making speeches where it was necessary, attending county conventions where I could be of any service and district conventions where the battle was raging—sometimes talking, sometimes horse-trading, compromising, working at political combinations that would promote the Roosevelt cause. In the end, we won. We carried all but two congressional districts and we carried the state convention. I was the progressive candidate for national committeeman. Henry J. Allen, of Wichita, headed the Kansas delegation pledged to Colonel Roosevelt. At the state convention we named not only the delegates but the presidential electors who should vote in the Electoral College for Colonel Roosevelt as the Republican nominee.

In the midst of this fight, I went East once or twice, possibly three times, to confer with the Colonel and with his national supporters about national strategy. The Colonel was carrying the primaries in the northern states, decisively; and it was evident that in the southern states, which never went Republican and in which the Republican party in too many cases was a corrupt alliance between the rich and the purchasable, the organization supporting Taft was naming the delegates. . . .

In May, when we held our last pre-convention conference at Oyster Bay, it was plain that we had the Republican sentiment of the country, as it was uncovered by direct vote of Republicans in state primaries, rather overwhelmingly for Colonel Roosevelt. It was also clear that the Republican national committee,

having the South, one-third of the convention as its pawn was instituting contests in convention states which would probably give the national committee an
opportunity to organize the national convention. For the national committee
named the temporary chairman who named the committee on credentials. The
committee on credentials seated such contestants as they deemed worthy or
necessary to promote their plans. There you have drama.

On the one side was the national committee. It was supporting President
Taft. . . . First, the committee would have back of it the South, although these
delegates represented no possibility of a Republican majority in their states in
the election. Secondly, the committee would have, on the early balloting, the
strength of its contested delegates. Thus the Taft conservatives, by controlling
the national committee, could shape the convention in its image.

Facing this phalanx of sheer political machine power was the sentiment of the
country as revealed by the primaries in the great Republican areas of the nation
which were for Roosevelt. Naturally passions mounted. Popular indignation, being thwarted by a hold-over national committee, was faced by the contempt of
this national committee as it went ahead with its plans to nominate Taft. . . .

Colonel Roosevelt was being staged as a martyr. He did not have a drop of
martyr's blood in his veins. . . . He wanted to be a victor. . . . He got mad,
deeply, terribly angry at the injustice which he faced. He could not think that a
national committee which he had swayed in the White House four years before
could treat him with such utter scorn, nor that it would risk Republican defeat
to retain its control of the national Republican organization.

He was a practical politician, was Colonel Roosevelt. He had fought it out in
the caucus at Oyster Bay, as I had. He had stood on a chair in state conventions
and howled with the winners. And on national committees he had gone to the
edge of the abysms and backed off before he bolted. For Theodore Roosevelt was
a party man. He was not a party man because of much conviction. We held
about the same ideas of party loyalty, that it was a necessary evil if one gave his
principles in government a chance for a fair trial. In other words he was an expe-
dient Republican, not a congenital partisan. He had used other people's party
loyalty for his own ends. . . . He found the national committee playing the same
trick on him.

He did not like it in prospect, as he saw the forces of politics shaping the tragedy of martyrdom for him while the powers controlling his party piled the fag-
gots of intrigue and corruption around his stake. When I saw him in those late
spring days, neither of us mentioned the possibility of a bolt. Each of us knew
that our progressive conference had decided upon it. He was undecided then, I
know, because he avoided the subject when we talked. We made the rather too
obvious pretense in those days of our party loyalty, whistling in unison through
the tall timber of darkening events to support our courage. . . .

It was in those spring conferences of the progressive Republicans in 1912 that I again met George W. Perkins, who had risen rather suddenly in the Roosevelt councils. . . . Personally we got along together rather well. But deeply and instinctively we distrusted one another. He represented money and the power of money. I felt that Morgan had cast Perkins into the progressive movement as an anchor to windward; that he was Roosevelt's friend—"just in case"!

He was a handsome young fellow, slim and trim, rather exquisitely undertailored. He was addicted to gray and white, and I liked a mohair suit he had so well that I came home and got one from our Emporia tailor. Perkins had good habits, mental, personal, political. He made quick decisions, spoke in a soft voice, smiled ingratiatingly, easily, was as careful of the punctilios as a preacher at the front door of the church, and I used to watch him fishing for men with a certain pride in his skill, which I greatly admired. But he was none the less a sinister figure in those conferences, and I knew it. I grumbled to Roosevelt about him, though I rarely made the mistake in politics of warning a man against his supporters. It is unlucky. But I felt that Roosevelt knew Perkins as I did. I hoped and rather believed he distrusted him as I did, but I also sensed that Roosevelt was using him and I used to wonder which one was fooling the other, he or Perkins. . . .

In the midst of it all we had bought a cabin on a hillside near Estes Park, Colorado. It was surrounded on three sides by snow-capped mountains that looked down into a valley, a peaceful green valley through which the Big Thompson River wound its way. It cost us only a few hundred dollars. . . . The cabin was only eighteen by twenty-four, with a fireplace in a little living room, two bedrooms, and a kitchen. Yet the fact that we bought it and had time to negotiate for it in the midst of the bedlam about us would seem to prove that there were areas of sanity somewhere within us, for there on that hillside we found a place of peace to which we were to withdraw in summers for thirty years and more. I pause to chronicle the beginnings of the house in Estes Park because the episode probably had a larger place in our real lives than had all the clash of that combat which was just before us on the big national stage where I strutted in a little brief authority, an accredited Kansas captain in a wild charge against the impregnable wall of conservative inertia that all the world was trying to batter down.

"Do you want to know about old Bill White?" said Henry Allen, riding on Roosevelt's train through Nebraska one evening late in the spring of 1912. "Well, I can tell you. He is down somewhere in Labette County in some little country town. And he is doing one of two things: He is standing on the rostrum of the schoolhouse assembly room making a speech for you, in a Palm Beach suit, sweating like a horse, stuttering and stammering to think of the word he wants to say, rabble-rousing to get a Roosevelt delegation out of that county. Or else he is sitting on the bed in a room in some dingy hotel at some crossroads town, fixing up a horsetrade so that Labette County can have a presidential elector or an alternate to the district convention, if they will instruct their delegates . . . to vote with the Roosevelt crowd. . . . And Old Bill's compromising. He is sweating just as hard but he isn't sputtering for the right word. He knows it!"

17

Armageddon

I went to Chicago in a dual capacity a week before the Republican national convention convened. I was to report the convention and its preliminaries for the George Matthew Adams Newspaper Syndicate, but I also went as a successful candidate for Republican national committeeman from Kansas, who would be elected by the Kansas delegation when it assembled. As a politician I went to the Roosevelt headquarters in the Congress Hotel and joined the conference of conspirators. As a reporter, I appeared at the Stratford Hotel where George Matthew Adams had quartered his other trained seals, George Fitch, Harry Webster, and J. N. Darling. Edna Ferber lived on the South Side in Chicago, and we proceeded to form a lively company. To me it was the comic relief of a nerve-tightening experience. . . . We ate together, worked together, wrote together. Later in the convention we sat together. I took my writing job most seriously. And in that pre-convention week I turned in a story a day, sometimes two stories, one for the morning and one for the evening paper. Adams had more than fifty American daily papers on his syndicate string, the best papers in the country.

Probably waiting for the curtain to rise on the great national tragedy is as good a place as any to introduce Edna Ferber. In that year she was in her early twenties. . . . She was a brunette, with a great mop of dark hair, blue-black, wavy, fine—the kind of lovely hair one is tempted to tousle. Her brow was low and broad. But her eyes—from them her spirit shone out. It was an eager spirit, young, curious, demanding, understanding, honest, and wiser than a thousand years. We men—most of us old enough to be her father—took over Edna as our "Little Eva."[1] It was George Fitch who called me "Uncle Tom." I was in my middle forties then. And he called George Adams, our boss, Simon Legree. I can remember yet across thirty years how we four men romped with her spirituality as

---

[1] Little Eva, Uncle Tom and Simon Legree were major characters in Harriet Beecher Stowe's best-selling antislavery novel, *Uncle Tom's Cabin* (1851).

with a pup, guying her, teasing her, helping her, tripping her, rolling her over, loving her to death. We called her "the angel child," which nickname she pretended to resent. Maybe she did—we could never tell. She was too smart for us. . . . After the hubbub and rancor around the political headquarters, it was a comfort, indeed a delight, to sneak off to the Stratford Hotel into another planet in another solar system.

That week before the convention opened, the national Republican committee, in its headquarters rooms, was slowly throwing out Roosevelt delegates, some of whom probably had questionable status, and substituting Taft contesting delegates, building up an impregnable majority in the convention for Taft. It was done with obvious *malice prépense*,[2] with a sort of Gargantuan impudence, profligate and heroically indecent, which angered the Roosevelt majority in the country and turned Michigan Avenue, where the delegates milled up and down between the hotels, into a hell's broth of wrath. . . .

The Roosevelt headquarters in the Auditorium Hotel consisted of a suite of four rooms . . . on one of the upper floors of the hotel. On the second floor was a row of offices near the Florentine Room. The Florentine Room was ordinarily a large dining room or ballroom. There a platform was erected and all day long orators were declaiming, men from all over the United States who wanted to relieve their emotions. It was a sort of steam gauge. Senators, members of the House of Representatives, governors, state bosses, all were called to this rostrum and talked to the crowd standing agape around it. When governors or senators spoke, or a leader like Pinchot or Garfield, the Florentine Room was crowded to suffocation. It was full of emotion, and reporters covered the proceedings there.

In the little office badges were distributed, names of delegates listed, workers assigned tasks among the doubtful delegates if there were any. . . . But bands had to be scheduled, and there were scores of them blaring up and down Michigan Avenue, marching through the hotels. Uniformed Roosevelt clubs had to be given something to do, and the turmoil channeled into something like order and purpose. Perhaps half a hundred men were working in those offices. On the lobby floor below, a few desks were manned by minor workers doing the thousand chores that are necessary for the organization of a first-class presidential candidacy in any convention.

It is hard to reconstruct for this story the emotions of that hour. The mounting hatred on both sides which has dissolved with the years was then a terrible reality. The Friday of the week before the convention met, Colonel Roosevelt decided to go to it. The decision broke a long precedent in convention ameni-

---

[2]*Malice prépense* is the common law term for malice aforethought, the traditional legal concept regarding the intentions of the accused that distinguishes murder from manslaughter.

ties. It just was not done. There again I was not in the group that urged him. I thought it was a mistake. . . . At any rate, when we knew he was coming, emotions began to rise among his friends and his enemies. The situation was genuinely tense.

Yet it was profoundly American. Gags, funny stories, tags evoking laughter ran through the crowds in Chicago. Someone had ten thousand handbills printed the day before he arrived in Chicago which announced that Colonel Theodore Roosevelt would walk on the waters of Lake Michigan at 7:30 Monday evening. And the bands were playing a popular song, "Everybody's Doin' It, Doin' It, Doin' It," which provoked smiles on the too tense faces of the mob that surged along the Avenue. So steam was released, but the engine of public opinion was running there and throughout the country with a rather too high gauge.

I was busy with my daily story for the Adams Syndicate and did not go to the train or try to see Colonel Roosevelt when he arrived, but the streets were packed and his car moved slowly through miles of cheering citizens. Police had to cordon his entrance to the hotel. They had to move him through the lobby into the elevator. If ever an American was a hero of a hot and crowded hour, it was Theodore Roosevelt that day in Chicago.

He spoke the next evening at the Auditorium. Borah was with him on the platform. I remember I had a front seat and heard the speech. It was one of his very best. Of course it could have been vapid and dumb and the crowd would not have known it. It would cheer anything he said. So as he spoke, some way the emotions of the crowd were wound tighter and tighter and released themselves in yells and roars. It was not an altogether pleasing spectacle, and I was disturbed, I suppose a little frightened, at the churning which he gave the crowd. He closed with the phrase which has lasted now through thirty years but which then literally sizzled in the hearts of his auditors and winged across the country solidifying the Roosevelt sentiment: "We stand at Armageddon and we battle for the Lord!"

That phrase, coming at the end of three-quarters of an hour's diatribe against privilege and of pleading for the cause of the underdog, set the issue of the year. . . . After the meeting closed, Borah and I walked for a few blocks along Michigan Avenue, trying to analyze the speech. Borah was an orator, and he knew how Roosevelt did it. He was tremendously impressed with it, but he was a little frightened, as I was. We had no idea of the hidden forces beneath our feet, the volcanic social substance that was burning deep in the heart of humanity. For three days before the Armageddon speech, the leaders on both sides of the convention contest had been sedulously organizing their forces. When they came to the convention, the Roosevelt leaders assumed that La Follette, who had the Wisconsin delegation and some delegates in the Dakotas and the far

Northwest, would join with the Roosevelt forces in organizing the convention against Taft. But La Follette balked. The Roosevelt forces agreed to take as temporary or permanent chairman anyone whom La Follette chose. The Wisconsin delegation would have been glad to see Governor McGovern as chairman, and he was eager to take the nomination. But the uncompromising spirit of the Wisconsin warrior balked. He could not be coaxed, bluffed, or bribed by offers of convention power, to ally himself with Roosevelt. So he went his own way. Rumor said, and it was fairly well substantiated, that he came to a little town outside Chicago where he could be quickly available at the convention and where he could see his own supporters easily. . . .

When the convention opened Tuesday morning, it had no surprises. The Taft men, through the national committee, put forward young Victor Rosewater, editor of the Omaha *Bee*, as their candidate for temporary chairman, and elected him after a few hours' turmoil and struggle during which time the Roosevelt floor manager and convention spokesman was young Herbert Hadley of Missouri. We had been in the university together and we were dear and beloved friends. He stood on the platform protesting every inch of the proceedings. He was most courteous. Indeed he breathed an air of chivalry that was pleasant to the heart. . . . His elocution was polished, his gestures pleasant, his manner firm and determined. He captured the imagination of the delegates. . . .

The next day, I was at the Roosevelt headquarters. When I went in Beveridge was standing on a chair in the outer room making big medicine oratorically to the waiting statesmen. Roosevelt called me into the inner room and asked: "What do you know about Hadley really?"

I told him about Hadley's determined rise, his obvious but decently repressed ambition; about his capacity for student poker; related the fact that he had been suspended in his senior year at K.U. for some harmless student revelry and had kept up his studies during his suspension and had taken his finals with honor, which amused Roosevelt. . . . All of this amidst the low murmur of the crowd on Michigan Avenue below us—amidst the tension and the sense of strife about the place, the slowly mounting fever that was all but crackling in our blood. Roosevelt, leaning forward on his chair, heard me, knowing that I was giving relevant testimony and competent about young Hadley. He chuckled as I talked.

"Well, they want to compromise on Hadley. He is going to see me in a few moments." He paused. "That story places him." Again he paused and said, snapping his teeth together as he often did when he was a bit perplexed: "I can take Hadley, but they must purge the roll of the convention if they compromise with me, take off the fraudulent delegates; let an honest convention assemble, and it can do what it pleases and I'll help Hadley."

He knew and I knew that that was idle talk. The organized leaders would not trust him. Moreover, they would not trust Hadley after the convention. . . . The story afterwards survived that Roosevelt would not compromise on Hadley, which was not quite true. . . .

The Republican national convention was meeting that week under a guard of nearly a thousand policemen. They crowded the aisles. They ranged through the galleries to maintain order. Not that disorder had broken out, but the marchers in the streets, the great throngs in the gallery were so overwhelmingly bent upon the nomination of Roosevelt that his inevitable defeat seemed a good reason for the cordon of police that ran through the hall like a blue smear around the buff upturned faces of the delegates. . . . I sat for the most part with the reporters where I could look down into the human caldron that was boiling all around me. The committee on credentials had done its work. It had seated enough contested delegates to nominate Taft. . . .

The Roosevelt delegates presented, as their candidate for permanent chairman, the name of Wisconsin's governor, McGovern, whom the Wisconsin delegates heroically deserted. The other La Follette delegates followed the La Follette suit. McGovern was defeated for the election as permanent chairman by Elihu Root, who took the chair. He became the symbol of the Taft machine. He was a man then in his sixties, probably the most learned, even erudite, distinguished, and impeccable conservative Republican in the United States. He had served as United States senator, as secretary of state, as secretary of war. He was the idol of the American bar. He had authority. When he clicked the gavel on the marble block that topped the speaker's table, order ensued almost hypnotically. The gaunt thin-lined features of this man, so conspicuously the intellectual leader of a convention which had been melted by rage into a rabble, stood there calm, serene and sure in his domination of the scene. He looked down upon the sweating, wrathful faces in the pit where the delegates sat, swept his eyes around the vast horseshoe of spectators who jammed the gallery until they sometimes crowded the police guards off their feet. But Root's hands did not tremble, his face did not flicker. He was master. He knew probably what we afterwards found out, that the railing approaches to his rostrum were wound with barbed wire. . . . In any struggle to . . . take possession by force of the organization on the platform, the attackers would have found their hands lacerated if they grabbed those railings or banisters, lacerated even before they got upon the platform, no matter from what angle they tried to rush the speaker's stand. Root seemed to us like a diabolical sphinx. He pushed the program of the convention through steadily and as swiftly as possible.

Hadley, floor manager for Roosevelt, matched Root's basilisk imperturbability with suavity and charm. He was punctilious where Root was grim. He even cracked a joke now and then. I knew when I saw Hadley that he was stricken with tuberculosis and often went to his post with a temperature of 101 or 102, and at the climax of his duty he was carrying 103. Few knew that. I told

Roosevelt, and he cried out for a moment, shocked and pained at the tragedy of it. But there on the floor of the convention he stood, an idol nonetheless, because hundreds, perhaps a few thousands, knew that Hadley had been the rejected compromise offered by the Taft delegates.

It is one of the mysteries of democratic action, this mob sentience, which so often in moments of grave portent casts the players on a tragic stage so nicely. Here for two long, hot, melodramatic days these two—Hadley and Root— stalked the stage, perfect incarnations of the opposing forces.

Root in his morning coat and gray trousers, a lean, almost hatchet-faced man in his late sixties, repressed, almost reticent in his stingy use of words exactly chiseled out of the moment's need, was the greatest corporation lawyer in the United States, a man born on an endowed college campus, representing the impeccable respectability of invested capital. All his life he had been on the money side of lawsuits, representing the invested economic surplus of a thrifty and not too scrupulous plutocracy. . . . Foreign travel had made him a cosmopolitan. Service in the United States Senate and in the Capital had given him that gentle, almost wistful cynicism that garbs the American aristocrat who stems back to Concord or to the James River. He was from every angle the perfect symbol of a propertied class struggling for its privileges which it honestly deems to be its rights. It was deeply symbolic that invested capital should be encased in dark-striped trousers and morning coat, wielding the gavel as a king would wave his scepter, with a dignity that made a show of indignation superfluous.

Beside him many times the convention saw the young Rooseveltian leader, Herbert Hadley. He wore a long gun-barrel double-breasted knee-length coat, and often in controversy smilingly pushed back a flap, shoved his hand in a trouser pocket, using the other for gesticulation, and smiled the guileless smile of lingering youth—boyish, disarming, as he spoke for the lost cause. He came to that rostrum because he had been fighting for ten years all that Root had defended for forty years. Hadley was a reformer. As prosecuting attorney in Kansas City he had been the foe of crooks, big and little; and as prosecuting attorney he had flashed on the national screen sharply, effectively, rather mercilessly cross-examining John D. Rockefeller the elder, who was the lion totem of the clan of predatory respectability in American industry. Hadley was the David to Rockefeller's Goliath. . . .

Slowly, motion by motion, phase by phase, the steamroller crushed its way toward the nomination of Taft. And here is a funny American expression: In the midst of all the rancor and wormwood pumping in the hearts of the delegates, every time a motion was offered by the Taft people, a thousand toots and imitation whistles of the steamroller engine pierced the air sharply, to be greeted with laughter that swept the galleries. An American crowd will have a terrible time behind barricades, or surging up Pennsylvania Avenue to overwhelm the White

House. It will probably laugh itself to death on the way. Kipling said it of the American: "His sense of humor saves him whole."

Looking back, I don't remember how I wrote my stories for the newspapers. I did them faithfully, and I think they were good stories. I can remember hours at the reporters' table as I watched the Taft steamroller crush its way through its program. I can remember gay mealtimes with the Adams trained seals and with other newspapermen who always congregated with their kind. I can remember conferences with the Kansas delegation. We stood almost solidly (two districts dissenting) with the Roosevelt forces. Henry Allen, who was chairman of our delegation and our most distinguished delegate, had been picked by Colonel Roosevelt's board of strategy to say farewell on behalf of the Roosevelt delegates to the victorious Taft forces when Taft's nomination was made. And I can remember well how proud our delegation was of Henry, and how delighted I was with his speech which we read together before he spoke it.

I can remember wiggling in and out of the crowded Florentine Room of the Roosevelt headquarters like an overfed ferret, nosing out little inside notes of news for my daily articles. I can remember quiet talks with Roosevelt in his room alone. He was becoming deadly as his defeat approached. We discussed the possible bolt. We discussed the formation of a new party. There again I rejected it, but there again I was determined to follow my leader after I had advised him against a course which seemed inevitable. He knew I would follow. Then a curtain falls and I do not remember when the decision was made that Roosevelt should bolt the nomination of Taft and run, either with a rump nomination or as the candidate of a new party. . . . But I do remember these things: Sitting at the reporters' table, I heard Henry Allen's ironic diatribe as he stood before Chairman Root and bade farewell to the Taft majority. It was a masterpiece of amiable sarcasm. And I was astonished to realize that I had not detected, when my eyes had read this speech, the fact that its climactic sentence lacked a verb. No one else noticed this. Afterwards Henry saw it and we had a pleasant titter about it. But the hour was too tense for grammar.

When Henry finished his tearless farewell, all Roosevelt delegates marched out of the building with as much dignity as men of wrath can assume in defeat. The Kansas delegates met immediately after the rout, and I resigned as Republican national committeeman for two good reasons: First, we wanted to hold the Kansas end of the Republican national committee, and I would not even pretend to support Taft under the wicked circumstances which surrounded his nomination; second, we elected a good smiling Republican who would go through the motions of supporting Taft with some sincerity and who was nevertheless politically aligned to our faction in Kansas.

I left the convention after the progressives walked out, but returned an hour later to see the final obsequies. It was a dreary performance, the nomination of

Taft and of James Sherman for vice president. Those who remained in the galleries stayed only to hoot ribaldly as the delegates on the floor, amid a wilderness of vacant chairs, went through the motions of reading their platform and nominating their ticket. Late in the afternoon they adjourned. I had a long day's story to tell to the readers who were taking my syndicated articles in two score newspapers. I did not drop into the Roosevelt headquarters in the Congress Hotel after the adjournment, but hurried to my room to write.

For some reason I did my own filing that night, which meant that . . . [when I finished] it was well along into the middle of the evening. I came back to the hotel and sat down alone to have the first good meal I had had since breakfast. . . . It must have been nine o'clock, perhaps later, as I was still feeding rather luxuriously and abundantly, when I noticed the dining room filling up. Ed Mullaney, one of the Kansas bolting delegates, came in, sat down beside me, and asked: "Why weren't you over to Orchestra Hall?"

I told him why, and he began to laugh. "Well," he said, "you missed the big show."

I said: "What show?"

"Oh," he said, grinning and knowing how funny it was, "we have organized the Progressive party. Roosevelt made a ripsnorting speech and the crowd tore the roof off and we are on our way!"

And I didn't know a thing about it. Neither did the readers of my story, and I was supposed to be on the inside of the whole progressive bolt! I had missed the story, and you could have bought me for a nickel. Experiences like that are good for a man when he gets puffed up, and I certainly was puffed up that week in Chicago, what with associating with the great, edging in on conferences, and waddling around with a fat man's strut.

It was too late to file another story. I hurried down to Roosevelt's headquarters. The Colonel yelled at me in his high falsetto, asking where I was and where I had been. Then he told me quickly what had happened after I had left the Kansas delegation. The bolt and the formation of the new party had been decided on several days before, but not the meeting that night at Orchestra Hall. The meeting was most dramatic, as they told me there in the Roosevelt headquarters, everyone sizzling with surging enthusiasm. Before bedtime I also was pretty well carbonated with hopes for the new party.

I was, of course, made national committeeman, and at an informal meeting of the national committee was elected a member of the national publicity committee. Practically all the rebels who walked out of the Republican convention that day joined the new party. And the unseated delegates from the Taft states joined the new party, so that it was not hard to organize it on the spot and call a national convention for mid-August, immediately after the Democrats had nominated their presidential ticket. I went to bed that night chagrined and disgusted with myself at missing the birth of the new party. I believed it was an historic event. . . .

The progressive movement was a ship in the midst of a sea of boiling indignation and surging optimism. I had not been for the bolt. I desired the new party only because I believed it was the fair and honest thing to do to leave the Republican organization, which was hopelessly reactionary. But at the very end, in the afternoon, when I resigned from the Republican national committee, I hoped that Roosevelt would not take the Progressive presidential nomination. I believed then—and events justified me—that we should have held him as our ace, which would also save him from the possible humiliation of defeat at the polls. I felt some way that our party would be the stronger and longer lived if it was not a personal party, not too much a camouflage upon a disgruntled bolt. I suppose that, deep down in my heart, my affection and protective care for the Colonel and his fortunes governed my political judgment, except that I wanted the new party. I did not want Roosevelt to bolt nor to run independently as a sorehead without the new party.

All this seems like raking over old ashes, yet it mattered intensely in that summer day of 1912. I had no other thought or hope or political desire except to get the new party started and at the same time to protect my friend from the consequences of his impetuous desire for revenge. He was burned up with it. Rage, futile, thwarted wrath, glowed in his face that night after the party had been launched in Orchestra Hall. He was not downcast; indeed he was triumphant, full of jokes and quips as though the tea kettle of his heart were humming and rattling the lid of his merry countenance. But rage was bubbling inside of him.

The thing I did not like there at the last was the presence of George Perkins, Morgan's partner, fluttering around the headquarters, smiling and simpering in triumph like a sinister specter—in his gray alpaca suit to match the slightly sprinkled gray of his brown hair and his gray moustache, and it seemed to me covering a steel-gray heart. He was not one of us, the mad mullahs of that selfless effervescing group, the men who had made the battle in the field, those who had carried the primaries in the Republican states of the North. I felt that Perkins was too close to the Colonel, and we—perhaps not I, for I had no sense of jealousy, but Beveridge, Bristow, Amos and Gifford Pinchot, Hiram Johnson, Dolliver, Cummins, Senator Clapp, Senator Bourne, Hadley, Harold Ickes, Governor Osborn of Michigan, the New England crowd, and the New Jersey progressives following George Record and Everett Colby—were not so close as they should have been to the Colonel that day nor, to peek ahead a little, in that campaign.

The only value this part of my story has is in revealing me as a rebel against the rebellion, suspicious even in my enthusiasm, but abating no ounce of energy even though I was standing beside myself, watching myself like a Big Brother.[3] I have always done that. Something in moments of tension has always split my personality. . . . It was so that night and the next day when the progressives crossed the Rubicon and I splashed along with them. Heaven knows, we didn't know why we were going. We knew nothing of the deep urge that was drawing us with the time spirit. But we thought we knew. The phrase was pat and apt that marked our destination: "To social and industrial justice."

I don't know how nor when I squeezed in two weeks that summer in Colorado in our newly bought cabin. But the fortnight filled the cisterns of my spiritual and physical energy, and I came back to Kansas full of a dozen maturing plans, mostly political. In early July I went to Baltimore with George Adams' trained seals to attend and report the story of the Democratic convention.

Adams had rented a three-story house in a good neighborhood half a block back of the Hotel Belvidere. The doctor who lived in it had moved out and left his cook and maybe a housemaid, both colored. We saw little of the maid, but the cook was our delight. She was a square-rigged, scow-bottomed, easy-going person whom we called Jemima, whether it was her name or not. She laughed easily and cooked like an angel. We bought our own groceries. Edna Ferber and I were the stewards and we liked company. We were given to breakfasts, held open house and invited the wide world, our world being more or less circumscribed by newspaper people and writers. We had breakfasts at which often ten or fifteen guests dropped in for pancakes or waffles, sausage and berries then in season—raspberries, strawberries, or huckleberries—or ham and eggs and hot biscuits and honey: whatever Edna and I could pick up at the market and tote home in our basket and whatever Jemima could make for our provender. We liked to have her serve at the table dressed as she was in the kitchen, and we kidded her and courted her and flattered her until she was quite one of us. . . . I think our Yankee manners shocked her a bit. . . .

We stowed Edna on the third floor by herself where she queened it with her typewriter. But below the third floor a man's bed was his own only if he got it, for our guests were forever coming in at all hours and flopping down on empty beds, as the convention tended to hold night sessions and as Fitch, Webster, Darling, and I were compelled by the irregular sessions of the convention to write our stories at midnight. The ménage in the doctor's house was utterly mad. The hotels were crowded and often the big overstuffed chairs in our parlor were filled for the night, and the sofas rarely were empty. . . .

I roamed through the hotel lobbies and into bedrooms of the political

[3]White here uses the phrase, which was capitalized in the original manuscript, that would be later immortalized as a symbol of state surveillance in George Orwell's novel *1984*. Critics of the New Deal in the 1930s also used the phrase in opposing the growth of what they considered an overprotective and potentially oppressive government.

hotels. . . . I was almost as much interested in the nomination of Woodrow Wilson by the Democrats as I was in the Republican nomination of Theodore Roosevelt. For it was obvious that Wilson, who had become the legatee of the Bryan estate in the Democratic party, was having the same fight in his party that Roosevelt had led in the Republican party. . . . I had met Wilson at Madison, Wisconsin, two years before. I had watched his career as governor of New Jersey. . . . I had no great personal liking for [him]. When I met him, he seemed to be a cold fish. I remember I came home from the meeting at Madison, Wisconsin, and told [Sallie] that the hand he gave me to shake felt like a ten-cent pickled mackerel in brown paper—irresponsive and lifeless. He had a highty-tighty way that repulsed me. When he tried to be pleasant he creaked. But he had done a fine liberal job in New Jersey. I liked the way he gathered the Irish politicians about him and let them teach him the game in his gubernatorial fights. In every contest he rang true.

A considerable majority of the states had, in the half decade before 1912, again and again supported liberal leadership in one party or the other. Even in the South, the leaven was beginning to work in states like Texas, the Carolinas, Tennessee, Kentucky. I reasoned that the conservative vote outside of the deep South was negligible and that if we had Roosevelt running against Wilson, the country was sure of a progressive president. And in my heart, loyal as I was to Roosevelt, it made no great difference to me whether Roosevelt or Wilson won. Although I was capable of emotional strain and surface prejudice, my ingrained habit of seeing both sides helped me to size up the realities of the political situation, and I gave my loyalty to the progressive cause rather than to the Progressive party.

Yet the picture of the Democratic party, when the national convention opened in Baltimore, indicated that Champ Clark, Speaker of the Democratic House, had a definite majority of the convention. Under the rules a Democratic nominee must have a two-thirds majority. That rule, for two generations and more, had given the South the veto power over all Democratic nominations. For the South always held two-fifths, or nearly that, of the delegates in the Democratic convention and, as the South generally voted as a block, the nominee had to suit the South. . . .

In the caucusing before the convention it was evident that the reactionary forces of the convention would support Clark. Tammany[4] was for Clark and the old-fashioned gold standard. Old-fashioned silk-stocking Democrats, symbolized by August F. Belmont and Thomas Fortune Ryan, were for Clark. So Bryan gave it out before the convention that he proposed to fight anyone whom Mur-

---

[4]Tammany Hall was the headquarters in New York City of the powerful Tammany Society, which frequently controlled the Democratic party in the city and state.

phy of Tammany, Thomas F. Ryan, and August Belmont supported. The convention had hardly opened before Bryan attacked his foes by name in a rather absurd resolution. It made a sensation, and the Clark forces finally decided to laugh it off by letting it pass unanimously without opposition. They made it ridiculous in the convention, but Bryan made it dramatic in the country. . . .

We reporters all knew that someone, maybe it was [his] brother Charley—it might have been Bryan—was promoting a rather futile cabal to nominate Bryan again that made no headway and excited no opposition save tolerant smiles. Bryan was a strange figure in that convention, a ridiculous man with tremendous power. The sixteen years that had elapsed since the boy orator of the Platte stampeded the convention at Chicago had broadened his girth, thinned his hair, taken youth out of him. He was slightly stooped and had not the cast or countenance of maturity, but a little too much weight in jowl and belly. He was beginning to dress, of summers, in an alpaca coat with a white vest and wrinkled trousers. He had never paid much attention to wherewithal he should be clad, and he had a frowzy look. It was evident from the parliamentary dowdiness of his resolution attacking Ryan and Belmont that his thinking was slightly askew. But his speech supporting his motion certainly had enough fire in it to draw howling approval from the galleries and also of what was evidently a majority of the convention.

It was a sinister exhibition, that response to the Bryan resolution. It was different from the clamor that greeted Roosevelt's leadership at Chicago, more emotional, more unrestrained, more savage. The academic group which was designed to control the Democratic party under the leaders like Wilson certainly had not made over the party. It was still Irish, and the rebel yell still ripped through the applause like a scythe down the swath.

On the first ballot, Clark took the lead. He registered a majority in the early balloting. As Clark was gathering his majority, it became evident that Wilson would be his opponent. Other Democratic candidates lost strength, which generally went to Wilson. After Clark had assembled his majority, he held it for several sessions.

To say that does not carry the sense of drama. To understand the drama we must realize that, ballot by ballot, the country was standing around the billboards of newspapers in great crowds, watching the Baltimore struggle. The cleavage between progressives and conservatives which had been opened by the Chicago convention was deepened and widened in the hearts of the American people by the spectacle at Baltimore. Clark, who was a better politician than Taft, had not revealed his conservatism. That showed forth in the character of his supporting delegates, and after he held his majority for a day the nation realized, as the convention had realized from the first click of the temporary chairman's gavel, that Clark and Bryan were fighting the battle that Roosevelt had lost to Taft.

I was almost as deeply moved, watching Wilson's strength develop, as I had been at Chicago where I had a personal stake in the ballot. . . . As the convention dragged on, far past the four or five days that it ordinarily took to hold a national convention, my respect for Wilson grew and my admiration waxed warm. And when the Nebraska delegation, after days and days of balloting for Clark, broke to Wilson, I stood on the reporters' table top and cheered until I was hoarse, with the galleries; while Tammany and the irreconcilable reactionaries in some of the southern states, and Tom Taggart, the Indiana boss, clung to the spars and lifeboats of the wrecked Clark liner, and all the country knew that Clark's day was done—that the progressives were about to win a victory in Baltimore to offset the defeat in Chicago. . . .

Wilson's strength in the convention slowly mounted until it tipped over the two-thirds majority needed for the nomination. But I did not exult much after that first demonstration of Wilson's power. It was tragic to see Clark's strength crumbling. I say tragic because it was indeed that disintegration of failure which one sees in well-built drama. Human nature is not always lovely in failure, and I sat watching the rise of Wilson and the fall of Clark—seeing men scurry from the Clark camp to the other to save their political hides, watching them sneak into the Wilson camp or go with banners.

I was not sure, as the Clark forces began to break, what really was back of the collapse. Was it the instinct to climb on the bandwagon? Was it the inner latent belief of those delegates who left Clark that the progressive cause was the righteous cause? Was it fear? What was it? It came to the same thing, that crystallization of the progressive elements of the Democratic convention which we witnessed in the Republican convention a few weeks before. But in the Republican convention they came convinced, instructed, militant. No votes were changed after the first click of the temporary chairman's gavel on the marble in the Republican convention at Chicago. But there at Baltimore, before my eyes, I saw the thing happen—the formation of a left-wing group led on the floor unofficially by Bryan, who even in victory looked like an adorable old rag baby but who had steel at the core.

To see that spectacle, in the longest convention I had ever reported, slowly unfold itself, take significance and definite meaning, was something well worth while. I shall never forget that metamorphosis from the mob to the marching cohorts of liberalism following Wilson, led by the spirit of Bryan. One would have said that, with the overthrow of a man like Clark, rather primitively human in his passions, his followers would have made a split in the Democratic party like that I had witnessed in Chicago. The Clark people were mad, but most of them who really understood what they were doing were first of all loyal Democrats who believed in party discipline. . . . However Clark might feel his own wounds (and he did feel them long and deeply—indeed, defeat broke his heart), his fellow Democrats soon became Wilson Democrats, and at the last I could see there, at my reporter's seat at the convention, that Wilson would go before the country with his party phalanx behind him.

In reporting the convention I did not conceal my frank bias for the Wilson cause. I was a liberal before I was a Republican or a Progressive, and was proud then of my heart's loyalty to the cause. Certainly I did not try to write a colorless story. I wrote frankly as a partisan of the liberals in both conventions, and while I told the truth as I saw it, my story was the story of the progressive split in each. There was no nonsense about concealing the cause of the rift, or smoothing it over as a personal triumph for either Taft or Wilson. I painted the conservatives black, and probably made the liberals white-winged angels—which they were not. They were only men, two-legged and frail, walking in strange new roads drawn by something they did not quite understand, following a pattern of political conduct that they could not quite resist, in a drama whose lines they improvised out of the promptings of their hearts.

18

The Birth
of a Party

It was no easy job, when I got home from Baltimore, to assume my part of the leadership which was organized in Kansas from the grassroots for the Progressive party in the campaign that was looming ahead of us. The first job was to hold local conventions to nominate delegates to the first Progressive national convention which was held in the late summer. Henry Allen, who had been the chairman of our delegation to the Republican convention, naturally was the leader of the delegation in the first Progressive convention. I was a delegate. . . .

The day before it met, the word "Bull Moose" became a tag for our party. Reporters asked Colonel Roosevelt, when he first arrived in Chicago for the convention, how he felt. He called out lustily, snapping his teeth, batting his eyes, and grinning like an amiable orangutan: "I feel as strong as a bull moose!" From that hour we, who followed in his train, were Bull Moosers, and proud of it.

It was when we were redecorating the Coliseum at Chicago that we discovered, underneath the bunting that wrapped the railings around the speaker's stand, the banisters, and the steps approaching it, closely wrapped barbed wire. . . . We were hopping mad when we discovered that barbed wire. It was a symbol of all the fraud and force and shenanigans and duress which we had encountered in the Republican national convention a few weeks before. When we decorated the Coliseum we took off the barbed wire and replaced the bunting.

The Bull Moose convention had little gallery support, but we managed to fill the delegates' chairs. I had seen many a protest convention. As a boy I had watched the Greenbackers. As a young man I had reported many a Populist convention. Those agrarian movements too often appealed to ne'er-do-wells, the misfits—farmers who had failed, lawyers and doctors who were not orthodox, teachers who could not make the grade, and neurotics full of hates and ebullient, evanescent enthusiasms. I knew that crowd well. But when the Pro-

gressive convention assembled at Chicago I looked down upon it from the reporters' stand and saw that here was another crowd.

Here were the successful middle-class country-town citizens, the farmer whose
barn was painted, the well-paid railroad engineer, and the country editor. It was
a well-dressed crowd. We were, of course, for woman suffrage, and we invited
women delegates and had plenty of them. They were our own kind too—women
doctors, women lawyers, women teachers, college professors, middle-aged leaders of civic movements, or rich young girls who had gone in for settlement work.
Looking over the crowd, judging the delegates by their clothes, I figured that
there was not a man or woman on the floor who was making less than two thousand a year, and no one, on the other hand, who was topping ten thousand.
Proletarian and plutocrat were absent—except George Perkins, who was too
conspicuous. He and his satellites and sycophants from Wall Street and lower
Broadway, who had known Roosevelt in Harvard, loved him, and misunderstood him. But they had their influence. . . .

Of course when the convention assembled, George Perkins—spic-and-span,
oiled and curled like an Assyrian bull, and a young one, trim and virile—was
conspicuous in all the preliminary proceedings. He was a man for detail, and he
did a right competent job of stage management in that dramatic hour when the
Bull Moose party was born, even though he could not fill the galleries. But on
the speaker's stand, we had notables from all over the land: college presidents,
heads of scientific foundations. Our prize exhibit was Jane Addams. I had something to do with bringing her to the convention, for I had known her many
years. . . . When she came down the aisle back of the speaker's stand where the
other notables wearing Bull Moose badges were arrayed in proud and serried
ranks, the delegates and the scattered spectators in the galleries rose and
cheered. Not even the Colonel got much more rousing cheers than Jane Addams when she rose to second his nomination.

The Colonel was there on the platform, and I saw his eyes glisten with pride
and exultant joy that she was fighting under his banner. I have rarely seen him
happier than he was that moment. The band played "Onward, Christian Soldiers," which probably Perkins or some of his newspapers friends had adopted as
our national anthem; and the crowd cheered and began to sing as the band led.
When our platform was read, it also was interrupted by cheers and outbursts of
the band, probably signaled by Perkins or his assistant stage managers. It was all
beautifully done, and after the platform had been adopted and the nominations
of Colonel Roosevelt for president and Governor Hiram Johnson of California
for vice president, we adjourned, singing "Praise God from Whom All Blessings
Flow."

I went to Chicago nearly a week before the convention assembled, for I was
interested more than anything else in the Progressive platform. . . . I sat in the

drafting committee on platform and was able to write in many of the ideas that had been embodied in the Kansas platform of 1910. We worked four days and the better part of three nights on that first Progressive platform. Dr. William Draper Lewis, dean of the law school of the University of Pennsylvania, was the chairman of the drafting committee. He had prepared a platform much more conservative than the Kansas platform. Several others appeared with ready-made platforms. Gifford Pinchot, who had consulted with Colonel Roosevelt as his old friend and supporter, appeared with a fine program which he and his brother Amos had submitted to the Colonel. After we had wrangled for a day or so over the Lewis, Kansas, and Pinchot platforms, Dr. George W. Kirchwey, dean of Columbia University Law School,[1] appeared with the most radical of all the platforms. He also had read it to Colonel Roosevelt. They had gone over it. The Colonel approved it. Apparently the Colonel was ready to approve anything that any responsible Progressive brought to him in sincerity. So by the time Dr. Kirchwey appeared in the committee he had the lasting blessing of our hero; and I should say, looking back over those years, that the Kirchwey draft was followed more nearly than any other draft in formulating the first Progressive national platform. For that day, it was radical

On the political side of current issues the platform declared for direct primaries, nationwide preferential primaries, the direct election of United States senators, the short ballot, and finally the initiative and referendum and recall in states. We declared for civil service reform, the exclusion of federal officeholders from party conventions, publicity for a limitation of campaign contributions, limitation of armament and two battleships a year while negotiations for limitation of armaments were going on. Our two controversies were over the tariff and the antitrust laws. We were in session two nights and a day. The tariff plank I submitted after a long wrangle. It was written by William S. Culbertson, a young man from Emporia who was working under Dr. Frank W. Taussig of Harvard, whom President Taft had drafted to study a possible tariff commission. The tariff plank pointed the way to a tariff commission.

The antitrust plank divided us even more seriously. We could not agree on the procedure that the government should use in attacking the trusts. One group of us—the left-wing Progressives—wished to catalogue specifically the evils of the trust which could be defined in law and made actionable. The right-wing Progressives, [including George Perkins], wanted a general definition of the kind of antisocial conduct which should be indictable. This side felt that to specify the kinds of indictable conduct would limit the courts in proceeding against the trusts. Looking back over the years, I realize that the differences between Perkins and Pinchot were purely academic, but they seemed vital at the time. The Pin-

---

[1] Kirchwey had in fact resigned the deanship of Columbia Law School in 1910.

chots certainly represented the views of the convention. Perkins, with equal certainty, represented the views of Colonel Roosevelt's New York friends, who were with him not so much on economic grounds as because they felt he had been unfairly cheated out of the nomination.

Colonel Roosevelt knew of the wrangle and the deadlock in the committee. Indeed in the convention hall the delegates were marking time, listening to speeches, cheering, raising a hullabaloo as all presidential conventions do while the committee on resolutions is out. The Colonel called some friends together and drafted a platform which Senator Joseph Dixon brought to the committee. Senator Beveridge came to explain the Colonel's position and asked us to adopt the plank. There was still a row. We modified the Colonel's plank and a compromise was reached. But it took time to modify it, so the convention went on and named the Colonel for president, amid wild enthusiasm.

When the row over the antitrust plank was raging, one of the funniest things I ever saw in politics turned up. I was sitting on a chair in the hall of the Blackstone Hotel, working on my newspaper story, and saw the Colonel pendulating between Perkins' room and Pinchot's room. He would toddle out of one room, looking over the top of his glasses, with the contested plank in his hand, and enter another room—maybe Perkins' room; and then in a few moments, like a faithful retriever, would come popping out, panting across the hall to Pinchot's room, still with the paper in his hand, grinning at me like a dog wagging his tail, as he tried to compromise the differences between the pinfeather wings of his new party. . . .

After the nomination of Hiram Johnson for vice president, Dr. Lewis, chairman of our platform committee, appeared, read the platform. When he came to the compromise plank it was evident that George Perkins was angry. . . . In the compromise, we had left the matter of specific listing of indictable acts rather vague. But Perkins was nevertheless angry. When Dr. Lewis finished reading that plank, Perkins rose, slammed his chair back, and walked out of the convention, a one-man bolt. It was the contention of Mr. Perkins' friends that the clerk of the committee gave Dr. Lewis the wrong plank to read. That is possible. It is not in my judgment probable. At any rate, a sizable row arose behind the curtains. The plank Lewis had read, which in my recollection was the one the committee had adopted, was given to the press. . . .

It was a merry row. Nevertheless the platform itself was notable and vastly more important than the row which it produced. To realize what that platform meant in the way of social and economic advance, one has to go back to 1912, twenty years before the New Deal, and grasp the fact that even then a considerable minority of the American people voting the Bull Moose ticket and another minority supporting the Democratic platform under Mr. Wilson that year voted for the same things. We, in our Progressive platform, declared in favor of work-

men's compensation laws, for the insurance against sickness and unemploy-
ment, the prohibition of child labor, minimum wages for women, safety and
health standards for various occupations, prohibition of night work for women
along with an eight-hour day for them, one day's rest in seven, and an eight-
hour day in continuous twenty-four-hour industries. When the New Deal came
with its program, it went little further than Colonel Roosevelt's Progressive
party had gone twenty years before. It was no wonder that Herbert Hoover,
who gave us a thousand dollars in 1912 to promote the candidacy of the Colonel and this platform, declared twenty years later that the reforms of the second
Roosevelt were long overdue. . . .

We were mighty well pleased with ourselves, filled with a glowing sense of duty
well done. We also believed that we had seen an historic occasion, the birth of a
party that was destined to rise and take in the country the place that the Republican party had occupied for fifty years. I know this, that a thousand delegates
carried home little mementos of the day and hour, effigies of the Bull Moose,
pictures of the Colonel, badges identifying themselves as delegates. They hoped
that these trinkets would be family heirlooms in another day and time. The occasion had all of the psychological trappings and habiliments of a crusade. We
were indeed Christian soldiers "marching as to war!"—and rather more than
mildly mad.

The morning after the convention adjourned, I had my first disturbing disillusion about the Progressive party. The platform which our committee had agreed
upon was published. But its antitrust section and the Pinchot plank had, during
the night, been definitely changed back to the Perkins plank, which appeared in
the morning press. Mr. Perkins' publicity agent, who was also secretary of the
national committee—Oscar King Davis—saw to it that, after the convention adjourned, the morning papers carried the Perkins plank in the platform.

We started a row and had the Colonel's promise that he would see that the official publication of the platform was corrected, which was done for one or two
editions. But I seem to remember that in later editions of the platform which the
national committee gave out, the antitrust plank was again modified to meet
somewhat the Perkins requirements. This was not the way Christian soldiers
marched. . . . It was a detour down a purple primrose path that we starry-eyed
martyrs disdained to tread. I set this episode down, trivial though it is, because
it shows that human organizations have human faults. Little lies, little greeds,
little cowardices appear even in the most high-toned endeavors and in the midst
of the grandest heroics. We who thought ourselves marching in the gleaming rai-
ment of saints in that day and hour blamed this diversion upon Perkins. I still
think we were not mistaken. I remember this, that the Colonel and I went to bat
on the proposition, and he could not believe that Perkins was responsible for
the change in the text of the antitrust plank. His soft side was loyalty to his

friends, and I thought, as we wrangled, that I should be the last to blame his soft side, otherwise I should have been cast in outer darkness long before. For he had had to defend me from the Perkinses in his life for fifteen years and still he tolerated me, and we could quarrel in mutual respect and affection.

It may be excusable to pause in this narrative for a moment and write in some account of the Colonel as he appeared to me in that convention. His wrath was submerged. He was ebullient, clicking his teeth sometimes like a snare-drum obbligato to the allegro of his blithe, humorous, self-deprecatory assurance. The squeaking falsetto in which he gently clowned himself was most disarming. He seemed full of animal spirits, exhaustless at all hours, exuding cheer and confidence. His paunch was widening a little. The cast of his countenance at rest was a little grimmer than it had been in those first days when I had known him as assistant secretary of the navy and as a young president. Into him had come not merely the sense of power but the unconsciousness of power. . . . There in Chicago, in the late summer of 1912, he was in command and yet was forever disclaiming, vaunting his modesty genially. Yet with all his physical virility, he was indeed the Bull Moose charging about the hotel corridors, stalking down an aisle of the Coliseum while the crowds roared, walking like a gladiator to the lions. In those days of the accouchement of the Bull Moose, he was superb. What if he tried to cover and to defend Perkins? What if he was a little obvious now and then as he grabbed the steering wheel of events and guided that convention not too shyly? I felt the joy and delight of his presence and knowing his weakness still gave him my loyalty—the great rumbling, roaring jocund tornado of a man, all masculine save sometimes for a catlike glint, hardly a twinkle, in his merry eyes.

The day after the Bull Moose convention adjourned in August 1912, the national central committee of the party met to organize. It was assumed by his supporters and by many other members of the committee that George Perkins would be made chairman of the executive committee of the national committee. I rebelled. I liked George Perkins personally. He had lived in Kansas long enough to acquire a folksy way with him. He exuded pleasantly the odor of great power that came from his Morgan connection. He had done a dozen little things to accommodate me and bind me to him which I could not forget. So in my rebellion I was tempted to stop or compromise. But I did not. I went clear through. Oscar King Davis, who was secretary, in his book[2] recalls that "characteristically" I took the floor in the central committee meeting and spoke against Perkins, warning the committeemen against him as a leader of our party. We had elected Joseph M. Dixon chairman, and Perkins was to be the inside mainspring of the party largely because he was furnishing and collecting the funds. My protest was

[2]*Released for Publication* (Houghton Mifflin, 1925). [White's note.]

probably crude and angry. O. K. Davis remembered it as a bit quixotic and smiled across the years at it. He wrote in his autobiography: "That eminent Kansas Progressive, William Allen White, Editor of the Emporia *Gazette*, who is so progressive that he never is long in any one place politically, seemed to be the leader of this opposition. He had the courage of his convictions too. He spoke right out in the meeting."

Harold Ickes, on the other hand, in a letter to me thirty years later, cast me as something of a hero, which I was not. I was just a scared but determined, fat, and preposterous-looking young fellow in his early forties trying to overcome his doubts by venting his wrath a little too raucously perhaps, but I did look Perkins squarely in the eye and as gently as I could, being full of indignation. I denounced him and opposed his selection as chairman of the executive committee. A small group, fewer than half a dozen out of the forty, followed me in the ballot. Harold Ickes, who held Jane Addams' proxy among others, and Myer Lissner, who also took the floor to support me, and one of the Pinchots stood by me.

Then, of course, what always happens to a man who proves he has more courage than judgment, happened to me: A dozen or twenty of the committee-men who voted against me came to me privately to congratulate me and express agreement with what I said, giving various perfectly good reasons why they did not vote with me. Something like that always happens to men or women who "go too far." Indeed, Perkins himself, immediately after the meeting adjourned, came over, put his arm around my shoulder, and said he hoped he would prove that I was wrong. We had no personal quarrel. We parted respected friends. He had his way of looking at things; I had mine. But I refused to follow him, then or ever. I wonder what he would have said in his memoirs about me and my kind. I have grasped the velvet glove of many iron hands but have enjoyed none more heartily than George Perkins'. I have looked into the gentle, warm, gray, stubborn beam in many eyes,[3] but none more deadly than George Perkins' happy smile. If I have painted him as a villain, I am sorry. He was just. He was playing his game righteously enough from his viewpoint, and I was playing mine. In the Punch-and-Judy show[4] of the moment, we two, a part of the century's struggle to realize humanity's ideals, were puppets in the pageant. We knocked our heads together for the delectation of the angels who saw far ahead the way the tide was washing. And little we knew about it.

From Chicago I went home and devoted the rest of the summer and the autumn until election helping the Kansas state Progressive chairman to organize

[3]Jesus said in his Sermon on the Mount, "Why beholdest thou the mote that is in thy brother's eye, but considerest not the beam that is in thine own eye?"

[4]Punch and Judy were the central characters of popular traditional British puppet shows that featured a heavy dose of violent slapstick.

Kansas for the Roosevelt ticket. We decided that we would raise our own funds. We wrote to the national committee that we would accept none of its money. We suspected it was Perkins' money—and were right about it. He had donated or collected most of the national committee's funds. So we raised ten thousand dollars, and it was my job to pass the hat for the Kansas campaign. This was all we needed, and we had a little money in the bank when we quit, less than two hundred dollars. We had every county organized thirty days after the Bull Moose convention had adjourned.

When we had refused in Kansas to take George Perkins' money . . . U. S. Sartin, the state chairman, and I felt free, and we notified the national headquarters that we did not want any more Perkins pamphlets. Perkins had printed a score of different pamphlets on public affairs—for instance, "What Perkins Thinks about the Tariff," "Perkins on the Trust," "George W. Perkins' Views on Labor," and so on down the line. They came in great bales by express collect to Emporia, and I refused to pay the charges and sent them back, after I had notified the national headquarters not to send them. The next time I saw George Perkins, I told him what I had done, to be sure that he knew, and he chuckled: "You old devil! You're an Injun. Don't you ever forget?" Whereupon we sat down and had a talk about the things on which we did agree, and they were many.

Early in the campaign I began to feel that we Bull Moosers were playing an unfair trick upon the Taft Republicans. It was this: The Republican presidential electors which we had chosen at the state convention in late May or early June were all Roosevelt supporters. They were going to vote for Roosevelt, all of them. Yet he was not the Republican nominee. They would be on the Republican ticket. If they remained there, the Taft men would be disfranchised. To me it was an open-and-shut proposition that this was unfair. And somewhat by bull strength, in spite of divided opinion in our party, I took those Rooseveltian electors off the Republican ticket. The Taft Republicans put up their own men as electors and transferred the Roosevelt electors to the Bull Moose ticket. While I was in the midst of it, before it had been done, I saw the Colonel and told him what I thought I should do, that it was plain, honest, political decency to do so. I knew that in doing so I had turned over the state to Wilson. For what with the confusion about the electors and also with the normal Republican strength of the state divided between the Bull Moose and the Taft men, the Democrats inevitably would win. When I had finished my story, the Colonel looked at me for a moment with his jaw agape; then it clicked shut and he asked: "White, do you really *have* to do that?"

I answered, "It's only honest, Colonel." He sighed, and I detected sadness in his voice: "Yes, I suppose so. It's only honest." But I knew what he thought. Still in the end, I am sure he was glad that I did it. . . .

During the early part of the campaign, the Bull Moose national committee provided Colonel Roosevelt with a special train in which he toured the country, accompanied by two or three score metropolitan newspapermen. His train came to Emporia one Saturday night, and he stopped with us. The campaign was at its height, and the visit of the Colonel to Emporia was an event of the greatest magnitude. Presidents Hayes and Grant had been here, and Taft had stopped for a few moments while the engine on his train took on water. But at the height and in all the excitement of the campaign, the nation's most spectacular figure spent Sunday in Emporia. The White family had its surrey with a fringed top and Tom who went "clop, clop, clop" down the street. We had a score, maybe two score, of automobiles in the town, and all the owners—Democrats, Republicans, and Bull Moosers—offered their cars to us. But we loaded the Colonel, on Sunday morning, in the old family surrey, much to the shame of the town; and I took D. A. Ellsworth, the town poet, and Fred Newman, the town banker, with me as I drove the Colonel around showing him the sights of the city. It was supposed that I would take him to our Congregational Church, and it was packed to the doors. But the Colonel asked if there was a German Lutheran Church in town. There was, and I took him there. [Sallie] did not go. She was afraid to leave the preparations for the Sunday dinner. So we four—the poet, the banker, the hero, and I—marched down the aisle of that little church where a score or so of worshippers were gathered, by no means a fashionable church. When the preacher saw what he had, he turned pale. He afterwards told me he felt like dropping dead, but he went through with the service and read his sermon without changing it. He made some slight reference to the Colonel's presence. Of course everyone in the congregation had stared at him in amazement. But the preacher lined out the hymns, and I was interested and delighted to note that the Colonel stood up with the congregation and sang three verses of "How Firm a Foundation, Ye Saints of the Lord," without taking up the book. As a song-bird, the Colonel was nothing to brag about. He had a rough bass about a half tone off key, and no ear for music, melody or harmony. But he bellowed through the hymn without "da-daing" on a line, so I was proud of him.

Emporia en masse entertained the two carloads of newspapermen on the wide verandas of the country club building and on the golf course, and brought two wagonloads of watermelons ripe and just off the vine, after cooling them overnight at the ice plant. A few of the sports produced liquor, but not much, and the newspapermen had to spend a dry Sunday. But they had a view of a midwestern town with its wide green lawns, its arched elm trees, its two colleges, its country club, and its lovely parks.

At our home after church we tried to shield the Colonel. We had put a great heaping platter before him on the table and did our own pushing and shoving. Little Mary, aged eight, would not come to the table because she thought she could get more fried chicken, without being noticed, by staying in the kitchen. Billy, his mother, the Colonel, and I devastated that heaping platter of fried chicken, mashed potatoes, and creamed gravy. The Colonel seemed to enjoy it. After his Sunday dinner, we put him to bed for an hour. He was tired. When he came downstairs after his rest, we three sat in the front room considering the cosmos. The talk drifted to the Republican convention. I asked him if he knew about the barbed wire around the bunting-covered railing that shielded the rostrum. His eyes snapped and he rose, backed himself in front of the living-room fireplace, and I never saw him so wrought with wrath:

"Yes, I knew about that barbed wire. Someone told me the day of the nomination. I wanted to take a pistol and go into the convention and, if trouble had started, if those policemen had tried to use violence on our men, I think I could have given a good account of myself!" He stopped. His teeth were set, and he cried: "And, by George, I wouldn't have wasted a bullet on a policeman. I would have got Root and got him quick!"

We sat through a moment's silence and, his rage being spent, he sighed and smiled, began clicking his jaws, walked back to his chair, and exclaimed without passion: "I suppose it's all right. It's all for the best!"

And the talk turned to the current campaign. . . . Ten minutes later he was telling us in his chuckling falsetto that in Denver the patriots referred to diminutive Judge Ben Lindsey—trim, slim, sawed-off dynamo in a Prince Albert coat to give him the dignity of his intellectual capacity—as "the bull mouse"! Then we reverted to his campaign. He was counting his chickens and felt that he had a reasonable hope to win the election. He counted Kansas in his column. I doubted it, but at the last I, too, felt Kansas would turn to him, for certainly the vocal part of the population was for Roosevelt overwhelmingly, and he did give Wilson a good race in Kansas. . . .

In the end Kansas went Democratic. . . . Wilson carried the state with Roosevelt running him a decent second and Taft a poor third. So it was in all the states of the North and West. The solid South did not crack or crumble. But it was evident that the progressive or liberal movement was overwhelmingly in the majority in the United States. The election of 1912 was the first election in which the liberal movement registered its strength. Bryan had never been able to command so many Democratic electoral votes as Wilson, who definitely inherited Bryan's strength. And no liberal Republican, not even Roosevelt in 1904 when his liberalism was revealing itself, ever before had called out the voting strength that Roosevelt commanded. So I was happy about the election, though I lost my first choice and my heart's political desire. I felt sure that the liberal movement in the United States had come to stay, that a party was organizing to carry its banner, and that in some way we should find a permanent vehicle in which to assemble the votes of the liberal majority in the United States. . . . The

National Bull Moose Committee had funds. It set up a Washington office where bills were drafted and lobbying was started to put through Congress the immediately realizable ideals of our platform. And so the year closed without an anticlimax.

The year 1913 found the White family—father, mother, the two children, their Grandma White, and our faithful Martha, who was nurse, cook, maid, friend, and companion—all settled in a beach house on the Pacific, at La Jolla, California. [Sallie] had uprooted us, bag and baggage, first because she thought I was tired and a new environment would refresh me; and second because she thought the novel we were working on was now ripe.

For four months I fiddled away on it, two morning hours six days a week. In the twilight we walked together along the ocean, talking over the story, developing the plot, trying to realize the characters. We knew exactly what we wanted to dramatize, but it was hard to fit the fable to fictional reality. Yet it was a lovely time. The children played in the ocean and in the sand by the bathing cove. Sallie and I bought vegetables and fresh fruits of the Chinaman who came to the back door every day. We made friends with the fishermen and got all kinds of rare sea foods—clams, abalone, sand dabs, or smelts that came scurrying into the cove when the whales were outside and wiggled to death on the beaches as the tide went out. From the Mexicans who lived in the villages along the road to San Diego we bought strange hot sausages and Spanish groceries that were good. . . .

Every week or so we went to San Diego to see a good play. . . . We had books and magazines aplenty, and just enough of give and take in parties to keep us interested in the life about us. Of course we became villagers in thirty days and were absorbed into the village life of the wandering tourist colony, a small but pleasant group—writers in exile, health-seekers, idlers, golf-playing retired professional men and merchants and farmers from the Middle West. . . . Emporia and Kansas and the Bull Moose party sloughed out of my conscience, and I took on the petty satisfying worries of my environment. . . . So the winter wore away, and in late spring we packed up our caravan and went home. . . .

The Bull Moosers in Kansas and everywhere were full of ebullient enthusiasm. Although no election was looming up that year, the Bull Moosers were holding meetings, particularly giving dinners, hearing speeches, and singing songs. Our national leaders were hurrying about from state to state addressing these glamorous dinners. It looked as though the Bull Moose party was sweeping everything before it. The Republicans had no such dinners, and the Democrats feeding at Woodrow Wilson's pie counter had no need for them. The thing we should have noticed was that at all these dinners in the county seats and at the banquets on formal occasions at the capitals, the same group of patriots was gathered around the board. Why that should have fooled us, I cannot imagine.

Two or three hundred people at a dinner is a small fraction of the electorate, and we held few public meetings, for no campaign was pending. We could not see that the strength of our cause was waning. We applauded wildly when our speakers demanded social and industrial justice; we were delighted when they talked about "distributive justice" and proved that the country had solved its problem of production of wealth and that the great problem of the distribution of wealth challenged the country. Yet we Bull Moosers—middle-class folks who had received all our share in the "distribution of the national income" and were fat and saucy in our attack upon aggrandized capital, were almost alone in our charge upon the citadel of privilege. . . .

While we sat at our feasts across the land, the whole cause and justification for our attack upon the established order was paling. Business [was] booming. We needed another linotype for the *Gazette*. Advertisers were crowding its pages. Often we had six pages and sometimes, maybe once or twice a month, eight pages. The farmers were getting good prices for their grain and livestock. They were to look back on those days from 1909 to 1914 as ideal years when farm prices were relatively just, compared with the prices of labor. The injustices of the distributive system were being corrected, not by laws but by speeding up the wheels of industry in the United States and to an extent around the world.

In our own country a new element had come into the industrial and commercial picture. The automobile age had arrived. Ford's assembly belt[5] was turning out Model T's. A kind of democracy was coming into the world and not through the ballot box, not by marching cohorts in the streets carrying banners, not even out of Congress or its laws. The thing which was changing our world was the democratization of transportation. The files of the *Gazette* showed that we had our first commercial garage in Emporia at that time. By way of humorous reference we called it "the garbage." In a few months a second garage appeared in the business part of town. We bragged that Lyon County had over fifty motorcars. Soon a motorized truck appeared on Commercial Street. The town was paving rapidly. All over the middle states, the prairie states, where roads had to be laid out on alluvial soil, the King road drag appeared. County and township road officers used it to smooth off dirt roads after a rain. It made going easy for the motorists who ventured to travel between towns. They organized by states and published road maps showing where the roads were dragged.

Then suddenly appeared a new advertiser in the *Gazette*. He was the Buick agent. Then came an advertisement for the Maxwell and the Winston, and the *Gazette* traded advertising from an automobile manufacturer for a motorcar, thirteen hundred dollars worth. But we felt the car was too expensive for us to

[5]The efforts of industrialist Henry Ford (1863–1947) to increase manufacturing efficiency culminated in the introduction in 1913 of the first factory assembly line, capable of mass-producing inexpensive standardized automobiles.

use, so Old Tom continued to clop up and down Exchange Street. We sold the motorcar to a doctor in a neighboring town and thus got cash for our advertising. Times were good and even a blighting drought in central Kansas in the summer of 1913 did not check the wave of prosperity.

That summer, taking the manuscript of our novel, we went to Colorado. We had enlarged our cabin, building a fourteen-foot porch on three sides of it. We also built a log cabin one hundred feet up the hill and two smaller bedroom cabins, so we were living like princes. . . . For a couple of months I went up from the main cabin of our Colorado home to the log cabin on the hill and pecked away at my typewriter on the novel. . . .

When I saw Theodore Roosevelt early in 1914, I sensed that he was fearful—perhaps the word "leery" expresses it—of the divine mission of the Progressive party. He began to realize even quicker than I did, and certainly before most of his crusading followers suspected, the approaching debacle. For a considerable percentage—anywhere between 40 and 60 percent—of the Roosevelt vote in 1912 was a protest vote against the outrageous action of the national Republican committee. Thousands, perhaps millions, of citizens who voted for Theodore Roosevelt for president in 1912 as the Bull Moose candidate had no idea of endorsing the radical Bull Moose platform. And being loyal Republicans who had sinned, they began to get most virtuous when they thought of their sins. So they began to be highly indignant at the thought of a third party. We, of the faithful, noted that we could identify the stray sheep of our party when they said, "Of course I was for Roosevelt, but—," and called them the "Roosevelt butters." And what a lot of them there were!

Despite the "Roosevelt butters" in many of the northern states which Roosevelt carried or where he ran second in 1912, the faithful, of whom I was one, began to hold national, state, and congressional district conferences or conventions to find candidates who would fill our ticket in the congressional and state elections of 1914. It was a tough job. It was one thing to drum up a crowd singing "Onward, Christian Soldiers," hurrahing for Roosevelt, and booing Taft after the dramatic swindle in the convention of 1912. It was quite another to go out in cold blood and get men to run on a third-party county ticket. The people who want county offices are timid folk, easily scared about their party standing. Yet my job as national committeeman, along with the Kansas state chairman, Mr. Sartin, was to get out a county ticket in every county and to get Bull Moose congressmen running in every district. We did it, and we also put out a state ticket with Henry J. Allen running for governor and Victor Murdock, who was a congressman in a safe Republican district, running for United States senator. I remember that when Henry promised me to run he said: "There's just one little thing: Will you call up Elsie and tell her?"

So I called up Elsie and I said: "Now look here, Elsie, don't be worried about Henry. He won't be elected. Not a Chinaman's chance. All we want—"

Then she cut in: "Now Will, if he is not going to be elected, why do you want him to run? It sounds foolish to me. No sense in it!"

But he ran, and with Elsie's consent, on high patriotic grounds. And, recalling the telephone dialogue, I know now that I also knew the truth about the Bull Moose party. . . . However, I felt in 1914 that we had the nucleus of a party, that we should not abandon it. In those days, former President Taft was gibing at us by saying we had an army of colonels, which was the ignoble truth. But I felt that if the colonels would stand the fire of 1914, they could rally, not to a victory in 1916, but to a substantial minority that might make a party of real principles four years later. . . .

For two years our general staff of colonels had been working with the progressive members of the Senate and the House of Representatives in Washington, forming a coalition between the liberal Republicans and Progressives on the one hand, and the progressive Democrats on the other. We sent emissaries to President Wilson persuading him to join us in putting through as much of the federal program as was possible. In his first term, therefore, we had established a Federal Trade Commission. We had set up the Tariff Commission with powers to change tariffs in certain cases in accordance with passing needs. We had established the parcel post in opposition to the railroads. We had written a strong railroad commission law. We had achieved the direct election of United States senators. We had written a law providing for minimum wages for women and children in industry and had passed a law prohibiting child labor—both of which the Supreme Court invalidated—and we had furnished public opinion which sustained the Supreme Court in establishing the eight-hour day in the railroad industry. This decision was a large legal hole in the dike upholding what was then the ten- and twelve-hour day. And by the time the war, with its reactionary wave, was well under way, we Progressives in the Bull Moose party and under the leadership of Woodrow Wilson, had come a long way in our first march from 1901, when Roosevelt had entered the White House. . . . Certainly in that body of legislation was evidence of a political revolution in the hearts of the American people. . . .

I set these things down here not to write a history of the Progressive party but merely to list the things in which I had been interested—the things that had been a part of my daily life in politics for fifteen years—the things that had brought me into friendly relations with liberal leaders in both parties. . . . I had little part in it except as legs, go-between errand-boy, compromiser. Probably also my irrepressible tendency to gibe and quip and relate many a wise saw and modern instance furnished comic relief for many a tedious hour in many a brittle situation. . . .

19

Decline
and Fall

In the late summer of 1914, the White family cut loose from politics and went to Colorado, where I worked again in the log cabin above our living rooms there on the novel that had been engaging me for so many years. And into that pleasant recreation plunged the World War. In the mountain valley below us and on the hills around us within a mile radius were half a dozen Kansas college professors and professional men. They gathered on our porch when Bill and Mary brought up the mail from the post office—we were taking four daily papers besides the *Gazette*—and we sat there with our families and discussed the news as it was blazoned in the headlines. The news was inconceivable. I remember Professor Hodder, of the history department of the University of Kansas, who had a low opinion of newspapers anyway, sitting tight-lipped and grim while we discussed the invasion of Belgium, the fall of Liège, the sack of Louvain, and all the horrors that followed that gray steel wave of Germans that washed over Belgium. For two days, maybe three, Hodder declared: "It can't be so. They aren't telling the truth. Why, there's a treaty between Belgium and Germany that would prevent it!" And so on.

When he had to accept the invasion of Belgium as a fact, despite the treaty, the foundations of his faith in modern civilization completely caved in, and he was a heartbroken man for nearly a week. But all those first scenes in Belgium in 1914 are associated in my memory with the front porch of our cabin, with the meadow and its waving grasses below, the long lateral moraine rising above the meadow and over that the snow-clad range, with Long's Peak arching far above the range in solemn majesty, flecked and speckled with white snow down its granite face. We, who were gathered there from the colleges around about to read the news and mull over the papers, had no idea of the significance of the war, what it would mean to modern civilization.

And I did not remotely dream that this war was a part of the revolution that I had seen gathering in Europe, that I was myself encouraging with all my might and main in my own land. It seemed like a quarrel between the crowned heads of Europe, the Hapsburgs, the Hohenzollerns, the Romanoffs.[1] . . . I realized with sadness that it would affect the United States indirectly by turning the minds of the people from reform to safety. . . . I was that wise. But after the war councils on the front porch were over, I climbed up to my desk in the log cabin and pecked away at my story or wrote letters to my fellow reformers in Kansas and elsewhere, bemoaning the wreck of matter and the crash of worlds.

In the autumn of 1914 the people of the United States must have taken a deep interest in the war. For I remember well that we Bull Moosers in our Kansas campaign for congressmen, senator, and governor in November, ascribed our defeat to the war. We had fine audiences, in some cases great audiences, for Henry Allen and Victor Murdock, our candidates for governor and senator. We brought one or two of our national orators like Beveridge or Pinchot or Raymond Robins to the state and had what might be called an outpouring of the masses at every meeting. But the Bull Moose vote confirmed Taft's diagnosis. We were afflicted with an army of colonels, and when I saw Colonel Roosevelt after the election, he was depressed about the third-party movement. I was not. I still felt that if we would stay with it, and were willing to lose another presidential election, we could establish ourselves as the second party. . . .

In the summer of 1915 the White family bought, partly for cash but mostly for advertising, its first motorcar. Poor Old Tom, the clop-clop, was pensioned in a pasture for life. Bill and a boy friend in the garage from which we bought the car—it was a Chandler made in Cleveland—hitched up and drove us to Colorado. It was a three-day journey, seven hundred fifty miles over dirt roads. A rain would hold us for hours—sometimes for twelve hours, sometimes half a day—and we were forever tinkering with the car along the way. Those were the days when the driver had to get out and get under. The tires were paper tires, apparently, for they were always blowing up and getting pinched in the rims. The Chandler was no worse than other cars. Man was merely learning how to make motorcars and in a few years he began to learn how to make roads out of taxes on gasoline. If ever there was an evolutionary process it was going on in transportation in that second decade of this century. . . .

It was that year that Bryan, on a lecture tour, came to our cabin and sat on our porch for an hour. I had come to have great respect for Bryan—I still do not know exactly what it was about him. I believe that he was as honest and as brave a man as I ever met, with a vast capacity for friendship. For his was an ardent nature. . . . We talked about the war. I was much nearer his views than Roosevelt's, and I suspected then he and I came more nearly agreeing than

---

[1]At the beginning of World War I these royal families occupied the thrones of, respectively, Austria-Hungary, Germany, and Russia.

Wilson and he. For he was beginning to be irked with Wilson's inner doubts about neutrality. Bryan's peace treaties, which were in his heart and in course of negotiation, seemed to me most wise. Of course I know now that the world was not ready for them. They were face-savers for many of our international neighbors, who must have smiled at Bryan as they were signing his treaties. Why did we not see? Why did he and I, sitting for an hour on the porch of our Estes Park home, talking about peace, run on and on, without ever realizing that treaties alone cannot maintain peace? Why did we not realize that treaties could only define peace which international economic adjustments must first establish? . . .

I have never met a man with a kindlier face, with a gentler, more persuasive voice, nor with seemingly more profound ignorance about sophisticated, mundane matters. He was a twelve-year-old boy in many things, yet a prophet far more discerning of the structure of the world that would be, and should be, and even now is (a house not made with hands) than were any of us—Roosevelt or Wilson or La Follette. . . . Bryan as we sat together, his rhetoric full of biblical metaphors and similes, his voice lovely to my ear with his modulating cadences, though he was not an oratorical talker, left an impression on my mind and heart that I have carried, even cherished, through all these years. I am ashamed now, and was ashamed then, that two decades earlier I had scorned him in "What's the Matter with Kansas?" as a boy orator. I wondered, as he sat there, if he remembered it. If he did, I am sure no rancor held over through the years, for he was most cordial and aglow with friendliness. . . .

After Bryan left, who should come wandering up to the porch a few days later, but Clarence Darrow![2] I had met Darrow in Chicago in 1897, a young lawyer in his forties. He was the perfect antithesis of Bryan, a cynic, a sophisticate, and a Sybarite.[3] We talked for an hour. I did not agree with the things Clarence Darrow said, but I tremendously enjoyed the way he said it. . . . In conversation he was a chuckler who talked in wise saws, cheered meticulously, grinned diabolically. He thought he was shocking me, and I believe he enjoyed it. He yearned for peace as much as Bryan, but had no hope for it and would have been angry at the terms upon which it could come. . . .

Darrow was intended by nature to be as tall as Bryan, but he stooped and slumped. His clothes were a mess, wrinkled, untidy—entirely clean but slomicky, if I may coin a word to fit his dishabille. He slouched when he walked, and he walked like a cat. I always thought of him as Kipling's cat who walked alone.[4] For he was essentially a lonesome soul, always seeking the unattainable, I think;

[2]In 1925 Bryan and Darrow would clash as opposing attorneys in the highly publicized Scopes "monkey trial," which tested a Tennessee law banning the teaching of theories of evolution.

[3]In ancient days Sybarites were inhabitants of Sybaris, in southern Italy, a region known for its luxurious and self-indulgent way of life.

[4]One of Kipling's *Just So Stories* for children was entitled "The Cat That Walked by Himself."

hobbled by his own cynicism but always stumbling on, looking for the ideal which he could not accept without quibble or gibe—a complex man, a rebel like Eugene Debs. Curiously, I associated Darrow and Bryan and Debs with the outposts of that American revolution which rose in the last decade of the nineteenth century and was going strong when these lines were written. If Bryan could have had some part of Darrow's capacity for intellectual doubt, if Debs could have had Bryan's indomitable energy and a little of Bryan's ignorance about realities, and if they could all have been rolled into one with the elements of each soul well mixed in the composite, what a man they would have made! I think Lincoln must have been such a mixture. . . .

The war was beginning to change our national economy. . . . As we rode to and from New York that year, we could see a change in American industry as we sped through the industrial sections of Ohio, Pennsylvania, and New Jersey. Things were humming. The British and the French were placing tremendous war orders in the United States. Accelerated business was increasing our national income. Labor and agriculture were getting more money, if not a larger share of the income, than they had during the decade and a half before. War was producing in the United States its own intoxication, a kind of economic inflation that had spiritual reflexes. . . . The Germans, because of the British Fleet, could not get their orders across the ocean, so naturally as the Allies were our customers, they became our friends. America began to swing away from Germany—all of America, from Hudson Bay to Patagonia. . . .

The Bull Moose party, which was founded upon a demand for distributive justice, or using government as an agency of human welfare, lost its cause. Prosperity was cheering up the farmers and the workers. Our little army of colonels drilled lonesomely on the parade ground of a lost cause. Yet during that mid-year of the second decade, we kept holding our conference dinners. We, the faithful, were still white hot with zeal for our party. We could not realize that when the economic set-up of the country changed, when prosperity came rolling in from the war, we did not touch the realities of the political situation. So we went on through that year like fairies dancing in some sylvan glade, apart from the busy world and its realities.

Colonel Roosevelt knew right well what was happening. Our failure at the polls in 1914 convinced him that we were "spurring a dead horse." Those were his words to me and a dozen others who talked about the party occasionally when he dropped in on a conference, but he was making it rather definitely known that he was done as our candidate. He did not wish to sacrifice himself on the altar of a futile party.

Moreover, the war was stirring him. At first he seemed to feel somewhat sympathetic to the Kaiser, but that lasted only a few weeks. The wave of rage in the United States at Belgium's fate at the hands of Germany carried the Colonel along with it, and by early winter he was well established as a Man of Wrath, raging at Wilson for his neutrality. And the more he raged, the more he forgot about the Bull Moosers—orphans in a storm. In his fulminations at Wilson, Colonel Roosevelt alienated many of his Progressive party supporters who agreed with the president that America should remain neutral. In the main, I was more inclined to follow Wilson's foreign policy than Roosevelt's militancy.

Anyway, social and industrial justice no longer interested Roosevelt. He had a war, a war greater than even he realized it would be, to engage his talents. He made a tremendous clamor for preparedness. . . . Finally the uproar was so definite that the Democratic national organization and the Democrats in Congress feared that Wilson might lose his leadership. I heard him recant, at a dinner arranged by the Manhattan Club at a New York hotel. The afternoon before the dinner Bob Collier, of *Collier's Weekly,* told me what was in the wind. Along with Norman Hapgood, and probably Mark Sullivan, we had a box seat in the gallery, where I was less than thirty feet from the speaker's table. Knowing what was coming, I watched the president closely. I never saw an unhappier face. It was dour. He scarcely spoke to those at his right and left. The gay quips and facile persiflage with which I had seen his countenance shine at the dinner in Wisconsin were missing. When he rose to talk I thought his glum face was a douser on the applause, for it was perfunctory. His voice was strained when he began. It relaxed a little as he went on, and by the time he had come to his climax announcing the national intention to rearm for national defense, he had cast off his black mantle and his voice was vibrant and his face was radiant for a few moments. But I felt he was taking his medicine without licking the spoon, and it was a bitter dose. I may have imagined it, but that night, as I watched the president—and I admired his belated stand for rearming, though I had not encouraged it—I felt he had entered a new phase of his leadership. Neutrality had gone out of his heart. He was a partisan of the Allies against Germany. He took the country with him eventually. . . .

Not long after that I saw the president again, from a window of the Macmillan Building on lower Fifth Avenue, marching at the head of the preparedness parade. He was in presidential regalia: silk hat and cutaway coat of the period, dark striped trousers, appropriate tie—a fine figure of a man. His head was thrown back in exultation, for he received a tremendous ovation during the mile and more of the march at the head of the bands, the drum corps, the soldiers, sailors, and civic organizations. And cheers along the line rose to greet him like a flowing wave of deep emotion that seemed to carry him along as one tiptoeing upon clouds. It was a happy day for him, and he turned a happy face to the multitude.

The country was tremendously stirred by the events in Europe—the horrendous battles, the slaughter; the danger threatening Western Europe, to which the United States was bound with many ties, first of blood and then of democratic interest. . . . Sympathy for the Allies, unashamed, unquenched, glowed in the hearts of the American people. [We] were beginning to understand the meaning of the war. We were not used to smelling blood from vast human slaughterhouses. Not since our Civil War had the ghastly facts of human butchery come so close to us as they were in those middle years of the century's second decade. The Boer War had not touched us seriously, nor the Spanish War, nor the Filipino Rebellion. They were remote, and the casualties were few. But this first World War was in our front yard, and we were horrified, frightened, and angry at the same time.

It must have been on that autumn visit to New York, when Sallie and I were staying at the National Arts Club where Mary Austin was functioning as high priestess, that we met Herbert Hoover. . . . Hoover was looming up as a national hero. He was beginning to feed the Belgians and was in New York arranging for an American end of the Belgian Relief Foundation. Vernon Kellogg had been with him in Europe, and his letters to us were filled with the glories of Herbert Hoover. . . .

Hoover sat in the midst of a small company, probably not more than a dozen or fifteen people, and we two Kansans were tremendously shocked when he declared that both the belligerents treated him badly in his efforts to feed the Belgians. We did not know then that he was constitutionally gloomy, a congenital pessimist who always saw the doleful side of any situation. But we were idealizing the British. We considered them and all their doings highly noble, and to hear him shake a dubious head about their intentions and their essential integrity as it related to Belgian relief frightened us.

Otherwise we found Herbert Hoover a most intelligent and gentle person who smiled naively with a certain vinegary integrity, and a mild delicious sense of humor like a vague perfume about his aura. In short, we fell for him. He seemed to have an adolescent sweetness with his perverse acerbity, flecked in its texture with an engaging and disarming smile. He was a complex person who curiously drew to him in a steel-bound loyalty the men whom he touched, but a man who never was able to make a mass appeal. After the crowd passed fifty the influence of his charm began to weaken. That whole group that gathered in the Arts Club that night was mesmerized by the strange low voltage of his magnetism. Sallie and I felt that we had met a Person—a person of some dignity and power. . . .

He was the link—a real living link—for us with the European struggle. It meant much to us, so the first man we had seen who was in the midst of the conflict was drawn into our hearts and lives. For after all one cannot impersonalize entirely a cosmic human drama like that war. Icons, images, symbols were all right, but here a flesh-and-blood hero stepped out of the great drama of Europe onto our tiny corner of a stage. So we set up a little altar to Herbert Hoover in our hearts—and after thirty years the candle before it is still burning.

When Woodrow Wilson spoke for preparedness at the Manhattan Club and when he had marched down New York's Fifth Avenue leading the long preparedness parade, the bell tolled for social reform in the United States. The struggle for industrial economic justice and progressive political change had ended. Not that President Wilson had consciously put the period at the close of fifteen years of liberal advance. The war did that. But when he—the liberal leader—was forced away from his liberal goal into the business of rallying his country into the quickstep of war, even though he still sincerely protested against entering the war, we poor panting crusaders for a just and righteous order were left on a deserted battlefield, our drums punctured, our bugles muted, our cause forgotten.

We did not know it. At least a few thousand of us, maybe a hundred thousand, felt that the need for justice was stronger than the urge for war. And we kept on during the whole year of 1916—indeed for another year beyond that—trying to mend our drums, trying to take the rags out of our bugles, and call men to our standards. The party Progressives still conferred in the nation and in the states, but it was harder every season to get enough people together for a dinner in the towns, the counties, and the districts. We party Progressives knew that it was an uphill fight. But we felt that if we could hold our party together through another presidential election, which we realized would return Wilson to the White House, it was worth the effort. . . . Roosevelt, in talks with his Bull Moose lieutenants and captains, made it plain that he did not want to be an accessory to the election of Wilson by running as a third-party candidate. And yet he did not say definitely "no." . . .

He and I had talked in the spring in Kansas City. . . . At parting, as I left the room he said: "No, White, I just mustn't do it. As things look now, it would be more than the Progressives ought to ask of me!" For by that time he had persuaded himself that he had been forced to bolt in 1912, when as a matter of cold fact, he went into the third-party bolt in a rage. . . . He had persuaded himself it was a matter of principle, and we all agreed with him after the fact; but in 1916 he felt that he had nobly led an assault upon privileged plutocracy and had done his full part in the progressive movement.

In the meantime . . . the more radical of our party leaders began to grow suspicious of Perkins and restless under his leadership. Gifford Pinchot was in open revolt, and they had a semipublic quarrel in which probably each was a little wrong. I was inclined to follow Pinchot, for I knew that he was right and that Perkins' leadership was hurting. . . . I was a compromiser who saw both sides and tried to bring together contenders who generally agreed on matters of principle and differed on methods of procedure. . . .

I realize, of course, that ways of thinking and patterns of political conduct do not come bang-up against a certain year or month or day and then suddenly turn or dissolve or shape new courses, but looking back to the summer of 1916 it seems to me that what may be called the liberal movement in the United States came to a rather definite and catastrophic climax in that month and year. Probably dissolution had been going on since 1912, but certainly in 1916, in two conventions at Chicago—the Republican and the Bull Moose—conservatism definitely and, for that decade, finally won. The story of the collapse of political liberalism that had been known very seriously as the insurgent movement of the Progressive party is so palpably dramatic, definite, and certain in its outward details that it will bear telling here, particularly as my life was so deeply affected by the circumstances that illustrate the change, a change that was for me tragic indeed.

During 1915, in the Republican party and in what might be called the Perkins wing of the Progressive party, two groups were trying to reunite the two parties. They had set the dates for the two conventions in the same week and on the same days of June, at Chicago. The Progressive harmonizers would have been willing to take the nomination of Theodore Roosevelt by the Republicans and accept their vice president. This suggestion of course was an insult to the Republicans who still hated Roosevelt bitterly. But the proposal was also offensive to many Progressives, probably to most of them. They hoped to nominate Colonel Roosevelt and adjourn and so, with a third ticket in the field, force Roosevelt's nomination on the Republicans. The Progressives, in their conference before the convention, planned to nominate Roosevelt and then either to empower their central committee to accept the Republican nominee for vice president, or to nominate a vice president and empower their committee to withdraw him and accept the Republican nominee, thus effecting a fusion.

The weakness of the Republicans was that they had no strong presidential candidate. Taft was out of the question. He would not accept the nomination, and his nomination would have been futile. Charles Evans Hughes,[5] chief justice of the Supreme Court, was considered by both parties, but while he made no direct statement, time and again he had indicated his distaste for the nomination. Yet those eastern Progressives who rallied around George Perkins were working with a group of Republicans led by Frank Hitchcock of New Mexico, a national committeeman and former postmaster under Theodore Roosevelt. They seem to have been working on Hughes. . . .

So the conventions opened. The supporters of Hughes in both parties knew

[5]Hughes was a Supreme Court justice at this time but did not become chief justice until 1930, serving until 1941.

exactly what they wanted and fairly well what they could expect of Mr. Hughes. The Progressives did not know what to expect of Colonel Roosevelt. . . .

Of this I am sure: I was struggling to cut down my weight. I was counting my calories fastidiously, and I remember vividly and with pride the fact that when I went up to Chicago in 1916 to attend the Bull Moose national convention and to report it and the Republican convention for the three score American metropolitan papers, a Chicago paper which carried my convention stories printed my picture from toe to top and noted that I had lost thirty pounds. I had what would be called today a new streamlined figure. But it was hard to hold.

We Kansans came to Chicago with what might be called a high grade delegation. . . . Watching the crowd gather for two or three days before the convention opened, I saw the same kind of delegates from the Midwest all the way from Ohio to Colorado. The Californians, too, were exceptional men. . . . But what jarred and angered me and made me mad was that the delegates to the Bull Moose convention from the East were big businessmen, who had come at Perkins' beck and call. This was not true of Massachusetts, but it was true of the metropolitan area—New Jersey, New York, Connecticut, and Delaware. Their names have faded now from the roll of fame, but I remember that a great steel master was one of them. A group of Wall Street brokers and bankers of some renown sat with New York when the convention opened. Obviously they regarded the western delegates as longhairs, and Perkins was holding fusion conferences with Republican delegates from which Victor Murdock, chairman of the Progressive party, was barred. Perkins was merely head of the executive committee or something of the kind. After that we held our own conferences. They were anti-fusion in their aims. . . .

The Republicans were bitter. Their permanent chairman was a man I had never seen before, Warren G. Harding. I drifted over to hear his opening speech. He was a handsome dog, a little above medium height with a swarthy skin, a scathing eye, and was meticulously clad in morning clothes with a red geranium as a boutonniere, and he had the harlot's voice of the old-time political orator. But he was bitter, scalding bitter, to Theodore Roosevelt. I distrusted him, and into my distrust came something unpleasantly near to hate, for I thought he was deliberately, cruelly unfair. Of course he represented the tip of the salient to the right. Two or three hundred Republican delegates, men like Borah and the Kansas Republicans, and Will Hays of the Indiana group, were reasonable men. Some of them told me later they were back of the movement which was urging Hughes to accept the nomination. . . .

It was evident to me then—and, looking back over the years in the light of what happened later in the week, I am satisfied—that Mr. Perkins and Frank Hitchcock knew definitely that Hughes would accept the nomination. Their strategy was to keep the Progressives from nominating Roosevelt and adjourning. They wanted the Republicans to nominate Hughes. And our group, the left-wing group in the Bull Moose party, was determined to nominate Roosevelt immediately after the platform had been adopted, even before if necessary, and let the Republicans decide who would be responsible for the reelection of Wilson. . . .

It is hard to bring back to these pages the rancor, the strife, the tumult that raged in that Progressive convention the first two days, Tuesday and Wednesday. These men and women—for women had come into the political picture by 1916, from all over the United States—were an earnest lot. They were full of emotion and zealous in their purpose. They were not party-minded. The party was too young for that. But most passionately they wished to see all that they stood for organized into a definite program under the aegis of the Progressive party. And they believed that finally Roosevelt, if he was nominated, would not desert them. In that week more than at any other time in his career Theodore Roosevelt was a little tin god to his idolaters. Not at any time in 1912, not even when he escaped an assassin's bullet,[6] was he so vividly lifted in the hearts of his followers as the hero-god of their hopes. . . .

I was in many conferences. I do not see exactly how I filed my daily story to the syndicate papers who were paying me so well. But I managed to meet my deadline every day with an hour out of politics. But the other twenty-three hours, it seems to me, were spent walking up and down hotel corridors, sitting in bedrooms that were stinking with stale smoke, serving on committees, intriguing, planning, conspiring to bring about the nomination of Theodore Roosevelt before the Republicans named their candidate. . . . I was to sit near the telegraph instrument at the back of the Auditorium stage where the Bull Moose convention was raging. Over that instrument information was ticking in about the happenings of the Republican convention at the Coliseum. Donald Richberg was to have a similar post in the Republican convention. He was to advise me, and I was to tell him what was going on. James R. Garfield, the floor leader at the convention, was not in our plot. We felt he would fall in with our plan, but we did not wish to embarrass him. . . .

When I got word that the Republicans were entering the order of nominating a candidate—which did not mean they were going to vote that day but rather make speeches for a time—I sent word (I think by Ickes) to our fellow conspirators. . . . We tried to make a premature nomination. Gifford Pinchot, I believe (or perhaps it was Amos), rose in the convention, got the chairman's eye, and was about to speak. Perkins, on the platform like a terrier at a rathole, instinctively realized what was ahead. He created a diversion, turned Chairman Robins

[6]During the 1912 presidential campaign, Roosevelt had been shot in the chest in an assassination attempt but had insisted upon delivering his scheduled speech.

around. In the diversion, the speaker was silent. A motion to adjourn came and left the speaker standing. The motion to adjourn may have been—I have always thought it was—on signal from Perkins, who feared that we of the left wing would force the nomination of Roosevelt a day before the Republicans were ready to ballot.

That afternoon a messenger from Perkins' room in the Blackstone told me that Colonel Roosevelt was on the wire, and I hurried to the telephone. The Colonel began reproaching me for not calling him. Our group had tried to call him several times but without success. I told him so. He began sputtering in his characteristic way, "Well, well now—here . . . ," and finally settled down to a coherent declaration: "That's strange. Didn't Perkins tell you last week that this phone was open to you?"

It was a direct line from Perkins' room to the president's library in Oyster Bay. I had not known that such a line existed and told him so. Again he burst into expletives and said: "I haven't heard from Jim, or Hiram, or Raymond, or Gifford"—meaning of course Jim Garfield, Hiram Johnson, Raymond Robins, and Gifford Pinchot—"and the private wire was put in with the explicit understanding that it would be equally free to you five people. I have not understood why you have avoided me."

I told him that I had been talking with the other four during the last week probably every hour of the day, and I was sure they did not know about it. His irritation was not feigned when he asked me to get each of them in the room and on the phone at once. Then he told me that he felt it would be a mistake to nominate him under any circumstances, and we argued that out. . . . He was firm but not cocksure of his position and began suggesting names for the Progressive nomination—names that shocked me. I cried out violently as he went over the list: Senator Lodge, John W. Weeks, even Root (that, softly and tentatively), and two or three other right-wing Republicans whose names would have doused that convention with chill anger. I told him so. We wrangled for a few minutes and then laughed it off, and I told him I would have Jim Garfield on in ten minutes, which I did, and the others in order, except perhaps Hiram Johnson, who at that time had developed relations with Perkins which made it difficult for a proud man to go into Perkins' room, hat in hand, and ask for the telephone.

Among other things that I tried to convey to the Colonel was that our convention was a gathering of rather highly placed people. This amazed him, and he came right back with the statement that I was the only one who told him so, as he understood it was a mob of irresponsibles. It was upon the basis of the information that came from Perkins' room, from a group of bankers, brokers, a few industrialists, newspaper proprietors like Munsey and Stoddard, that the Colonel had formed his judgment and written the letter which was in Perkins' hand two days before the nomination of Hughes. Sometime during those two days I heard of the letter, and the Colonel may have told me of it over the phone. Knowing of it confidentially, I could not use the information. He may have told Jim Garfield and Gifford Pinchot, and certainly did so if he told me. The convention was not in session when we talked to him, and did not convene until Saturday morning. In the meantime, we gathered the conspirators, a score or two of us, and made our Saturday plans. . . .

Bainbridge Colby was to nominate Roosevelt as quickly as possible after the convention preliminaries were finished. Our platform had been adopted by the committee. There was no question about it. We were ready to go. Then Colby from the floor asked for recognition. He was out of order, of course. We were stalling around on some parliamentary subterfuge waiting for Heaven knows what. Colby was to nominate Roosevelt right out of the blue. We knew that once the name came before the convention on any kind of motion, it would prevail. The nomination would be made.

When Robins recognized Colby, Perkins, sitting on the platform back of the chair, instinctively knew what was up. He literally leaped to the speaker's stand and began crying out in a [distraught] and almost hysterical voice. Harold Ickes recalls that no one knew exactly what he was trying to say. Robins shoved Perkins back into his chair, and Colby in less than a hundred words put Roosevelt's name before the convention. Such a burst of cheering, so full of joy, so charged with exultation, I never had heard. I had been attending conventions and had heard the claque of candidates roar on sometimes for an hour, but that ten-minute burst for Roosevelt there in the Auditorium was a cry that I had never heard before. Governor Hiram Johnson seconded the Colby resolution. By ayes and nays on the spot the nomination was made. In a few moments the nomination of John M. Parker,[7] former governor of Louisiana, for vice president, followed.

The nomination of Roosevelt was made at noon—nearly exactly noon. I am satisfied that what Perkins was trying to say as he cried vainly before the convention was that he had a letter from Colonel Roosevelt declaring that he could not accept the nomination of the convention. . . . But we, the conspirators, carried out our plot. The job was done. Then a most amazing thing happened. Hughes had not been nominated by the Republicans. Perkins could not be sure that he would be nominated, though it was strongly presumed that he would be. But after the nomination of Roosevelt and after our noon adjournment, during which time Hughes was nominated by the Republicans, Perkins still withheld the letter from Roosevelt. We gathered there that afternoon and started a money-raising campaign. Still Perkins withheld the letter. We were going on into

[7]Actually, Parker would not become governor of Louisiana until 1920.

the campaign. Every hour that we sat there raising money—and we raised something over a hundred thousand dollars and were pledging strongly—I watched the proceedings from a box where I sat with Ida Tarbell and some friends from the *American Magazine*. . . . I was glowing with a kind of terror such as a train dispatcher might feel who had two engines approaching on the same track. I knew of the letter. From hour to hour I wondered if it had been withdrawn, and tried to think what could have happened that caused its withdrawal. The Republicans completed their ticket and adjourned. We remained in session until late afternoon, raising money, making plans, rejoicing.

At last the collision came. The letter was presented. In amazement that great throng heard it. The last words, "But your candidate I cannot be," fell upon them like a curse. For a moment there was silence. Then there was a roar of rage. It was the cry of a broken heart such as no convention ever had uttered in this land before. Standing there in the box I had tears in my eyes, I am told. I saw hundreds of men tear the Roosevelt picture or the Roosevelt badge from their coats and throw it on the floor. They stalked out buzzing like angry bees and I followed them.

In the late afternoon a few of us gathered at the University Club. We were heartbroken. We tried to make plans. We could not. It was a dour and terrible hour, the ebb tide for our cause. We looked out across the stark ugly stretches of the dirty marsh where once our current flowed so strong, and in the agony of disillusion and despair we saw the dark rocks and the crawling things that had been underneath that ebbing tide.

I wrote my story for the papers. . . . It was nearly midnight when I got back to the University Club where I was staying, called Sallie on the phone in Emporia, and spent nine dollars and eighty-five cents bawling like a calf into the receiver. At least I had release and relief. She cut me off when she thought I had spent enough money, and I went to bed at peace and slept. It was the end of a great adventure, politically and emotionally probably the greatest adventure of my life.

My despair came because I did not realize what had happened. It was merely ebb tide. Since the Civil War had destroyed slavery in this country and the tide went out with Reconstruction and the corruption of Grant's day, a new tide had been flowing in and for fifteen years since the century's turn had been pounding upon the rocks of privilege and of social and economic injustice, crumbling them here and there and making inroads upon bastions and ramparts. This progressive movement was a part of a revolution. As I stood there heartbroken upon the shore at ebb tide, I did not realize how soon and how strong the tide would come flowing in, and what rocks and docks and earthworks would melt in that flowing current.

20

A World
Aflame

The nomination of Chief Justice Charles Evans Hughes by the Republicans followed the nomination of Roosevelt. It was the best nomination the Republicans could have made. Most of the Colonel's insurgent friends of 1908 favored Hughes instead of Taft for president. The whole La Follette group preferred Hughes to Taft. I did, and the second- or third-string leaders around President Roosevelt.

Hughes had made a great reform governor of New York. He had cleaned out a nest of scalawags in the life insurance business in New York City and state. He had made a successful fight with the direct primary. . . . His gubernatorial record appealed to the Progressives. He had been aloof from the two factions in 1912. He was a man of unblemished political character and personal integrity. Having been a Supreme Court justice, he added distinction to the Republican ticket. But, the day after the nomination of Hughes by the Republicans, the Progressive national committee met and endorsed Hughes by only a narrow margin.

I did not vote. I was too deeply wrought up to abandon even the remote hope of a Progressive party by joining the Republicans. The Progressives held their national committee together. I was a national committeeman. I was certain only of one thing: that if the party could be salvaged as a going concern I should be ready to join it and do my part in saving it. . . . I had met Mr. Hughes once or twice some eight or ten years before, and had the highest esteem for him. I conceded to every good point which his supporters urged and which the Colonel pressed home. But I was heartbroken, too freshly widowed to be in a mood for political romance.

The Democratic national [convention] met in St. Louis the week after the Republican convention, and I attended as a reporter, taking Bill with me. It was a tame convention. Wilson was renominated without much enthusiasm. He had alienated the machine Democrats, but they had to take him. The cogs, levers, wheels, and pulleys of the mechanics which carried the Wilson nomination to consummation creaked, wheezed, groaned, and squeaked painfully as the processes drew to a close. Bill and I lunched, dined, and breakfasted with the newspapermen and the Democratic statesmen. I remember we had one evening with Martin Littleton, a New York congressman who delivered the speech which started the slogan "He kept us out of war." It was consciously built up, and it reminded me of college oratory. But it did rouse the only spark of enthusiasm that glowed in the Democratic convention, and became the strongest vote-getting feature of Wilson's second campaign. He himself never used the slogan nor gave it endorsement—never made the promise to keep us out of war. He was entirely free to go to war if he chose to—meanwhile letting the people be deceived, as they were, by the use of the slogan, which covered billboards all over the land and was the holy text of Democratic orators. . . .

I have no doubt that Mr. Hughes desired to keep us out of war as definitely as President Wilson. I, in those days, hoped ardently that we could avoid entrance into the conflict. And as the campaign warmed up in September, it was evident that the war issue would not be squarely met. At a national meeting of the German-American Alliance, resolutions endorsing Hughes shook the Colonel and his friends. Still the Colonel went out in a special train touring the country, particularly the West, speaking for Hughes. I joined his train at Kansas City and rode to Emporia with him. He was angry with Hughes for not taking a more decisive stand in favor of bringing the United States into the war. . . .

One of the few times when Roosevelt cut me to the quick was on that train. I forget who was standing about when we talked, but it was a group of his followers. When he was fulminating against the pacifists, he cried out: "Poor bleeding Jane Addams!" I could not forget that day four years ago when Jane Addams amid a volcano of emotion and applause had stepped to the platform to second Theodore Roosevelt's nomination as the Progressive presidential candidate and his eyes were filled with glistening grateful tears. It was not anger at him that I felt there on the train but a deep pitying sadness that a man could so soon forget.

So I left his train at Emporia when he headed West. I did very little in the national campaign one way or another, but devoted the *Gazette*'s political activities to the reelection of Arthur Capper, governor of Kansas. A fortnight or so before the election, Sallie and I went to New York on a business trip. There Colonel Roosevelt invited us over to Oyster Bay and we spent a delightful evening with him and Mrs. Roosevelt at dinner and around the hearth in his workroom. He brought home the day's mail, as was his custom, to Mrs. Roosevelt. She went over it, they discussed it, and we all fell to talking about other days. Politics were adjourned. But just before bedtime, perhaps as we were standing before the fire ready to go to our rooms, Sallie let drop the innocent remark that she was going to vote for Wilson. The roof lifted from the house. The Colonel let out a blast of pain and rage and sorrow. Then we had a laugh and went our ways. We were to take an early train the next morning and have breakfast before sunup. While we were dressing, in burst the Colonel, coatless and vestless, not noticing that Sallie was in her petticoat. He began: "Oh, my dear, my dear, it can't be, it really can't be, not really, that you are going to vote for Wilson!"

It occurred to him in a moment or two that Sallie was not fully dressed. He threw up his hands in horror and went out and talked with the bedroom door ajar until she was ready to come out and go to breakfast. Then he and she had it out over the meal, and Mrs. Roosevelt and I enjoyed our victuals. As he waved us off in the car bound for the station, his last words were a welding of imprecation, pleading, and anguish for her not to do a thing like that. It was not that he had such faith in Hughes, but he could not endure anyone whom he loved giving aid and comfort to a man whom he despised. . . .

When the returns were all in they proved clearly that Wilson was elected by the votes of the Progressive states—states normally Republican in the Middle West . . . the very states where Roosevelt's leadership had impressed the people in other days. Hughes was not sufficiently aware of the importance of Progressive issues to appeal to these Republican states. . . . The war in Europe had submerged them, but it had not obliterated them. The American people were still liberals in 1916. . . .

When Wilson took us into the war, the *Gazette* supported every measure which he deemed necessary. And we favored the vigorous prosecution of the war. Kansas and all the midwestern states that had voted for Wilson developed a robust war spirit and enlistments preceded the draft. We bought war bonds to our full quota. We exceeded our quota for the Red Cross and the Y.M.C.A. Drives and campaigns gave us delight. We treated roughly laggards who withheld their subscriptions to the war effort. We were suspicious of families with German names. And I was on all of the money-raising campaigns, chairman of a "Special Gifts" committee—which means I helped to look after the larger givers. Every country editor's job is to conduct, directly or indirectly, his town's drive for progress and benevolence, and it was no new experience for me to pound the streets of Emporia with a subscription paper in my hand. I had done it for twenty years.

Yet for all my patriotic interests, I stood, I hope, rather sturdily for the rights of free expression. The protestants against war throughout the country, the pacifists like my friends David Starr Jordan and La Follette and Jane Addams, had my sympathy and support. I remember one winter day when Scott Nearing, a pacifist Socialist, came to Emporia to see me. I invited him home for dinner, and Bill, my son, who was in high school, was seriously alarmed lest I should get into trouble harboring an enemy of the government. He went to his mother about it and shook his head with solemn warning. But Nearing was the first of a rather sad little procession of the despised and rejected men in those days who beat a path to our front door. All my life, because in some way I have had to see both sides I have in all my political activities rested under the suspicion of trafficking with the enemy. I could not do much for them except hold their hands and let them weep on my shoulder. I kept La Follette's picture in the *Gazette* office, and whenever I would leave town for a day or two I would go back and find it turned to the wall. I never could find out who did it. I did not care much.

In those days when I was supporting Wilson and the war, I came to dislike him—this man who was president—for his cold, mean, selfish policy toward those whom he liked to segregate and hate as his enemies, those who he probably fancied had forced him into preparedness, notably Roosevelt. I can still in my mind's eye recall the picture that I had from the day's press reports when Roosevelt, who more than any other thing on earth desired to fight for his country, walked up the curved pathway to the White House, swallowing his pride—and it was certainly a bitter mouthful—and asked the president to be allowed, under any terms, to recruit a regiment for France. The frigid malevolence with which Wilson denied this strong man's plea, made in what Wilson, being sensitive and wise, knew was excruciating abasement, carved deeply in my heart a picture of Woodrow Wilson that I could not erase when I wrote a book about him. His salving over his humiliation of Roosevelt with the oily pretext that it was in the interest of military discipline was for me worse than his real reason, wicked as I felt it to be. As commander in chief, Wilson could directly or indirectly have easily curbed any untoward military conduct of Theodore Roosevelt. It was ungenerous and worse—it was stupid—of Wilson to think that Roosevelt would be intriguing and caballing in France. . . .

In the summer of 1917 I went to war. I put on the uniform of a Red Cross lieutenant colonel. Henry Allen of Wichita and I went together. We were designated as inspectors of Red Cross activities in Europe. What we really intended to do was to come home and write articles and make speeches about Red Cross activities. We did not inspect much. We did not have special intelligence enough to help much even if we had inspected the Red Cross activities in Europe. But we did see the American soldier coming fresh off the boat; we did see the front line from the Vosges to Belgium; and we got the feel of the American soldiers in France. Every day I wrote home to Sallie and the children a confidential letter for their eyes only. I had no thought of publishing the letters. But they were impressions hot off the griddle with no attempt at literary flavor.

When I came home Sallie insisted that I sit down and make a book of them. So I wrote *The Martial Adventures of Henry and Me*. It was a trivial book, and the theme of it was in the first paragraph: the story of two fat middle-aged men who went to war without their wives. I rigged up a rather cobwebby romance to give the book a backbone; I knew that sketches would not be read. But I felt that if the experiences I had enjoyed—and I really did enjoy them even though I was frightened—were hung on the thread of a tenuous love affair, the book would have a chance. . . . The tale had its value because of two things: The scenes were described in the colloquial language that a man uses to his family; and it was a book without hate, parts of it funny. It sold well, forty or fifty thousand copies. But the English would have none of it. The humorous parts offended them. They could not conceive of a writer joking with death. . . .

I came home from Europe in the early autumn, and every day kept hammering away at the novel *In the Heart of a Fool*. It had taken shape and was being trimmed down. I never worked more faithfully nor harder upon any job. When I write that I was working on the novel, I mean that I was working an hour or two every morning. . . . After my morning's work on the novel or on magazine articles I went to the office and did a hard day's work writing editorials, talking over business problems, cheering up the men who sold advertising, writing local stories, and serving on various committees which fostered the town's needs. It was not a lazy man's job on Commercial Street as editor of the Emporia *Gazette*, a job which has engaged me for nearly half a century. But it has been a happy job, and I have waxed "healthy and wealthy" and, I hope, wise in doing it. . . .

The year 1917 saw me through my forty-ninth year. . . . According to Kansas standards I was well-to-do. We lived well at home; travelled decently, never in luxury; enjoyed what the world had to offer, but not extravagantly; watched our pennies and put whatever money we had above our daily needs right back into the *Gazette* office. . . .

I was reading fairly widely in biology because Kellogg, whom I saw two or three times a year, stimulated that part of my curiosity, and I liked it. And I was reading a lot of books on psychology, normal and abnormal. I had a whole case of books which Bill and Mary called "Daddy's nut books." And of course there was music. Every year we brought to Emporia a symphony orchestra. Once Damrosch came with his orchestra from Minneapolis, and St. Louis orchestras came. And wherever we could find music in New York or Kansas City, we went. At home we spent hours—all of us—listening to the phonograph, familiarizing ourselves rather consciously at first, but later in delight, with what might be called the musical classics. More than all of that, our home was filled with wayfarers, people who came to visit, people who could talk, who knew things and kept us in touch with the world.

During the First World War the moving picture was just beginning to sap the income of the theater in American country towns. The theater was disintegrating. Special railroad rates were being abandoned; it was hard to move scenery and a large company. Emporia's Opera House was gathering cobwebs. But when

we went to New York—which was two or three times a year—we saturated ourselves with the theater and its diversions.

In 1917 politics seemed to have sagged nationally, and in Kansas the Republicans were engaged in harmonizing and held many conferences which I did not
attend. I knew that sooner or later I would harmonize. When I got ready, I
would try to make my own terms. . . . I was busy promoting the candidacy of
Henry J. Allen, the Bull Moose leader and my dear friend since college days,
who was being drafted as a harmony Republican candidate for governor. I summoned twenty or thirty politicians of both sides to Emporia, and Sallie fed
them, and we organized the Allen campaign. I was one of three who agreed to
raise the money for it. The standpat Republican leader, Mort Albaugh, who was
also Henry's personal friend, set up an office in Topeka. Henry was in Europe in
the Red Cross and was to be nominated and elected *in absentia*. It was easy. To
raise the ten thousand or so that we needed for the campaign was as easy as
picking cherries. The money came from sources which we were glad to publicize,
mostly in hundred-dollar contributions or less. This ease and felicity on the
money-gathering side of the Allen candidacy proved to me, at least, that it was
popular, that Allen's political boom was a winner. Speaking generally I should
say politicians who want to win should beware of a cause that does not speak
fluently in money. People who won't give, won't vote. . . .

[Henry Allen's candidacy] was symbolic of the harmony movement over the
country. The Rooseveltians were moving in. Everywhere men like Allen were assuming local leadership of the Republican party. The regulars were losing control not of the party organization but of popular leadership outside it. Half a
dozen former Bull Moosers were going to the United States Senate. Half a score
of gubernatorial candidates were appearing from the Bull Moose ranks. The
chairman of the Republican national committee, Will H. Hays of Indiana, was a
Republican Rooseveltian in the convention of 1912, and he was trying harmony
in the party from the Rooseveltian angle. . . . Allen was elected governor by a
decisive majority.

Times were easy in Kansas. The farmer was getting good prices for what he
had to sell, grain and livestock. The Emporia banks were lending money upon
fairly easy terms. The merchants and professional people were doing well. The
Gazette's circulation and advertising rates were going up proportionately. The
new press that we had bought a few years before was becoming inadequate to
take care of the increasing subscription list. [It] had risen to five thousand, all in
Lyon County. Sugar rationing and meatless days did not trim down the advertising of the Emporia merchants, even though all of us in town who had as
much as two thin dimes to rattle in our pockets invested one of them in a war
bond and divided a nickel of the other among war activities like the Red Cross,

the Y.M.C.A., and the Salvation Army. The war years were boom years. As a nation we were exporting tremendous quantities of war material and munitions.

Somewhere after the beginning of 1916 and before the end of 1918 the United States went into a new phase of its economy. It became a creditor nation and not a debtor, and curiously an exporter and not an importer. From an economic standpoint it was a sign of insanity. A nation should not be sending out its capital and its goods at one and the same time. To be a world creditor we should at least have been a world importer, thus allowing our debtors to pay us. But no, we had to have our cake and eat it. We had to be a great exporter nation and a great creditor nation and we began erecting a house built on sand. But in Emporia, in the *Gazette* office and in all the publishing offices where I sold my wares, this economic madness was creating a rather exhilarating delusion of grandeur. We were drunk and dressed up, all of us. . . .

Occasionally I made a commencement address at some of the second-grade colleges and received an honorary degree in addition to a decent stipend. I never used the degree, but I was making a collection. By the time I was fifty I had degrees from Washburn College and Baker, the University of Kansas, Columbia University, and Oberlin. And strange as it may seem, considering my average grade of B at the university, I delivered a Phi Beta Kappa address at Columbia and was often invited to talk at academic gatherings. . . .

But in those academic shades, talking to men who were far removed from politics as I knew it, I came to have an uneasy but growing sense that the egoistic forces of this country were organizing. . . . Talking to college professors who made charts and wrote books around them, the economists, the sociologists, the political scientists, I began to be conscious, if I did not fully realize and understand, that some relation was being established between our expanding industrial life and the direction our country was taking in the world of international politics. I did not see it clearly, but I sensed that in those middle and latter years of the second decade of this century the old ways of our country were passing.

We were moving into a new and strange time. Mark Hanna had tried hard to plutocratize the Republican party around the interests of manufacturers. In his day the National Association of Manufacturers was organized. . . . Then along came Theodore Roosevelt, who tried to overturn Mark Hanna's industrial empire. The power—first challenged by him—was checked in the first decade of the century. But the war came in the second decade, stimulating our industrial growth; and with the growth of industry came political power. . . . [I] was disturbed as I went about the country at odd times living with the gentle far-visioned people in the academic world, who saw and were making me see, more and more clearly, how the centrifugal egoistic forces of American life were generating more and more irresponsible power—were hungrier and more insatiable every year to increase that unleashed power. . . .

21

The Peace
That Passeth
Understanding[1]

Then came the Armistice, and I was keen to go to
Europe and write about the peace. I asked Walter Lippmann to intercede for me
at the White House, thinking I might get a passport and a minor place in the
president's peace party; but the president did not see it. So I turned to the Red
Cross, where John S. Phillips . . . was editor of the *Red Cross Magazine*. He commissioned me to go to Europe and write some articles on the European postwar
demobilization. And he got me a passport when passports were hard to get.
Having the passport, I went to the syndicate which had been selling my stuff to
newspapers, and they sold my articles from the peace conference, giving me the
right to use the cable three times a week. . . . Sallie insisted—and she was wise—
that I take Bill along. He was then eighteen. I was able to get him demobilized
quickly from the Student Army Training Corps, and in early December he and I
appeared in New York, got into our Red Cross uniforms, and were ready to sail.
All this was done in thirty days after the Armistice. It was fast work. . . .

[This chapter] will be an attempt to tell something not of what really happened but of the atmosphere of Paris in those days—the Paris of the Peace Conference. No one who was there enjoyed it more than I did. No one, I am sure,
took less to it and brought away more. And I am sure that no one grew in
strength and grace and, I hope, in wisdom as I did, for few of them started so far
back in the muck and mire of ignorance as I. The only thing I took worth baggage room to Paris that year was an open mind.

I had told the Colonel [Roosevelt] that I would be in New York sailing for Europe, and he wrote asking me to call and see him. When I got to town I found a
message asking me to come to see the Colonel at the Roosevelt Hospital at noon.

---

[1]From a traditional Christian blessing: "The peace of God, which passeth all understanding,
keep your hearts and minds in the knowledge and love of God."

Bill and I showed up at the hospital and the girl at the desk gave us a rather glassy eye. She called the Colonel's nurse, who said that he was not so well that day and was sleeping and could not be seen. While we were talking, Mrs. Roosevelt appeared and said that the Colonel was under the influence of a narcotic. We chatted for a moment, and I asked her to tell the Colonel that General Wood was a bona-fide candidate for the presidency, and that if the Colonel had any idea of running he should talk frankly to General Wood. That was the chief thing I would have said to the Colonel. Whereupon we departed. . . .

When we returned to the National Arts Club after lunch, the people in the reception office were in a great flutter. Three messages had come in two hours from the Roosevelt Hospital. . . . The Colonel was still an important national figure, and messages from him at fifteen-minute intervals to our rather modest club produced an impression. About four o'clock Bill and I, having placed our trunk in the ship's hold at the dock, appeared at the hospital again.

As we came in the door, the girl at the desk came out into the lobby. She said: "Mr. White, you don't know how glad I am to see you!"

Before I knew it, an intern had grabbed my hand and said: "Come right along—hurry! The Colonel is anxious!"

Then appeared Dr. Lambert and took me by the arm and said: "You've saved our lives. That man has had this whole hospital upside down for three hours."

Whereupon Mrs. Roosevelt came hurrying down the corridor and cried: "Theodore will be so glad to see you, and it was so good of you to come again."

The doctor cut in: "I would rather see you than any other man in America right now. Maybe we can get that man's temperature down. He seems to have been raising Ned all over the place."

When we went in, the Colonel was propped up in bed, sweet as a cherub, reading. It was marvelous to see how that dynamo could send the juice over that hospital, across the town, down to the National Arts Club, and impress a personality through a dozen people most vividly. He seemed to be glad to see Bill, whom he had known since he was a baby. For a few moments Archie and Kermit, or perhaps one of them, I am not sure, appeared, and the Colonel's pride in his soldier boys was a delight to witness. The affection between them was unassumed, and when his sons left he bragged about them with glistening eyes. . . .

We sailed on a small French ship with a crooked beam, the *Chicago*, which listed seven ways from Sunday, and I was seasick much of the time. . . . Bill and I shared our cabin with Norman Angell, who was also a tablemate, and I came to admire and trust him and have held him in affectionate esteem through all these years. He was going to write about the Peace Conference for a string of British papers. As we dropped south toward Bordeaux, our landing place, the weather moderated and we walked the deck a great deal, tromping on shell-pink clouds of iridescent dreams about world peace. There was rumor and gossip about the League of Nations which Wilson was determined to establish and Angell had a lot of ideas about the League—better ones, I discovered later, than Wilson had. . . . It was a highly profitable journey. . . . It was my introduction to international politics. When we landed at Bordeaux, between Christmas and New Year's, I was full of enthusiasm—fired with a desire to see and be a part of what then seemed to be one of the greatest adventures that man had ever embarked upon since he dropped his tail and went to Eden.

At Paris they sent Bill and me and Norman Angell to a little hotel called the Normandie. Coal was short in Paris that winter, and the Normandie was so cold that it reminded me of the icehouse on the Walnut River at El Dorado. We shivered there for nearly a week; then Norman Angell, who knew Paris better than we did, found out that the Hotel Vouillemont, across the Boissy-d'Anglais from the Crillon, had recently been occupied by the American Navy, which moved out leaving an ample stock of coal. We found good rooms there. . . . There lived Ray Stannard Baker, who was the president's mouthpiece to the press, and Ida Tarbell, who was writing something about the peace for the *American Magazine*. Dorothy Canfield used to come occasionally. Half a dozen men who were more or less attached to the American delegation to the conference lived there: James Scott Brown, an advisor on international law; some Quakers who were doing reconstruction work in terms of many millions of dollars in devastated France; and, for a time, Oswald Garrison Villard; and one or two correspondents from the London papers who knew vastly better than I did what the conference was about. I must set these names down here, not in pride but to show how I got what little education I had, as I wrote my stories from Paris for the McClure Syndicate. . . .

We had been in the Hotel Vouillemont only three days when I came down to breakfast and saw in the morning edition of the Paris *Herald* the news that Colonel Roosevelt was dead. I can remember, across the years, standing there with that paper in my hand; dumb, speechless, and probably tearful. I could not have read that news without sorrow. Again and again I looked at the headlines to be sure that I was reading them correctly. Ray Baker came along, and I cried: "Ray, Ray, the Colonel is dead—Roosevelt!"

He must have seen the grief in my face. He had the paper in his hands also, for he had read it at breakfast. He put his hand on my shoulder and said: "Yes, Will, it's a great blow. We are all sorry." Then he and Ida Tarbell and I sat down to talk it all over, and get used to a world without Roosevelt in it. Not since my father's death had grief stabbed me so poignantly as those headlines cut into my heart that gray, cold Paris morning. . . .

I am satisfied that, if the Colonel had lived, he would have been the Republican nominee and the country would have had, in workable terms, from a Republican administration, much of the social program that came a dozen years later under the second Roosevelt. It would have been adopted in normal times. We should have had the little end of the wedge. It would not have disturbed economic and industrial traffic, and a great cataclysm might have been avoided.

The Paris of the Peace Conference in the winter of 1918 and 1919 was crowded. Ten thousand civilian visitors must have come there from every nation in Europe. For every nation on this globe had some vital interest at that conference. Each nation sent its delegation and its delegation brought its hangers-on—men and women whose special interest made it profitable, even necessary, to come to Paris so that the special national interests would not be ignored in the conference. Probably nowhere else on earth were ever assembled so many self-seeking visitors who knew, or thought they knew, exactly what they wanted. The air was filled with international horse-trading. The world's great commodity interests there probably for the first time met face to face. And from that Paris conference sprang the international agreements, patent pools, cartels, trusts, interlocking international directorates that began to rise in the third decade and were organized compactly in one huge worldwide compact of plutocracy. That organism—somewhat financial, somewhat social, and of necessity more or less political—was growing conscious across national lines, even across ocean boundaries. . . .

There at Paris these thousands of representatives of the nations and those who came to guard them, had to be fed, lodged, entertained, transported around the city, and diverted with the idea that they were achieving something worthwhile. So the air was filled with gaiety, theaters were crowded, concert halls played to capacity houses, restaurants within a mile of the Place de la Concorde were always showplaces jammed with people who wanted to be seen. And the two opera houses, the Opéra Comique and the Opéra, were sold out days in advance. Traffic on the boulevards was congested. The city was a place of parties, receptions, teas, conferences, caucuses, secret gatherings. And out of it all, where the horde of visitors went about their foolish futile errands, grew that world which wrecked itself in a quarter of a century; largely, I think, because the same unrestrained forces of amalgamated self-interest found that winter in Paris—in all its gaiety and beauty, and outward sense of joy and inner sense of power—the formula of destruction which was to shatter the world.

I did not know that at the time. I worked hard, six or eight hours a day. I attended regular press conferences held by the Americans and by the British. Occasionally I went to the French, who were such obvious liars that their perfidy palled after it ceased to be amusing. And when there was a special conference or a semipublic meeting of any consequence, I made it my business to attend. I used the cable three times a week, writing my letters in cablese, skeletonized. And I told seriously, honestly, and briefly what was going on at the conference in those days. Reading those stories today I see they are dull and unimportant. I realize now that I did not know the truth and that few, if any, of the American correspondents knew it. We had access to the facts. Ray Baker was illuminating when he talked and most obliging when we asked questions. But we did not ask the right questions apparently. We did not comprehend the significance of the conference even if we sensed its importance.

Every day I saw Colonel Edward M. House, who had been the President's emissary to Europe during the war. I walked with him late afternoons along the banks of the Seine and we discussed the passing show in the various secret conferences. I am sure that he was candid with me. I am certain that he had no guile. So far as he knew what was pending and why it was important, he told me. Much that he told me was in confidence. If he knew something about the undercurrents of the great Peace Conference I would have known it. . . . I was exposed to all the facts. I should have known the truth.

Moreover, every day I saw and talked with the American correspondents; the wisest of them all was Frank Simonds, who was beginning to know the truth, who tried to tell me the truth. But he was such an inveterate pessimist that I could not believe the truth when he told it to me. He saw the rocks and the wreck ahead. He wrote it to his papers. And much thanks he got for it. The president became bitter against him and he lost caste and standing as men always do who proclaim the unpleasant and terrible truth. I remember that Frank Simonds one day in February showed me his cable. The first lines contained the phrase: "The League of Nations is dead. The treaty of peace is impossible."

That was the burden of his song. After Wilson refused to consider the use of force as a guarantee of the decisions and pronouncements of the League of Nations, Simonds felt that without a common police force to implement the treaty of peace and to make good the decisions of the League of Nations, the League would fall into a political mechanism to promote the balance of power, the old organ of European political stability. He also was sure that without an international police force, the terms of the treaties soon would be violated because no one cared to stop the intrigue of special privilege in and upon the conquered countries which would sooner or later render the peace of Paris a mockery. Now all these things I sensed, suspected vaguely, understood but did not quite know as I went about my job in Paris in those days. . . . After all, I was just Republican precinct committeeman in the Fourth Ward of Emporia, Kansas, who had been on the state committee and had been on the national committee, and so walked with what I thought was a heroic tread. But the vast complexity of European politics, built on centuries of tradition, usage, prejudice, and conflicting desires, was not even remotely in any corner of my consciousness. So I wrote the day's story without realizing the larger story of which the report of the day's routine was a small and insignificant part.

But one must not get the impression that I, or anyone else at Paris, was devoted solely to considering and reporting high and mighty matters. Paris was gay. Bill was with me. He was studying French with a tutor four days a week and soon had the language in hand. . . . We went together to the theater and to the good restaurants, often picking up friends; and because I was lonesome for the female society of my kind, we generally picked up interesting women of whom there were great lonesome droves in Paris, members of the various recon-struction units, wives, sisters, and daughters of delegates and experts attending the conference, and occasionally the classical detached expatriated American mother and daughter living on the Continent because prices were cheap and domestic duties were few. . . .

The French were hospitable. They were forever entertaining the press of the world and were particularly eager to please the representatives of the American press, and especially courteous to those of us who were filing news by cable. So Bill and I saw everything that was going on. The French nation rented a gor-geous palace of a rather vulgarly rich man—a palace he had adorned in the dec-orations with naked women spreading over fireplaces, or standing on the newel posts, or bending over doorways and windows. It was a forest of obtrusive nu-dity, and it became known in the parlance of the American press delegation as "the House of a Thousand Teats." There the French gave us dinners, shows, lectures, and receptions to meet the great and the near-great. I remember a lovely evening I had there with Henri Bergson, the philosopher whose *Creative Evolution* I had taken two years to read. He was a charming man who reminded me, because he was blond and slight and soft-voiced and with a certain sup-pressed humor, of James Whitcomb Riley. We three—the merchant, my host, and Bergson (and possibly Bill)—ranged over the whole earth and the fullness thereof in our talk at the dinner, and I went home late with my head in the stars. . . .

For all the festive face of Paris, in her heart of hearts turmoil was raging. It was man's first experience in organizing world affairs. The Roman Empire, after all, was mostly a Mediterranean concern. Napoleon scarcely left the boundaries of Europe. The British Empire represented only a minority of mankind. But here for the first time man was trying to organize the whole globe into some kind of political entity. These thousands, perhaps hundreds of thousands, of men and women who were gathered there in Paris in the early winter and spring of 1919 were literally of "every kindred, every tribe on this terrestrial ball."[2] With their self-interests, which were unrestrained, was their satellite special interests which were greedy and unashamed in their greed; and they were trying to integrate, trying sincerely to form, some kind of unity. But it is evident now that some-

[2]From the last verse of the eighteenth-century hymn "All Hail the Power of Jesus' Name," by Edward Perronet.

thing more than goodwill is needed. Their noble emotions which might have united them were not matched . . . by their minds. The problem was too big for man, acting in his collective capacity with his limited knowledge and experience, to solve.

I gathered . . . with what terrible earnestness Woodrow Wilson was trying to comprehend the problem. I think he knew—he must have known—his limitations, any man's limitations facing that problem. In the end, the problem was checked up to three men, to Wilson, Clemenceau, and Lloyd George. The preliminary work—what might be called the predigestive process—was done in scores of committees, and by these committees checked up to a rather large council of the Allies. There the work of the committees was digested. But giving the blood, putting on the flesh, and making the bone of the world structure was in the womb of the Big Three.

Premier Clemenceau represented the continent of Europe. He knew it as well as one man could know it. He was a cynic but not a pessimist, for he had a great faith. But chiefly his faith was in France and the French way of life. At first probably he despised Wilson as a canting Presbyterian moralist. He sneered at him in several public utterances before he met him at the conference at the Table of Three—sneered politely with a gay French touch, but nevertheless his sneers were poison barbs.

Lloyd George was a horse-trading Welsh politician—expansive, emotional, but canny in the deep and bitter experiences of a lifetime in the peculiarly shady politics of the British parliament. He knew little about continental Europe and apparently cared less. His eyes were greedy for advantage to the British Empire. He wanted colonies. He wanted British mandates which were quit claims rather than fee simple deeds to possession. Lloyd George knew Wilson and his kind better than Clemenceau, for Wilson was a Scotch-Irish parson in his eyes. He understood Wilson's aspirations, shared them with a sort of academic enthusiasm. Lloyd George, in the Council of the Three, worked more often with Wilson than with Clemenceau, but when the interests of the British Empire were at stake, he deserted Wilson with the sweet and lovely complacency of the courtesan who has her children to support.

Wilson was not exactly an innocent, but his life as a college president had not equipped him with political experience. He was sitting in a game with two sharpers who knew the cards, who had marked the decks and knew the value of the chips. Yet he was for all that, by reason of the nobility of his ideals, the brave, fine way he stuck to them, and even for what he achieved, a truly great and noble figure in Europe that year.

Wilson proclaimed during the war, at the end of the war, and when he went to Europe, that the United States wanted no territory, desired no colonial influence, hoped only to establish an organization to guarantee world peace. For that he would do anything; indeed his stern Presbyterian morality once in a long while was bent to what he thought was a larger good. The difference between the complacency of Lloyd George and the surrender of Wilson was that the Britisher knew he was harloting, and Wilson believed he was serving the will of God.

The secret treaties which the Allies had made before America's entrance into the war, with Italy and with Japan, rose to meet President Wilson early in the sessions of the conference. After the Covenant was drawn and he came home, the president denied that he knew of those treaties until he went to Europe. There again I think the Scotch-Irish parson was telling the truth. He had heard of them. They seemed trivial at the time they came into his ken. Other matters, which seemed much more important to him than the text of the treaties which were published in the New York papers, were worrying him deeply. So in the conference there at Paris, when the treaties rose and stood in his path as he walked sternly toward his ideal of justice, he was concerned with these complications, bedeviled by their consequences in the work before him, and necessarily detoured more or less around the straight path to his objective. Woodrow Wilson was fundamentally honest, a man of high and noble purpose at that conference. And he sat there at that cosmic poker game with the fate of humanity in the run of the cards. He made his bets with his hand face upward on the table for all to see. He really had only one chip in the game, to secure justice for humanity in some kind of a vital political organism that would live and breathe with the righteousness that was in his own heart. But alas, the thing he fathered had his own weaknesses. He begot it too good for this world. . . .

I suppose the story of the Commission to Prinkipo belongs here. Certainly it is a part of my primary education in European politics. It was an insignificant affair and it fizzled. Yet in its pattern and in its failure lay all the evils and tragic weaknesses that made the Peace Treaty of Versailles a mockery. . . .

I began to realize early in January that the fundamental clashes in the conference were between the French demand for security against another German invasion, versus the feeling of Wilson and Lloyd George that the best security France could have would come if the Allies treated Germany fairly and if the conference left a fairly free Europe, free to organize itself as a going civilization. This clash explains much, though of course not all, of the political maneuvering at Paris in the winter and spring of 1919. France desired to control eastern and central Europe. France feared Bolshevism[3] in that area with a jibbering terror. Lloyd George and Wilson were uneasy about the Bolsheviks, but the whole political policy of France at the peace table was to put a ring around Germany and

[3]The Bolsheviks, a revolutionary communist party, had seized power in Russia in October 1917.

erect a barrier against Russia. Preferably France would have liked to overthrow the Bolshevik regime and restore, if not the Romanoffs, at least some semblance of the Kerensky Republic.[4] Clemenceau was willing to trade security against Russia and Germany for anything that Great Britain desired, or that Wilson cared to put into the bargain. So, in the end, the British extended their colonial empire. Wilson got, with certain reservations, his League of Nations; France, the establishment of a balance of power in central Europe and a free hand to deal with Russia either by diplomacy or force. . . .

It was in late January that Ray Stannard Baker told me that Lloyd George and President Wilson had persuaded the French to set up a conference with the Russians at Prinkipo in the Sea of Marmara, an island off Turkey where Lenin and Trotsky would either send envoys or go themselves, and where they would meet representatives from the little nations that had broken off from the Bolshevik rule, Estonia, Latvia, Lithuania, an Arctic Republic under the leadership of Chaikovskii and, as I recollect, a government more or less on paper in the Ukraine. . . . The idea of the conference at Prinkipo was to bring these small nations to a definite agreement with Russia which should guarantee the peace of the Baltic and afford a certain amount of security to the Allies of France in her scheme of European balance of power, the Balkan countries, Rumania, Austria, Czechoslovakia.

After explaining the purpose of the conference to me, Mr. Baker said: "Will, would you go as one of the American representatives to that conference?" I was bowled over. What did I know about European politics except that in a general way I knew, or thought I knew, those matters that I have just related. I was abysmally ignorant. In politics one must know two things: the issues at stake, and the men who dominate those issues and dramatize them. I knew vaguely about the issues, but not how they affected each of the principalities, and I knew nothing of the Powers. But here was a chance to serve and to learn. With some proper protestations and modesty which probably I really felt, I yielded. Baker told me that my American conferee would be Professor George D. Herron and asked me if I knew him. I had never met him, but I knew about him. Baker told me the names of the men who were being considered as the French delegates to the Prinkipo Conference and the names of the British. I did not know the Frenchmen, but the British names were fairly familiar. I have forgotten them now. Which makes no difference, for the episode was a mere bubble on the stream of contemporary events. But I was pleased and in my pride cabled Sallie.

The conference was set for mid-February and a day or so after the announcement was made of my appointment and Herron's, Professor Herron appeared in

---

[4]The Bolsheviks had overthrown a provisional government headed by Aleksandr Kerensky that had succeeded the abdication of Czar Nicholas II in March 1917.

Paris. I saw that he was lodged at the Vouillemont where we could talk things over. . . .

What strange yoke-mates we were! I often wondered, as we tried to team up, what he though of this off-ox. I was given to quips and jests and jollity, to quick and sometimes illogical decisions. I was utterly ignorant of things that were commonplace in his erudition and his practical political experience in Europe. . . . I must have been a cross to poor Herron, who never left a sentence unfinished nor a logical process incomplete, to whom all food was alike, and all social gatherings where men met in camaraderie were a pain in the neck. But he knew the situation which we were tackling.

Almost the first thing he told me after he had been in town two or three days was that the French were working on the delegates from the White Russian countries . . . trying to get them to refuse to go to a conference with the bloody Bolsheviks. The French persuaded these delegates that it would be terrible to sit at a table with representatives of robbers, murderers, and arsonists who had overthrown the Russian government and brutally murdered its Czar. But they were bewildered and impoverished, living at mean, smelly little hotels or pensions, and I had the bright idea, which worked well for a few weeks, to round up each delegation and feed it. So two or three nights in a week Herron and I picked out a good gay restaurant and invited the delegates from some of these countries to dine with us, taking along a friendly interpreter. Having given them a square meal, we sailed in, and in most cases undid the work of the wily French, and pledged one by one, these delegates, to come to Prinkipo. At the dinners, Herron was most competent. He knew the best restaurants in Paris, though he ate with no discrimination. But he talked convincingly, and I was a sort of a snare-drum obbligato to his tuba solo and added the condiments to our conversations.

In the meantime Lloyd George and Wilson had sent emissaries—Lincoln Steffens and Bill Bullitt—to Russia to find out whether or not Lenin and Trotsky and Chicherin, their foreign minister, would send delegates to Prinkipo. . . . They were in Russia two weeks and came home full of strange tales. Steffens, in particular, was bug-eyed with wonder [at the Russians' social miracle]. . . . Like the ancient mariner,[5] Steffens was always stopping the wedding guests and telling them his Russian story until they beat their breasts in despair. One day at the Crillon, six or eight of us were sitting in the big fat leather chairs in the lobby around Steff, listening to his Marco Polo[6] story. One of Steff's favorite phrases in that stirring tale was "I have seen the future, and it works!" It was an

[5]In Samuel Taylor Coleridge's poem "The Rime of the Ancient Mariner" (1798), an aged seaman buttonholes a young man on his way to a wedding and tells him a long and fantastic story of his experiences.

[6]Marco Polo (c. 1254–1324), a Venetian, was one of the earliest European travelers to China.

impressive sentence and Steff knew it. I had heard him spring it several times, and I liked it. But it was beginning to pall on the other newspapermen, and so was Steff's wonder tale. . . . They were just a shade weary, and probably envy for his luck tinged their skepticism. . . . At the climax, or near the climax of his story, to prove with a sentence the reality of his Utopia, he exclaimed: "Gentlemen, I tell you they have abolished prostitution!"

I do not remember whether it was Larry Hills of the New York *Sun*, or James of the New York *Times*, or Herbert Swope of the *World*, or Arthur Krock—but one of them held up his hand, stopped Steff, and cried: "My God, Steff! What did you do!" Steff, who was never a philanderer, blushed like a beet and rose and trotted away, for he was too little to stalk. And the Crillion forum broke up amid triumphant cackling which purged us all of envy of Steff. . . .

Time passed, and with it the date for the conference. President Wilson and Lloyd George kept trying to get the French to set a new date. They were slippery. No new date ever was set. And so the conference just fizzled out. . . .

Bill and I took [a trip to] Germany in late January of 1919. . . . With us in our car was Burge McPhall, a former *Gazette* reporter who had been with Pershing's army for the Associated Press during the last three months of the war and on the front when the Armistice was signed. Cyril Brown, a reporter for the New York *World* was also with us, and we picked up a reporter for the London *Daily Mail* and another for the London *Daily Express*. . . .

Near Coblenz was the headquarters of General Joseph T. Dickman, who lived at general headquarters for the Third Army, the army of occupation. We found him a fine old German-American with a deep contempt for French works and ways. . . . Quite apart from him as a museum piece was the building wherein he held forth. It was a modern office building, a sort of federal building, which had been occupied by the German government. On the walls of General Dickman's office were pictures of Bismarck, the elder Kaiser, Kaiser Wilhelm II, and steel engravings showing various days of triumph for the German army. Not a thing had been changed. The war maps of Germany hung on the walls alongside the pictures of their idols. When the Germans moved back into that office they found the building as they had left it. For the Americans observed a biting, scrupulous honor about things all over Germany. We noticed as we rode about that no German sign was painted out, no German monument was changed. The Americans put up their own military signs and painted upon them their own military instructions. They touched nothing that the German armies had established. . . .

We bunked up one night at an American army post in a little town where a company of our young soldiers were quartered in a cloister. They insisted that the nuns had invited the soldiers to come as guests. The nuns kept house for the boys, who were as happy and comfy as bugs in a rug. The nuns moved about the place cheerful and happy, and when one remembers the stories that were told, either true or false, about the nuns in Belgium, one gets an idea of the deeply different relations between the American army of occupation in Germany and the German army of occupation in Belgium.

General Headquarters had to issue an order forbidding our soldiers to fraternize with the populace, and the order had about as much force as if they had posted a notice commanding the wind to be quiet, the water to be still, and the sun to change its course. That non-fraternizing order from G.H.Q., of course, was posted all over the place in that village where the nuns were hostesses, and the priest in the village had spoiled all the fun for the boys and the town girls by calling all the girls together and warning them about the wiles of our boys. But in the next village the priest had taken no such precautions, and the boys were having the time of their young lives, all quite against regulations. They were popular in that village even though the order against fraternizing was strict.

The company band played in the public square two or three times a week, and we saw the populace turn out to listen. The whole village crowded about. Certainly we could see no aloofness, no fear. There was, of course, a little shyness. They were village people, these were strangers, but certainly not conquerors. The soldiers played with the children and smiled at the girls, who were clearly on amiable terms with the village. . . .

We went into the back areas, up the hills about the Rhine. There, in little villages miles from the railroad, our boys were quartered. The gray gloomy villages were not spotlessly clean. Water ran down the gutters in which the natives washed tons of turnips—apparently the chief fodder item for their cows. Sometimes we stopped and talked to the villagers along the way. Politically they were all Centrists and Catholics, and they were against the Kaiser and the Bolsheviks. Amidst our soldiers, by the thousands, women were walking these lonely roads, as carefree as the men—which probably more than anything else indicates how little our army is a conquering army. . . .

One German peasant asked us, "We notice always your American officers talk with the men, play games with them." It was baseball and basketball mostly, for in order to get up teams, the G.H.Q. had commandeered all college and professional baseball and football and basketball players even up to colonels. The peasant said, "Your soldiers treat the men as though they were folks. We do not understand that. With us the men are not folks, only officers are folks. The rest are cattle. We see your men obey their officers in the drill, and our soldiers tell us your men have fine discipline in battle. We do not understand this!"

Then we undertook a right difficult job of getting it through that peasant's head that our men obeyed their officers because they respected and admired their officers, not because they feared their officers. Then, by way of trying a little missionary work, we tried to explain that to bring obedience based on respect rather than on fear into the world was what brought us into the war. All this greatly puzzled him. He made us repeat it over and over, and looked at us like a smart collie dog, as though he almost understood, and he went away repeating the phrase, "obedience based upon respect and not fear," chewing it all over. I wonder if he ever got it. Also we were fooled by his phrase *Herrenvolk*, which we thought meant "folks"—folksy folks, common people—when apparently he referred to a master race. . . .

In due course we came to Cologne, . . . and on the whole broad countryside around Cologne was a series of gay bright peasant villages, very different from the gray bleak places in the hills around Coblenz. This Rhine country apparently was Germany's Colorado and California combined, their spare bedroom. Along the way on the hillside were sunny homes of the rich Berliners and Hamburgers. Every village had its restaurant. Even then, in the mid-winter of 1919, the restaurants were open with little food. Yet every town was spick and span and modern, and for the first two hours out of Cologne, everywhere American soldiers colored the landscape. The children seemed to take to these grinning, cheerful-looking American boys as big brothers. They had no trouble with the civilian population, for they were natural-born fraternizers and couldn't help it. . . .

As we were passing up the Rhine Valley, we came to the headquarters of General Douglas MacArthur. Burge McPhall had known Douglas MacArthur in Washington and also at the front before the Armistice. So we stopped, and before we knew it we had accepted the general's invitation to lunch. He had commandeered a beautiful home—larger than Al Gufler's in Emporia, and most exquisite, high above the road overlooking the Rhine and the hills beyond. . . . Inside, everything was white, very severe, all straight lines, all repressed, as if the architect had said to himself, "I'll not be French; I'll not be French," a thousand times over. The draperies and hangings were severely plain but beautiful to a degree; and every form of house luxury that you ever heard of was found there, but always hidden, suppressed, covered from ostentation. The repression of it all was Spartan. . . .

Into this austere and formal situation flashed General Douglas MacArthur, aged thirty-eight, a bachelor, with the grace and charm of a stage hero. I had never met before so vivid, so captivating, so magnetic a man. He was all that Barrymore and John Drew hoped to be. And how he could talk! . . . His staff adored him, his men worshipped him, and he seemed to be entirely without vanity. He was lounging in his room, not well (an ulcer in his throat), and he wore a ragged brown sweater and civilian pants—nothing more. . . .

As we came into Cologne I saw with astonishment that the men were practically all back from the German army. Never before in my life had I seen so many men. The streets were black with them. They were not at work, I was told—at least, only on part time—and the soup kitchens were running at full blast. They were being fed, but they were demanding work. The walls were covered with political posters, and little knots of men and surrounding spectators gathered on every corner. No big public meetings were allowed, but it was evident that northern Germany was seething. The whole population was fighting the Reds. The Catholics were the strongest anti-Red group, the regular Socialists were next strongest, and the Social Democrats and the Democratic People's party seemed next. The walls were bristling with proclamations, and politics was red-hot. Men, women, everyone was talking politics, and the streets were crowded. . . .

Cologne was a splendid city. They had built it according to modern city planning. In the dry-goods districts some architect had done marvelous things. The store buildings were modern Gothic and conformed to a plan which was binding the commercial exterior of the town to the cathedral. The hotels were wonders of comfort—New York had nothing more gorgeous. The whole place seemed to be the expression of a spirit of the times; and there on those beautiful buildings and about in the squares were bas-reliefs of great hulking giants breaking clubs, statues of the Hohenzollerns showing their power, or Bismarck with his sneer, and one saw the worm in the bud. Their crass philosophy was imprinted everywhere for them to bow before. Possibly all these placards on the walls, these angry street crowds and the gaunt windows of the food shops might turn the Germans from their idols of wood and iron and stone. I didn't know, but I seriously doubted it. . . .

It is curious to go back to the notes, the letters, and articles I wrote in January 1919 about this trip to the American front in Germany. It is evident that the people of our country felt that a policy of kindness toward the German people in their humiliation and distress would bring response in kind. The soup kitchens which were running full blast in Germany were for the most part financed by the Americans, entirely by the Allies. Germany was prostrate, and our soldiers, who obviously represented the attitude of the people of the United States, were on German soil not as conquerors but as guests. Their attitude was entirely misunderstood. Apparently the Germans felt that our kindly consideration was the result of fear. . . .

The German mind in 1919 was not ready to receive the ideas of democracy. It was not a part of their tradition, and the conduct of their conquerors could not be explained in terms that they could comprehend. We, the victors of 1918, made our blunder by assuming that the language of democracy was understood by a people who had never in all their history fought for the freedom of the common man, for the rights of the people. We thought that liberty could be passed around as alms or material benefits. We did not realize that men can have freedom only when they have found it worth the sacrifice. Ours was a sad and tragic blunder in 1919, and the world paid for it for a generation. Maybe the debt is not paid yet.

22

Through
the Valley
of the Shadow

When I returned from Europe in 1919 the fight upon the League of Nations was raging. It was led by "a group of irreconcilables," most of whom were Republicans. Lodge was their leader. A majority was visible in the Senate through many informal ballots for the League of Nations with reservations. The reservations were supposed to be written and submitted by a group of Republicans: Nicholas Murray Butler, Charles Evans Hughes, Elihu Root, and William H. Taft. It was fairly obvious that Wilson was deeply irritated by the reservations. When he came home in February, certain modifications were suggested by this group or by their Republican senatorial representatives, and he accepted them. To surrender again was temperamentally impossible for him. He was equally angry with the reservationists who had a majority in the Senate and with the irreconcilables who were in a minority but who, voting with the reservationists, made a decisive senatorial majority against the League.

The treaty with the League attached was pending in the Senate. I felt it my duty under the auspices of an organization quickly created for the purpose (called, I believe, "the League of Nations Association") to go out and make speeches favoring the adoption of the League. I paid my own expenses. . . . (I set it down only to warn young men against the temptation of letting anyone pay any expenses when one is on any kind of a political or propaganda mission. One surrenders his freedom while he is in service and his right afterwards to change his mind and criticize or even denounce the cause he has espoused if it goes wrong or if he discovers that it is making mistakes. In politics, a man must pay for his freedom with his own checkbook.)

I went into Wisconsin and, as I recollect it, into Michigan; made a speech or two in Missouri and in Kansas. It was obvious that I was fighting for a lost cause, which did not discourage me. But I found everywhere the rigid belligerent attitude of the president toward the reservationists was weakening his hold upon the people. Soon after I came home from my speaking campaign, the president was stricken. We did not know at first how heavy the blow was, but as the autumn deepened and the winter opened, it was obvious that Woodrow Wilson's work was done.

The syndicate which had been employing me in Paris asked me to cover the story of a conference which President Wilson had called in Washington to consider the twelve-hour day in the steel industry. . . . The eight-hour day was largely adopted by industries like transportation, communications, textiles, copper, mining, and smaller manufacturing concerns, . . . but steel was on a twelve-hour day; this was a national disgrace, so Wilson called a conference. He named delegates to represent the steel industry. They were under the leadership of Elbert H. Gary, who was the head of the so-called Steel Trust. Labor was represented by Samuel Gompers, head of the American Federation of Labor. The public was represented by a number of distinguished citizens who were not public officials, among others young John D. Rockefeller, Jr., and my dear friend, Ida M. Tarbell. . . .

The first or second day of the conference, while I was at a window of the conference room (held, I think, in the Pan-American Building) looking over the lovely formal garden, young John D. Rockefeller, Jr., came up and our elbows touched. After some casual conversation he batted his eyes, grinned, and said: "You know Miss Tarbell very well, I believe." I was glad to say that I did, and after some sparring he indicated that he was a bit puzzled as to what attitude he should take toward her. Young John D. essentially was a gentle person, a kindly, warm-hearted man. It was evident, even if he had not said so in terms, that his natural instinct to be friendly with people in general was making it rather difficult in the case of Miss Tarbell. For after all, her book about his father and the methods of Standard Oil in the seventies and eighties and nineties was an unpleasant fact. . . . I told him that personally she was a sane common-sense person with really as much sensitivity about the situation as he had, and that he could afford to go ahead, meet her casually and naturally, and they two could find a path of approach to a pleasant relationship and a useful cooperation. I believe he really was trying to find out what kind of a person she really was.

Shortly afterwards, I met Gary, whom I knew was fond of Miss Tarbell. I told him about young John D.'s uneasy feeling, and the Judge and I had a quiet chuckle about it, knowing that the two who had been antagonists could, if they were thrown together and used their common sense and their instinctive kindness, find a way of approaching the job before them easily and naturally. One noon, when the conference was in recess, we saw young John D. hurrying out in the street to hail a cab for her. Franklin Lane, secretary of the Interior, who gave a dinner for the delegates, placed the two side by side. I always thought Judge Gary put him up to it. At any rate, as the dinner proceeded the Judge enjoyed the spectacle of the two leaders of the right and the left chatting amiably together, and Miss Tarbell told me afterwards that the old Judge nearly winked his eyelids loose at her and at Rockefeller over the beatific picture they made, each trying to outdo the other in politeness as the evening wore on.

The last session of the conference was notable. I sat at the press table not twenty feet away from one of the most dramatic public spectacles in what might be called a Grade C drama that I witnessed. On the front seat sat Judge Gary, who upheld the twelve-hour day and had defended it through the long conference. Samuel Gompers, the leader of the organized labor, had attacked it during all the conference. Gary had summed up his final word in a formal but not convincing speech. He knew precious well that the debate was against him and that his position was untenable. Gompers was on the program to reply to Gary. . . .

They were powerful men, leaders who had real following and spoke each for his class. Judge Gary was the most notable figure in the conference. . . . He dressed as if sitting for his portrait, with clothes creased, linen immaculate, and hands manicured. They generally rested clasped together in his lap as though sustaining his stomach, which was not large and needed no support. He impressed one as being a nerveless man. He sat there for thirty minutes without moving a muscle except once or twice to brush his chin while Samuel Gompers stood arraigning Judge Gary's Steel Trust and all its men in a powerful speech. . . .

Gompers himself was . . . Judge Gary's antithesis. During the conference Gompers rarely sat still. One might know how the conference was going by looking at his half-bald head, which flushed pink and paled white like the bulb of a barometer as the proceedings went forward, pleasing or displeasing. He did not fidget, but he rarely held the same position ten minutes at a stretch. . . . His face was mobile, his mouth was large and strong, his jaw was brutal and indomitable. . . .

I wrote the story of Judge Gary's ordeal under Gompers' fire . . . and the story was a picture of two iron men at a moment of crisis. . . . After the story had been published I received a letter written on rather elegant stationery in that angular handwriting that was fashionable for women at the turn of the century:

Dear Mr. White:

I read what you said about the imperturbability of Judge Gary under the lash of Gompers. You spoke of his color not changing and of the control he had over his features.

Well, you missed the point. You should have watched his ears. When the Judge is moved, his ears turn white. I am sorry you didn't watch his ears.

So was I. That letter, which was anonymous, remained photographed in my memory, and the handwriting, so obviously of the fashion of the late nineties, stuck in my memory. . . .

It was in the autumn of 1919 that Will Hays, chairman of the Republican national committee, began trying to work for harmony in the Republican party. He set up a harmony platform committee under Ogden Mills, which would try to work out before the Republican presidential convention of 1920, a set of Republican principles that would be acceptable to the progressive and the conservative wings. He named me on the committee. It was a good committee, if I do say so. On it were open-minded, intelligent men from both wings of the party. We worked hard on a short, simple, definite statement of Republican issues and were fairly well agreed upon it. . . .

I went as a delegate to the national Republican convention of 1920, [committed to the candidacy of General Leonard Wood]. The Kansas delegation elected me to serve on the committee on resolutions, the platform committee. But before the convention assembled, it was evident that the national Republican committee, which had wrecked the party in 1912 by nominating Taft, was dominated by the Senate group who had fought Wilson on the issue of the League of Nations. . . . The liberal group still known as the progressive crowd made its first fight in the convention to control the committee on resolutions and to write the platform which Chairman Hays had asked Ogden Mills to arrange. Mills was defeated as a candidate for chairman of the resolutions committee by Senator James Watson, an avowed spokesman of the reactionary senatorial group. We Progressives were able to muster less than a dozen men in the committee who represented our faction in the Republican party. . . . We managed to slip into the platform five demands of the National League of Women Voters. . . . But we were overwhelmed in most of our suggested planks by reactionaries. For two whole nights and a day and part of two other days we worked on the platform. In the meantime I was writing a story every day and sometimes two stories, one for the evening and one for the morning papers of the syndicate which was taking my stories. . . .

Governor Allen had been chosen by General Wood to put the general in nomination for the presidency and Henry was working on his speech day and night. He wrote at least two, and if I am not mistaken three, speeches which were inevitably rejected by the Wood forces. I say inevitably because any board of political strategy supporting a candidate wants nothing forthright, no commitments. They desire circumlocutions. One of the troubles with Governor Allen's orations was that they were too eloquent. A story began to creep through the delegates that the reactionary forces in control of the convention would like to nominate Allen for vice president to appease the progressives, so the Wood people watched every syllable of his speech to see that he did not glow and lure the delegates. It was a funny proceeding, which I watched out of the corners of my eyes from time to time as I worked in the committee room and on my stories, for Henry and I were dear and close friends and could laugh at the tragedy of his position: temptation glittering before his eyes, the suspicion of the Wood supporters clouding every moment, and the final acceptance by Wood's supporting strategy of a dull, unconvincing, purely political speech which gave Wood no standing. Whereupon Wood's friends blamed Allen for not rousing the convention. The governor's position was one of those seriocomic predicaments which no dramatist can originate but which arise out of the play of human ambitions, temperaments, and untoward circumstances, to drive earnest men and women and sometimes strong ones into distraction and folly. . . .

In the meantime, I was watching . . . the backstage machinations of what was known as the Senate cabal. It was in control of the convention. I have never seen a convention . . . so completely dominated by sinister predatory economic forces as was this. . . . One day Henry Allen came to me and said that he had been called to a room in a business block and taken onto a high mountain by a group representing oil, who questioned him closely about his views on foreign policy and particularly Mexico. This was in relation to his possible candidacy for vice president. That candidacy was one of those things that he did not encourage, and so far as he could he let it alone. But his name was buzzed about in high places, so that oil thought it worthwhile to probe him. Every delegation that I knew much about was loaded with one, two, or a half a dozen representatives of national commodity interests—oil, railroads, telephones, steel, coal, and textiles. We had been warned five months before the convention by Harry Daugherty, an Ohio lobbyist, that Harding would be nominated in a "smoke-filled room" after the delegates had been allowed to play for a while with their own candidates. . . .

The convention waited a day for the report of the platform committee. Senators Borah, Medill McCormick, and I managed to wangle into the platform a phrase granting to labor "collective bargaining" in labor disputes with "representatives of their own choosing." That was Gompers' phrase. . . . Also we managed to get in something that Gompers did not like, a promise pointing to the recognition of Russia and a mild endorsement of what was then known as the World Court. But the committee deadlocked and spent most of its time on a plank relating to foreign relations. Borah was an out-and-out isolationist. So was McCormick. We—and there were a dozen of us active and fairly determined in the committee who favored the League of Nations Covenant as it was amended by the reservationists—tried all sorts of formulas, some frankly compromising phrases, others slick and greasy, which might get by. But Borah's eye caught our subterfuges and finally we asked Senator Lodge to take the matter up with Elihu Root, who was sailing for Europe.

Root was an internationalist, but he realized the problem before him to get any sort of a formula in the Republican platform that would not close the door absolutely to negotiations to join the League. He sent back a plank. It was fearfully and wonderfully made. It meant nothing except that it frankly did mean nothing, and we accepted it. It was that or defeat on the floor. For the Republican party of 1920 had the same bitter hatred of Wilson and anything Wilson stood for which twenty-four years later was to mark the Republican party as it entered the campaign of 1944. It was "isolationist" for spite and hatred, governed by its emotions, and not amenable to reason. Out of that witch's pot of mad malice rose the stench which produced Harding's election and became the Harding administration.

I do not think that the propertied interests of the country deliberately started this wave of wrath against Wilson to create in Chicago the situation which gave them control of the Republican party. Things are not so simple. Wilson had his blame in the matter, and the anger and bitterness of the Republicans only met Wilson's suspicious jealousies, bitterness, and cold malevolence toward his opponents. Perhaps even without that vicious quarrel the result in 1920 would have been the same. As we rose out of the war, the world's creditor nation, custodians of the world's debt, we had not learned as a people how to behave as a creditor. Perhaps our own pride and fear and newly acquired and not quite understood leadership of the world gave us a vulgar, rapacious arrogance which dramatized itself in the idolatry of the power of money. And if it had not produced Harding it might, indeed probably would, have expressed itself in some other way as evil, as tragic, and as shameful. I do not know.

I only know that I was unhappy as I watched the convention, as I sat night after night until dawn in the resolutions committee, and as I sat with the Kansas delegation in the great hall where the thermometer rose to 100, to 101, 102 degrees Fahrenheit, and the multitude sweated, stank, and lifted from the floor sheeplike faces which fell under the hypnosis of the American madness of the hour.

For two long days the deadlock between General Wood and former Governor Lowden gathered strength. Then it clinched and set like a bone. Kansas was more or less pledged to Wood and we voted generally as a unit for Wood. Saturday morning—the morning of what was to be the last day of the convention— Senator Curtis came to the Kansas delegation and told us frankly that it had been decided (the phrase was his) to give Harding a play, after trying for a ballot or two to name Wood. The delegation was for the most part glad enough to take orders. I sat in the meeting of the delegation in our hotel that morning, and when the Curtis orders came, I blew off. I cried: "If you nominate Harding, you will disgrace the Republican party. You will bring shame to your country."

James Stewart of Wichita, who more than anyone else represented property . . . sneered across the room: "Ah, White, you are a dreamer. Try to be practical once."

And then I blew off again. But in my malediction I was prophetic and did not quite realize it. The end of the whole business was that I got practical, and I told the leader of the delegation that I would go along with them to Harding to make it unanimous if, and only if, they would promise to go with me to Herbert Hoover if Harding could not make it. It was a long chance. They took it. Early in the afternoon, when Wood failed to take the necessary gain in the balloting, Curtis came to our delegation and told us that now was the time to break for Harding. Kansas was to lead the break, and I was up against it. I remember sitting there sweating, fanning myself with my new twenty-five-dollar Panama, with my coat over the back of my chair, in a blue-and-white striped silk shirt of great pride, red-faced, perturbed, and most miserable in body and spirit. I didn't want to vote for Harding.

I had warned the delegation that morning against Harding, and yet these were my friends. Some of them had run errands for me in politics, others had done me many favors, and Mulvane, who was the only real political adversary I had in the delegation with influence there, had promised to go to Hoover if Harding failed. If Harding succeeded, my opposition would not head him off. I was torn, as I often am in politics, between the desire to jump in the fiery furnaces as a martyr and the instinct to save my hide and go along on the broad way that leadeth to destruction. But in the end I toddled along, followed the Kansas banner in the parade, ashamed, dishevelled in body and spirit, making a sad fat figure while the bands played, the trumpets brayed, and the crowd howled for Harding; and in that hour the Republican party bade farewell to the twenty years of liberalism which had grown up under the leadership of Theodore Roosevelt. As I marched, I saw Harding in Chicago back in 1916, in the measly opportunist convention where the whole desire of the party had been to head off Roosevelt. As I marched I saw that figure of Harding, all properly tailored, with suitable dove-colored trousers and morning coat, with a red geranium in his lapel, mouthing those mean miserable strafings at T.R. which gave him his first prominence and distinction as a national Republican leader. And indeed, as I trudged along in the Kansas delegation leading that parade to Harding, my heart was bowed down with a weight of woe. I kept feeling that I would have looked better sulking in my seat, letting the hope of Hoover, with which I licked my spiritual wounds, go glimmering. I kept asking myself, "Is the long chance of Hoover worth this?" And my striped blue silk shirt and my red necktie, all bedraggled with sweat, didn't revive my drooping spirits as I marched and the crowd yelled and danced on the grave of the Colonel who had been my leader and my friend for a quarter of a century. A sad spectacle I made, and time has not softened the shabby outlines of the picture in all these long years. . . .

So, in the heat and confusion and insanity of that afternoon, Kansas voted for Harding. The Kansas banner led the Harding parade. I marched with the Kansas delegation, hoping in my heart that Harding would fail in a ballot or two and that I could collect my promise. I think it might have been done. Anyway, on the next ballot and the final ballot, I cast one of the nine votes in that convention for Herbert Hoover and tried to purge my soul. I was being practical, God help me, and I was greatly ashamed. . . .

Harding was nominated and Senator Medill McCormick told us in the Kansas delegation that on the slate it was written that Lenroot should be nominated for vice president. Curiously, the delegates in the convention . . . rose and flouted the bosses and nominated Calvin Coolidge. . . .

I have often wondered, looking back over the years—nearly a quarter of a century now—why I faltered that hot afternoon in Chicago. The promise of Mulvane to support Hoover if Harding failed should not have held me in the Harding parade. But there I marched! I believe now that the death of Theodore Roosevelt and the rout of his phalanx of reform, together with the collapse of Wilsonian liberalism when America rejected the League of Nations, the eclipse of the elder La Follette's leadership—all created in my heart a climate of defeat. My purpose was enervated.

Indeed, the whole liberal movement of the twentieth century which had risen so proudly under Bryan, Theodore Roosevelt, and La Follette was tired. The spirits of the liberals who called themselves progressives were bewildered. The fainthearted turned cynics. The faithful were sad and weary, however bravely we shouted. I did not sink low enough to carp, but as I trudged up the aisle of the convention hall when Kansas took her banner to Ohio for Harding, I was too heartsick to rise and fight. I hope now, looking back to that sordid hour in Chicago, that I am not merely rationalizing my conduct to justify its turpitude!

23

Mostly
Personal

Two or three weeks later, the Democratic conven-
tion was meeting in San Francisco, and my contract with the newspaper syndicate required me to go there. Of all the national conventions which I have
attended in the last forty-four years, that convention at San Francisco was physically the most pleasant. Of course, the weather was irreproachable. The San
Francisco restaurants are the best on the continent. The San Francisco people
are most hospitable. . . .

The convention also was a delight. We who reported it saw, or thought we
saw, many evidences, unmistakable evidences, that President Wilson, stricken as
he was, hoped for a third-term nomination that would vindicate him and give
him a chance to rescue his discarded and discredited League. . . . But the delegates paid no heed to Wilson's desires. Late evidence has indicated that the cal-
lousness of the convention hurt him deeply. But there was a gay debate between
Bryan and Bourke Cockran about Prohibition; and young Franklin Roosevelt,
in his prime, a state senator from New York State, stood before the convention
and made an impassioned plea for the nomination of Governor Al Smith,
which also the convention ignored after some rather obvious clack and a considerable real enthusiasm for the man who dared to oppose Prohibition when it
was young and strong. In the end the convention made a synthetic nomination:
Governor James M. Cox, a newspaperman in an Ohio town, who made his living as Warren Harding made his. Cox was more of a person than Harding and
has survived with much more repute than his fellow Ohio editor, but his nomination did not stir the convention or the country profoundly. . . .

That summer . . . in Estes Park was pure joy. The two children, Bill and Mary,
and their mother and one of her sisters [were with us], and, I think, my mother
and Sallie's mother. It was a gala time by day. Up in a log cabin, one hundred
feet above the living quarters, I hammered away at my typewriter, writing something, perhaps a part of a book, perhaps a magazine article. But Bill was twenty

305

and Mary was sixteen, and they were forever going out to parties and dressing, and little dances were springing out of the cracks of the boards on the wide porches and in the living room. The phonograph was forever chirping its gargantuan cricket song, either for dance or diversion. . . . Friends were continually coming and going. We gave a tea for Jane Addams, I remember, and had faculty people from the neighboring valley crowding on the front porch, and Mary was there, lovely, being a child and stuffing herself with food in the kitchen but being quite a young lady on the porch serving our guests. And Bill was fishing and supplying the frying pan and tramping all over the hills, sometimes gone for a day or two camping. And the Estes Park markets in the village were filled with fresh Colorado fruits and vegetables, and we rarely sat down to a meal without company. It was a gay, boisterous summer, the last we were ever to have as a united family. . . .

We knew that Bill was going to Harvard and that the family would be rather badly battered. So Sallie and I cherished every happy day of it. Mary came home for meals after spending her mornings in the Y.W.C.A. grounds, half a mile away, and spouted a fountain of miscellaneous and generally useless information about that citadel of morality—the term was hers, though she was really a devout little person and, they told us, sometimes led the exercises of the young women of the Y.W.C.A. gathered there for state convention. But she had lively and devilish comment to make on everything. Bill packed his lunch and his fishing outfit and came home with his creel full in the afternoon and had little to say about strange adventures which we heard from others. He certainly never tattled on the gang he ran with. And by the same token we knew that he was safe and sound and fine in his relations with them and with us. It is odd how two children out of the same womb with the same environment could be so different and yet so dear.

That summer in the park, where we all huddled together in three little cabins around a living-room cabin, was a fair and sunny one which we will cherish through the years as our brightest memory of the family. And it seems to have a necessary place here in the narrative if my life is to have any sort of record or interpretation in these pages. Above everything else, from childhood on, I have been a family man. An event has never happened in my life that I have not waited for its completion by mulling it over and finally giving it substantial reality in the family. Then it became set in its proper direction and place in my life. . . .

Bill's Harvard days were the making of him, and we took a sort of postgraduate course in sophisticated living, for we had to see his coonskin coat, his ramshackle Ford, his unbuttoned sophomore galoshes, his tail coat and white tie in his junior year, his success as a co-author of two Hasty Pudding Club musical comedies, his course with Professor Copeland, affectionately known as "Copey," and his editorial work on *The Lampoon*, and his blossoming into some of the college clubs. All these things came to us intimately and with a freshness that was amazing and delightful. He certainly earned his way through Harvard with the joy he gave his doting parents. . . .

Bill came home from Harvard for Christmas. Mary, well along toward her seventeenth birthday, was going out to little high school dances. She had passed through the riotous period of her life while Bill and I were in Paris, when her mother got her first gray hairs keeping vigil over the child with her rollicking, irresponsible habits which hid a great tenderness under a vast humorous impudence that was not so easy to curb and channel as it seemed. But the worst was over. . . .

She was a born tomboy. . . . She rode her horse, first a Shetland pony, then a spirited single-footer, all over town and was a familiar figure everywhere. She shared; whenever she saw bug-eyed kinds on the other side of the track looking wistfully at her, she got off her horse, put them on, and led it by the bridle or let them ride around the block. She hated special privilege instinctively and once told her teacher with welling eyes, "I'm so tired, so darn tired of being William Allen White's little girl!"

And she meant it. She wanted to be Mary White in her own right. She was five feet three, and disliked that too. She wanted to be as big as her ideas. I never knew how my father, who was only an inch or two taller than Mary, felt about being a little sawed-off man until I noticed in the early spring of 1921 that Mary was beginning to walk with the same curious little swagger, bending her body not from her hips but from her dorsal vertebrae just a little bit, and it was amusing how much her back view looked like his. She was constantly, in those days, reminding me of him in physical habits and sometimes in her bubbling humor and impish mischievousness. Because of this odd physical and spiritual resemblance between the ancestor and the descendant, I often dreamed of my father in those days—vivid and generally joyous dreams. I did not understand it then. Now I can see that it was natural enough. The dreams came because Mary was continually dropping little hooks of reminder into my subconscious mind, and in sleep the images took form.

In May 1921, I was called away on business—among other things, to make a speech in the East and to see La Follette. I went away on a late afternoon train, and Mary and her mother drove me down to the train. They stood on the platform while I hurried back to the observation car and waved them out of sight. The picture they made there, with the background of the sunset behind the roundhouse, has always remained with me. They were smiling and waving and stood until after the train had passed entirely out of their sight. A week later perhaps, a telegram from Sallie told me that Mary had fallen from her horse and was hurt, but not seriously. She told me to go on with my engagements. I went

to Atlantic City where I had promised to speak at the annual American Booksellers Association convention, and there received a telegram to hurry home,
that Mary was in danger. When I changed cars at Chicago, Harold Ickes and
Edna Ferber were on the platform to tell me that Mary was dead. It was a long,
sad, agonizing journey home. The Santa Fe stopped the train for me at Exchange Street so that I would not have to go clear to the station, and there Sallie
met me. Her face was brave and I knew her heart was staunch, and when I
kissed her I knew it was all right.

Bill came home from Harvard a few hours later. The day after her funeral I
knew that I must write something about Mary. I had at first thought I would
make a little book, but I could not wait. The things that I wished to say were
boiling in my heart, so I went to the office and hammered out her obituary.[1] Sallie came and we went over it together and revised it three times in the proof before the type was put into the forms. I had said my say and some way felt eased
in my soul.

The town was deeply moved by it. I could tell that. As I walked about the next
day, I could see in the faces of people, though most of them stopped to tell me,
how the editorial about Mary had touched them. In a day or two, of course, the
town forgot the editorial. Then the Kansas City *Star* picked it up, and Franklin
P. Adams reprinted it in his "Conning Tower" in the New York *Tribune*. From
there it went through the daily press of the country. And then a woman's magazine repeated it, then another, and another. Christopher Morley was writing an
anthology and asked to include it. Alexander Woollcott put it into his first
"Reader" and read it over the radio. Other radio entertainers used it and within
a year it had been in four books of reading for high schools and colleges.

Mary had been entered at Wellesley before her death. In 1926, which would
have been her graduating year, her class adopted her and dedicated the Wellesley Annual to her. She was carried on the rolls of the class of 1926 for many
years. In the meantime, year after year, the piece appeared in innumerable anthologies. We kept tally on it for twenty years and it had been in more than
forty of those school readers or anthologies of Americana, in the best of them
and in the humbler ones. It has been a comfort to her mother and me to know
that for a decade, at least, Mary will survive. She would be now in her forties. If
the article never appears in another book, she would survive in the hearts of
youth well into her fifties. Hardly a day, never a week, passes that boys and girls
in high schools and colleges do not write to me about Mary. . . . She survives, I
think, as she would like to survive—in the hearts of her kind, high school and
college students. It is a strange immortality. Probably if anything I have written

[1]The 1946 edition of the *Autobiography* relates the composition of the obituary somewhat differently: "Sallie and I walked down to the *Gazette* office together, and I hammered out her obituary."

in these long, happy years that I have been earning my living by writing, if any-thing survives more than a decade beyond my life's span, it will be that thou-sand words or so that I hammered out on my typewriter that bright May morn-ing under the shadow and in the agony of Mary's death. Maybe—and when one thinks of the marvels of this world, the strange new things that man has discov-ered about himself and his universe, it could well be true—maybe in some dis-tant world among the millions that whirl about our universe, Mary will meet her mother and me and, just as she grinned and looked up at her mother that evening when we climbed the mountain in Colorado with her hand around my finger, she will grin: "Daddy and I have had an adventure!"

It would be a gay and happy meeting.

MARY WHITE

May 17, 1921.

The Associated Press reports carrying the news of Mary White's death declared that it came as the result of a fall from a horse. How she would have hooted at that! She never fell from a horse in her life. Horses have fallen on her and with her—"I'm always trying to hold 'em in my lap," she used to say. But she was proud of few things, and one of them was that she could ride anything that had four legs and hair. Her death resulted not from a fall but from a blow on the head which fractured her skull, and the blow came from the limb of an overhanging tree on the parking.

The last hour of her life was typical of its happiness. She came home from a day's work at school, topped off by a hard grind with a copy on the High School Annual, and felt that a ride would refresh her. She climbed into her khakis, chattering to her mother about the work she was doing, and hur-ried to get her horse and be out on the dirt roads for the country air and the radiant green fields of the spring. As she rode through the town on an easy gallop, she kept waving at passers-by. She knew everyone in town. For a decade the little figure in the long pigtail and the red hair ribbon has been familiar on the streets of Emporia, and she got in the way of speaking to those who nodded at her. She passed the Kerrs, walking the horse in front of the Normal Library, and waved to them; passed another friend a few hundred feet farther on, and waved at her.

The horse was walking, and as she turned into North Merchant Street she took off her cowboy hat, and the horse swung into a lope. She passed the Tripletts and waved her cowboy hat at them, still moving gaily north on Merchant Street. A *Gazette* carrier passed—a High School boy friend—and she waved at him, but with her bridle hand; the horse veered quickly, plunged into the parking where the low-hanging limb faced her and, while she still looked back waving, the blow came. But she did not fall from the horse; she slipped off, dazed a bit, staggered, and fell in a faint. She never quite recovered consciousness.

But she did not fall from the horse, neither was she riding fast. A year or so ago she used to go like the wind. But that habit was broken, and she used the horse to get into the open, to get fresh, hard exercise, and to work off a certain surplus energy that welled up in her and needed a physical outlet. The need has been in her heart for years. It was back of the impulse that kept the dauntless little brown-clad figure on the streets and country roads of the community and built into a strong, muscular body what had been a frail and sickly frame during the first years of her life. But the riding gave her more than a body. It released a gay and hardy soul. She was the happiest thing in the world. And she was happy because she was enlarging her horizon. She came to know all sorts and conditions of men; Charley O'Brien, the traffic cop, was one of her best friends. W. L. Holtz, the Latin teacher, was another. Tom O'Connor, farmer-politician, and the Rev. J. H. Rice, preacher and police judge, and Frank Beach, music master, were her special friends; and all the girls, black and white, above the track and below the track, in Pepville and Stringtown, were among her acquaintants. And she brought home riotous stories of her adventures. She loved to rollick; persiflage was her natural expression at home. Her humor was a continual bubble of joy. She seemed to think in hyperbole and metaphor. She was mischievous without malice, as full of faults as an old shoe. No angel was Mary White, but an easy girl to live with, for she never nursed a grouch five minutes in her life.

With all her eagerness for the out-of-doors, she loved books. On her table when she left her room were a book by Conrad, one by Galsworthy, *Creative Chemistry* by E. E. Slosson, and a Kipling book. She read Mark Twain, Dickens, and Kipling before she was ten—all of their writings. Wells and Arnold Bennett particularly amused and diverted her. She was entered as a student in Wellesley for 1922; was assistant editor of the High School Annual this year, and in line for election to the editorship next year. She was a member of the executive committee of the High School Y.W.C.A.

Within the last two years she had begun to be moved by an ambition to draw. She began as most children do by scribbling in her school books, funny pictures. She bought cartoon magazines and took a course—rather casually, naturally, for she was, after all, a child with no strong purposes—and this year she tasted the first fruits of success by having her pictures accepted by the High School Annual. But the thrill of delight she got when Mr. Ecord, of the Normal Annual, asked her to do the cartooning for that book this spring, was too beautiful for words. She fell to her work with all her enthusiastic heart. Her drawings were accepted, and her pride—always repressed by a lively sense of the ridiculous figure she was cutting—was a really gorgeous thing to see. No successful artist ever drank a deeper draft of satisfaction than she took from the little fame her work was getting among her schoolfellows. In her glory, she almost forgot her horse—but never her car.

For she used the car as a jitney bus. It was her social life. She never had a "party" in all her nearly seventeen years—wouldn't have one; but she never drove a block in her life that she didn't begin to fill the car with pick-ups! Everybody rode with Mary White—white and black, old and young, rich and poor, men and women. She liked nothing better than to fill the car with long-legged High School boys and an occasional girl and parade the town. She never had a "date," nor went to a dance, except once with her brother Bill, and the "boy proposition" didn't interest her—yet. But young people—great spring-breaking, varnish-cracking, fender-bending, door-sagging carloads of "kids"—gave her great pleasure. Her zests were keen. But the most fun she ever had in her life was acting as chairman of the committee that got up the big turkey dinner for the poor folks at the county home; scores of pies, gallons of slaw, jam, cakes, preserves, oranges, and a wilderness of turkey were loaded into the car and taken to the county home. And, being of a practical turn of mind, she risked her own Christmas dinner to see that the poor folks actually got it all. Not that she was a cynic; she just disliked to tempt folks. While there, she found a blind colored uncle, very old, who could do nothing but make rag rugs, and she rustled up from her school friends rags enough to keep him busy for a season. The last engagement she tried to make was to take the guests at the county home out for a car ride. And the last endeavor of her life was to try to get a rest room for colored girls in the High School. She found one girl reading in the toilet, because there was no better place for a colored girl to loaf, and it inflamed her sense of injustice and she became a nagging harpy to those who she thought could remedy the evil. The poor she always had with her and was glad of it. She hungered and thirsted for righteousness; and was the most impious creature in the world. She joined the church without consulting her parents, not particularly for her soul's good. She never had a thrill of piety in her life, and would have hooted at a "testimony." But even as a little child, she felt the church was an agency for helping people to more of life's abundance, and she wanted to help. She never wanted help for herself. Clothes meant little to her. It was a fight to get a new rig on her; but eventually a harder fight to get it off. She never wore a jewel and had no ring but her High School class ring and never asked for anything but a wrist watch. She refused to have her hair up, though she was nearly seventeen. "Mother," she protested, "you don't know how much I get by with, in my braided pigtails, that I could not with my hair up." Above every other passion of her life was her passion not to grow up, to be a child. The tomboy in her, which was big, seemed loath to be put away forever in skirts. She was a Peter Pan who refused to grow up.

Her funeral yesterday at the Congregational Church was as she would have wished it; no singing, no flowers except the big bunch of red roses from her brother Bill's Harvard classmen—heavens, how proud that would have made her!—and the red roses from the *Gazette* forces, in vases, at her head and feet. A short prayer; Paul's beautiful essay on "Love" from the Thirteenth Chapter of First Corinthians; some remarks about her democratic spirit by her friend John H. J. Rice, pastor and police judge, which she would have deprecated if she could; a prayer sent down for her by her friend Carl Nau; and, opening the service, the slow, poignant movement from Beethoven's Moonlight Sonata, which she loved; and closing the service a cutting from the joyously melancholy first movement of Tchaikovsky's Pathetic Symphony, which she liked to hear, in certain moods, on the phonograph; then the Lord's Prayer by her friends in High School.

That was all.

For her pallbearers only her friends were chosen; her Latin teacher, W. L. Holtz; her High School principal, Rice Brown; her doctor, Frank Foncannon; her friend, W. W. Finney; her pal at the *Gazette* office, Walter Hughes; and her brother, Bill. It would have made her smile to know that her friend Charley O'Brien, the traffic cop, had been transferred from Sixth and Commercial to the corner near the church to direct her friends who came to bid her good-by.

A rift in the clouds in a gray day threw a shaft of sunlight upon her coffin as her nervous, energetic little body sank to its last sleep. But the soul of her, the glowing, gorgeous, fervent soul of her, surely was flaming in eager joy upon some other dawn.

24

The Downhill Pull

In the fall of 1920, I [had been] faced with the unpleasant duty of either supporting Harding or bolting him. I did neither. Perhaps one editorial may be found in the files of the *Gazette* faintly indicating my support of the Republican national ticket, though I bore down hard many times on the need of electing the Republican state and congressional tickets, and I was always strong for the Republican county ticket. It generally carried with it the election of a county commissioner. This board distributed the county printing which was not a rich plum but palatable.

During that campaign I was one of those who signed a letter to Harding asking him to support a League of Nations. The letter was written and was passed around among the signatories by Herbert Hoover. It was signed by Root and Hughes and, as I recollect it, by Taft and a rather substantial group of conservative Republicans. Harding naturally made an equivocating reply, and even if he had answered it with a straightforward "yes," it would have meant nothing. His "yes" would have been based on expediency rather than conviction.

He had no conviction. He had passing opinions, poor fellow. He was densely ignorant. At best he was a poor dub who had made his reputation running with the political machine in Ohio, making Memorial Day addresses for the Elks, addressing service clubs—the Rotarians, Kiwanians, or the Lions—uttering resounding platitudes and saying nothing because he knew nothing. . . . In the end, even the morning of the election, I did not know exactly how to vote for president. But I screwed up my courage and voted for Harding, thinking of the shortcomings of Cox. I fear these shortcomings were exaggerated. I did not realize how bad Harding would be.

But it was not in the stars to elect anyone in 1920 who advocated anything seriously. The country, after eight years of Wilson and with the four short years of breathing space with Taft before Wilson, and seven years of Roosevelt—almost twenty years in which they were keyed up to principles, years in which causes were followed and battles fought for issues rather than men—was tired of issues, sick at heart of ideals, and weary of being noble. . . . However, it was Harding who was elected rather boisterously, and the gaudy, bawdy, hell-roaring third decade of the century opened.

After Harding was decently seated in the White House, an ironic thing happened. In his first message to Congress, he ignored practically all of the five demands which organized womanhood of the country had been able to slip into the Republican platform and recommended specifically the one demand which Senator Smoot had rejected—the demand for federal aid for maternity hospitals and nurses. Nothing could illustrate more beautifully the breakdown of party government. Nothing could prove so clearly how little relation a party declaration has to actual party performances. The planks which we liberals had slipped into the Republican platform were ignored. A short, equivocal plank on the tariff had embellished the Republican platform, and most of the first sessions of Congress when the Republicans came in were devoted to the tariff. Our egregious compromise on the League of Nations resulted in a number of curious feints from President Harding toward adherence to the World Court. But he backed, sidestepped, and sparred for position so obviously that nothing came of his foolish gestures. He was sadly beset. Secretary Hughes and Mr. Hoover in his cabinet, and Republican leaders like Taft and Root outside of the cabinet, were urging him to join the World Court. And in the Senate the irreconcilables bedeviled him incessantly to keep out. He did not know what to do. So he went flutter-ducking around, trying to satisfy both sides, and fooled no one.

But President Harding did one important thing. He called the Disarmament Conference. In November 1921, the response of the people to that call, a glorious flare-up of faith which Wilson had fanned to flame in 1917 and 1918, was lovely to behold. Probably the American people even then would have followed some strong leader into a crusade for organized world peace. The nation rejoiced in pride at America's part in summoning the conference. And I went to the conference as a reporter for a group of twenty-seven newspapers with something like the exultation of spirit that had taken me to the Peace Conference at Paris. In Emporia, between the call of the conference and its date of meeting, everywhere I met joyous comments. The Democrats were, of course, saying, "I told you so," and the Republicans also pointed with pride to what Harding had done.

As I sit writing these lines here in my middle seventies, my memory goes back down the long line of political spectacles that I have seen. . . . But of all the human conclaves I have ever witnessed, the gathering of the Disarmament Conference in Washington furnished the most intensely dramatic moment I have ever witnessed. . . . It lacked the color of pageantry. A small room seating fewer than three thousand people held, in encompassing galleries, the American Senate,

the American House of Representatives, the American Supreme Court, the diplomatic corps from the various foreign embassies and legations, a fringe of newspapermen, and a group of distinguished sons-in-law from the State Department.
The spectators were mostly clad in conventional black. A few women wearing
blues and crimsons made bright flecks in the somber tones of the galleries. The
delegates in the pit assembled about a U-shaped table. They also wore the conventional black of the statesman, excepting a few turbaned East Indians and less
than half a dozen admirals who speckled the drab scene. Democracy, which rejects distinctions among men, rejects the colors which mark the distinctions,
and so it is for the most part drab. The U-shaped table at which the delegates to
the Disarmament Conference sat was a solid affair of walnut, constructed for
the occasion, which gave an air of sincerity and permanence to the scene. . . .

One conspicuous delegate appeared in America who was entirely absent, conspicuously ignored, and rather bitterly snubbed at Paris. It was God. No one,
not even President Wilson, introduced God to the delegates at Paris. After a
Baptist minister at Washington, in a formal invocation, gave official credentials
to God in the Disarmament Conference, President Harding opened it with the
words, "Inherent rights are of God and the tragedies of the world originated in
their attempted denial." Later in his speech, the president asked: "How can humanity justify or God forgive the World War unless its fruits shall be fruits of
permanent peace?"

The speeches of all the delegates, that first day of the Washington Conference,
were couched in language filled with biblical allusions, and the eloquence
of every speaker had an evangelical swing, peculiarly American, middle-class
American, the patois of King Demos indicating a deep emotional conviction, a
religious conviction about the business in hand. For all the high hats of Congress, the Supreme Court, and the diplomats, the Washington Conference was
at heart deeply middle-class, thoroughly democratic. The ancient instinct of
American politicians to cheer broke out early in the first meeting of the conference. President Harding, groomed within an inch of his life, made the opening
speech of the conference. . . . He walked to the desk like "a bridegroom coming
out of his chamber," said his little speech—which was unimportant, rather
stilted and delivered in a throaty oratorical voice, lacking somehow in sincerity,
but the cheering arose as he sat down. The Senate had the temerity to begin the
cheering. The House joined, and the Court, the diplomatic corps, and the reporters respectfully followed in the clamor. The European delegates were
shocked. Cheering is bad form at diplomatic functions across the ocean.

Then followed Hughes, and it was from Hughes' speech that the thrill of the
day emerged. Here were delegates from England and her colonies, from Japan,
from France, from Belgium, from America, summoned to hear a disarmament
proposal, and the American spokesman, Charles E. Hughes, secretary of state,

rose and threw into the conference a sharp challenge of sincerity. Excepting President Harding and one admiral present, no man in the hall knew how deeply Hughes proposed to cut the armament of the world.

Compared with the president, Hughes was slighter, and his face, ruddy with health in his mid-fifties, glowed with the kind of spiritual exultation which gave tone and timbre to his voice. No throaty oratorical nonsense was there. His words rang out with a trumpet clearness of a challenge. As he went into the details of his proposal, the sheer audacity of his deliverance—an audacity backed by the financial power and economic resources which gave America the leadership of the world—created a genuine hush of awe in the room. The well-masked faces of the diplomats cracked under the impact of Hughes' speech. One could see them moistening their lips, craning their heads forward. One knew that the American secretary of state was reaching their spirits as men, not as diplomats. With characteristic American dignity and self-respect, Hughes had not communicated to the representative of any other nation an inkling of the American proposal. Just before the conference met, Secretary Hughes talked for three hours with Mr. Balfour, the British leader, about affairs of the convention and had given him no intimation of his intentions. Balfour, of course, knew that he was going to fire a bomb, but not that the bomb would blow nearly two million tons of war-craft out of the waters of the world. The gloomy British reporters seated in the press galleries, who came to America peddling pessimism, were shocked to a faster heartbeat, and when the Senate led the galleries, standing to release its exuberance by cheering for ten minutes, the British delegates led the visitors from the Allies in a mad chorus of approval, like a great political convention. The drab lining of those galleries, looking down upon the pit where the delegates sat, was resonant with enthusiasm. . . . Into the outburst of the crowd spilled the joy that had tightened its nerves as it listened. Hats waved, handkerchiefs fluttered, men shook one another's hands, hugged one another, slapped one another, exhibited every kind of animal delight of which human beings are capable in their high moments. There was an agenda or program of the conference, but after Hughes had spoken, democracy took charge of the rules and order of business, and as the cheering died the galleries—after the ancient fashion of American political conventions—began calling out for speakers. First of all, the senators insisted upon hearing M. Aristide Briand. And when the other parts of the room had quieted, from the Senate sections came cries of "Briand, Briand." The senators pronounced it with a long i, and the French did not understand that the senators were calling for "Breeand." Such is the difference in pronunciation of vowels among our Allies. I sat next to William Jennings Bryan, . . . [who] thought it was he who was called for. He whispered: "White, shall I get up?"

I said: "No, they don't mean you."

"Yes," he said. "But they are calling my name."

"They mean Breeand, the French premier," I said.

"Do they pronounce it that way?" said Bryan.

And when the clatter for "Briand, Briand, Briand," spread over the hall and became a roar, William Jennings Bryan rose up beside me and started to lift his hand. I gave his coattail an awful yank, for the Senate, seeing him, broke out in a raucous: "No, no, no! Sit down, sit down! No, no, no!"

And what with the yank of his coattail and the shock of those riflelike noes, Bryan fell back into his chair, smiling kindly but dazed and confused by the proceedings. Arthur Balfour rose when order had been restored, spoke in the exact but hesitant British manner, with no emotion, in splendid English, perfect taste and real distinction, and so quieted the crowd. When the meeting adjourned, the American reporters—perhaps a hundred of us—went to our press headquarters in a nearby building to write our stories of the morning. One after another entered the room literally bubbling with happiness. I have never seen newspapermen thrown off their feet in a mass as they were. These were old stagers in the craft, for no callow youth was assigned to this important task. Here I met men whom I had been seeing at conventions and conferences for thirty years, the most skillful newspapermen of America, inured to all sorts of excitement and generally emotion-proof. But they went about shaking each other's hands, slapping one another's back, delighted beyond words, not merely with the splendid drama of the Hughes speech but with the deep implications for peace that came in the Hughes proposal. It was from this gathering of newspapermen that I had realized how tremendous had been the drama of that moment.

Looking back nearly a quarter of a century upon that scene, I can understand why, with all the enthusiasm in the heart of mankind for peace, the efforts of the Disarmament Conference failed. In brief, men wanted peace but were not willing to pay the price of justice—and peace without justice is a mockery. Men thought that by disarming the world, peace would come. Delegates to the Disarmament Conference from all over the earth, who for a few moments rose and cheered with unquestioned sincerity as Charles Evans Hughes made his great speech, represented millions of people who were not ready for peace. Their national plans and aims were bars to peace on earth because those aims and aspirations were not based upon goodwill to men.

No one can doubt that the world wanted peace. The 1920s were full of manifestations of man's desire for a peaceful world. But also the nations of the earth and their leaders, political, social, industrial, and financial leaders, had dreams of wealth and power, plans narrowly centered in nationalism. And the whole bright bubble of peace by disarmament, which gleamed and glimmered in the hearts of men in the 1920s, was a sad illusion and mirage that had no reality.

We who were pacifists, and I was one, believed that it was only the admirals and generals and the armament makers who brought war to the world. We did not know that war came inevitably out of the hearts of greedy men who led nations into the paths of potential conquest and exploitation and oppression and deep injustice, we could not know—we whose voices were lifted in cheers that day in that little room in Washington. How the angels must have wept or smiled, God knows which, as we lifted our voices in that futile cheer which was a prayer for peace that could not come to the world because of the evil deep in our own hearts. Still the yearning was there, the ancient hope of the Hebrew prophets for that day when men would turn their spears into plowshares and their swords into pruning hooks, and war should be no more.[1] But man was not yet ready. He had not yet purged his heart or prepared his life for peace.

Sitting in a mahogany-paneled room in New York, the national directors of the Federal Reserve Bank, in 1921, decided by formal resolution to deflate the currency. After the war, labor troubles broke out all over the country. The high wages which prevailed during the war, wages symbolized by silk shirts on workers and a great herd of new and secondhand Fords stampeding over the country, persuaded the American banking interests that their job as vicegerents of God in the United States required them to do something about labor. They felt that deflation would take the crimp out of the arrogant labor leaders and help Harding restore the country to normalcy. But they made a bad guess.

Deflation did not hit labor, but it did hit the American farmer, and it hit especially hard the cattleman of the Middle West. . . . The credit structure which reached small-town merchants cracked. Stores closed, banks were tottering, business slacked. Car loadings on the railroad dropped. Railroad men were laid off. The railroad business slackened and in the summer of 1922 a shopmen's strike was called in the Middle West.

The outlook for the strikers was never hopeful. Remember that the farm boy, who was learning as much about the car and the tractor as he used to know about the horse, had been coming into town to work in the garages since the war. . . . When the workmen walked out of the shops, the boys from the garages walked in, and more farm boys walked into the garages. There was an exhaustless source of fairly skilled labor at hand to break the shopmen's strike. Whatever justice there may have been in some of their demands, the strike was illtimed. Also there was a silly terror of Bolshevism in the hearts of the American people. The cruel raids of Attorney General Palmer had been continued somewhat by Attorney General Daugherty, who persecuted Reds and radicals far beyond the danger which they threatened. . . .

---

[1]The Old Testament prophet Isaiah proclaimed, "They shall beat their swords into plowshares, and their spears into pruning hooks; nation shall not lift up sword against nation, neither shall they learn war any more" (Isaiah 2:4).

The strike affected Emporia, for we had one of the largest shops on the Santa Fe system. The railroad had installed a company union. The men didn't like it. They wanted to join a union that would be recognized by the Railway Brotherhoods, and when the strike was called the leaders of the Emporia shopmen came to the *Gazette* office to talk the thing over with me.

I assured them that we would print the news, that we would always give them a chance to present their side through the *Gazette*, and that when any statement came from the railroad we would show it to them and print their answer with the statement, which was only fair. I said that frankly I could not advise them one way or the other about striking, but if they struck we certainly would not criticize them and would see that they had every chance to present their case to the people of the town and county.

They struck. We printed the news. Bill, who was summering in Emporia, was put on the job of covering the strikers' meetings. They admitted him to the meetings and he made a full, honest, and intelligent story of what happened. The strikers were pleased. No violence of any kind occurred in Emporia. In other towns where the newspapers hooted at the strikers and refused to give them space to present their side of the case, cars were tipped over and heads were bashed and there was trouble in the wind. Trains were delayed.

In the meantime, Governor Allen had taken the railway side of the case. He believed that the strikers were stirred up by labor agitators. . . . In Kansas, we had enacted an Industrial Court to adjudicate labor disputes in essential industries. . . . And although this was a national strike and the Kansas Industrial Court could have done nothing to settle it, Governor Allen, under the impulse of terror which filled the hour when the strike was called, set out to use the machinery of the Industrial Court and the strong arm of the state. Troops were sent to various railroad division points, and considerable flurry was manifest over the state.

In all the towns, a considerable group of merchants had been carrying the shopmen on their credit books for anywhere from thirty to ninety days. They knew these men. Ordinarily in Emporia they paid their debts, as in the other country towns. The shopmen met the merchants in the churches and lodges, and they all were on friendly terms. Over the state the strikers distributed a large placard about two feet long and one and a half feet wide, on which was written, "We are for the strikers 100 percent." The strikers asked merchants to put these placards in their windows as a neighborly act.

The placards offended Governor Allen. He felt that they heartened the strikers and justified them in their violence. He issued an order demanding that the merchants take the placards down. I told him over the telephone that I thought it was pretty awful, but he couldn't see it that way. I also told him that I was going to put a placard up in my window, not endorsing the strikers 100 percent but at least giving them encouragement in struggling for what they regarded was their rights. We were affectionate friends all during the controversy and remain so today. He said, "Bill, if you do that, I'll have to arrest you." And I said, "Come on and arrest me and we'll test this matter in the courts. I think your order restricts the liberty of utterance."

There it stood. The next day, after Sallie and I thought it over and slept on it, I put a placard in the *Gazette* window which read: "So long as the strikers maintain peace and use peaceful means in this community, the *Gazette* is for them 50 percent, and every day which the strikers refrain from violence, we shall add 1 percent more of approval." Then I signed it.

It was a poster of the size which the governor had ordered down and of the same character, except in degree. The fact that we were friends and political associates made my action news. The next day photographers were down from Topeka and Kansas City, snapping pictures of the poster. It became a national episode.[2] The Kansas press was largely with Governor Allen. The national press, and particularly the liberal press, was with me. And a great hullabaloo occurred across the land.

In the meantime Governor Allen came down to visit the Kansas State Teachers' College and, of course, I invited him to lunch and, of course, we had our pictures taken together, for the photographers followed him to Emporia like trailing clouds of glory. This made national headlines and first-page news. But it also raised a doubt in the minds of labor as to my sincerity. Men who are striking and risking their jobs don't like to see their friends fraternizing with the enemy. . . .

It is difficult at this time to revive the picture presented by our controversy. For a moment it was a national cause. I received scores, probably hundreds, of letters and telegrams endorsing my position, and a few of course denouncing me. I received offers from lawyers to take the case to the United States Supreme Court and I was vociferous about one thing: I wanted the case tried on its merits and started on its way through the courts. In the meantime, at the height of it, the Kansas gubernatorial primary occurred. I was supporting my old friend Roscoe Stubbs, who was trying to come back as a candidate for governor. I was his most conspicuous supporter. Middle-class opinion in Kansas said thumbs down to my poster. Poor old Stubbs went to slaughter in the primary, and I was sorry.

About that time an old friend whom I had known and worked with for many years, a former Bull Mooser, Fred J. Atwood of Concordia, Kansas, wrote me a warm and sincere letter of protest. It was kindly and came out of the affection in his heart. I answered him and then it occurred to me that my answer to him

---

[2]On July 22, 1922, Governor Allen ordered White arrested and charged him with violating the antipicketing law and conspiring with the strikers to stop the trains.

would be my answer to everyone who differed with me. I took the carbon copy of my answer, marked it for the editorial page and headed it "To an Anxious Friend." Two or three days after the letter had gone to Atwood, I worked over the phraseology of that editorial. I cut out every adjective and used a verb instead, which greatly strengthens one's style. I shortened it, avoiding repetition, and finally ran it out. I think I transferred it from the editorial page to the front page. Here it is:

TO AN ANXIOUS FRIEND

July 27, 1922.

You tell me that law is above freedom of utterance. And I reply that you can have no wise laws nor free enforcement of wise laws unless there is free expression of the wisdom of the people—and, alas, their folly with it. But if there is freedom, folly will die of its own poison, and the wisdom will survive. That is the history of the race. It is proof of man's kinship with God. You say that freedom of utterance is not for time of stress, and I reply with the sad truth that only in time of stress is freedom of utterance in danger. No one questions it in calm days, because it is not needed. And the reverse is true also; only when free utterance is suppressed is it needed, and when it is needed, it is most vital to justice.

Peace is good. But if you are interested in peace through force and without free discussion—that is to say, free utterance decently and in order—your interest in justice is slight. And peace without justice is tyranny, no matter how you may sugar-coat it with expedience. This state today is in more danger from suppression than from violence, because, in the end, suppression leads to violence. Violence, indeed, is the child of suppression. Whoever pleads for justice helps to keep the peace; and whoever tramples on the plea for justice temperately made in the name of peace only outrages peace and kills something fine in the heart of man which God put there when we got our manhood. When that is killed, brute meets brute on each side of the line.

So, dear friend, put fear out of your heart. This nation will survive, this state will prosper, the orderly business of life will go forward if only men can speak in whatever way given them to utter what their hearts hold—by voice, by posted card, by letter, or by press. Reason has never failed men. Only force and repression have made the wrecks in the world.

It went over the country like wildfire. Editors supposed that I had written it to my friend Henry Allen, although there was nothing to indicate this in the editorial. The moderation and strength of this boiled-down, concentrated, passionate reply to my opponents gave it wings. Like "What's the Matter with Kansas?" it went all over the country. In due course, it received the Pulitzer Prize for the best editorial of the year.

In the meantime, the strike ended. Late in the autumn, the attorney general of Kansas moved to dismiss the governor's suit. With all the earnestness of a hardened martyr, I tried publicly and privately to stop the dismissal, but when the attorney general refused to prosecute there was nothing else for the court to do. But the court did accompany its order of dismissal with a statement that I had appeared and demanded a trial insistently and with obvious sincerity. The court was aware that I was anxious to settle the constitutional question raised by my arrest. Then the court dismissed the case. And of course hundreds of Americans, including many of the shopmen whose rights I had tried to defend, refused to believe that the suit was anything but a publicity stunt, a put-up job between two friends to get our names in the newspapers. Which didn't matter, so far as I was concerned. I had done what I had to, had presented the case, and had won it as far as I was concerned, and lost as far as the governor was concerned. No rift ever came to our friendship. Each thought he was right and still thinks he was right, and there was never any question of hard feeling on either side; which is the way, it seems to me, all controversies should proceed to settlement under the democratic process.

At the end of Harding's first year in the White House it was evident that the man tremendously desired to do what he regarded as the right thing, that he saw—as clearly as he could see anything—an opportunity to make a name in history. . . . The Emporia *Gazette* printed an editorial . . . calling attention to the conspicuously decent things which had been accomplished. It pleased him. It pleased Mrs. Harding also. Both of them wrote letters of grateful appreciation. Once or twice later they sent or wrote friendly messages and in mid-winter of 1923 when I happened to be in Washington for a few days . . . the president sent for me. I do not know how he learned that I was in town. Certainly I did not seek to see him.

But I went over one Friday about nine o'clock. It had been more than four years since I had been in the White House. . . . I came a few moments early expressly to visit with my old friends Ike Hoover and Jud Welliver before the time of my appointment with the president. Welliver was employed in a secretarial capacity. We talked about Harding, and Jud broke forth after a moment's preliminary sparring with something like this:

"Lord, Lord man! You can't know what the president is going through. You see he doesn't understand it; he just doesn't know a thousand things that he ought to know. And he realizes his ignorance, and he is afraid. He has no idea where to turn. Not long ago, when the first big tax bill came up, you remember there were two theories of taxation combating for the administration's support. He would listen for an hour to one side, become convinced; and then the other side would get him and overwhelm him with its contentions. Some good friend would walk into the White House all cocked and primed with facts and figures to support one side, and another man who he thought perhaps ought to know would reach him with a counter argument which would brush his friend's theory aside. I remember he came in here late one afternoon after a long conference in which both sides appeared, talked at each other, wrangled over him. He was weary and confused and heartsick, for the man really wants to do the right and honest thing. But I tell you, he doesn't know. That afternoon he stood at my desk and looked at me for a moment and began talking out loud:

" 'Jud,' he cried, 'you have a college education, haven't you? I don't know what to do or where to turn in this taxation matter. Somewhere there must be a book that tells all about it, where I could go to straighten it out in my mind. But I don't know where the book is, and maybe I couldn't read it if I found it. And there must be a man in the country somewhere who could weigh both sides and know the truth. Probably he is in some college or other. But I don't know where to find him. I don't know who he is and I don't know how to get him. My God, but this is a hell of a place for a man like me to be!'

"He put his hand to his head, smiled at his own discomfiture, turned and walked heavily away. I see something like that going on in him all the time; the combat between folly and wisdom. I never knew a man who was having such a hard time to find the truth. How Roosevelt used to click into truth with the snap of his teeth! How Wilson sensed it with some engine of erudition under the hood of his cranium! But this man paws for it, wrestles for it, cries for it, and has to take the luck of the road to get it. Sometimes he doesn't, and sometimes he does, and much he knows about it when it comes."

At the end of our talk I went into the presidential office, where the president stepped forward cordially to greet me. He had been sick. There was a dark cast to his olive skin. . . . For a moment or two, while he was offering cigars and moving festively out of the preliminaries of a formal conversation, he was socially and spiritually erect. But as we sat in the south sunshine flooding through the windows of his office, he warmed and melted and slouched a little. I had no idea why he had sent for me. I have precious little idea now, only a theory. I have a notion that he was lonesome and that he wanted to talk about the newspaper business. At least he talked of little else. He began by asking me what we were paying for print paper, where we got it, how many carloads we used a year, going into the terms of our contract which by some miracle I had in my mind.

Then he began rather abruptly: "Here's another thing. What do you do with all the people that want to subscribe to your paper outside of the trade territory of the Emporia merchants? I am being swamped by subscribers from Oregon and Maine who want to read the Marion *Star* every day, on the theory that I knock off two or three hours down here and write the editorials for it. If these subscribers don't let me alone, they will bust the paper. The white paper and postage costs more than the subscription price. They are no good to the Marion dry-goods stores. They don't buy anything there, and I can't raise my advertising rate. And I can't reorganize my whole business to make a paper that would interest the advertising agencies in New York and Chicago to bring me a lot of foreign advertising." (By "foreign advertising," he meant advertising from outside Marion—chewing gum, pianolas, pipe organs, toothpaste, Grand Rapids furniture, life insurance, and the like.) . . .

I told him that we had a little weekly, four pages, without any advertising, and we charged enough for the weekly to pay for the white paper, and let it go at that. This weekly contained the editorials and a little local news for people who have moved away from Emporia, and just about pays expenses. The idea struck him as worth considering, and he talked a little more about it. Then he went on to ask about our profit-sharing plan, of which he had read something in the trade papers. He outlined his plan of distributing stock in the Marion *Star* to his employees and explained that it worked well. He went into the matter of wages for reporters, linotype men, floor men, and the foreman, and we compared notes. While one of the White House servants was putting wood in the grate, we both watched him critically. Then the president rose and walked over to the fire, stood with his hands behind him warming his back. One could see that he was physically subnormal. He had a powerful frame, strong, rather sloping shoulders, with just a hint of a stoop in them that tall men often need to get their eyes in focus with the common world a few inches below them. As he stood there by the glowing fire and mused a moment, he said: "Well, when I first took this job, I had a lot of fun with it. I got a kick out of it every day for the first six months or so. But it has fallen into a routine, more or less."

He spoke slowly, dropping into a reminiscent mood, and went on: "You know every day at three-thirty, here in the midst of the affairs of state, I go to press on the Marion *Star*. I wonder what kind of a layout the boys have got on the first page. I wonder how much advertising there is; whether they are keeping up with this week last year. I would like to walk out in the composing room and look over the forms before they go to the stereotyper. There never was a day in all the years that I ran the paper that I didn't get some thrill out of it."

He grinned and paused, and it wasn't for me to talk. I fancy he was getting out of me exactly what he wanted—an audience who would understand the touch of homesickness which had come to a man away from his life's work, a man who had been confined to his room and was a bit under himself physically. Suddenly he broke a minute's silence, left the fire, came over, sat down, crossed his legs, and asked abruptly: "Say, how do you get the county printing?"

I told him that there was a gentlemen's agreement between the Democratic paper and the *Gazette* that when the Democrats elected the county officers, whose business it was to let the county printing, that we did not bid; or if we did bid, we bid the full legal rate. So the Democrats let the printing to the Democratic paper. And when the county was Republican, the Democrats decently refrained from disturbing the legal rate by a cutthroat bid.

"That's fine, fine!" he answered, and a querulous strain rasped in his voice. "Do you know how we used to get it? Well, we all go in and bid and choose among ourselves the low bidder before we bid, and he adds enough to his bid to give us all a little slice of the profits above his low bid."

He paused a second and then turned toward me a troubled face, and he cried: "And that's the hell of it. Right now, at the moment, there is a bunch down at the Willard Hotel coming up here to see me this afternoon, good friends of mine from Ohio, decent fellows that I have worked with thirty years. Some of them have supported me through thick and thin. Well, there is an energetic young district attorney down East here—maybe New York, or Boston, or Philadelphia, it don't make any difference where—and he has gone and indicted those fellows; is going to put them in jail for violating the antitrust law or some conspiracy law for doing exactly in crockery what I have done in printing for twenty years. *And,*" he added, "they know all about my method, and they are going to ask me to dismiss the indictment. I can't do that. The law is the law, and it is probably all right, a good law and ought to be enforced. And yet I sit here in the White House and have got to see those fellows this afternoon and explain why I can't lift a hand to keep them from going to jail. My God, this is a hell of a job! I have no trouble with my enemies. I can take care of my enemies all right. But my damn friends," he wailed, with a sort of seriocomic petulance, "my Goddamn friends, White, they're the ones that keep me walking the floor nights!" . . .

We talked on, never touching politics; talked of homely country things for the better part of an hour. And then a doorman announced that the cabinet was gathering. He took me out and introduced me to a number of members that I had not met, and there for the first time I saw Secretary Fall. The man's face, figure, and mien were a shock to me, that such a man could be in a president's cabinet; a tall, gaunt, unkept, ill-visaged face that showed a disheveled spirit behind restless eyes. He looked like the patent medicine vendor of my childhood days who used to stand, with long hair falling upon a long coat under a wide hat, with military goatee and moustache, at the back of a wagon selling Wizard Oil—a cheap, obvious faker. I could hardly believe the evidence of my eyes. How he must have twisted the nerves of Secretary Hoover! How Hughes must have sensed him and pitied him!

The rest of the cabinet, excepting Hughes and Hoover and Hays, were for the most part starched-shirt-fronts, human bass drums, who boomed out in front of the plutocratic sideshow with bellying banners, shouting the wonders of the fat boy of prosperity and the octopus of big business, and the fire-eater and sword-swallower of a starved but greedy militarism. . . .

I left the White House with a feeling that it was the scene of a terrific struggle. Fall was the symbol of one of the forces, Hoover of another, that were grappling for supremacy with the confused mind of the president. His heart was all right. His courage was fairly good. But his confusion lay in his lack of moral perceptions. He did not know where to place his loyalty. He was deeply fond of his friends the grafters—the petty politicians in every state, who were looking for pickings through the Republican national committeemen or through some subterranean avenue to quick easy money or a soft cynosure.

The president was under many obligations to Harry Daugherty. Daugherty's standing in the Republican national committee, and his acquaintances gained as the attorney for a number of great corporations in various states, had given him easy access to delegations under the senatorial control in the Chicago convention. Over the protests of a powerful group of highly respectable Republicans, the president had appointed Daugherty, and the latter's friends had moved into the attorney general's office, making it a rendezvous for questionable characters and a nest of scandal. Cheap and sometimes corrupt little men were using the powerful leverage of Daugherty's name for unbelievably corrupt semipublic transactions. The spy service of the Department of Justice was set upon those who protested against the dubious transactions of the attorney general, or indeed upon those who protested against any irregular practices anywhere in the federal government. . . .

The hour I had spent with Harding convinced me that he realized the conflict around him and that, insofar as a man with his sordid background could, he was trying to line up with the righteous forces striving to break away from the hands of the past that were drawing his administration down to shame. I remember well walking down the avenue from the White House, troubled in my own heart about the proper attitude to take toward him. Obviously, I could not sit by, grinning at the tragedy. It was a question whether or not to join those who were trying to destroy him in order to expose the corruption which his friends were shielding, with his too obvious acquiescence if not connivance, or whether to join the forces that were trying to win him from his old ways, his vicious companions, and strengthen his purpose to serve his country.

It was plain that his purpose needed strengthening. The Washington of the newspapermen—the writers, the liberal senators, the western congressmen—was abuzz with a thousand little stories, rumors, and suspicions of irregularity, sometimes amounting to crookedness, often merely the petty performances in the various departments, the Interior Department, the Navy Department, the War Department, the attorney general's office. But there were counter stories, little hero tales of the president's kindness, of his dawning consciousness of the truth and his growing resolve to serve it. At the end of my walk I decided to line up with the Hoover-Hughes crowd and try to salvage something from the threatened wreck. . . .

I wrote a piece about Harding emphasizing his good intentions, his kindly nature, his lonely position, his country-town view of life; spoke of his associates in Ohio, of the Saturday night poker game in Marion, and the good fellowship which organized it and kept it going; and tried to explain him in terms of the leading citizen of a country town moving cautiously and rather alone in a new, unfriendly environment. . . .

Sometime that spring while I was in Washington I met, on the sidewalk in front of the White House, a group of friends. They seemed to be in [the] charge of Oswald Garrison Villard. Monsignor Ryan was in the group. They stopped me and I learned that they were on their way to meet President Harding by appointment, to plead with him for the pardon of Eugene Debs. They insisted that I should go along. I knew Debs. I believed that he had been unjustly imprisoned, so I joined them. In the White House office we stood in a group, and just as the president came in Villard said: "White, you speak first."

I tried under my voice to say I had formed no speech, but I cut loose. The president listened attentively and obviously with more than casual interest. Villard followed me, and Monsignor Ryan followed Villard. We spoke briefly three or four minutes each. The president asked questions, and as Ryan closed at the end of a dozen minutes and our time was running out, the president said pleasantly that he was glad to have the matter presented, that he thought he understood the Debs case, and that he would give it his immediate attention. Whereupon a woman, one of those human hellcats who have no sense of the proprieties, stepped forth and cried: "Mr. President, that's no way to answer us. We demand a yes-or-no answer now!"

We were shocked. One of us tried for a second or two to disavow the woman's outburst. But the president straightened himself up. The stoop seemed to come out of his shoulders. A certain gentle dignity enveloped him. He said: "My dear woman: You may demand anything you please out of Warren Harding. He will not resent it. But the president of the United States has a right to keep his own counsel, and the office I occupy forbids me to reply to you and I should like to if I were elsewhere!"

A little flutter of applause came from our group. He smiled and nodded for me to stay after the others were gone. I started to congratulate him. He smiled and laughed quietly: "I hope you thought I got away with it all right. Of course, I want to do something for old Debs. I think I can." After a pause he grinned and said: "But, God, that was no way to get it."

After that we chatted for a second and I left him. I saw him next and finally a few months later in the West—first at Kansas City and then on the train crossing Kansas on his way to Alaska. He was cordial, kindly, extremely courteous, but obviously under some strain. Three times he said: "White, I want to have a long talk with you."

It did not seem to be easy to arrange it that day, but I felt that something was on his mind. . . . He had tried to get me to come to dinner with him. I sent to the hotel at dinner time, explaining that I could not come because I would have to turn down an old friend who had prepared a dinner. Harding, Mrs. Harding, and Senator Capper were dining alone in the hotel suite. As I came in, Harding rose, came from the little dining room of the suite carrying his napkin, and greeted me most cordially. He invited me on the trip that I took the next day. While we were talking, Mrs. Fall, the wife of the secretary of the Interior, came to the door. He excused himself a minute, took her into an adjoining room, and did not return. Finally I made my excuses to Mrs. Harding and to Senator Capper and went on my way. Senator Capper told me afterwards that Mrs. Fall and the president stayed closeted in that room until the very moment he went to make his speech, and that he came out obviously frustrated, worried, and excited. What she told him must have been on his mind when he saw me on the train the next day. . . . I remember sitting in the private car between Emporia and Hutchinson, and he again said this: "I have no trouble with my enemies. I can take care of them. It is my friends." And he repeated it again, "My friends, that are giving me the trouble!"

Is it a wonder that he died that summer?[3] How could the doctors diagnose an illness that was part terror, part shame, and part utter confusion! For the first time in his life he had encountered a moral issue that he could not dodge.

And I left him at Hutchinson with an uneasy feeling. He had no sense of his physical strength. He went into the wheat field on a hot day, not to boast as a farmer but to prove himself a good fellow. That was the strength and the weakness of him—his unquenchable kindness, which too often shadowed his higher loyalty.

Sallie and I came home in mid-spring of 1923 to Emporia, after three months abroad, to find the town in a building boom. . . . The economic revolution was going full tilt. A whole class was moving up in its standard of living, in its self-respect, in its attitude toward life. The serving class in America was passing. The machine was becoming the servant. The servant was joining the master class. New houses all over Emporia were replacing the old houses and the character of

---

[3]When White saw him, Harding was on the first leg of a 1,500-mile, two-month tour of the western states and Alaska. To show his solidarity with the nation's farmers, Harding appeared at the Kansas state fairgrounds at Hutchinson and, under a baking noonday sun, drove a wheat binder around a field. Continuing to push himself at a grueling pace throughout his long trip, Harding collapsed on July 29 and died in San Francisco on August 2, 1923. The cause of his death was stated to be cerebral embolism, but he may have suffered a heart attack.

every street was changing. The odd thing about this building boom that came to the country towns in the early part of the third decade of this century was that the big houses, which might be called the three-girl houses, were practically extinct in country towns. The one-girl house, or the no-girl house, was rising on the outskirts of every town in the smart suburbs. The girls who thirty years before went out to service were working in stores or offices, having graduated from high school either in their rural neighborhoods or in the nearest town. They were marrying clerks and office men and skilled workers, and the wages of women doing housework were rising faster than the wages of men in the stores and offices.

Our first three-story, brick apartment building in the town was ready for occupancy—another sign, a social sign, that the economic revolution was achieving its purpose. The home was changing. Old America, the America of "our Fathers' pride," the America wherein a frugal people had grown great through thrift and industry, was disappearing before the new machine age. Mass production was accumulating and distributing wealth by some inner automatic process quite beyond government and law, as though the mass of machinery on this continent was one vast machine which was spewing out of its hopper a glittering shower of goods, chattels, and material hereditary appurtenances which were being carried by tubes and wires and shafts and funnels and trolleys to all parts of the earth, to all estates and conditions of men, distributing it by some prescience accurately, if not quite justly, to the homes of the multitude.

The *Gazette* was, of course, one of the little cogs of the distributing machine. The advertising patronage of the paper was growing rapidly, crowding extra pages in every day. A new linotype which we had bought in the previous year did not relieve the pressure in the composing room. Merchants were spending their money freely to attract buyers. And from the East came thousands of dollars in advertising, calling attention to national products—automobiles, radios, phonographs, tobacco, oil, transportation—a long list of things which once were luxuries and were becoming the common comforts of the people.

[The *Gazette*] was a different organization from that I had come to a generation before, with a forty-five-dollar weekly payroll, a bookkeeper, and a reporter, each of whom did more or less of the other's work, when advertising—like kissing—came by favor, and subscribers expressed their politics in their preference for a newspaper. Our politics had nothing to do with our subscription list, and our advertisers cared precious little personally for the editor or his views on any question except the price of advertising. Journalism was ceasing to be a profession and was becoming a business and an industry. That also was a fruit of the revolution.

The miracle of the radio was becoming a commonplace in the humblest home. Kansas was presently to have enough automobiles to put every man, woman, and child in the state on wheels at the same time. Everyone was working, and the country, spiraling upward toward the Coolidge bull market, throbbed with a new youth. But alas, where was mine? I was already into my sixth decade, which by any definition you care to take is the downhill pull.

A milestone in my life had been that bright, crisp day in February 1918, when I celebrated my fiftieth birthday. It shocked me. Sallie had arranged a dinner for a dozen of our old friends. Before they came I went upstairs to dress and, coming down before the guests were assembled, I amazed the family by sitting down midway on the stairway landing and bursting into tears. To be fifty was definitely to leave youth and young manhood and to begin to be an old man. Always I had dreaded the responsibility of maturity. I mourned because I was grown up. For I had liked to hide my blunders and my conscious idiocies behind the shield of pretense that I was young, naive, inexperienced. I was given the impish mischief, and under fifty it might be excusable. But I felt, there on the stairs, that I had crossed the deadline; that the whole gay panorama of childhood, boyhood, youth, young manhood, and mature adolescence was gone. Fifty years meant something so new and so sad that I felt upset in bewilderment and something like sorrow. I had crossed the meridian, and I did not like the new country.

And where, in these glittering twenties, were the hopes which I and my kind had held so high in the first two decades of the new century? Looking around me in the gathering roar of prosperity, the only rising political force seemed to be the dark bigotry of the Ku Klux Klan. The Ku Klux Klan had captured the [Emporia] city building at the spring election, and the paper, having been defeated in the mayoralty fight, was enjoying that complacent advantage which every newspaper enjoys when it gets licked. And other sinister forces of oppression to the free human seemed to be gathering across the seas. Where were our hopes and dreams of yesteryear?

Looking back now more than thirty years, I can shut my eyes and see that Bull Moose convention of 1912, see their eager faces—more than a thousand of them—upturned, smiling hopefully, with joy beaming out of them that came from hearts that believed in what they were doing; its importance, its righteousness.

It seemed to matter so much, that convention of zealots, cleansed of self-interest and purged of cynicism. I never have seen before or since exactly that kind of a crowd. I impressed it on my memory because I felt as they felt—those upturned, happy faces.

And now they are dust, and all the visions they saw that day have dissolved. Their hopes, like shifting clouds, have blown away before the winds of circumstance. And I wonder if it did matter much. Or is there somewhere, in the stuff that holds humanity together, some force, some conservation of spiritual energy, that saves the core of every noble hope and gathers all men's visions some day, some way, into the reality of progress?

I do not know. But I have seen the world move far enough under some, maybe mystic, influence to have the right to ask that question.

Biographical Notes

FRANKLIN P. ADAMS (1881–1960) was a journalist and radio personality.

GEORGE MATTHEW ADAMS (1878–1962) headed a syndicate that distributed feature articles to newspapers.

JANE ADDAMS (1860–1935) founded Hull House in Chicago and was an influential figure in the creation of the new profession of social work.

JOSEPH ADDISON (1672–1719) was an English essayist and poet, whose writings in the eighteenth-century magazines *The Tatler* and *The Spectator* helped establish the essay as a major literary form.

GEORGE ADE (1866–1944) was a humorous newspaper columnist and playwright.

JOHN B. ALDEN (1847–1924) published cheap editions of classical and popular literary works.

NELSON W. ALDRICH (1841–1915), a Rhode Island businessman and conservative Republican politician, was a member of the U.S. Senate from 1881 to 1911.

THOMAS BAILEY ALDRICH (1836–1902) was a poet and short-story writer and the editor of *Atlantic Monthly* from 1881 to 1890.

HENRY J. ALLEN (1868–1950) was a Kansas journalist and politician.

WILLIAM B. ALLISON (1829–1908) was a Republican senator from Iowa.

NORMAN ANGELL (1872–1967) was an English writer and lecturer on international affairs. He received the Nobel Peace Prize in 1933.

DANIEL R. ANTHONY, JR. (1870–1931), was a Kansas journalist and Republican congressman.

SUSAN B. ANTHONY (1820–1906) was a prominent leader of the women's rights movement in the nineteenth century.

J. OGDEN ARMOUR (1863–1927), the son of Philip Armour (1832–1901), succeeded him as head of the Armour and Company meat-packing empire.

MARY H. AUSTIN (1868–1934), an American writer, is perhaps best known today for her studies of life in the desert Southwest.

FRANCIS BACON (1561–1626) was an English philosopher.

LUCIEN BAKER (1846–1907) served as Republican senator from Kansas from 1895 to 1901.

ARTHUR JAMES BALFOUR (1848–1930), Conservative British politician, was prime minister from 1902 to 1905 and lord president of the cabinet from 1919 to 1922 and 1925 to 1929.

J. M. BARRIE (1860–1937), a Scottish dramatist and novelist, was popular for the sentimentality and fantasy of works such as *Peter Pan* (1904).

JOHN BARRYMORE (1882–1942) was a popular theater and film actor.

LUDWIG VAN BEETHOVEN (1770–1827), a German, was one of the major composers of the nineteenth century.

AUGUST F. BELMONT (1853–1924) was a New York financier.

ARNOLD BENNETT (1867–1931) was a naturalistic English writer.

HENRI BERGSON (1859–1941), an influential French philosopher, emphasized the role of intuition and the irrational in human experience.

ALBERT J. BEVERIDGE (1862–1927) was a lawyer, Republican politician, and historian.

OTTO VON BISMARCK (1815–1896) had been prime minister of Prussia and founder and first chancellor of the German Empire.

JAMES G. BLAINE (1830–1893) was a powerful Republican politician and unsuccessful candidate for president in 1884.

WILLIAM E. BORAH (1865–1940) was a lawyer and longtime Republican senator from Idaho from 1907 to 1940.

JONATHAN BOURNE, JR. (1855–1940), was Republican senator from Oregon from 1907 to 1913.

GEORGE P. BRETT (1858–1936) was president of the Macmillan Company.

ARISTIDE BRIAND (1862–1932), an advocate of the League of Nations, was premier of France in 1921 and recipient of the Nobel Peace Prize in 1926.

ROBERT BRIDGES (1858–1941) edited *Scribner's* from 1887 until 1930.

JOSEPH L. BRISTOW (1861–1944), a Kansas newspaper publisher, served as U.S. senator from 1909 to 1915.

CYRIL BROWN (1887–1949) was an American journalist.

JOHN BROWN (1800–1859), a fanatic abolitionist, was hanged for leading the raid on the U.S. armory at Harper's Ferry, Virginia, on the eve of the Civil War.

CHARLES W. BRYAN (1867–1945) was political adviser to his older brother William Jennings Bryan and governor of Nebraska (1923–1925 and 1931–1935).

WILLIAM JENNINGS BRYAN (1860–1925) was a Nebraska politician who won the Democratic nomination in 1896 after giving an impassioned speech against the gold standard.

JAMES BUCHANAN (1791–1868) was Democratic president of the United States just before the Civil War (1857–1861).

WILLIAM C. BULLITT (1891–1967) was attaché to the American delegation at Versailles.

JOSEPH R. BURTON (1850–1923) was Republican senator from Kansas from 1901 to 1906.

ASA S. BUSHNELL (1834–1904) was an Ohio businessman and Republican governor of Ohio (1895–1899).

BENJAMIN BUTLER (1818–1893) was presidential nominee of the Greenback party in 1884.

NICHOLAS MURRAY BUTLER (1862–1942), educator and philosopher, became president of Columbia University in 1902.

GEORGE GORDON, LORD BYRON (1788–1824), was an English poet who created in his life and his works the romantic "Byronic" hero, a brooding, defiant young man.

PHILIP P. CAMPBELL (1862–1941) was a Kansas attorney and Republican politician.

FRANK J. CANNON (1859–1933), a journalist, was the first senator from Utah (1896–1899).

JOSEPH G. CANNON (1836–1926), a longtime Republican congressman, was Speaker of the House from 1903 to 1911.

ARTHUR CAPPER (1865–1951), Kansas newspaper and magazine publisher, was Republican governor of Kansas (1915–1919) and U.S. senator (1919–1949).

WILL CARLETON (1845–1912) was an American poet who expressed in his work the simple sentiments of common people.

THOMAS CARLYLE (1795–1881), a Scottish-born British writer and critic of nineteenth-century industrialization, wrote a popular history of the French Revolution.

ANDREW CARNEGIE (1835–1919), Scottish-born founder of Carnegie Steel, was also widely known as a philanthropist.

WILLA CATHER (1876–1947) was a prominent American novelist.

NIKOLAI V. CHAIKOVSKII (1850–1926), a Russian radical and leader of the cooperative movement, had opposed the Bolsheviks and briefly headed the government of the Northern Region of Archangel while that region was occupied by Allied troops.

GEORGII V. CHICHERIN (1872–1936), a Bolshevik leader, headed the Soviet foreign office.

FREDERIC CHOPIN (1810–1849) was a leading Romantic composer.

MOSES E. CLAPP (1851–1929) was Republican senator from Minnesota from 1901 to 1917.

CHAMP CLARK (1850–1921) was Democratic congressman from Missouri and served as Speaker of the House from 1911 to 1919.

WILLIAM A. CLARK (1839–1925), a Montana businessman, was Democratic U.S. senator (1899–1900 and 1901–1907).

GEORGES CLEMENCEAU (1841–1929) was premier of France (1906–1909 and 1917–1920).

GROVER CLEVELAND (1837–1908) was twice Democratic president of the United States (1885–1889 and 1893–1897).

W. BOURKE COCKRAN (1854–1923) was a New York City lawyer and Democratic politician.

BAINBRIDGE COLBY (1868–1950), lawyer and Progressive politician, became secretary of state under Wilson in 1919.

EVERETT COLBY (1874–1943) was a progressive New Jersey Republican politician.

ROBERT J. COLLIER (1876–1918) succeeded his father in 1909 as publisher of *Collier's Weekly*.

WILKIE COLLINS (1824–1889), an English writer, was an early master of the mystery story.

ROSCOE CONKLING (1829–1888) was a New York politician who as U.S. senator from 1872 to 1908 was a staunch opponent of civil service reform.

JOSEPH CONRAD (1857–1924), a Polish-born former ship captain, was a prominent British fiction writer.

CALVIN COOLIDGE (1872–1933), a Massachusetts politician, became president when Harding died in 1923.

JAMES FENIMORE COOPER (1789–1851), an early American novelist, wrote many highly popular adventure tales, including many—such as *The Last of the Mohicans* (1826)— about the frontier.

MELVIN T. COPELAND (1884–1975) taught business administration at Harvard from 1919 to 1953 and directed its Bureau of Business Research.

FRANCOIS COPPEE (1842–1908), a French poet and playwright, wrote sentimental works lamenting the sufferings of the poor.

WILLIAM SHEFFIELD COWLES (1846–1923) was a commander in the U.S. Navy in 1901, becoming a captain in 1902 and rear admiral in 1908.

JAMES M. COX (1870–1957), an Ohio newspaper publisher, was congressman (1909–1913) and governor (1913–1915 and 1917–1921).

CHARLES R. CRANE (1858–1939) was a prominent businessman, philanthropist, and supporter of reform causes.

FRANCIS MARION CRAWFORD (1854–1909) was a novelist and historian.

WILLIAM S. CULBERTSON (1884–1966), lawyer and public administrator, was a member of the U.S. Tariff Commission from 1917 to 1925.

CHARLES CURTIS (1860–1936), a conservative Kansas Republican, served as congressman (1892–1907), senator (1907–1929), and vice-president under Herbert Hoover (1929–1933).

WALTER DAMROSCH (1862–1950) was a composer and conductor.

J. N. ("DING") DARLING (1876–1962) was a political cartoonist and conservationist.

CLARENCE S. DARROW (1857–1938) was an attorney noted for his defense of controversial figures.

ALPHONSE DAUDET (1840–1897) was a member of the French naturalist school of fiction that drew upon simple stories of everyday life, often set in provincial France, and made frequent use of ironic endings.

HARRY M. DAUGHERTY (1860–1941), a Republican politician, was appointed attorney general in return for his support of Harding. His administration was notorious for inefficiency and corruption, and he was dismissed by President Coolidge in 1924.

OSCAR KING DAVIS (1866–1932) was a journalist and served as secretary and publicity chief of the Progressive national committee in 1912.

RICHARD HARDING DAVIS (1864–1916) was an American journalist and novelist, best known for his dashing war correspondence.

CLAUDE DEBUSSY (1862–1918) was a French composer.

THOMAS DE QUINCEY (1785–1859) was an English Romantic poet, essayist, and critic.

CHARLES DICKENS (1812–1870) was an English novelist whose works, including *Oliver Twist*, *Great Expectations*, and *A Christmas Carol*, were among the most popular of the Victorian period.

JOSEPH T. DICKMAN (1857–1927) was a major general in the U.S. Army.

JOSEPH M. DIXON (1867–1934) was Montana's congressman (1903–1907) and senator (1907–1913).

JONATHAN P. DOLLIVER (1858–1910) was a Republican senator from Iowa.

IGNATIUS DONNELLY (1831–1901), Populist reformer and politician, wrote the popular anti-utopian novel *Caesar's Column* (1891).

STEPHEN A. DOUGLAS (1813–1861) was the Democratic candidate for president in 1860.

JOHN DREW (1853–1927) was a popular theater actor.

FINLEY PETER DUNNE (1867–1936) was a humorist whose popular essays on the passing scene recorded the wise and witty comments of fictional saloon keeper "Mr. Dooley."

GEORGE ELIOT (1819–1880) was the pseudonym of English Victorian novelist Mary Ann Evans, whose *The Mill on the Floss* appeared in 1860.

RICHARD T. ELY (1854–1943), economist and social reformer, was a founder of the "new economics" school that challenged the laissez-faire principles of classical economics.

RALPH WALDO EMERSON (1803–1882) was an influential American essayist, poet, and lecturer.

ALBERT B. FALL (1861–1944), New Mexico lawyer and Republican politician, was Harding's secretary of the Interior. His illicit deals allowing oil drilling on government lands spawned the Teapot Dome scandal; convicted of accepting a bribe, he served a one-year sentence in federal prison.

EDNA FERBER (1887–1968) was a short-story writer, Pulitzer Prize-winning novelist, and playwright.

EUGENE FIELD (1850–1895) was a journalist and author of the popular poems "Little Boy Blue" and "Wynken, Blynken, and Nod."

GEORGE HELGESON FITCH (1877–1915) was a journalist and humorist.

STEPHEN C. FOSTER (1826–1864) was a popular antebellum American songwriter.

ALICE FRENCH (1850–1934), whose pseudonym was Octave Thanet, wrote stories depicting life in the Midwest and South.

HENRY B. FULLER (1857–1929), a novelist, was best known for his realistic studies of life in Chicago.

FREDERICK FUNSTON (1865–1917), later a U.S. Army general, became a hero of the American war in the Philippines.

JOHN GALSWORTHY (1867–1933) was a popular English novelist.

JAMES R. GARFIELD (1866–1950) was commissioner of Roosevelt's new Bureau of Corporations (1903–1907) and secretary of the Interior (1907–1909).

HAMLIN GARLAND (1860–1940), author of short stories and novels, was known for his realistic studies of the struggles of midwestern farmers.

WILLIAM LLOYD GARRISON (1805–1879) published the abolitionist newspaper *The Liberator*.

ELBERT H. GARY (1846–1927) was a corporation lawyer, financier, and chairman of the board of United States Steel.

RICHARD WATSON GILDER (1844–1909) was a poet and editor of *Century Magazine*.

PATRICK GILMORE (1829–1892) was a highly popular Irish-born American bandleader.

CHARLES SUMNER GLEED (1856–1920) was a Kansas lawyer, businessman, and Republican politician.

OLIVER GOLDSMITH (1731–1774) was an eighteenth-century English poet.

SAMUEL GOMPERS (1850–1924) was president of the American Federation of Labor from 1886 until his death.

JAY GOULD (1836–1892) was notorious for his unscrupulous practices in the stock market and in railroad management.

ULYSSES S. GRANT (1822–1885) was a Union general during the Civil War and president of the United States (1869–1877).

THOMAS GRAY (1716–1771) was an English poet.

HORACE GREELEY (1811–1872) was editor of the New York *Tribune* and unsuccessful presidential nominee of the liberal Republican and Democratic parties in 1872.

CHARLES H. GROSVENOR (1833–1917) was a Republican congressman from Ohio.

HERBERT S. HADLEY (1872–1927) was Missouri attorney general (1905–1909) and governor (1909–1913).

MARCUS ALONZO HANNA (1837–1904) was a businessman and politician and was widely known as William McKinley's mentor.

NORMAN HAPGOOD (1868–1937) was editor of *Collier's Weekly* from 1902 to 1912.

WARREN G. HARDING (1865–1923), a newspaper publisher and senator from Ohio, became president of the United States in 1921.

THOMAS HARDY (1840–1928) was a major English novelist and poet.

BENJAMIN HARRISON (1833–1901) was Republican president from 1889 to 1893.

RUTHERFORD B. HAYES (1822–1893) was the Republican presidential nominee in 1876, winning in a close election decided by the House of Representatives. He served from 1877 to 1881.

WILL H. HAYS (1879–1954), Republican politician, became the first chairman of the Motion Picture Producers and Distributors of America, Hollywood's official spokesman.

FELICIA HEMANS (1793–1835) was a popular British poet.

THOMAS A. HENDRICKS (1819–1885) was Tilden's vice-presidential running mate in 1876.

WILLIAM ERNEST HENLEY (1849–1903) was a British poet, critic, and editor.

GEORGE D. HERRON (1862–1925), a one-time Congregational minister, was a lecturer and writer on socialism and international affairs and had lived in Europe since 1901.

LAURENCE HILLS (1879–1941) was chief correspondent at Versailles for the New York *Sun*.

FRANK H. HITCHCOCK (1867–1935), an attorney, served as postmaster general under Taft and managed Hughes's presidential campaign in 1916.

EDWARD W. HOCH (1849–1925), a Kansas publisher and politician, was governor from 1905 to 1909.

FRANK HEYWOOD HODDER (1860–1935) was professor of history at the University of Kansas.

OLIVER WENDELL HOLMES, JR. (1841–1935), was justice of the Supreme Court.

HERBERT C. HOOVER (1874–1964), a millionaire mining engineer and public administrator, was president of the United States from 1929 to 1933.

EDWARD M. HOUSE (1858–1938) was an influential though always unofficial adviser to several Texas politicians and, after 1911, to Woodrow Wilson.

EDGAR WATSON HOWE (1853–1937) was a Kansas journalist and novelist.

WILLIAM DEAN HOWELLS (1837–1920), an American novelist and critic, was an influential early advocate of realism in literature.

CHARLES EVANS HUGHES (1862–1948), was a Republican politician, Supreme Court justice, secretary of state (1921–1925), and chief justice of the Supreme Court (1930–1941).

HAROLD L. ICKES (1874–1952), a reform-minded journalist and politician, later served as secretary of the Interior under Franklin Delano Roosevelt.

JOHN J. INGALLS (1833–1900) was Republican senator from Kansas from 1873 to 1891.

AUGUSTE F. JACCACI (1857–1930) was an Italian-born artist and graphic designer.

ANDREW JACKSON (1767–1845) was an American general and president of the United States from 1829 to 1837.

EDWIN L. JAMES (1890–1951), Paris correspondent for the *New York Times* (1919–1925), was later its managing editor.

HIRAM W. JOHNSON (1866–1945) was the reform-minded governor of California (1911–1917) and later U.S. senator (1917–1945).

SAMUEL JOHNSON (1709–1784), poet, essayist, and lexicographer, is considered the major English literary figure of the latter eighteenth century.

WILLIAM AGNEW JOHNSTON (1848–1937) had been elected to the Kansas Supreme Court in 1884; he served as its chief justice from 1903 to 1935.

DAVID STARR JORDAN (1851–1931) was the first president of Stanford University and a long-standing advocate of international peace.

RUDYARD KIPLING (1865–1936), an Indian-born Briton, wrote highly popular poetry and stories, often about his experiences in Asia, that celebrated the British Empire and preached the "white man's burden" to civilize the world.

GEORGE W. KIRCHWEY (1855–1942) was a law educator and prison reformer.

PHILANDER CHASE KNOX (1853–1921) served as attorney general under Theodore Roosevelt.

ARTHUR KROCK (1887–1974), a reporter and editor, won three Pulitzer prizes for his coverage of Washington.

ROBERT M. LA FOLLETTE (1855–1925), Republican congressman (1885–1891), governor of Wisconsin (1901–1906), and U.S. senator (1906–1925), was an unsuccessful Progressive candidate for president in 1924.

FRANKLIN K. LANE (1864–1921), a lawyer and Democratic politician, was Wilson's secretary of the Interior.

ANDREW LANG (1844–1912) was a Scottish scholar and poet.

THOMAS W. LAWSON (1857–1925) was a financier and journalist.

MARY ELIZABETH LEASE (1853–1933) was a prominent Populist lecturer who urged farmers to "raise less corn and more hell."

GUSTAVE LE BON (1841–1931) was a pioneering French social psychologist.

NIKOLAI LENIN (1870–1924) was a leader of the Bolshevik government after the Russian Revolution in 1917.

IRVINE L. LENROOT (1869–1949), a progressive ally of La Follette in Wisconsin, was U.S. senator from 1918 to 1927.

WILLIAM DRAPER LEWIS (1867–1949) was a lawyer and scholar.

ABRAHAM LINCOLN (1809–1865) was the first Republican president of the United States, serving from 1861 until his assassination in 1865.

BENJAMIN B. LINDSEY (1869–1943) was a Denver judge and social reformer.

MEYER LISSNER (1871–1930) was a Los Angeles lawyer and civic leader.

FRANZ LISZT (1811–1886) was a nineteenth-century Hungarian composer and pianist.

MARTIN W. LITTLETON (1872–1934) was a lawyer and Democratic politician.

DAVID LLOYD GEORGE (1863–1945), a Welsh-born British politician, was prime minister of Great Britain from 1916 to 1922.

HENRY CABOT LODGE (1850–1924) was a conservative Republican senator from Massachusetts (1893–1924).

CHESTER I. LONG (1860–1934) was Republican congressman (1895–1897 and 1899–1903) and senator (1903–1909) from Kansas.

HENRY WADSWORTH LONGFELLOW (1807–1882) was a popular American poet.

ALICE ROOSEVELT LONGWORTH (1884–1980), the only child of Theodore Roosevelt and his first wife, Alice Hathaway Roosevelt, was well known as a flamboyant personality.

NICHOLAS LONGWORTH (1869–1931) was Republican congressman from Ohio and Speaker of the House from 1925 to 1931.

GEORGE H. LORIMER (1867–1937) was editor-in-chief of the *Saturday Evening Post* from 1899 to 1936.

FRANK O. LOWDEN (1861–1943) was governor of Illinois from 1917 to 1921.

JAMES RUSSELL LOWELL (1819–1891), a poet and critic, was editor of the *Atlantic Monthly*, professor of literature at Harvard, and U.S. ambassador to Spain and Britain.

SAMUEL WARD MCALLISTER (1827–1895) was a leader in New York society.

DOUGLAS MACARTHUR (1886–1964) was promoted to brigadier general during World War I. He commanded U.S. Army forces in the southwest Pacific during World War II.

SAMUEL SIDNEY MCCLURE (1857–1949), an Irish-born American editor, founded the highly influential *McClure's Magazine* in 1893.

JOSEPH MEDILL MCCORMICK (1877–1925) was a Chicago newspaper publisher and Republican U.S. senator from 1919 to 1925.

FRANCIS E. MCGOVERN (1866–1929) was progressive governor of Wisconsin from 1911 to 1915.

WILLIAM MCKINLEY (1843–1901), an Ohio lawyer and politician, was president of the United States from 1897 to 1901.

JEAN PAUL MARAT (1743–1793), a Swiss-born French politician and physician, was a leading figure in the early French Revolution.

MARIA THERESA (1717–1780) was archduchess of Austria and queen of Hungary and Bohemia.

GUY DE MAUPASSANT (1850–1893) was a French naturalist writer.

OGDEN L. MILLS (1884–1937) was a New York lawyer and Republican politician.

DWIGHT LYMAN MOODY (1837–1899) was an American evangelist who during the post–Civil War decades conducted a series of successful revivals in the United States and Britain.

CHRISTOPHER MORLEY (1890–1957) was a prolific writer of essays, articles, plays, novels, and poetry.

JOHANN JOSEPH MOST (1846–1906) was a German-born anarchist who became a leader of American revolutionaries upon his emigration in 1882.

DAVID W. MULVANE (1863–1932) was a Topeka lawyer and politician.

FRANK A. MUNSEY (1854–1925) was a magazine and newspaper publisher and financier.

VICTOR MURDOCK (1871–1945) was a Wichita journalist and Republican politician.

CHARLES F. MURPHY (1858–1924) was a New York saloon keeper and head of the Tammany organization from 1902 to 1924.

SCOTT NEARING (1883–1983), social scientist and author, was fired by the University of Pennsylvania in 1915 and the University of Toledo in 1917 because of his controversial public statements on behalf of socialism and pacifism.

WILLIAM ROCKHILL NELSON (1841–1915) founded the Kansas City *Star* in 1880.

GEORGE W. NORRIS (1861–1944) was Republican congressman (1903–1913) and senator (1913–1943) from Nebraska.

EDGAR W. "BILL" NYE (1850–1896) was a journalist and humorous writer and lecturer.

CHASE S. OSBORN (1860–1949) was a journalist, prospector, and Republican governor of Michigan from 1911 to 1913.

ALBERT BIGELOW PAINE (1861–1937) was a journalist and biographer.

A. MITCHELL PALMER (1872–1936) had as attorney general from 1919 to 1921 conducted widespread raids on aliens and suspected radicals that aroused concerns for civil liberties.
ALTON B. PARKER (1852–1926) was the Democratic presidential nominee in 1904.
JOHN M. PARKER (1863–1939), a Louisiana businessman, was governor of Louisiana from 1920 to 1924.
VERNON L. PARRINGTON (1871–1929), a teacher and historian, wrote the influential reform-minded survey of American literature *Main Currents in American Thought* (1927–1930).
DONALD CULROSS PEATTIE (1898–1964) was a free-lance writer best known for his works on natural and historical subjects.
ELIA W. PEATTIE (1862–1935) was a writer, critic, and playwright.
GEORGE R. PECK (1843–1937), an attorney, was general solicitor of the Santa Fe Railroad (1882–1884 and 1886–1895).
WILLIAM A. PEFFER (1831–1912) was a Kansas lawyer and Populist U.S. senator (1891–1897).
GEORGE W. PERKINS (1862–1920) was a partner in the banking house of J. P. Morgan and Company.
JOHN J. PERSHING (1860–1948), a U.S. Army general, commanded the American Expeditionary Force in World War I.
JOHN S. PHILLIPS (1861–1949), editor and publisher, was S. S. McClure's partner in his publishing enterprises.
WENDELL PHILLIPS (1811–1884), leader of the antebellum abolitionist movement, became a critic of Gilded Age capitalism.
FRANKLIN PIERCE (1804–1869), a Democrat, was elected president of the United States in 1852 and served from 1853 to 1857.
PONTIUS PILATE was Roman governor of Judea under Emperor Tiberius in the first half of the first century A.D. and presided over the trial of Jesus.
AMOS PINCHOT (1873–1944), a lawyer and Republican politician, was his older brother Gifford's chief adviser.
GIFFORD PINCHOT (1865–1946), professional forester and conservationist, was governor of Pennsylvania (1923–1927 and 1931–1935).
ORVILLE H. PLATT (1827–1905) was a Republican senator from Connecticut.
THOMAS COLLIER PLATT (1833–1910) was a powerful New York politician and served as U.S. senator briefly in 1881 and from 1897 to 1909.
PRESTON B. PLUMB (1837–1891) was Republican senator from Kansas from 1878 to 1891.
PLUTARCH (c. 46–c. 120) was a Greek historian.
EDGAR ALLAN POE (1809–1849) was an American critic, poet, and short-story writer.
ALEXANDER POPE (1688–1744) was a prominent eighteenth-century English poet and critic.
CHARLES READE (1814–1884) was an English novelist who exposed in his works the injustices of British society.
GEORGE L. RECORD (1859–1933) was a leader among progressive politicians in New Jersey.
THOMAS B. REED (1839–1902), a Republican politician from Maine, was Speaker of the House (1889–1891 and 1895–1899).
RICHARD I (1157–1199), king of England after 1189, was glorified for his courage by troubadours and later writers such as Sir Walter Scott and became popularly known as Richard the Lion-Hearted.
DONALD R. RICHBERG (1881–1960) was a Chicago labor lawyer and an activist in the progressive movement.
JOHANN PAUL FRIEDRICH RICHTER (1763–1825), known as Jean Paul, was a German Romantic novelist.

JAMES WHITCOMB RILEY (1849–1916) was a popular American poet known for his dialect verse.

RAYMOND ROBINS (1873–1954) was a religious leader, social reformer, and progressive politician from Illinois.

JOHN D. ROCKEFELLER (1839–1937) was a founder of the Standard Oil Corporation, which formed the model for the giant industrial corporations that emerged in the late nineteenth century.

JOHN D. ROCKEFELLER, JR. (1874–1960), an industrialist and philanthropist, was son of a founder of the Standard Oil Corporation.

ALICE ROOSEVELT. *See* Alice Roosevelt Longworth.

ARCHIBALD ROOSEVELT (1894–1979) was the third son of Theodore Roosevelt and his second wife, Edith Kermit Roosevelt.

FRANKLIN DELANO ROOSEVELT (1882–1945), a Democrat, would be president of the United States from 1933 until his death.

KERMIT ROOSEVELT (1889–1943) was the second son of Theodore Roosevelt and Edith Kermit Roosevelt.

THEODORE ROOSEVELT (1858–1919), historian, Republican politician, and reformer, was president of the United States from 1901 to 1909.

THEODORE ROOSEVELT, JR. (1887–1944), was the oldest son of Theodore Roosevelt and Edith Kermit Roosevelt.

ELIHU ROOT (1845–1937), an attorney and Republican politician, was secretary of war (1899–1903), secretary of state (1905–1909), and senator from New York (1909–1915).

VICTOR ROSEWATER (1874–1952) was a journalist and Republican politician.

DANTE GABRIEL ROSSETTI (1828–1882) was the leader of the English Pre-Raphaelite movement.

ANTON RUBINSTEIN (1829–1894) was a Russian pianist and composer.

JOHN AUGUSTINE RYAN (1869–1945), a prominent Catholic social reform advocate, was named a domestic prelate by Pope Pius in 1933.

THOMAS FORTUNE RYAN (1851–1928) was a New York financier.

LADY MILLICENT FANNY ST. CLAIR-ERSKINE (1867–1955), wife of the fourth Duke of Sutherland, was a noted writer.

JOHN P. ST. JOHN (1833–1916) was Republican governor of Kansas from 1879 to 1883 and Prohibition party candidate for president in 1884.

GEORGE SAND was the pseudonym of Amandine Aurore Lucie Dudevant (1804–1876), a French Romantic writer.

JOHN SINGER SARGENT (1856–1925) was a prominent society portrait painter.

WILLIAM SHAKESPEARE (1565–1616) is considered one of the greatest playwrights and poets of the English language.

JAMES S. SHERMAN (1855–1912) was Republican congressman from New York and Taft's vice president (1909–1912).

JOHN SHERMAN (1823–1900) was a Republican U.S. senator (1861–1877 and 1881–1897).

JOHN M. SIDDALL (1874–1923), associate editor of the *American Magazine* in 1906, became editor-in-chief in 1915.

FRANK H. SIMONDS (1878–1936) was a journalist and military historian.

JERRY SIMPSON (1842–1905) was a Populist member of the House from Kansas (1891–1895 and 1897–1899). Republicans gave him the nickname "Sockless Jerry" because he denounced them for wearing expensive silk stockings, which he could not afford.

E. E. SLOSSON (1865–1929), a chemist, author, lecturer, and editor of *The Independent*, was noted as a public interpreter of the sciences.

REED SMOOT (1862–1941) was a Utah businessman and Republican U.S. senator from 1903 to 1933.

HERBERT SPENCER (1820–1903), an English philosopher and social scientist, applied Darwin's new theories of evolution to human society.

WILLIAM E. STANLEY (1844–1910) was governor of Kansas from 1899 to 1903.

ELIZABETH CADY STANTON (1815–1902) was a national leader of the women's rights movement in the nineteenth century.

RICHARD STEELE (1672–1729) was an English essayist and dramatist.

ROBERT LOUIS STEVENSON (1850–1894) was a popular Scottish writer and the author of adventure stories such as *Kidnapped* (1886).

FRANK R. STOCKTON (1834–1902) was a popular short-story writer, best remembered for his story "The Lady or the Tiger?"

HENRY L. STODDARD (1861–1947) was publisher of the New York *Evening Mail*.

WALTER ROSCOE STUBBS (1858–1929) was in turn railroad contractor, stockman, politician, and reform-minded governor of Kansas (1909–1913).

EUGENE SUE was the pseudonym of French novelist Marie-Joseph Sue (1804–1857), who focused upon the seamier side of city life.

MARK SULLIVAN (1874–1952) was a journalist who wrote for *Collier's* from 1906 to 1919.

EMANUEL SWEDENBORG (1688–1772) was a Swedish religious philosopher and mystic.

HERBERT B. SWOPE (1882–1955) won the first Pulitzer Prize for reporting in 1917 for his coverage of wartime Germany.

CHARLES P. TAFT (1843–1929) was editor of the Cincinnati *Times-Star* and William Howard Taft's half-brother.

WILLIAM HOWARD TAFT (1857–1930), an Ohio-born lawyer and politician, served as both president of the United States (1909–1913) and chief justice of the Supreme Court (1921–1930).

THOMAS TAGGART (1856–1929) was an Indiana banker, hotel proprietor, and Democratic politician.

IDA M. TARBELL (1857–1944) had written a series of popular biographies of Napoleon and Lincoln for *McClure's Magazine* and in 1903 would publish an influential exposé of the Standard Oil Corporation.

FRANK W. TAUSSIG (1859–1940) was professor of economics at Harvard (1882–1935) and would be the first chairman of the U.S. Tariff Commission (1917–1919).

HENRY M. TELLER (1830–1914) was Republican senator from Colorado (1877–1882 and 1885–1909).

ALFRED TENNYSON (Baron), (1809–1892) was a major nineteenth-century English poet. He published *Poems by Two Brothers* with his brother Charles Tennyson (1808–1879) in 1827.

WILLIAM MAKEPEACE THACKERAY (1811–1863) was an English novelist known for his satirical treatment of upper-class life.

OCTAVE THANET. *See* Alice French.

JAMES MAURICE THOMPSON (1844–1901) was a lawyer, engineer, and author of popular novels.

JOHN M. THURSTON (1847–1916) was Republican senator from Nebraska from 1895 to 1901.

SAMUEL J. TILDEN (1814–1886) was Democratic presidential nominee in 1876, losing to Rutherford B. Hayes.

ANTHONY TROLLOPE (1815–1882) was an English novelist who vividly depicted details of Victorian society in his works.

LEON TROTSKY (1879–1940) was a leader of the Bolshevik government after the Russian Revolution in 1917.

MARK TWAIN was the pseudonym of American humorist and novelist Samuel Langhorne Clemens (1835–1910).

ROBERT T. VAN HORN (1824–1916) was a newspaper publisher and an early promoter of Kansas City.

THORSTEIN B. VEBLEN (1857–1929), an American economist, was a trenchant critic of nineteenth-century capitalism and author of *The Theory of the Leisure Class* (1899), which attacked the "conspicuous consumption" of the wealthy.

VERGIL—in Latin, Publius Vergilius Moro (70–19 B.C.)—was a Roman poet and author of the epic poem the *Aeneid*.

OSWALD GARRISON VILLARD (1872–1949) published and edited the New York *Evening Post* (1897–1918) and the *Nation* (1918–1932).

RICHARD WAGNER (1813–1883), a German, was one of the leading composers of the late nineteenth century.

LEW WALLACE (1827–1903) was a lawyer, Civil War soldier, and governor of both Indiana and New Mexico in addition to being the author of the best-selling novel *Ben-Hur: A Tale of the Christ* (1880).

EUGENE F. WARE (1841–1911) was a Kansas poet in addition to being a journalist, lawyer, and politician.

BOOKER T. WASHINGTON (1856–1915) was a black leader and educator.

JAMES E. WATSON (1863–1948) was an Indiana senator from 1916 to 1933.

HAROLD T. WEBSTER (1885–1952), a newspaper cartoonist, later created the comic-strip character Caspar Milquetoast.

JOHN W. WEEKS (1860–1926), a businessman and Republican politician, was senator from Massachusetts (1913–1919) and secretary of war under Presidents Harding and Coolidge.

JUDSON C. WELLIVER (1870–1943) was a journalist who directed public relations for Harding.

H. G. WELLS (1866–1946), an English writer, was an early master of the new genre of science fiction.

WALT WHITMAN (1819–1892) published the first of many editions of *Leaves of Grass* in 1855. His unorthodox, at times sensuous poetry was considered by some to be vulgar and immoral, but his celebration of the common man earned him the title of "the bard of democracy."

JOHN GREENLEAF WHITTIER (1807–1892) was an American poet and leader of the abolitionist movement.

WILHELM I (1797–1888) was king of Prussia and the first German emperor (*kaiser*).

WILHELM II (1859–1941) was the German emperor (kaiser) until he abdicated and fled to the Netherlands in the last days of World War I.

WOODROW WILSON (1846–1924) was a university professor and president, governor of New Jersey (1911–1913), and president of the United States (1913–1921).

LEONARD WOOD (1860–1927), military surgeon and soldier, was army chief of staff and had led the prewar preparedness movement.

ALEXANDER H. WOOLLCOTT (1887–1943) was a newspaper columnist, drama critic, and radio commentator.

FRANK LLOYD WRIGHT (1869–1959), probably the most influential American architect of the twentieth century, originated a low, spreading style for domestic architecture known as Prairie Style.

Editorial
Notes

In the following notes the first page and line listing refers to this edition; the second page listing refers to the 1946 edition of the *Autobiography*, published by Macmillan. If no other annotation is made, the second page listing refers to a deletion (indicated in this edition by ellipsis points).

CHAPTER 1. "AS IT WAS IN THE BEGINNING!"

P. 1, l. 12: pp. 3–20; l. 23: p. 20.
P. 2, l. 7: p. 21; l. 40: pp. 22–25.
P. 3, l. 25: p. 26; l. 27: p. 26.
P. 4, l. 20: Seventeen sentences moved from pp. 23–24; ll. 23, 28, and 34: p. 23.
P. 5, l. 12: pp. 27–28; l. 14: Two sentences moved from p. 25.
P. 6, l. 18: pp. 29–32; l. 19: p. 32; l. 21: Two sentences moved from p. 9; l. 31: pp. 32–33; l. 32: p. 34.
P. 7, l. 4: p. 34; l. 15: p. 35; l. 19: pp. 35–36; l. 25: p. 36.
P. 9, l. 9: pp. 38–39; l. 35: p. 39.
P. 10, ll. 16 and 25: p. 41; l. 37: Two sentences moved from p. 42.
P. 11, l. 16: Five sentences moved from p. 43; l. 23: p. 42; l. 34: p. 42; l. 39: p. 43.
P. 12, l. 3: Ten sentences moved from pp. 57–58.
P. 13, l. 36: p. 44.
P. 14, ll. 7 and 12: p. 45.
P. 15, l. 13: p. 46; l. 33: pp. 48–53.

CHAPTER 2. THE STORY OF WILL (SOMETIMES BILLIE)

P. 17, l. 6: pp. 57–58; ll. 12, 14, and 20: p. 58.
P. 18, ll. 1 and 4: p. 59; l. 24: pp. 59–60; ll. 29 and 37: p. 60.
P. 19, ll. 4 and 7: p. 61; l. 34: p. 63.
P. 20, l. 5: pp. 63–64; ll. 18, 28, and 31: p. 64.
P. 21, l. 14: pp. 65–66; l. 41: p. 66.
P. 22, ll. 9 and 13: p. 67; l. 29: p. 68.
P. 23, l. 2: p. 68; ll. 10, 11, and 17: p. 69.
P. 24, ll. 7 and 8: p. 70.
P. 26, ll. 36 and 38: p. 73.
P. 27, l. 39: pp. 74–75.
P. 28, ll. 5 and 12: p. 75; l. 14: p. 76; l. 33: pp. 76–78; l. 36: Seven sentences moved from pp. 79–80.
P. 29, l. 16: pp. 79–80.

P. 30, ll. 19, 22, and 26: p. 81.
P. 31, ll. 22 and 26: p. 82.
P. 32, l. 41: pp. 83–84.
P. 33, ll. 7, 8, and 12: p. 84; ll. 20 and 24: p. 85; l. 33: pp. 86–88.

CHAPTER 3. I CHOOSE A FOSTER FATHER

P. 34, l. 18: p. 88; l. 23: p. 89.
P. 35, l. 7: p. 89; l. 13: pp. 89–90; l. 20: Six sentences moved from pp. 90–91; l. 26: p. 90; l. 28: pp. 90–91; l. 34: Two sentences moved from p. 89; l. 39: pp. 90–91.
P. 36, ll. 5, 11, 15, 17, and 19: p. 91; ll. 25 and 29: p. 92.
P. 37, l. 2: p. 92; l. 3: Four sentences moved from p. 98; l. 7: p. 92; ll. 21 and 26: p. 93; l. 38: p. 94.
P. 38, ll. 8, 10, and 12: p. 94; ll. 20, 22, and 31: p. 95.
P. 39, ll. 8, 12, and 25: p. 96.
P. 40, ll. 8 and 16: p. 97; l. 26: p. 98; l. 39: p. 100.
P. 41, l. 10: One sentence moved from p. 100; ll. 16, 23, 27, and 28: p. 101; l. 36: Seven sentences moved from pp. 103–104.
P. 42, l. 1: pp. 103–104; l. 9: p. 104; l. 13: p. 102; ll. 20 and 24: p. 104; l. 35: Six sentences moved from pp. 103–104.
P. 43, ll. 7, 11, and 14: p. 105; l. 39: p. 106; l. 41: Twenty-three sentences moved from pp. 102–103.
P. 44, l. 1: p. 102; ll. 33, 34, and 36: p. 106.
P. 45, l. 6: pp. 106 107.

CHAPTER 4. DESTINY ROLLS MY DICE—"COME SEVEN"

P. 47, ll. 5 and 19: p. 109; l. 25: pp. 110–111.
P. 48, l. 1: p. 111; l. 10: pp. 111–112; l. 21: One sentence moved from p. 112; l. 29: p. 113; l. 34: Five sentences moved from pp. 111–112.
P. 49, l. 1: Nine sentences moved from p. 112; l. 7: p. 112; l. 19: p. 113; l. 32: p. 114.
P. 50, l. 23: p. 115.
P. 51, l. 2: p. 115.
P. 52, l. 9: p. 117.
P. 53, ll. 11 and 18: p. 118; l. 20: One sentence moved from p. 118.
P. 54, l. 2: pp. 120–121; l. 17: p. 121; l. 20: pp. 121–122; l. 23: p. 122; l. 38: pp. 122–123.
P. 55, ll. 2, 6, and 8: p. 123; l. 27: pp. 124–125.
P. 56, l. 4: pp. 125–126; l. 7: p. 127.
P. 57, l. 22: p. 128; l. 29: p. 129.
P. 58, l. 2: p. 130; l. 11: p. 131; l. 19: p. 132.
P. 59, l. 26: pp. 133–134; l. 38: p. 134.
P. 60, l. 11: pp. 134–135; ll. 18 and 33: p. 135; l. 36: pp. 135–136; l. 37: p. 136.
P. 61, ll. 12 and 14: p. 136; ll. 23 and 30: p. 137.
P. 62, l. 11: pp. 137–138.

CHAPTER 5. A REPORTER IN COLLEGE

P. 63, l. 14: pp. 139–140; ll. 14, 16, and 18: p. 140.
P. 64, l. 4: p. 140; l. 6: Three sentences moved from pp. 140–141; l. 16: pp. 140–141; ll. 22 and 27: p. 141.

P. 65, ll. 2, 4, and 12: p. 142; l. 13: pp. 142–143; l. 16: p. 143; ll. 27, 32, and 35: p. 144.

P. 66, ll. 1, 6, and 22: p. 145; l. 26: pp. 146–147; ll. 30 and 32: p. 147.

P. 67, l. 3: p. 147; ll. 15 and 29: p. 148; l. 31: pp. 148–149.

P. 68, l. 23: Eleven sentences moved from pp. 177–178; l. 24: pp. 177–178; l. 28: p. 178; l. 41: p. 150.

P. 69, l. 7: pp. 150–151.

P. 70, l. 32: p. 152; l. 34: p. 153.

P. 71, ll. 5 and 7: p. 153; ll. 12 and 19: p. 154; l. 37: p. 155.

P. 72, l. 14: One sentence moved from p. 160; l. 15: p. 155; l. 16: Twelve paragraphs moved from pp. 164–167; ll. 19 and 28: p. 164; l. 32: pp. 164–165.

P. 73, l. 3: p. 165; l. 4: Two sentences moved from pp. 164–165.

P. 74, l. 3: p. 166.

P. 75, l. 4: p. 156.

P. 76, ll. 9 and 20: p. 157; l. 22: pp. 157–158; l. 25: p. 158; l. 32: p. 159; l. 35: pp. 159–161.

P. 77, ll. 5 and 15: p. 162; l. 19: pp. 162–163; ll. 21, 27, and 35: p. 163; l. 39: p. 164.

P. 78, l. 2: pp. 164–167; ll. 9 and 11: p. 168; l. 15: pp. 168–169; ll. 20 and 24: p. 169; l. 35: pp. 169–170; ll. 40 and 41: p. 170.

P. 79, l. 4: p. 170; l. 10: p. 171; ll. 21, 22, and 24: p. 172; l. 27: p. 173; l. 37: pp. 174–175.

CHAPTER 6. I BECOME A BLIND LEADER OF THE BLIND

P. 81, ll. 4 and 13: p. 176; l. 15: pp. 176–177.

P. 82, l. 2: p. 177; l. 5: Two sentences moved from p. 180; l. 10: pp. 177–179; ll. 12 and 22: p. 179; l. 26: pp. 179–180.

P. 83, l. 2: p. 180; l. 13: p. 181; l. 28: p. 182.

P. 84, l. 3: p. 182; ll. 4 and 11: p. 183; l. 12: pp. 183–184.

P. 85, l. 3: pp. 184–186; l. 6: p. 186; l. 22: pp. 186–187; l. 30: p. 187.

P. 86, l. 11: p. 187; ll. 14, 20, and 30: p. 188; l. 32: pp. 188–189; l. 37: p. 189.

P. 87, l. 9: pp. 189–190; ll. 15, 21, and 25: p. 190; l. 34: pp. 190–191; l. 35: p. 191.

P. 88, l. 29: p. 192.

P. 89, l. 2: pp. 192–193; ll. 7, 20, and 23: p. 194; ten sentences moved from pp. 215–216.

P. 90, l. 9: p. 195; l. 17: pp. 195–196; l. 30: p. 196.

P. 91, l. 4: p. 197; l. 19: pp. 197–198; l. 33: p. 198.

P. 92, ll. 4 and 8: p. 198; ll. 10, 11, and 27: p. 199; l. 33: pp. 199–200; l. 37: p. 200.

P. 93, l. 30: p. 201.

P. 94, l. 2: p. 201.

CHAPTER 7. A GILDED METROPOLIS

P. 95, l. 6: p. 205.

P. 96, l. 3: pp. 205–206.

P. 97, l. 13: p. 207.

P. 98, ll. 11 and 22: p. 208; l. 26: One sentence moved from p. 207; ll. 26 and 31: p. 209; l. 26: p. 208.

P. 99, l. 3: p. 209; l. 23: p. 210; l. 24: Eight sentences moved from p. 213.

P. 100, ll. 1 and 2: p. 210; ll. 11 and 23: p. 211; l. 32: pp. 212–213; l. 34: Three sentences moved from p. 217.

P. 101, l. 28: p. 214; l. 35: Eight sentences moved from p. 220.

P. 102, l. 11: pp. 214–215; l. 12: One sentence moved from p. 221; l. 23: pp. 215–219; l. 25: pp. 220–221; l. 32: p. 221.

P. 104, l. 12: Thirty-four sentences moved from pp. 217–219; l. 22: p. 217; l. 34: pp. 217–218.
P. 105, l. 5: p. 218; l. 14: pp. 218–219.
P. 106, ll. 15 and 17: p. 223; l. 17: pp. 223–224; ll. 21, 26, and 32: p. 224.
P. 107, ll. 24 and 34: p. 225.
P. 108, l. 2: pp. 225–226.

CHAPTER 8. I CROSS THE RUBICON

P. 111, l. 20: p. 229.
P. 112, l. 2: p. 230; l. 5: One sentence moved from p. 230; l. 8: p. 230; l. 10: Seven sentences moved from p. 237; l. 15: One sentence moved from p. 230; l. 37: Sixty-three sentences moved from pp. 237–239.
P. 113, l. 39: p. 238.
P. 114, l. 38: p. 230.
P. 115, l. 6: p. 232; l. 12: pp. 231–232; l. 15: Fifteen sentences moved from p. 240; l. 17: p. 240; l. 37: p. 232.
P. 116, ll. 19 and 27: p. 233.
P. 117, ll. 5, 11, and 29: p. 234; l. 35: pp. 234–241; l. 41: p. 241.
P. 118, l. 13: pp. 241–243; ll. 19, 26, and 30: p. 243.
P. 119, l. 21 and 29: p. 244.
P. 120, l. 36: p. 246.
P. 121, l. 4: pp. 246–247; l. 15: p. 247.
P. 122, l. 10: p. 248.
P. 123, l. 21: p. 249.
P. 124, ll. 28 and 39: p. 251.
P. 125, l. 22: p. 252; l. 37: p. 253.
P. 126, l. 22: p. 254; l. 26: pp. 254–255; ll. 28, 32, and 33: p. 255.
P. 127, l. 5: p. 255; ll. 21, 25, and 38: p. 256.
P. 128, ll. 7, 13, and 33: p. 257.
P. 129, l. 5: p. 258.

CHAPTER 9. THE NEW EDITOR AND HIS TOWN

P. 130, l. 28: pp. 259–260.
P. 131, l. 4: Two sentences moved from p. 260; ll. 11, 14, and 15: p. 260.
P. 133, l. 4: pp. 262–263; ll. 13 and 18: p. 263; l. 20: Twenty sentences moved from pp. 267–268; l. 34: p. 267; l. 37: pp. 267–268.
P. 134, l. 16: p. 264; l. 35: Eleven sentences moved from p. 262.
P. 135, l. 8: p. 262; l. 20: p. 264.
P. 136, l. 7: pp. 266–268; l. 35: Two sentences moved from p. 271; l. 37: p. 269.
P. 137, l. 13: p. 270; l. 14: p. 271; l. 19: pp. 271–272; l. 32: p. 273; l. 35: Four sentences moved from p. 272.
P. 138, l. 6: Eight sentences moved from p. 266; l. 7: p. 266; ll. 16 and 21: p. 273; ll. 31 and 39: p. 274.
P. 139, l. 4: p. 274; l. 9: pp. 274–275; ll. 18 and 29: p. 275.
P. 140, ll. 6, 11, 16, and 25: p. 276.
P. 142, l. 26: p. 278.
P. 143, l. 12: p. 279; ll. 23 and 27: p. 280.
P. 147, l. 16: p. 283.

CHAPTER 10. I AWAKEN TO FAME

P. 148, ll. 2 and 5: p. 284.

P. 149, ll. 4 and 14: p. 285; l. 22: pp. 286–287; l. 27: p. 287.

P. 150, ll. 14, 19, 22, and 26: p. 288.

P. 151, l. 26: pp. 289–290; l. 36: p. 290.

P. 152, l. 5: p. 290; ll. 15, 30, and 36: p. 291.

P. 153, ll. 4, 5, 7, 8, 19, and 25: p. 292; l. 33: p. 293.

P. 154, l. 12: p. 293; l. 19: pp. 293–294; ll. 39 ad 41: p. 294.

P. 155, l. 3: p. 294; l. 38: p. 295; l. 40: pp. 295–297.

P. 156, l. 2: p. 297.

P. 157, l. 6: p. 298; l. 9: pp. 299–300; ll. 14 and 19: p. 300; l. 21: Six sentences moved from p. 301; l. 29: p. 300.

P. 158, l. 5: p. 301; l. 8: pp. 301–302; l. 19: pp. 302–307.

CHAPTER 11. AT THE CENTURY'S TURN

P. 159, ll. 4 and 5: p. 311; l. 6: pp. 311–312; l. 23: p. 312.

P. 160, l. 1: p. 312; l. 2: Thirteen sentences moved from pp. 319–320; l. 12: p. 319; l. 24: p. 320; l. 29: p. 313; l. 31: Five sentences moved from p. 303; l. 37: Two sentences moved from p. 323.

P. 161, l. 7: pp. 313–314; ll. 12 and 26: p. 314; l. 29: pp. 314–315; l. 30: p. 315; l. 34: Three sentences moved from p. 315.

P. 162, l. 11: p. 315; l. 34: p. 316.

P. 163, ll. 3 and 10: p. 316.

P. 164, l. 10: pp. 317–320.

P. 165, l. 13: p. 322.

P. 166, l. 12: p. 323; l. 14: pp. 323–324; ll. 17 and 19: p. 325.

P. 167, l. 6: p. 326; l. 11: pp. 326–327.

P. 168, l. 4: pp. 328–329; l. 5: p. 329; l. 11: Eight sentences moved from p. 327; l. 19: p. 327; ll. 23, 24, and 27: p. 329; l. 36: p. 330.

P. 169, l. 28: p. 331; ll. 30, 34, and 36: p. 332.

P. 170, ll. 13 and 24: p. 333; l. 41: p. 334.

P. 171, ll. 3 and 6: p. 334; ll. 24, 28, and 32: p. 335.

P. 172, l. 9: p. 335.

P. 173, l. 3: p. 336.

CHAPTER 12. I DISCOVER REFORM

P. 174, ll. 6 and 10: p. 338; l. 16: pp. 338–339; l. 17: p. 339

P. 175, l. 40: p. 340.

P. 176, l. 16: p. 341; l. 27: pp. 341–342.

P. 177, l. 2: p. 342; l. 14: p. 343.

P. 178, l. 7: pp. 345–346; l. 10: p. 346; l. 36: p. 347.

P. 179, l. 25: p. 348; l. 27: p. 349.

P. 180, l. 14: pp. 349–350; ll. 16 and 17: p. 350; l. 21: pp. 350–351.

P. 181, l. 10: p. 351.

P. 182, l. 40: p. 353.

P. 183, l. 3: p. 353; l. 20: p. 354.

P. 184, l. 3: p. 355; l. 13: pp. 355–364; ll. 20 and 33: p. 365.

P. 185, l. 16: p. 366; l. 35: Eight sentences moved from pp. 367–368; l. 37: p. 367.
P. 186, l. 20: p. 367; l. 36: pp. 368–369.
P. 187, l. 9: p. 369; six sentences moved from p. 443; ll. 19 and 20: p. 369.

CHAPTER 13. HAPPY DAYS

P. 188, l. 2: pp. 372–376; thirty-nine sentences moved from pp. 355–357; l. 6: pp. 355–356;
l. 10: p. 356; l. 16: Two sentences moved from p. 356.
P. 190, l. 20: p. 377; l. 33: p. 378; l. 36: Forty-four sentences moved from pp. 375–376;
l. 38: p. 375.
P. 191, l. 38: p. 378.
P. 194, l. 12: p. 381; l. 15: Nineteen sentences moved from pp. 372–374; l. 18: p. 372; l. 24:
One sentence moved from p. 373; l. 26: pp. 372–373; ll. 27 and 35: p. 373.
P. 195, l. 3: pp. 373–374; l. 5: Two sentences moved from p. 391; l. 11: pp. 374–376; l. 14:
Nine sentences moved from p. 391; l. 16: p. 391; l. 27: Thirty-one sentences moved
from pp. 392–394; l. 41: pp. 392–393.
P. 196, l. 10: p. 393; l. 14: p. 394; l. 25: p. 381.
P. 197, l. 16: p. 382; l. 19: Sixteen sentences moved from pp. 370–371; ll. 21 and 33: p.
370.
P. 198, l. 28: pp. 382–383; l. 37: pp. 383–384; l. 39: One sentence moved from p. 383.
P. 199, ll. 3 and 11: p. 385; l. 18: pp. 385–386.
P. 200, l. 3: p. 386; l. 41: pp. 387–388.
P. 201, ll. 4 and 5: p. 388; l. 10: pp. 388–389,
P. 202, l. 3: pp. 389–394.

CHAPTER 14. I JOIN A REBELLION

P. 203, l. 18: p. 395.
P. 204, l. 9: p. 395.
P. 206, l. 13: p. 397; l. 27: pp. 399–401; l. 30: Twelve sentences moved from pp. 402–403; l.
39: p. 403.
P. 207, l. 24: p. 401; l. 36: pp. 402–403; l. 37: Eighteen sentences moved from pp. 399–401
and 399.
P. 208, ll. 1 and 4: p. 399; l. 6: pp. 399–400; l. 33: pp. 400–401.

CHAPTER 15. THE EUROPE WHICH HAS VANISHED

P. 209, l. 6: p. 404; l. 25: p. 405.
P. 210, l. 14: p. 405; ll. 19, 23, and 32: p. 406; l. 40: One sentence moved from p. 406.
P. 211, l. 5: Three sentences moved from p. 406; l. 18: pp. 407–408; l. 22: pp. 408–409; l.
24: Nine sentences added from manuscript.
P. 212, l. 5: p. 409; l. 9: p. 410; l. 13: pp. 410–418; ll. 14, 16, and 18: p. 418.
P. 213, ll. 7 and 9: p. 419; l. 14: pp. 419–420; ll. 16, 35, and 36: p. 420.
P. 214, l. 4: p. 421; l. 5: Three sentences moved from p. 423; l. 7: p. 423; l. 33: Four senten-
ces moved from p. 421; l. 36: pp. 422–423.

CHAPTER 16. THE BATTLELINES FORM

P. 215, ll. 5, 21, and 22: p. 423; l. 24: p. 424; l. 27: One hundred three sentences moved
from pp. 428–433.

P. 216, ll. 8 and 10: p. 428; l. 18: p. 429.

P. 217, l. 1: One sentence moved from p. 429; ll. 5, 10, 11, 17, and 22: p. 430.

P. 218, ll. 2 and 5: p. 431.

P. 219, l. 2: pp. 432–433; l. 13: pp. 424–425; ll. 16 and 22: p. 425; ll. 34 and 37: p. 426.

P. 220, ll. 15 and 19: p. 427.

P. 221, l. 11: pp. 428–435.

P. 222, ll. 2 and 13: p. 436; l. 17: pp. 437–438; l. 37: pp. 438–439.

P. 223, l. 20: pp. 439–440; ll. 28 and 38: p. 440.

P. 224, l. 4: p. 441; ll. 26 and 33: p. 442.

P. 225, ll. 1 and 4: p. 443; l. 17: pp. 444–445; l. 21: p. 445; l. 30: Five sentences moved from p. 446; l. 41: p. 446.

P. 226, l. 5: One sentence added from manuscript; p. 446; l. 16: p. 447; l. 17: pp. 447–448.

P. 227, l. 8: pp. 449–450; l. 27: pp. 450–451; l. 31: p. 451; l. 34: pp. 451–452; l. 36: p. 452.

P. 229, l. 37: pp. 454–455.

P. 230, l. 16: p. 456; l. 21: pp. 456–457; l. 37: p. 457.

P. 231, l. 8: p. 457; ll. 17, 19, and 32: p. 458; l. 41: p. 459.

P. 232, l. 3: p. 459; l. 19: pp. 459–461; l. 23: p. 461.

P. 233, l. 4: p. 461.

CHAPTER 17. ARMAGEDDON

P. 234, ll. 11 and 19: p. 462; l. 24: One sentence moved from p. 462; two sentences moved from p. 463.

P. 235, ll. 4, 14, 16, and 26: p. 463.

P. 236, l. 2: p. 464; l. 33: pp. 465–466.

P. 237, l. 10: pp. 466–467; ll. 19, 20, and 29: p. 467; l. 41: p. 468.

P. 238, l. 2: p. 468; l. 9: p. 469; l. 12: p. 469; l. 31: p. 470; l. 34: One sentence moved from p. 483.

P. 239, ll. 15 and 34: p. 471.

P. 240, l. 24: p. 472.

P. 241, ll. 8 and 11: p. 473.

P. 242, l. 2: p. 474.

P. 243, l. 3: p. 475; ll. 27 and 28: p. 476; l. 36: p. 477.

P. 244, ll. 1 and 5: p. 477; l. 6: Ten sentences moved from p. 479; l. 7: p. 479; l. 20: Three sentences moved from p. 479; l. 33: p. 478.

P. 245, l. 5: p. 478; l. 6: Two sentences moved from p. 477.

P. 246, l. 4: p. 479; l. 13: p. 480.

P. 247, l. 1: pp. 480–481.

CHAPTER 18. THE BIRTH OF A PARTY

P. 248, l. 8: p. 482; l. 17: p. 483.

P. 249, l. 15: p. 483; l. 24: p. 484; l. 41: pp. 484–485.

P. 250, l. 39: Three sentences moved from p. 487.

P. 251, l. 15: Three sentences moved from p. 487; l. 23: p. 487; ll. 26 and 34: p. 486.

P. 252, l. 10: pp. 487–488; l. 12: Six sentences moved from p. 484; l. 27: One sentence moved from p. 486; l. 33: p. 489.

P. 253, l. 14: p. 490.

P. 255, l. 11: Eight sentences moved from pp. 492–493; l. 41: pp. 492–493.

P. 257, l. 19: p. 495; ll. 27, 28, and 41: p. 496.

P. 258, ll. 22 and 23: p. 497; l. 28: pp. 497–498; ll. 30 and 31: p. 498.

P. 259, l. 10: p. 499; l. 12: Six sentences moved from p. 498.

P. 260, l. 8: p. 500; l. 10: pp. 500–502.

P. 261, ll. 7 and 12: p. 504; l. 31: pp. 504–505; ll. 33 and 37: p. 505; l. 41: pp. 505–506.

CHAPTER 19. DECLINE AND FALL

P. 263, ll. 2 and 4: p. 507; l. 19: pp. 507–508; l. 32: p. 508; l. 37: pp. 508–509.

P. 264, ll. 9 and 15: p. 509; l. 22: pp. 509–510; ll. 27 and 31: p. 510.

P. 265, ll. 10 and 11: p. 512; l. 14: Three sentences moved from p. 512; ll. 19 and 22: p. 512; l. 39: Six sentences moved from p. 507.

P. 266, l. 9: p. 513; l. 29: p. 514.

P. 267, l. 2: p. 514; l. 3: Two sentences moved from p. 514; ll. 13, 17, and 36: p. 515.

P. 268, l. 23: p. 516; l. 26: pp. 516–517; l. 27: Six sentences moved from p. 521; l. 31: p. 512; ll. 35 and 39: p. 517; l. 41: pp. 517–519.

P. 269, l. 36: p. 521.

P. 270, l. 2: p. 521; l. 3: Five sentences moved from p. 518; ll. 11 and 13: p. 521; l. 25: p. 522; l. 37: pp. 522–523.

P. 271, ll. 5 and 17: p. 523; ll. 24, 31, and 35: p. 524.

P. 272, l. 24: p. 525.

P. 273, l. 7: p. 525; l. 32: p. 526.

P. 274, l. 4: p. 526; l. 24: p. 527.

CHAPTER 20. A WORLD AFLAME

P. 275, l. 9: p. 528; l. 20: pp. 528–529.

P. 276, l. 13: pp. 529–530; l. 22: pp. 530–531.

P. 277, ll. 14, 17, and 19: p. 532; l. 21: pp. 532–533.

P. 278, l. 26: p. 534.

P. 279, l. 4: p. 535; l. 8: pp. 536–538; l. 13: p. 538; l. 19: pp. 538–539; l. 20: p. 539; l. 21: One sentence moved from p. 540; l. 24: pp. 539–540; l. 39: Five sentences moved from p. 539.

P. 280, l. 6: pp. 540–541; l. 21: p. 542; eight sentences moved from p. 546; l. 29: p. 546; l. 36: One sentence moved from p. 538; l. 37: One sentence moved from p. 539.

P. 281, l. 1: One sentence moved from pp. 538–539; l. 13: pp. 542–543; ll. 20, 23, and 32: p. 543; l. 36: pp. 543–545; l. 41: pp. 545–546.

CHAPTER 21. THE PEACE THAT PASSETH UNDERSTANDING

P. 282, l. 5: pp. 545–547; ll. 10 and 14: p. 547; l. 17: Five sentences moved from p. 551.

P. 283, l. 8: pp. 547–558; l. 11: p. 548; l. 33: pp. 548–549; l. 35: p. 549.

P. 284, l. 3: p. 549; l. 14: p. 550; l. 25: pp. 550–551; l. 38: pp. 551–552.

P. 285, l. 1: Four sentences moved from p. 549; l. 19: p. 553; l. 39: Eight sentences moved from p. 550.

P. 286, l. 12: p. 554; l. 33: Four sentences moved from p. 558.

P. 287, ll. 3 and 10: p. 555; l. 27: pp. 555–556.

P. 288, l. 2: p. 556; l. 5: pp. 556–557; l. 34: Three sentences moved from p. 551.

P. 289, l. 24: p. 558; l. 28: p. 559.

P. 290, l. 8: pp. 559–560; l. 16: p. 560.

P. 291, l. 2: pp. 560–562; ll. 6, 13, and 30: p. 562; l. 32: pp. 562–563.

P. 292, ll. 3 and 4: p. 563; l. 12: pp. 563–564; l. 15: pp. 564–567; ll. 16 and 21: p. 567; ll. 25 and 37: p. 568.

P. 293, l. 8: One sentence moved from p. 567; l. 20: pp. 569–570; l. 29: p. 570.

P. 294, l. 7: One sentence moved from pp. 575–576; pp. 570–571; l. 8: p. 571; ll. 19, 25, and 31: p. 572; l. 35: p. 573; l. 38: pp. 573–574.

P. 295, l. 10: pp. 574–575; l. 24: p. 575; l. 34: pp. 575–576.

CHAPTER 22. THROUGH THE VALLEY OF THE SHADOW

P. 297, l. 18: pp. 577–578.

P. 298, ll. 10, 12, and 19: p. 578; l. 31: p. 579.

P. 299, l. 15: pp. 579–580; ll. 17, 24, 25, and 29: p. 580; l. 31: pp. 580–581; ll. 32 and 33: p. 581.

P. 300, l. 5: p. 581; l. 14: p. 582; l. 21: pp. 582–583; ll. 27, 28, and 33: p. 583.

P. 301, ll. 14, 15, 17, and 18: p. 584; l. 30: pp. 584–585; l. 34: p. 585.

P. 303, l. 4: p. 586.

P. 304, l. 3: pp. 587–588; ll. 10, 13, and 14: p. 588; l. 16: Eleven sentences moved from pp. 587–588.

CHAPTER 23. MOSTLY PERSONAL

P. 305, l. 7: p. 590; ll. 11, 23, and 24: p. 591.

P. 306, l. 4: p. 592; l. 13: pp. 592–594; l. 36: p. 595.

P. 307, l. 4: pp. 596–603; l. 11: p. 603; l. 12: pp. 603–604.

P. 308, l. 11: One sentence added from manuscript; l. 36: p. 605.

CHAPTER 24. THE DOWNHILL PULL

P. 313, l. 1: One hundred twenty-three sentences moved from pp. 596–602; l. 20: p. 596.

P. 314, l. 2: p. 597; l. 37: p. 598; l. 40: pp. 598–599.

P. 315, l. 12: p. 599; l. 31: p. 600.

P. 316, ll. 26 and 39: p. 601.

P. 318, l. 22: p. 610; ll. 30 and 37, p. 611.

P. 319, l. 21: p. 612; l. 23: Three sentences moved from p. 611; p. 611.

P. 320, l. 24: pp. 612–613.

P. 322, ll. 23 and 27: p. 615; l. 31: pp. 615–616.

P. 323, l. 28: p. 617.

P. 324, l. 8: p. 617.

P. 325, l. 25: p. 619.

P. 326, ll. 2 and 23: p. 620.

P. 327, l. 3: p. 621; l. 9: pp. 621–622.

P. 328, l. 5: p. 623; l. 18: p. 624; l. 19: Five sentences moved from p. 623; l. 31: p. 625.

P. 329, l. 25: Four sentences moved from p. 625.

P. 330, l. 26: One sentence moved from p. 625.

Selected
Bibliography

BOOKS BY WILLIAM ALLEN WHITE

Rhymes by Two Friends. Fort Scott, Kans.: M. L. Izor & Sons, 1893. In collaboration with Albert Bigelow Paine.

The Real Issue: A Book of Kansas Stories. Chicago: Way and Williams, 1896.

The Court of Boyville. New York: Doubleday & McClure Co., 1899.

Stratagems and Spoils: Stories of Love and Politics. New York: Charles Scribner's Sons, 1901.

In Our Town. New York: McClure, Phillips & Co., 1906.

A Certain Rich Man. New York: Macmillan Company, 1909.

The Old Order Changeth: A View of American Democracy. New York: Macmillan Company, 1910.

God's Puppets. New York: Macmillan Company, 1916.

The Martial Adventures of Henry and Me. New York: Macmillan Company, 1918.

In the Heart of a Fool. New York: Macmillan Company, 1918.

The Editor and His People: Editorials by William Allen White. Compiled by Helen O. Mahin. New York: Macmillan Company, 1924.

Politics: The Citizen's Business. New York: Macmillan Company, 1924.

Woodrow Wilson: The Man, His Times, and His Task. Boston: Houghton Mifflin Co., 1924.

Calvin Coolidge: The Man Who Is President. New York: Macmillan Company, 1925.

Some Cycles of Cathay. Chapel Hill: University of North Carolina Press, 1925.

Boys—Then and Now. New York: Macmillan Company, 1926.

Masks in a Pageant. New York: Macmillan Company, 1928.

What It's All About: Being a Reporter's Story of the Early Campaign of 1936. New York: Macmillan Company, 1936.

Forty Years on Main Street. Compiled by Russell H. Fitzgibbon; foreword by Frank C. Clough. New York: Farrar & Rinehart, 1937.

A Puritan In Babylon: The Story of Calvin Coolidge. New York: Macmillan Company, 1938.

The Changing West: An Economic Theory about Our Golden Age. New York: Macmillan Company, 1939.

Defense for America. Edited, with an introduction, by William Allen White. New York: Macmillan Company, 1939.

The Autobiography of William Allen White. New York: Macmillan Company, 1946.

OTHER WRITINGS BY WILLIAM ALLEN WHITE

White's hundreds of published articles, as well as writings about him, are included in the comprehensive *A Bibliography of William Allen White*, prepared by the Kansas State Teachers College [now Emporia State University]. 2 vols. Emporia: Teachers College Press, 1969.

BOOKS ABOUT WILLIAM ALLEN WHITE

Clough, Frank C. *William Allen White of Emporia*. New York: McGraw-Hill Book Company, 1941.

Griffith, Sally Foreman. *Home Town News: William Allen White and the Emporia* Gazette. New York: Oxford University Press, 1989.

Hinshaw, David. *A Man from Kansas: The Story of William Allen White*. New York: G. P. Putnam's Sons, 1945.

Jernigan, E. Jay. *William Allen White*. New York: Twayne Publishers, 1983.

Johnson, Walter. *William Allen White's America*. New York: Henry Holt and Company, 1947.

McKee, John DeWitt. *William Allen White: Maverick on Main Street*. Westport, Conn.: Greenwood Press, 1975.

Rich, Everett. *William Allen White: The Man from Emporia*. New York: Farrar & Rinehart, 1941.

Index

Abilene *Reflector*, 101
Abolitionists, 89, 198
Adams, Franklin P., 308
Adams, George Matthew, 234, 243
Addams, Jane, 206, 249, 254, 276–77, 306
Addison, Joseph, 70
Ade, George, 150
Advertising, xi, 161, 189–90, 259, 263, 324, 329
Aeneid (Vergil), 44
African-Americans, 13, 19, 165
Albaugh, Mort, 164–65, 187, 280
Alden, John B., 38, 40, 41
Aldine Club, 196
Aldrich, Nelson W., 219
Aldrich, Thomas Bailey, 112
"All Coons Look Alike To Me" (song), 166
Allen, Elsie, 260–61
Allen, Henry J.: controversy with WAW, 319–21; as governor of Kansas, 300–301; as political ally of WAW, 181, 203, 222, 230, 232–33, 240, 248, 260–61, 263, 280; visit of to Europe with WAW, 278
"All Hail the Power of Jesus' Name" (song), 287n
Allison, William B., 169
"America" (song), 142, 160
American Booksellers Association, 308
American Magazine, 200–201, 213, 274, 284
American Press Association, 87
Angell, Norman, 283–84
Anthony, Daniel R., 185
Anthony, Susan B., 19
"Aqua Pura," 138
Arkansas Traveler, 38
Armour, J. Ogden, 82
Armstrong, Walter, 100–101
Associated Press, 60, 87, 148–49, 194, 292, 309
Atchison *Globe*, 66
Atlantic Monthly, 44, 137
Atwood, Fred J., 320
Austin, Mary H., 197–98, 267
Autobiography of Benjamin Franklin, The, xiv–xv

Automobiles, 165, 188, 259–60, 263, 318, 329–30

Bacon, Francis, 104, 178n
Baker, Lucien, 153–55
Baker, Ray Stannard, xii, 200, 210, 284, 286, 290
Balfe, Michael W., 138n
Balfour, Arthur James, 316–17
Banks, and politics, 133–34, 161–64, 182, 191–92
Barnum, P. T., xiv
Barrie, J. M., 199
Barrymore, John, 294
Bartlett's *Familiar Quotations*, 67
"Battle Hymn of the Republic" (song), 158n
Beach, Frank, 310
Beethoven, Ludwig van, 121, 312
Belgian Relief Foundation, 267
"Bells, The" (Poe), 36n
Belmont, August F., 244–45
Bemis, Edward W., 116
"Ben Bolt" (song), 20n
Bennett, Arnold, 310
Bergson, Henri, 287
Betts, Bill, 21
Betts brothers, 8
Beveridge, Albert J., 201, 228–29, 237, 242, 251, 263
Bible, language of, xvii, 19, 45, 166
Bimetallic League, 167
Bismarck, Otto von, 292, 295
Black, Fannie DeGrasso, 17
Blaine, James G., 25, 43–44, 97, 115
Blair, Dow, 9
Blitz, Pinky, 113
"Blub Blub, Judge," 183
Bohemian Girl, The (opera), 138
Bolsheviks, 289–91, 293, 318
Book-of-the-Month Club, x
Borah, William E., 185, 225, 228, 236, 270, 301–2
Bourne, Jonathan, Jr., 228–29, 242

357

Brett, George P., 207
Brewer, David Josiah, 223n
Briand, M. Aristide, 316–17
Bride of Triermain, The (Scott), 95n
Bridges, Robert, 150, 160
Bristow, Joseph L., 203–6, 213, 219, 222, 225, 228, 242
Brown, Cyril, 292
Brown, Ed, 165
Brown, Francis, xix
Brown, James Scott, 284
Brown, John, 222
Brown, Rice, 312
Browning, Robert, 107n
Bryan, Charles W., 245
Bryan, William Jennings, 186, 304, 305; description of, 167–68, 263–65; at Disarmament Conference, 316–17; as leader of liberal Democrats, 206, 257; at 1912 Democratic convention, 244–46; as presidential candidate, 142, 146, 149, 207
Bryant, William Cullen, 110n
Buchanan, James, 228
Bull Moose party. *See* Progressive party
Bullitt, William C., 291
Bulwer-Lytton, Edward Robert, 29n
Bunyan, John, xiv
Burton, Joseph R., 153, 177, 179, 184
Bushnell, Asa S., 141
Butler, Benjamin, 83
Butler, Nicholas Murray, 174–75, 297
Butler County *Democrat*, xi, 23n, 47–55
Butts, Alex, 114–15, 118
"Bye, Baby Bye, Oh, Why Do You Cry, Oh!" (song), 74
Byron, Lord, George Gordon, 28, 41, 60n

Caesar, Julius, 29n
Campbell, Philip P., 185
Campbell (reporter at Kansas City *Star*), 114
Canfield, Dorothy, 65, 284
Canfield, James H., 65, 77, 89
Cannon, Frank J., 140–41
Cannon, Joseph G., 207, 210, 219, 228
Capper, Arthur, 135, 276, 328
Carlton, Will, 29, 87
Carlyle, Thomas, 70, 104
Carpenter, Mrs., 41–42
Carroll, Lewis, 156n
Carruth, Frances, 66
Carruth, William Herbert, 66, 77
"Casabianca" (Hemans), 9
Cather, Willa, 119, 120n
"Cat That Walked by Himself, The" (Kipling), 264n
Century Club, 172, 198

Century Magazine, 55, 137, 198
Certain Rich Man, A, xvii, 194–95, 207–8, 213–14, 215, 219
Cervantes Saavedra, Miguel de, 38n
Chaikovskii, Nikolai V., 290
Chicago, 150–51
Chicago (ship), 283
Chicago *Evening Post*, 165
Chicherin, Georgii V., 291
Chopin, Frederic, 121
Christian Century, xviii
Clapp, Moses, 228, 242
Clark, Champ, 244–47
Clark, William A., 184
Clemenceau, Georges, 288–90
Clemens, Samuel. *See* Twain, Mark
Cleveland, Grover, 31, 43–44, 71, 74, 102, 109, 114–15, 117
Clover, Sam, 165
Cockran, W. Bourke, 305
Cockrane, Alexander G., 183n
Colby, Bainbridge, 273
Colby, Everett, 242
Coleridge, Samuel Taylor, 291n
College Life, 55
College of Emporia, xvii, 40–45, 57
Collier, Robert J., 196, 266
Collier's Weekly, 196, 201, 266
Collins, Wilkie, 18
Colorado, White vacations in, 79–80, 120–21, 194, 195, 225, 232, 243, 260, 262, 263–64, 305–6
Committee to Defend America by Aiding the Allies, ix, xii
"Confessions of an English Opium Eater, The" (De Quincey), 41
Confessions of Saint Augustine, xiv, xvii
Congreve, William, 60n
"Conning Tower" (newspaper column), 308
Conrad, Joseph, 310
Coolidge, Calvin, 304, 330
Cooper, James Fenimore, 13, 41n
Copeland, Melvin T., 306
Coppée, François, 149
Courier, 63
"Court of Boyville, The," xv–xvi, 138, 157
Cowles, William Sheffield, 174
Cowles, Mrs., 174
Cowley, Dol, 37
Cox, James M., 305
Cox, Joe, 52–53
Crane, Charles R., 200
Crane, Cyrus, 63
Crawford, George, 135

Crawford, Francis Marion, 200
Creative Chemistry, 310
Creative Evolution, 287
Cretic (ship), 210–11, 213
Cross, Charles S., 133, 134, 161–64
Cross, Harrison C., 43
Crowd, The (Le Bon), 137
Gruden's *Concordance of the Bible*, 67
Culbertson, William S., 250
Cummins, Albert B., 242
Curtis, Charles, 90, 148, 153–55, 179, 180–83, 185, 219, 302–3
Czolgosz, Leon, 172

Damrosch, Walter, 117, 279
"Danny Deever" (Kipling), 112n
Darling, J. N., 234, 243
Darrow, Clarence, 150, 264–65
Darwin, Charles, xvi
Daudet, Alphonse, 149
Daugherty, Harry M., 301, 318, 326
Davenport, Joseph J., 113
Davis, D. M., 161
Davis, Oscar King, 252–54
Davis, Richard Harding, 101, 149
Dean (Kansas City *Journal* drama critic), 96–97, 100
Death Comes for the Archbishop (Cather), 120
Debs, Eugene V., 265, 327
Debussy, Claude, 121
Dennis, Jim, 72, 74
Denny, Ed, 52
Depression of 1890s, 120–22, 139
De Quincey, Thomas, 41, 70
Detroit Free Press, 38
Devil's Pool, The (Sand), 14n
Dewey, George, 160
Dickens, Charles, 13, 18, 36n, 38n, 44, 104, 226, 310
Dickman, Joseph T., 292
Disarmament Conference, 314–18
Dixon, Joseph M., 228, 251, 253
Dodwell, Jimmie, 60
Dolliver, Jonathan P., 169, 228, 242
Donnelly, Ignatius, 104, 116
Don Quixote (Cervantes), 38
Douglas, Stephen A., 228
Drew, John, 294
Du Maurier, George, 20n
Dunne, Finley Peter, 150, 200
Dupee, Ed, 9

East Side Literary, 121, 127
Ecord, Mr., 310

El Dorado: early schools in, 8; founding of, 1–2; in 1870s, 10, 12–13, 17; in 1880s, 21, 35, 55, 58–61
El Dorado *Daily Republican*, 35, 57–61, 63, 67, 81–82, 84, 86–87, 91–92, 109, 217
Eliot, George, 14
Ellet, General, 26
Ellsworth, D. A., 256
Ely, Richard T., 89
Emerson, Ralph Waldo, 42–43, 45, 54, 59, 67
Emporia: celebration of Whites' return from Europe, 214; during World War I, 277, 279–81; in 1868, 1; in 1880s, 40, 56–57; in 1890s, 133–37; in 1900s, 188–94; in 1913, 259–60; in 1920s, 319, 328–30
Emporia *Daily Republican*, 127, 134
Emporia *Gazette*, 185, 188, 224, 262, 278, 313, 322; and county printing, 324–25; coverage of Cross suicide, 163; growth of, 160–61, 189–90, 208, 259, 279, 280, 329; office in 1890s, 130; purchase by White, 127–28
Emporia National Bank, 128, 133, 160, 164
Emporia *News*, 1, 55–57, 114, 127
English, Thomas Dunn, 20n
Eskridge, Charles V., 134, 136, 149, 164
Everybody's, 201
"Everybody's Doin' It, Doin' It, Doin' It" (song), 236
Evolution, xvi
Ewing, Albert, 9, 15, 21, 29, 31, 38, 39, 40

Fall, Albert B., 325–26
Fall, Mrs., 328
Farmers' Alliance, 83–91, 212. *See also* Populists
Farming: during World War I, 280; in 1880s, 69, 83, 85; in 1900s, 190; in 1920s, 318
Faust, Tony, 138
Federal Reserve Bank, 318
Ferber, Edna, 234–35, 243, 308
Field, Eugene, 87, 111
Field, Roswell, 111
Finney, W. W., 312
First National Bank of Emporia, 161–64
Fitch, George, 234, 243
Fleming, Tom, 177–78
Flint Hills, 61–62
Flock, The (Austin), 197
Florence, El Dorado and Walnut Valley Railroad, 37
Foncannon, Frank, 312
Ford, Henry, 259
"For to Admire" (Kipling), 211n
Foster, Stephen C., 37
Franklin, Benjamin, xiv–xv
Franklin, Ed, 79
Franklin, Will, 79

French, Alice (Octave Thanet), 151, 159
"Frenzied Finance" (Lawson), 201
Frieburg, Cass, 47, 59
Frost, Harry, 101
Fuller, Henry B., 150
Fulton, Thomas Parker, 23–25, 47–49, 52–53, 55
Funston, Frederick, 65, 79–80, 99–100

Galsworthy, John, 310
Gardner, George, 60–61
Garfield, James R., 235, 271, 272, 273
Gargantua and Pantagruel (Rabelais), 14n
Garland, Hamlin, 104, 150
Garrison, William Lloyd, 89, 198
Gary, Elbert H., 298–300
George Matthew Adams Newspaper Syndicate, 234, 236
German-American Alliance, 276
Germany, White's visit to in 1919, 292–96
Gibson, Colonel, 26
Gilder, Richard Watson, 198–99
Gilmore, Patrick, 100, 117
Gladheart, Jerry, 75–76
Gleed, Charles S., 92, 96, 99, 101, 109
Glick, George W., 31
"Go Down, Moses" (spiritual), 37
Goldens and Spooners (theater company), 24
Goldsmith, Oliver, 70, 115
Gompers, Samuel, 298–99, 301
Gould, Jay, 183, 185
Grand Army of the Republic, 136
Grangers, 83, 89, 212
Grant, Ulysses S., 49, 256, 274
Gray, Thomas, 70
Great Expectations (Dickens), 36n
Greeley, Horace, 9, 89
Greenbackers, 83, 89, 212, 248
Grosvenor, Charles H., 140–41
Gufler, Al, 294

Hadley, Herbert S., 237–39, 242
"Hail Columbia" (song), 160
Hamlet (Shakespeare), 9
Hanna, Marcus Alonzo (Mark): and McKinley, 122, 138–42, 148, 166, 172; and plutocracy, 173, 182, 281; and White, 151–55, 158; and Roosevelt, 156, 174
Hapgood, Norman, 266
"Happy Is the Bride That the Sun Shines On" (song), 118
Hard Times (Dickens), 226
Harding, Warren G., 270, 301–4, 313–16, 318, 322–28
Harding, Mrs., 322, 328
Hardy, Thomas, 199, 200

Harger, Charles, 101
Harper & Brothers, 126
Harper's Bazaar, 29
Harper's Magazine, 42, 137, 199
Harrison, Benjamin, 71, 102, 117, 153
Harvey, Charley, 21
Harvey, Ed, 37
Harvey, Fred, 185
Harvey Houses, 118, 210
Hasty Pudding Club, 306
Hatten, Frank, 26
Hatten, Katherine, 142
Hayes, Rutherford B., 9, 256
Hays, Will H., xii, 270, 280, 300
Hazard of New Fortunes, A (Howells), 200
Heaton, Leila, 9, 14, 15
Heber, Reginald, 147n
Hemans, Felicia, 9n, 18
Hendricks, Thomas A., 9
Hendy, Rankin, 43
Henley, William Ernest, 40, 137
Henry Holt & Company, 138
Herbert, Ewing, 54–57, 89, 101, 126, 128
Herron, George D., 290–91
Hidden Hand, The (play), 24
Higginbotham, Jim, 181
Hill, Adams Sherman, 41n
Hill, David J., 41n
Hills, Laurence, 292
Hitchcock, Frank, 269, 270
Hobson, Mrs. Charley, 17
Hoch, Edward W., 187
Hodder, Frank Heywood, 225, 262
Hohenzollerns, 263, 295
Holmes, Oliver Wendell, Jr., 210
Holtz, W. L., 310, 312
"Home Sweet Home" (song), 214
Hood, Calvin, 188, 190; and factional politics, 133, 153–54, 161–62, 164, 182, 179, 191–94, 222–24; and White's purchase of *Gazette*, 128, 133–34
Hoover, Herbert, 252, 267–68, 303–4, 313, 314, 325–26, 327
Hoover, Ike, 322
House, Edward M., 286
House family, 72–74
Howe, Edgar Watson, 36, 66–67, 138, 165
Howe, Julia Ward, 158n
Howe, Old Man, 21
Howells, William Dean, 200, 210; meeting with White, 157–58, 197, 198; praise of White's work, 150, 194; read by White, 44–45, 66, 67, 137
"How Firm a Foundation, Ye Saints of the Lord" (song), 256
Huck Finn (Twain), xv, 55

Hughes, Charles Evans, 269–71, 275–76, 297, 314–17, 325–27
Hughes, Walter, 312
Hugo, Victor, 38n
Hurd, Franklin, 213
Hutchinson, Paul, xviii

Iacocca, Lee, xiv
Ickes, Harold, 242, 254, 271, 308
Imperialism, 159–60
Independent, 137
Indians, 4–5, 165
Ingalls, John J., 19, 87–89
In Memoriam (Tennyson), 89n
Innocents Abroad (Twain), 19
In Our Town, 194, 198
"In the Court of Boyville," xv–xvi, 138, 157
In the Heart of a Fool, 225, 279
Isolationism, ix, 302

Jaccaci, Auguste F., 157, 196
Jackson, Andrew, 26
James, Edwin L., 292
James, William, 150n
Jobes, C. S., 162–63
Joe (foreman of Butler County *Democrat*), 53
"John Brown's Body" (song), 213
Johnson, Hiram, 228, 242, 249, 251, 272
Johnson, Samuel, 70
Johnson, Tommy, 112, 114, 115, 118, 121
Johnston, William Agnew, 203
Jones, Mrs., 41, 42
Jones, Robert, 41
Jordan, David Starr, 277
Judge, 42
Jumping Frog of Calaveras County (Twain), 19

Kaisers. *See* Wilhelm I; Wilhelm II
Kansas City, in 1980s, 93–96, 113, 121–22, 125–26
Kansas City *Journal*, 91–92, 96–102, 109–11
Kansas City *News*, 64
Kansas City *Star*, 60, 87, 91–92, 111–27, 138, 204, 308
Kansas City *World*, 138
Kansas Day Club, 101–2
Kansas Industrial Court, 319
Kansas State Agricultural College, 61
Kansas State Teachers College (Normal), 41, 134, 137, 320
Kansas University, 55, 63–66, 78–79
Katy Railroad. *See* Missouri, Kansas and Texas Railroad
Kellogg, Vernon, 89, 117, 197, 267, 279; as college friend of White's, 41–43, 55, 61, 63, 65–66, 71–80

Kelly, Hortense, 135
Kerensky, Aleksandr, 290n
Kerrs, the, 309
"King of Boyville, The," 149
Kipling, Rudyard, 199, 200, 310; quotations from, 112, 135, 211, 240, 264; read by White, 90, 101, 137, 149
Kirchwey, George W., 250
Knowles, Charley, 204
Knowles, John, 16
Knox, Philander Chase, 176
Krock, Arthur, 292
Ku Klux Klan, 330

Labor Movement in America, The (Ely), 89
La Follette, Robert M., 203, 213, 275, 307; and bid for presidential nomination, 226–27, 236–37, 238; and progressive movement, 186, 204–6, 220–22, 304; in World War I, 277–78
Lalla Rookh (Moore), 29
Lambert, Dr., 283
Lambert, Ike, 160, 192–93
Lampoon, The (Harvard), 307
Land of Little Rain, The (Austin), 197
Lane, Franklin K., 299
Lang, Andrew, 137
"Larboard Watch" (song), 72, 74
Larriway, Orin, 60
Lawrence *Journal*, 64, 65, 66, 71–76, 79, 92, 119, 128
Lawrence *Tribune*, 71
Lawson, Thomas W., 201
League of Nations, 284, 286, 288–89, 297–98, 300, 301, 304, 305, 313–14
League of Nations Association, 297
Learnard, Oscar E., 71–72, 74–75, 77, 79
Lease, Mary Elizabeth, 105, 147
Leaves of Grass (Whitman), 90
Le Bon, Gustave, 137
"Legends of Evil, The" (Kipling), 135n
Leland, Cyrus, 164, 187, 217; and McKinley candidacy, 122–24; as political boss, 88, 103–4, 127, 138, 153–55, 177; and White, 128, 160
Lenin, Nikolai, 290–91
Lenroot, Irvine L., 304
Leon *Indicator*, 204
Leslie's Monthly, 42, 200
Lewelling, Lorenzo D., 110–11
Lewis, William Draper, 250–51
Life, ix, xv, 149–50
Lincoln, Abraham, 26, 228n, 265
Lindsay, Jessie, 225
Lindsay, Milton, 120
Lindsey, Benjamin B., 257

Lippmann, Walter, 282
Lissner, Myer, 254
Liszt, Franz, 121
Littleton, Martin, 276
Lloyd George, David, 212, 288–92
Lobdell, Charley, 60
Lodge, Henry Cabot, 272, 297, 302
London *Daily Express*, 292
London *Daily Mail*, 292
London Illustrated News, 42
Long, Chester I., 180–83, 185, 203–8
Longfellow, Henry Wadsworth, 41
Longworth, Alice Roosevelt, 187, 207
Longworth, Nicholas, 207
Lord, Lillie, 24
Lord's Prayer, 312
Lorimer, George H., 160, 167, 194
Lowden, Frank O., 302
Lowell, James Russell, 112
Lucile (Bulwer-Lytton), 29

McAllister, Samuel Ward, 124
MacArthur, Douglas, 294
Macbeth (Shakespeare), 160n, 205n
McClure, Samuel Sidney, xvi, 157–58, 199–200, 206
McClure's Magazine, xvi, 149, 157–58, 167, 169–70, 175, 178–79, 196, 199–200, 206
McClure Syndicate, 284, 298, 305
McCormick, Joseph Medill, 301, 304
McGinley, Jack, 130–31, 134–35
McGovern, Francis E., 237, 238
McGuffey's Readers, 13, 170, 173
McKinley, William, 168; death of, 172–74; presidential candidacy of, 138–39, 142, 149; and White, 122–25, 152–56, 169–71, 177
Macmillan Company, xi, xix–xx, 207, 211
McPhall, Burge, 292
Maine (ship), 159
Main Travelled Roads (Garland), 104
Marat, Jean Paul, 142
"Marguerite" (song), 37
Maria Theresa, 36
Marion *Star*, 323–24
Marsh, Arthur Richmond, 65–66
Martha (White family cook), 258
Martial Adventures of Henry and Me, The, 278–79
Martin, Charley, 135
Martin, John (Democratic politician), 31
Martin, John (Emporia businessman), 135
Martindale, William, 133, 134, 161
Maupassant, Guy de, 149
"Mazeppa" (Byron), 60n
Meffert, Delta, 193
Meffert, William, 193

Mill on the Floss, The (Eliot), 14
Miller, Frank, 149
Mills, Ogden L., 300
Misérables, Les (Hugo), 38
"Miss Devilette" (story), 101
"Missionary Hymn" (Heber), 147n
Missouri, Kansas and Texas Railroad (Katy), 175, 223
Missouri Pacific Railroad, 68, 180, 182, 183n, 185
Mitchell, Charles B., 118
Modern Instance, A (Howells), 44
Moody, Dwight Lyman, 43
"Moonlight Sonata" (Beethoven), 312
Moore, Thomas, 29n
Morgan, J. Pierpont, 182, 185, 201–2, 232
Morgan, W. Y., 127–28, 132–33, 134
Morley, Christopher, 308
Morrill, E. N., 103, 122, 128
Most, Johann, 63
Mother Goose, 14
Motion Picture Producers and Distributors Association, xii
Motion pictures, xii, 188, 279
Mourning Bride, The (Congreve), 60n
Muckraking, 166–67, 196, 201, 216
Mugwumps, 92, 199
Mullaney, Ed, 241
Mulvane, David W., 177, 179, 303–4
Munsey, Frank A., 272
Murdock, Alice, 10, 17, 35
Murdock, Marie Antoinette O'Daniel, 35–37
Murdock, Marshall, 84
Murdock, Mrs., 35
Murdock, Thomas Benton: as El Dorado newspaperman, 27, 34–37, 57–58, 61, 92; joins progressive movement, 217–19; as Republican politician, 67–69, 81–86, 88, 124
Murdock, Victor, 185, 222, 225, 228, 260, 263, 270
Music, 3, 8, 16, 17–18, 27, 37–38, 71, 117, 279

Napoleon, 203n
National Arts Club, 197, 267, 283
National Association of Manufacturers, 281
National League of Women Voters, 300
Nau, Carl, 312
"Nearer My God to Thee" (song), 172
Nearing, Scott, 277–278
Nelson, William Rockhill, 92, 112–15, 117, 121–22, 125–27
New Deal, 222, 243, 251–52
Newman, Fred, 256
Newman, George, 166, 188
Newspapers: descriptions of, 23–24, 47–55, 55–

61, 96–103, 108–11, 130–37; and politics, x–xi, 23, 48, 58–59, 76–77, 97, 99, 101–2. *See also names of specific papers*
Newton *Republican*, 109
New York City, 157–58, 195–201
New York *Nation*, 66, 99, 137
New York *Sun*, 292
New York *Times*, xix, 213
New York *Tribune*, 308
New York *World*, 111, 292
Nicholas II, 290n
1984 (Orwell), 243n
"Nobody Knows the Trouble I See" (song), 37
Normal. *See* Kansas State Teachers College
Norris, George W., 225, 228
Norton, Tom, 109–11
Nye, Edgar W. "Bill," 38, 59

O'Brien, Charley, 310, 312
O'Connor, Tom, 310
"Of Truth" (Bacon), 178n
"Oh, Alice, Where Art Thou?" (song), 74
"Old Ark's A-Moverin', The" (song), 37
Old Order Changeth, The, 215
Olin, Professor, 39
Omaha *Bee*, 237
"Onward, Christian Soldiers" (song), xvii, 249, 260
Oregon Short Line Railroad, 184
Orwell, George, 243n
Osborn, Chase S., 242
Othello (Shakespeare), 26n
Outlook, 137
Owsley (Kansas City official), 113

Paine, Albert Bigelow, 87, 106, 126
Palmer, A. Mitchell, 318
Panic of 1907, 195–96, 205, 208
Parades, 26, 32, 44, 85–86, 212–13, 266
Parallel Lives (Plutarch), 30, 33
Paris, during Peace Conference, 284–92
Paris *Herald*, 284
Parker, Alton B., 207
Parker, John M., 273
Parrington, Vernon L., 149
Pathetic Symphony (Tchaikovsky), 312
Peace Conference, 282–92
Pearl Harbor, xviii
Peattie, Donald Culross, 150
Peattie, Elia W., 150
Peck, George R., 88, 89, 217, 218
Peffer, William A., 145
Periodical Publishers Association, 226
Perkins, George W., 201–2, 232, 242, 249–55, 268–73
Perronet, Edward, 287n

Pershing, John J., 292
Phi Delta Theta, 63, 65, 100, 128
Phillips, John S., 157, 196–97, 200–201, 210, 282
Phillips (Lawrence marshal), 74
Phillips (telegraph editor on Kansas City *Star*), 114
Phillips, Wendell, 89, 198
Pierce, Franklin, 228
Pilgrim's Progress (Bunyan), xiv
Pinchot, Amos, 242, 250, 254, 271
Pinchot, Gifford, 235, 242, 250, 254, 263, 268, 271, 272–73
Pippa Passes (Browning), 107n
Platt, Orville H., 176
Platt, Thomas Collier, 169, 171–72, 175, 178–80
Plumb, Amos H., 128
Plumb, George, 128
Plumb, Preston B., 19, 91, 128, 223, 224
Plutarch, 30, 33
Poe, Edgar Allan, 36, 199n
Political Economy (Walker), 86
Poor Richard, xv
Pope, Alexander, 70
Populists, 117, 212, 248; beliefs of, 89–90, 104–5; Kansas convention of 1892 of, 109–10; as political movement, 102, 116, 127, 139; and White, 91, 142–47, 149. *See also* Farmers' Alliance
"Praise God from Whom All Blessings Flow" (song), 249
Prentis, Noble, 114–15, 120
Progressive party, ix, xv, xviii, 241–43, 248–57, 260–61, 263, 265–66, 268–74, 330
Progressivism, x, xvii–xviii, 167, 185–87, 203–8, 211–12, 215–33, 261, 277
Prohibition, 19, 31, 49, 305
Puck, 42
Pulitzer Prize, x, 322
Pygmalion and Galatea (play), 24

Quantrill, William Clarke, 41–42

Rabelais, François, 14n
Radio, 329
Railroad: influence of, x, 13, 21, 85–86, 116, 122, 128, 175, 318–19; and newspapers, 97, 119, 134; and politics, 37, 58–59, 68–69, 71, 82, 88, 102, 116, 134, 180–85, 223–24
Rank, Joe, 66
"Raven, The" (Poe), 36, 199n
Reade, Charles, 18
"Reader, The" (radio program), 308
Real Issue, The, xv, 121, 138, 143, 148, 149–50, 153, 157, 161

Record, George L., 242
Rector, Dora, 28
Red Cross, 277, 278, 280, 282
Red Cross Magazine, 282
Reed, Thomas B., 104–5, 139, 148, 158, 172–73, 179
"Regeneration of Colonel Hucks, The," 91–92
Religion: attitudes toward, xvi–xviii, 14, 19, 45–46, 166–67; and progressivism, 216–17; and revivals, 43, 54
Rhetoric (Hill), 41
"Rhymes and Rhythms" (Henley), 40n
Rhymes by Two Friends, 126, 138
Rhymes of Ironquill, The (Ware), 36, 87
Rice, John H. J., 310, 312
Rich, Everett, xi
Richardson (city editor of Kansas City *Star*), 127, 138
Richberg, Donald, 271
Richter, Johann Paul Friedrich (Jean Paul), 54
Riley, Agnes, 19–20, 29, 31, 38–39, 42, 61–62, 70
Riley, James Whitcomb, 29, 67, 87, 100, 153, 287
"Rime of the Ancient Mariner, The" (Coleridge), 291n
Robins, Raymond, 263, 271–73
Rockefeller, John D., xvi, 239
Rockefeller, John D., Jr., 298–99
Rock Island Railroad, 68, 180, 185
"Rock of Ages" (song), 32
Roget's *Thesaurus*, 67
Romanoffs, 290
Roosevelt, Alice. *See* Longworth, Alice Roosevelt
Roosevelt, Archibald, 283
Roosevelt, Edith Kermit, 176, 210, 276–77, 283
Roosevelt, Franklin Delano, 285, 305
Roosevelt, Kermit, 283
Roosevelt, Theodore, 196, 199, 201, 213, 215, 244, 275, 313, 323; as candidate of Progressive party, 248–49, 251–53, 255–57; and conflict with Taft, 225, 226; death of, 284–85; as president, 87, 174–75, 183, 205, 209–10; political ambitions of, 168–69, 227–33, 283, 284; and progressive movement, x, 186, 207, 220–22, 248–53, 281; and refusal to run for president in 1916, 260, 265, 268–74; at Republican presidential convention of 1912, 234–43; White's friendship with, xvii, 156–58, 166, 178–80, 282–83; and Wilson, 276–77, 278
Roosevelt, Theodore, Jr., 176
Root, Elihu, 176, 238–40, 257, 272, 297, 302, 313, 314
Rosewater, Victor, 237

Rossetti, Dante Gabriel, 150
Rubaiyat of Omar Khayyam, The, 62n
Rubinstein, Anton, 121
Ruddick, Lizzie, 31, 39
Runyon (editor of Kansas City *Star*), 112, 113
Rural Free Delivery, xi
Ryan, John Augustine, 327
Ryan, Thomas Fortune, 244–45

St. John, John P., 19
St. Louis, 138
St. Louis *Globe-Democrat*, 60, 64, 65
St. Nicholas Magazine, 126
Salvation Army, 281
Sand, George, 14, 340
Santa Fe, N.Mex., 119–20
Santa Fe Railroad, xv, 37, 68–69, 88, 92, 97, 118–19, 134, 150, 165, 180, 319
Sargent, John Singer, 176
Sartin, U. S., 255, 260
Saturday Evening Post, 160, 167, 185, 194
Schmucker, Lew, 38, 39, 99–100, 134, 143, 148–50, 165–66
Scott, Walter, 95n
Screech Owls, 37, 40
Scribner's Magazine, 137, 150, 160, 199
"See the Conquering Hero Comes" (song), 179
"Self Reliance" (Emerson), 42–43
Shakespeare, William, 70–71, 104, 160, 205n
Sherman, James S., 207, 241
Sherman, John, 146
Siddall, John M., 200
Siestad (clerk at Kansas City *Star*), 114
Simonds, Frank H., 286
Simpson, Jerry, 104–5, 110, 116
Slosson, E. E., 310
Smith, Al, 305
Smith, Mary Riley, 29
Smoot, Reed, 314
Snow, Byron, 9
Snow, Francis H., 66, 71
Social Darwinism, xvi
Socialists, 208, 211–12
Soden, W. T., 190–91
Solomon, 30
Song of Hiawatha, The (Longfellow), 29
"Song of Myself" (Whitman), 90
Spanish-American War, 159–60
Sparticus, the Gladiator (play), 24
Spencer, Herbert, xvi, 167
"Spoopendyke Papers," 38
Spring Chicken Club, 27, 42, 89
Standard Oil Company, xvi, 298
Stanley, William E., 180–82
Stanton, Elizabeth Cady, 19
"Star Spangled Banner, The," 160

Steele, Richard, 70
Steffens, Lincoln, 200, 291–92
Stevenson, Robert Louis, 199, 200
Stewart, James, 303
Stewart, Phil, 168
Stockton, Frank, 149, 200
Stoddard, Henry L., 272
Stone & Kimball, 150
Story of a Country Town, The (Howe), 36, 66
Stout, Ralph, 114, 118
Stowe, Harriet Beecher, 234n
Stubbs, Walter Roscoe, 187, 200, 203, 211–12, 213, 217, 222, 225, 320
Sue, Eugene, 41
Sullivan, Mark, 266
Sutherland, Duchess of (Millicent Fanny St. Clair-Erskine), 196
Sutliffe, Helen, 71, 78
Swedenborg, Emanuel, 198
"Swing Low Sweet Chariot" (song), 37
Swope, Herbert B., 292

Taft, Charles P., 219
Taft, William Howard, 169, 261, 263, 269, 275, 313, 314; and Roosevelt, 219–22, 224, 225–26, 229, 231; and election of 1912, 250, 255, 257; and 1912 Republican national convention, 235, 237–41, 247, 300; as president, 206–7, 209; and League of Nations, 297
Taft, Mrs., 219
Taggert, Thomas, 246
Tale of Two Cities, A (Dickens), 38
Tammany Hall, 244, 246
Tarbell, Ida M., 157, 200, 210, 274, 284, 298
Taussig, Frank W., 250
Tchaikovsky, Peter Ilich, 312
Teller, Henry M., 140
Telyea, Peter, 26
Tennyson, Alfred, 18, 41, 89
Tennyson, Charles, 18
Texas Siftings, 38
Thackeray, William Makepeace, 104
"Thanatopsis" (Bryant), 110n
Thanet, Octave. *See* French, Alice
Theater, 71, 117, 188, 279–80
Thompson, James Maurice, 150
Through the Looking-Glass (Carroll), 156n
Thurston, John M., 140
Tilden, Samuel J., 9, 25
"To an Anxious Friend," 321–22
Tolle, George, 47, 52
Tom Sawyer (Twain), xv, 19
Topeka *Capital*, 135, 204
Topeka *Commonwealth*, 35
Trilby (Du Maurier), 20n
Tripletts, the, 309

Trollope, Anthony, 18
Trotsky, Leon, 290–91
Trusts, 116, 208, 285
Tucker, Charley, 76
Twain, Mark (Samuel Clemens): biography of, 126; meeting with White, 196–97; White reads, 19, 38, 39, 59, 66, 67, 310; on White's work, 194

Uncle Tom's Cabin (Stowe), 24, 234n
Union Labor party, 83
Union Pacific Railroad, 68, 183, 185
University of Kansas. *See* Kansas University
University Review, 65

Vandergrift, Fred, 99–100, 117
Van Horn, Robert T., 97–98
Van Schaick, John, 149
Veblen, Thorstein, 116
Vergil, 44
Vernon, Charles, xi, xvii
Villard, Oswald Garrison, 284, 327

Wagner, Richard, 117
Walker, Francis, 86
Wallace, Lew, 120
Walnut Valley Times, 27, 34
Wandering Jew, The (Sue), 41
Ware, Eugene F., 36n, 87, 106, 143–44
Warrens, the, 188
Washington, Booker T., 153
Watson, Carrie, 70
Watson, James E., 300
Watt, Jack, 75
Way, Irving, 150
Way & Williams, 138, 150
Webster, Harold T., 234, 243
Weekly University Courier, 65
Weeks, John W., 272
Welliver, Judson C., 322
Wells, H. G., 310
Western Artists and Authors Society, 106
Western Union, 110, 124, 163, 185
"What's the Matter with Kansas?" 143–49, 152–53, 156, 166, 167, 172, 178, 264, 321
"When the Mists Have Cleared Away" (song), 32
White, Allen (father), 132, 212; character of, 6, 7, 8, 11, 32–33; death of, 31–32; influence on son, 8, 15, 18, 19, 20; last days of, 30–31; move to El Dorado, 1; move to a farm, 6–7; new house of, 10–12; opening of hotel, 22; political activities of, 2, 19, 25–26, 31
White, Mary (daughter), 279; accompanies family, 210–11, 213–14, 225–26, 258, 262, 305–6;

White, Mary, *continued*
  birth of, 194, 195; death of, xvii, 307–12;
  during Roosevelt visit, 256–57
White, Mary Hatten (mother), 1–4, 8, 12, 111,
  117, 127; character of, 6, 7, 10–11, 18, 22,
  32, 44; takes in boarders, 34; accompanies
  White, 64, 81, 102, 119–21, 134, 210, 213–
  14, 225, 258, 305
White, Sallie Lindsay (wife), 169, 206, 207, 244,
  282, 307, 309; courtship and wedding of,
  100–101, 105–8, 111, 117–21; edits *Autobiography*, xiii, xx; as hostess, 256–57, 258, 280,
  330; illness of, 107, 142–43, 147; as partner
  in White's career, 128, 134–36, 137, 148, 149,
  157, 194, 195, 225, 274, 278, 290, 308, 320;
  and travels with White, 150, 151, 178–79,
  184, 197–99, 209–14, 267–68, 276–77, 305–6,
  328
White, William Allen: birth and childhood, 1–
  16; boyhood and youth, 17–80; early experiences in journalism, 23–25, 47–54, 57–61,
  71–76, 79; as editor of El Dorado *Republican*,
  81–94; education of, 8, 13–15, 38, 63–66, 70–
  71, 78–80; marriage of to Sallie Lindsay,
  117–21; and purchase of *Emporia Gazette*,
  127–37; reading of, 18–19, 66–67, 70–71,
  137, 166–67, 197, 226, 279, 287; religious beliefs of, xvi–xviii, 14, 43, 45–46, 54–55, 166–
  67; travels of to Europe, 209–14, 278, 282–
  96; writing of for Kansas City *Journal*,
  92–111; writing of for Kansas City *Star*, 111–
  27. Works of: "Aqua Pura," 138; *Autobiography of William Allen White, The*, xi–xviii;
  Certain Rich Man, A, xvii, 194–95, 207–8,
  213–14, 215, 219; *In Our Town*, 194, 198; "In
  the Court of Boyville," xv–xxvi, 138, 157; *In
  the Heart of a Fool*, 225, 279; "King of Boyville, The," 149; *Martial Adventures of Henry
  and Me, The*, 278–79; *Old Order Changeth,
  The*, 215; *Real Issue, The*, xv, 121, 138, 143,
  148, 149–50, 153, 157, 161; "Regeneration of
  Colonel Hucks, The," 91–92; *Rhymes by Two
  Friends*, 126, 138; "To an Anxious Friend,"
  321–22; "What's the Matter with Kansas?"
  143–49, 152–53, 156, 166, 167, 172, 178,
  264, 321
White, William Lindsay (son): accompanies
  White, 275–76, 277, 282–84, 287, 292; as
  child, 169, 178–79, 194, 195, 210–11, 213–
  14, 225–26, 257, 258; as youth, 262, 263,
  277–78, 279, 311, 319; at Harvard, 306–8,
  312; edits *Autobiography*, xii, xix–xx
White Committee, ix, xii
Whitley Opera House, 137
Whitman, Walt, 90
Whittier, John Greenleaf, 29, 112
Wichita *Eagle*, 204
Wilhelm I, 292
Wilhelm II, 211, 265, 292, 293
Wilhite, Mit, 166
Williams, Chauncey, 150–51, 153, 165
Williams, Helen, 150
Wilson, Woodrow, 216, 313, 314, 323; conflict
  over League of Nations, 297–98, 302, 305;
  election as president in 1912, 255, 257, 258;
  nomination by 1912 Democratic national
  convention, 244–47; at Paris Peace Confer-
  ence, 286, 288–92; reelection in 1916, 275–
  77; war policies of, 227, 264, 266, 268, 278
Wood, Leonard, 283, 300–302
Woollcott, Alexander, 308
Woman of Genius, A (Austin), 197
Women, 19, 53–54, 135, 137, 189, 249, 271
Works of Thomas De Quincey, 41
World Court, 301, 314
World War I, xviii, 262–63, 277–78
World War II, ix, xiii, xviii
Wright, Frank Lloyd, 150

Yearout, Minnie, xii
Yonkman, George, 37
Young, Merz, 10, 21
Young Men's Christian Association, 277, 281
Young Women's Christian Association, 306,
  310
Youth's Companion, 29